Nutrition f
HEALTHCARE
PROFESSIONALS

AN INTRODUCTION TO DISEASE PREVENTION

DAVID BISSONNETTE

Kendall Hunt
publishing company

Cover Image © Shutterstock.com

Kendall Hunt
publishing company

www.kendallhunt.com
Send all inquiries to:
4050 Westmark Drive
Dubuque, IA 52004-1840

Copyright © 2016, 2019 by St-Jude Nutrition Medical Communications LLC

PAK ISBN 978-1-5249-8377-2
Text alone ISBN 978-1-5249-8379-6

Published in the United States of America

DEDICATION

This book is dedicated to Jesus and his dear mother, Mary, without whom nothing would have been completed.

CONTENTS

FOREWORD

This is an introductory textbook on nutrition for healthcare professionals; it is written in a way that invites students in dietetics, nutrition, nursing, health sciences, and medicine to think critically about nutrition within the field of medicine and public health. After all, it is precisely the increasing prevalence of obesity in the United States and all the secondary diseases that derive from it, such as heart disease and type-2 diabetes, that have set off alarm bells nationwide. Health professionals are warning that obesity and type-2 diabetes have reached epidemic proportions, affecting the lives of both the adults and the youth. If we remain unable to turn this thing around, it will, without a doubt, forcibly change the quality of life and the health of our nation. Since the early 1980s, we have been consuming an overabundance of food that has led to excessive intakes of fat, sugar and salt. Moreover, suboptimal fiber intakes now threaten the gastrointestinal health of millions. We are now looking at a generation with food habits that are so impoverished that they are threatening its very health.

As healthcare professionals, you are preparing to provide medical services of various types to a culture that has sickened itself with cheap processed foods and lifestyles of physical complaisance. The consequences are dire as greater numbers of patients will be seeking help to manage heart disease, obesity, gastrointestinal diseases of various types, cancer, depression, and type-2 diabetes; the financial cost to the system will be staggering and oppressive. These are the most significant diseases afflicting our society currently, and they will likely impact your life in some manner, either affecting you directly, or impacting family members and friends. They will also affect your careers as healthcare professionals, because of the onslaught of medical train wrecks that will be lining up for help in clinics and urgent cares all over the country. The tsunami has already begun. You can ask any family physician, physician assistant, or nurse practitioner who has been working in the trenches for longer than 10 years. America is not just sick, but it is profoundly ill, and nutrition is at the epicenter of the disaster. And so it is timely to be studying nutrition, as you will be introduced to several of the most pertinent concepts of nutrition and to the many diseases associated with diet. It is my hope that this textbook will provide you with a rich learning experience, and that you will go away, after studying this book, with a more in-depth understanding of the role of nutrition in individual and public health.

This book comes with a video streaming web address and access code—located inside the textbook's front cover—for viewing the streamed documentary: A DIABETIC NATION: An American Tragedy (run time: 1 hour and 47 minutes). It explores the impact of nutrition on the obesity and diabetes epidemics in the United States. Students are encouraged to access a second documentary, currently distributed by Films for the Humanities and Sciences: OBESITY IN AMERICA: A National Crisis, which thoroughly investigates the prevalence, causes, assessment methods and most effective treatments of obesity.

Nutrition for the Prevention of Disease

1.1 THE ROLE OF NUTRITION IN HUMAN HEALTH

1.1.1 The Prevalence and Impact of Chronic Disease

For most of the 20th and 21st centuries, chronic diseases have been affecting American society, and have been growing in prevalence at alarming rates, reaching, in many instances, epidemic status. NHANES data from 2015-2016 confirms that 71.2% of US adult men and women are considered overweight or obese (Fryar et al., 2018) and that as many as 39.8% are obese (Hales et al., 2017). This was a significant increase from the 2011-12 NHANES data, which reported 34.9% of American women and men (≥20

years old) were obese, and a noticeable jump from the 13.4% obesity prevalence seen in the 1960s (Fryar et al., 2018; May et al, 2013, Ogden et al., 2014). Most concerning is that as many as 33.4 % of children, ages 2 to 19, were in 2014, either overweight (16.2%) or obese (17.2%) (Fryar et al., 2016). The 2015-16 NHANES survey confirms that the percentage of obese youth has now jumped to 18.4% (Hales et al., 2017). This prevalence is shocking given that body weight disturbances of this magnitude are at the center of numerous secondary diseases, such as heart disease, cancer and type-2 diabetes, that not only greatly diminish quality of life, but also increase mortality rates. Indeed, a mean 47.45% of all mortalities in the United States can be attributed to either cardiovascular disease or some forms of cancer (Heron, 2013), and while close to 25% of all deaths are linked directly to cancer (Heron,

2013; Cordain et al., 2005)—a number that has not changed much since the turn of the new Millennium—as many as 90–95% of all cancer cases are caused by environmental influences and a mere 5–10% appear linked to genetic defects (Anand et al., 2008; ACS, 2004). Although these statistics are alarmingly elevated, the sobering conclusion that can be drawn is that most cancers are in fact, preventable. The preventability of cancer has been known for some time. Back in the 1980s Doll and Peto (1981) demonstrated that between 80–85% of cancer cases diagnosed in the United States could have been prevented by modifying lifestyles, and in the 1990s roughly 30–40% of cancer cases worldwide were attributed solely to diet (Anand et al., 2008). This finding was supported later on by Preetha Anand and colleagues who estimated, in their 2008 review of the literature, that between 65–85% of all cancers were caused by obesity, diet, or tobacco (Anand et al., 2008). The association between cancer and diet is most evident in colorectal cancers, specifically, as an impressive 70% of deaths have been tied to dietary habits (ACS, 2008). In fact, the overall risk of colorectal cancer increases with obesity, physical inactivity, smoking, heavy alcohol consumption, and diet. Specifically, the work out of Harvard's School of Public Health has attributed greater cancer risk to individuals whose diets are high in red or processed meats, in addition to being inadequate in fruits and vegetables (Willett, 2000; ACS, 2008). Although fiber intake appears to have some protective effects against cancer, the strongest protection seems to come from the phytochemicals found in fruit and vegetables more than the fiber components (Willett, 2000). In light of these strong epidemiological correlations, nutrition has become a primary focal point in preventative health care. This is especially true for the aging "babyboomers" who are now particularly at risk of chronic diseases such as osteoporosis and cardiovascular disease (Warburton et al., 2007) and for whom the cumulative risk of all cancers up to 70 years of age tends to increase (White et al., 2014). Yet despite this public awareness and concern, cancer rates continue to grow. A total of 1,529,560 new cancer cases were recorded in 2010, an amount that does not include the two million additional basal and squamous cell skin cancers that are not normally reported to the national cancer registry (ACS, 2010). That number grew to 1,658,370 cancer cases by 2015, and by 2017 the number jumped to 1,688,780 cases (ACS, 2017, 2015). The growing prevalence of cancer carries significant and burdensome financial implications for the U.S. economy. According to the NIH, it cost $263.8 billion dollars in direct and indirect medical expenses to manage cancer in 2008 (ACS, 2010).

Cancer is not only a U.S. problem; it has insidiously made its way into almost all cultures and societies around the world. The World Health Organization estimates that in 2001 there were 10 million cases of cancer worldwide; they expect the number to grow to almost 20 million cases per year over the next 20 years (WHO, 2001). Because the lifetime cumulative risk of being diagnosed with some kind of cancer, in the US, is 41% (Howlader, et al., 2012), the impetus to find the elusive elixir that will quell this plague is very powerful. While a general cure has not been found yet, diet is most certainly central to the discussion; indeed, very few doubt that a chronic mismanagement of diet carries negative repercussions on human health. This is because there is a wealth of information easily accessed via the Internet, bookstores, and libraries that are popularizing healthy nutrition practices and lifestyles.

1.1.2 The Role of Nutrition in Healing and Prevention

The notion that nutrition is preventative and medicinal is as old as at least the Greek Classical period (500-336 BC). Aristotelian medical theory advanced that diseases originated from an imbalance of the fluid humors of the body: yellow bile, black bile, blood, and phlegm (Webster, 2008; Lagay, 2002) and that disturbances in the humors occurred from three basic causes: first, excesses or deficiencies, whether they be in diet, drink, or exercise; second, violent causes such as wounds, trauma, or extreme fatigue; and third, atmospheric conditions. It was the pre-Socratic philosopher, Empedocles of Agrigentum (500–430 BC), who proposed that the four elements of water, fire, earth, and air could explain the entire universe, including the biological system (Maher, 2002). This Empedoclean model suggested that nature and humans appeared to be intertwined and connected to the four seasons, and thus to the four humors. The four characteristics of these seasons were cold, hot, moist, and dry, offering, as it were, some natural principles of balance and contrasts that provided a rational belief structure that explained the inherent dangers associated with excesses or clear deficiencies. Consistent with this idea of equilibrium, Plato, in the *Timaeus*, (Plato, 2005) describes four principles of disease. The first was based on the notion that any excesses or deficiencies in the four humors would result in changes in the cold, hot, moist, and dry properties of the body, thus leading invariably to disease. The second principle, defined by Plato as the diseases of the "secondary formations," describes the consequence of insufficient food or drink to replenish the blood. A third origin of disease is considered from breath, phlegm, and bile. Here Plato describes lung diseases and the transformation of body fluids during the disease processes as visible signs of the loss of body balance. Fourth, he proposes that diseases can be caused by imbalances of the soul and mind (Bissonnette, 2013; Plato, 2005).

Hippocrates (460-370 BC), the father of medicine, built his practice around the idea that body balance was necessary for optimal health. He writes: *"Diseases that are generated by repletion are cured by depletion, and all which arise from depletion are cured by repletion; all which arises from exertion are cured by inactivity and all which arises from inactivity is cured by exertion"* (Brothwell & Brothwell, 1969). Elizabeth Craik, a reputed British classics scholar who teaches at the University of Saint Andrews, writes about Hippocratic balance, describing it in terms of a balance for the individual's physical condition and the elements in diet and in food (Craik, 1997). What is surprising is that the Greek notions of biological balance, and of the interdependency of the mind and body were ideas derived from rational thought and observations, rather than from experimentation; and yet despite the erroneous understanding of the pathophysiology of diseases, there was a great deal of truth rooted in the principle of biological homeostasis (Pang et al., 2014). In fact, scientific discussions and experiments are currently framed around the precepts of metabolic balance. Today we also believe that nutrition is an integral part of an individual's health, and of the collective health of a society for that matter. But conceivably, the Greeks, much like modern society today, understood that both the body and the mind needed to be in some kind of homeostasis to attain optimal health. The Greek physicians also understood that balance for the individual was dependent on routines for eating frequencies and on the types of foods that varied with seasons, customs, and geography. Our biology, Hippocratic medical practitioners believed, basically commanded what we should be eating; not providing what it needed could lead to illness and deficiency diseases. This physical balance was therefore achievable so long as excesses in food intake were balanced with abstinence, and increases in weight gains were tempered by weight loss (Plato, 2005). Early writings, from the classical Greek period, reveal that obesity was a known phenomenon, although clearly not as prevalent as today, and that its cause was clearly understood to be from an imbalance between quantity of food consumed and physical activity. Not surprising then that Greek writings refer to "Diaita" as a way of living that considered diet, exercise, baths, and emetics as an important dietary modality for treatment (Craik, 1997). Foods and concoctions were made up of food and plant mixtures that were purely medicinal in nature. Hence, diet and medicines were considered of equal importance by Greek and Roman physicians in battling the diseases of the time. In Oribasios' *Medical Complications* (Grant, 1995) a recipe for insomnia, written by a third-century BC physician, illustrates that in ancient Greece the soporific properties of poppy were clearly appreciated. Similarly, the Hippocratic obstetrician would have utilized a mixture of cheese, barley, and poppy to displace the womb during pregnancy (Grant, 1995). Medical conditions most certainly afflicted Greek society, and the Hippocratic physician played an important role in managing and curing them. However, was Hippocrates inspired to create the field of medicine in pursuit of therapies for a minority of people who were ill or was it by necessity to manage a growing prevalence of disease within Greek society?

1.1.3 The Neolithic Revolution and the Rise in Human Disease

Up until the archeological discovery, by Professor Joseph Carter in the early 1990s, of the 223 skeletal remains from the Metaponto Greek colony (580 BC and 250 BC) in the south of Italy, it was generally believed that diseases and nutritional deficiencies were fairly uncommon during the Greek classical period (Rensberger, 1992). Back then, the Greeks had broad food habits, consisting of a wide diversity of cereals, fish, domesticated animals, fruits, and vegetables. Nutritional deficiency diseases were also thought not to be very prevalent even during the Neolithic revolution (6000-3400 BC) in Ancient Greece. A Greek Minoan family, around 3000 BC for instance, would have had a typical diet consisting of chickpeas, leeks, millet, lentils, and bread, mixed with olive oil and goat cheese, and served with wine (Brothwell & Brothwell, 1998; Kishlansky et al., 1991). Additionally, meats, consisting of sheep, goat, cattle and swine would have been widespread as early as Neolithic times (7000 BC) and thus, when combined with vegetables and cereals, would have provided a broad and nutrient-rich diet (Brothwell & Brothwell, 1998). The Aegean people's (2300-1550 BC) proximity to the sea gave them access to abundant fish and seafood (Kishlansky et al., 1991), and thus would have limited actual meat consumption to only special feasts, a practice amounting nonetheless, to a nutritiously varied diet (Maher, 2002).

Although eating traditions—acquired and learned through the ages—may have safeguarded populations against the devastating consequences of poor nutrition and food poisonings, to some degree, sedentism, husbandry, and agricultural economies, embraced during the Neolithic Revolution, appear to have been responsible for the decline in human health (Cordaine et al., 2005; Brothwell & Brothwell, 1998). For instance, ergotism epidemics, originating from the fungal infestation of cereals like rye, by the *Claviceps purpurea* fungus, would have wiped out entire communities during Neolithic times (10,700-3,000 BC). Similarly, hydrogen cyanide, found in manioc tubers, would have poisoned many, before farmers understood the importance of pulping and soaking the roots in water to detoxify them before consumption. Indeed, cereal agriculture, introduced during the Neolithic revolution, was likely a vector for a variety of plant diseases, such as ergot and barley smut, that afflicted many populations up to the Early Bronze Age (3300-2100 BC) (Brothwell & Brothwell, 1998).

Overall, however, more recent work reveals that nutritional deficiencies, in Greek society, were likely more widespread than originally thought. The skeleton remains, unearthed following 18 years of excavations at Metaponto, an Italian colony of Greece (700-690 BC), by Professor Joseph C. Carter, a Centennial Professor of Classical Archaeology from the University of Texas, Austin, showed widespread

malnutrition in addition to adult diseases such as anemia caused by Thalassemia, possibly syphilis, tuberculosis and perhaps leprosy. Living conditions were likely pretty awful back then, asserts Professor Carter (Carter, 2006; Rosensberger, 1992).

As nomadic groups transitioned to sedentism, populations would have grown in size, therefore necessitating the planting of crops and the domestication of animals as food sources. This would have been necessary in order to feed a growing population that was less nomadic, and more inclined to build fundamental dwellings, and develop both agricultural (Richards, 2002) and fishing economies (Svizzero, 2014). It is now widely believed that this transition, from hunter-gatherer—seen as a more subsistence economy—to agriculturalist, would have taken place between 5000 to 12,000 BC; over an estimated 7000 year period there would have been a co-existent mix of agriculture and hunter-gatherer economies (Svizzero, 2014). But even after the Neolithic period began, claims Don Brothwell, a renowned archeologist from York University in the UK (Brothwell & Brothwell, 1998), early human agricultural settlements would have still relied on small game hunting, but to a much lesser degree than in Pre-Neolithic or Paleolithic eras. As food became more available, through stable agriculture, there would have been not only a trend towards wealth accumulation, but also a particular focus on production, storage, and surplus for trade purposes (Svizerro, 2014). Concomitantly, the population likely further increased in size, affecting an inevitable move toward urbanization and crowding conditions, a vector for infectious disease. The fundamental dietary adaptations, to accommodate the increased population density, would have been the source of higher rates of disease, morbidity, and mortality at the population level (Boaz, 2002; Gould, 2002; Nesse, 1994).

Some of the diseases were known to be of nutritional origin and were treated with nutritional remedies by the doctors of that period. A treatment of ox liver was found in Hippocrates' writings, in Roman texts and specifically in Chinese literature, dated AD 610, for the treatment of night blindness, which is caused by vitamin A deficiency. Even an Egyptian medical treatise, named the *Ebers papyrus*, dating back to 1600 BC, contained a description of ox liver as a treatment for night blindness, which preceded a more devastating blindness called **xerophthalmia** that arose from the drying of the cornea. Beriberi, a nutritional disease resulting from thiamine deficiency, and which had serious neurological symptoms ending with swelling and death, was documented in China during a nine-month siege of the city of Tsai Chseng around 529 (Brothwell & Brothwell, 1998). Hippocrates also documents bleeding and ulceration of the gums, typical of **scurvy**, whereas **pellagra**, a **niacin deficiency**, was prominent among corn- or maize-dependent economies, such as those of the Mayans and Aztecs (Brothwell & Brothwell, 1998). Rickets, produced by vitamin D deficiency, and characterized by the bowing of the long bones, caused by insufficient calcification of the bone matrix, seemed to have occurred quite infrequently among the early populations of China and Scandinavia. The earliest vestiges of bowed tibias, dating back to Neolithic times, were uncovered by archeological excavations in Denmark (Brothwell & Brothwell, 1998). However, the abundant vitamin D–rich fish oils, consumed by fish-eating populations of that era, living by the sea, in addition to the frequent sun exposure in southern climates, most certainly ensured sound bone health. Evidence of rickets did however increase later, in Rome (100-200 AD), because of the child-rearing practice of keeping the children indoors and protected from the sun.

Archeologists can, however, only speculate about the health impact of starchy and sugary foods—introduced in the early to middle Neolithic period—on dental caries since tooth decay is not strictly limited to agricultural societies, but has also been associated with the Pleistocene period, which significantly predates the Neolithic era (Brothwell & Brothwell, 1998). Nevertheless, other dental and bone diseases provide reasonable suspicion that there could have been important dietary inadequacies plaguing early Neolithic societies. For instance, **hypoplasia**, characterized by deformed tooth enamel, was identified in about 58-88% of dental samples between the Mesolithic and Bronze Age; in addition, **symmetrical hyperostosis**—seen only at the start of the Neolithic Era—presented as an osteoporotic pitting of the skull (Brothwell & Brothwell, 1998).

Carrera-Bastos and colleagues (2011) argue that the propensity for disease arose from new dietary habits that would have opposed the genome selected during the Paleolithic era in Africa, which would have occurred 2.5 million years ago. This change

from hunter-gatherer to agriculturist would have occurred only within 666 generations or 11,000 years ago (Carrera-Bastos et al., 2011). This must have theoretically created an evolutionary discordance between the genome and the environment (Cordaine, et al., 2005)—a selective pressure, as it were, that would have attempted to establish a new genomic set point—but because of the relative recency of the change, instead engendered disease. Indeed, the diet initiated by the Neolithic revolution was different than the pre-agricultural Hominin diet in that it contained more cereals, grains, and meats.

1.1.4 The Rise of Disease Prevalence in Western Societies

Current U.S. dietary traditions, it could be argued, are the consequence of the combined impacts of the Neolithic, Industrial, and Modern eras (Carrera-Bastos et al., 2011), culminating in a diet with up to 70% of the calories consumed from dairy products, mostly refined cereal grains, sugars, vegetable oils, and alcohol (Cordaine et al., 2005). But it is most certainly the Industrial Revolution, which only began seven generations ago, and the modern era, which have been shaping our diets and lifestyles for four generations, that have had the most significant impact in defining the Western lifestyle; that recency is what precludes any meaningful genetic adaptation that would have permitted the survival of the genus *Homo* to such dramatic dietary changes and transformation as we have seen with the late 19th and throughout the 20th centuries (Carrera-Bastos et al., 2011). It is rather the implementation of significant public health measures in the last two centuries that have prevented death rates from consistently soaring, not any kind of genetic adjustment to what some have described as recent radical changes to diet and lifestyle (Carrera-Bastos et al., 2011). Indeed, Sir Edwin Chadwick's School Meals Program, the School Medical Service, and the National Insurance Act, implemented in the early 1900s, were instrumental in reforming the English people's access to diet and medical services. It was, however, the implementation of a sophisticated system of sewers in London that mostly reformed public hygiene practices, and caused death rates to plummet in England, and eventually in the United States during the 19th and 20th centuries (Summers, 1989; Margotta,

1996). Although death rates have been tempered by improved public health, and by pharmaco-therapeutic strategies to manage diseases and conditions in recent times, chronic diseases, nevertheless, have increasingly been afflicting Western societies, the United States in particular, over the last century, but specifically since the 1980s. Indeed, national health expenditure data from the Centers for Disease Control and Prevention, describe an increase from $256 Billion to $2.9 Trillion by 2013 (CDC, 2013) followed by a subsequent jump to $3.5 Trillion in 2017 (Martin et al., 2018), representing nearly a 21% increase in just four years.

Some scholars have proposed that it was, specifically, the consumption of porridge and breads in Europe, rice in Asia, and maize in the New World, that caused the deterioration of human health and stature early in the Neolithic period (Richards, 2002). Others (Cordain et al., 2005) have convincingly concluded, from extensively reviewing the literature, that the Neolithic diet fundamentally harmed human health by changing several long-standing parameters of the diet, most notably: 1) glycemic load, 2) fatty acid composition, 3) macronutrient composition, 4) micronutrient density, 5) acid-base balance, 6) sodium-potassium ratio, and 7) fiber content.

Glycemic Load—The glycemic load (G.L.) measures the potential for a food to increase blood sugars based on the carbohydrate content per serving and the glycemic index (G.I.). The latter was developed by Dr. David Jenkins out of his lab at the University of Toronto's Nutritional Science department back in 1981 (Jenkins et al., 1981). The G.I. measures the ability of a standard quantity of carbohydrate-based foods to increase blood glucose levels within a defined period of time consequently leading to a ranking of carbohydrates following a scale of 0 to 100 (Holesh and Martin, 2019); as such, a G.I less than 55 would be considered a low G.I food (oatmeal, oat bran, muesli, legumes and most fruits), whereas a food with a G.I between 55 to 69 would be classified as having a medium G.I. (quick oats, brown rice and whole wheat bread). Finally, high G.I. foods consisting of white bread, corn flakes, white potatoes, rice cakes, pretzels and popcorn would have a G.I varying between 70 and 100 thereby increasing the risks of obesity, heart disease and type-2 diabetes (Holesh and Martin,

2018). Dr. Jenkin's research demonstrated that sugary products and refined grains invariably generated higher glycemic indexes (G.I.) than raw unprocessed fruits (Cordaine et al., 2005; Foster-Powell, 2002). There have been several large-scale studies linking the chronic intake of foods with high glycemic loads to greater risks of diseases like type-2 diabetes and cardiovascular diseases (Foster-Powell et al., 2002). This makes sense from an evolutionary perspective if one considers that the typical diet of the hunter-gatherer communities consisted primarily of foods with low glycemic load indices (Cordaine et al., 2005) that tended to be less than 10 (Table 1.1). Indeed, archeo-botanists tell us that hunter-gatherers consumed a lot of berries, fruits, and nuts complemented with meats, which clearly resulted in a very low overall G.L. The transition to an agricultural society, however, cannot be seen as all bad as there is good evidence supporting the cultivation of legumes such as soy beans, lentils, peas, and vetch early in the Neolithic period around the sixth and seventh millennia (Brothwell & Brothwell, 1998). As compiled in Table-1.1, legumes have G.L.s that are considerably low, with values varying between 0.6 and 6.6, and thus representing but a small insulinotropic effect. This is good news for long-term health as diets that maintain low blood glucose and insulin levels tend to not cause negative effects on metabolism and health (Cordain et al., 2005).

The G.I. values in Table-1.1 are based first, on the determination of a G.I. standard using glucose, and second, on the relative degree to which blood sugars are generated from the ingestion of an assortment of carbohydrate-based foods that are simple or complex. Given that glucose has a G.I. equal to 100, then it is possible to derive from this number, the relative blood glucose values generated from other carbohydrate foods. For instance, Rice Krispies cereal from Kellogg's has a G.I. equal to 82 out of 100 whereas a doughnut has a G.I. of 76 and white bread has one equal to 70. But most surprising, a baked potato has a G.I. of 85 whereas most fruits register a G.I. between 38 and 59 out of 100.

Now the G.L. can be calculated following two methods (GL[1] or GL[2]) as seen in Table-1.1. First, to calculate GL[1], the known grams of carbohydrates per serving are divided by 100 and then multiplied by the G.I. (Glycemic index × Grams of carbohydrates per serving / 100g of food product). In the case of General Mills' Cheerios, the G.I. is equal to 74. Considering that a standard serving size of Cheerios is one ounce weight or roughly 30g and that it contains 20g of carbohydrates, it is possible to establish the G.L. by multiplying the G.I. of 74 by 20g and then dividing it by 100g in order to derive a G.L.[1] of 15 (74 × 20/100).

The second method (G.L.[2]) is calculated by multiplying the G.I. of 74 by the grams of carbohydrates found in one serving of the product. Afterwards, that value is divided by the weight of one serving of cereal or 30 grams. The Glycemic Load (G.L.) can now be calculated: (74 × 20g)/30g = 49. As students review Table-1.1, they will observe that the G.L.[2] tends to more realistically reflect the true glycemic load. It should become apparent that processed foods such as breakfast cereals with very little fiber tend to have a G.L. that varies between 60 and 72 using method 2, whereas the high fiber cereals will have G.L.s that are between 23 and 38, which is about two to three times less. Similarly, the glycemic load of many highly processed foods is also much more elevated than what would normally be seen with the ingestion of a healthy variety of fruits and vegetables (Foster-Powell et al., 2002). And while baked breads and pastas have more elevated G.Ls (11 to 38) compared to fruits and legumes (1 to 10), it is the sweets in combination with the highly-processed foods that deliver a very debilitating glycemic punch because of their prominence in the U.S. diet and their unusually high glycemic loads of 40 to 105 (Table-1.1). Loren Cordain, and colleagues (2005) describe, in their review, a U.S. food

Table 1.1
Glycemic Index (G.I.) and Glycemic Load (G.L.) of Common Foods

Food Items	G.I. (Glycemic Index)	G.L. (Glycemic Load)[1]	G.L. (Glycemic Load)[2]
BREADS & CEREALS			
Bagel (white)	72	25	36
Bread (white processed)	70	10	33
Bread (50% oat bran)	44	8	26
Bread (French baguette)	72	27	38
Bread (whole wheat)	71	9	31
Bran Buds (Kellogg's)	58	7	23.2
Corn Flakes (Kellogg's)	81	21	70
Couscous (cooked)	65	23	15.2
Fruit Loops (Kellogg's)	69	18	60
Raisin Bran (Kellogg's)	61	12	38
Rice (basmati white-boiled)	58	22	14.7
Rice (brown)	55	18	21
Rice (long grain parboiled)	56	23	15.3
Rice Krispies (Kellogg's)	82	22	72
Spaghetti (whole grain)	37	16	10.5
Spaghetti (white)	44	21	12

Food Items	G.I. (Glycemic Index)	G.L. (Glycemic Load)[1]	G.L. (Glycemic Load)[2]
FRUITS			
Apples (raw & fresh)	38	6	5
Apricots (raw & fresh)	31	9	4
Banana (raw)	52	12	10
Cherries (raw)	22	3	2
Oranges (raw & fresh)	42	5	4
Peaches (raw & fresh)	42	5	4
Pears (raw & fresh)	33	4	3.5
Pineapple (raw & fresh)	59	7	6.4
Plums (raw)	39	5	4
Strawberries (fresh)	40	1	1
NUTS			
Nuts (cashews)	22	3	5.72
Peanuts	14	1	1.7
VEGETABLES/LEGUMES			
Baked Beans (canned)	48	7	4.8
Carrots	47	3	3.5
Corn (sweet)	54	9	11.5
Lentils (green, canned)	30	5	3.4
Parsnips	97	12	14.6
Peas (green)	48	3	4.2
Pinto Beans (canned & cooked)	45	10	6.6
Potato (baked russet with no fat)	85	26	17
Potato (white, mashed)	74	15	10
Potato (white, instant, mashed)	85	17	11.3
Potato (white, boiled)	50	14	9.3
Potato (French fries)	75	22	14.5
Romano Beans (canned)	46	8	5.5
Soy Beans (boiled)	18	1	0.6

Food Items	G.I. (Glycemic Index)	G.L. (Glycemic Load)[1]	G.L. (Glycemic Load)[2]
SUGARS			
Fructose	19	2	19
Glucose	99	10	99
Honey (average)	55	10	40
Maltose	105	11	105
Sucrose (table sugar)	68	7	68
JUNK/SNACK FOODS			
Corn chips	63	17	33
Jelly Beans	78	22	73
Mars Bar	65	12	40
Nutella	33	4	19.8
Pop-Tarts	70	24	49
Potato chips	54	11	23

Adapted from Foster-Powell et al., 2002; $GL^1 = GI \times$ grams of carbohydrates per serving then divided by 100. $GL^2 = GI \times$ grams of carbohydrates per serving as listed on the products Nutrition Facts Panel and then divided by the portion size.

market in which 39% or more of the food supply is contributing towards heightened insulin resistance (Del Prato et al., 1994). This is not surprising as nutritive sweeteners (sucrose, syrups, honey, and glucose) in addition to high fructose corn syrups of varying glycemic loads (HFCS-42 & HFCS-55) make up approximately 18.6% of all calories consumed in the United States. It is specifically the HFCS that represent quite a paradox as they appear to worsen insulin insensitivity in hyperinsulinic men, despite having both low G.Is and G.Ls. Fructose action appears to take place at the biochemical level, causing a metabolic shift from a preferred state of fat oxidation to one that favors esterification or fat deposit. Regardless, there is no precedent in human evolutionary history for so much sugar consumption by such a large population—152 lbs. of sugar per capita in the United States in the year 2000—which is a deviant intake that has only been seen within the last 200 years of human existence (Cordain et al., 2005).

Fatty Acid Composition—The modern Western diet contains, on average, far greater amounts of total fat—40% of calories—compared to 21% of calories in hunter-gatherer societies through to the mid-1800s (Simopoulos, 1999). It has been postulated that with the increased processing of food that took place since the Industrial Revolution, omega-6 polyunsaturated fats in addition to quantities of saturated fats (SAFs) and trans-fatty acids (TFAs) have jumped to greater prevalence in the diet than healthy standards allow (Cordain et al., 2005; Simopoulos 2002). The SAFs from fatty meats, baked goods, cheese, milk, margarine, and butter are all thought to contribute towards the development of cardiovascular disease (CVD) when the cumulative amounts of SAF become >10% of calories (Cordain et al., 2005); this is a fat profile not likely to have been prominent in the diet of Pleistocene Hominids of the Paleolithic era. It is commonly believed that these prehistoric hominids relied on wild lean animals from successful hunts and not on fatty meats, which emerged as more of a dietary tradition later on with the domestication of livestock in the Neolithic era. Consequently, the proportion of polyunsaturated fats (PUFAs) and monounsaturated fats (MUFAs), coming from plants, relative to SAFs originating from meats, would have been much greater than in our modern age. Moreover, more than 50% of the carcass fat on wild animals would likely have consisted of MUFAs and PUFAs (Cordain et al., 2005). Therefore, by no means could it be argued, that SAFs were prominent enough, in the Paleolithic era, to have exerted negative selective pressures, on the genome of the hominid of that time thereby causing disease and death (Cordain et al., 2005). It was likely the dietary changes, occurring 150 years ago with the Industrial Revolution, that incited the prevalence of chronic disease to sharply increase in modern society. During that time, not only did the proportion of SAFs rise with fattier meats in the mid to late 1800s, but also the ratio of omega-6 (n-6 PUFAs) relative to omega-3 fatty acids (n-3 PUFAs) greatly increased during the early mid-1900s. It jumped from 1–2:1 in the diet of the hunter-gatherer, through to the beginning of the 1900s, to an outlandish population mean around 12.4–16.7:1 in the 1960s to 90s—some individuals reaching as high as 25:1—with the advent of liberal recommendations to replace the intake of saturated fats with polyunsaturated (n-6) fats, like sunflower seeds, safflower seeds, cottonseed, and soybeans; the purpose was to decrease blood cholesterol and the risk of heart disease (Kris-Etherton, 2000; Simopoulos, 2002, 1999). This dietary change, in the Western diet, was facilitated by a wide availability of omega-6 fatty acid-rich oils, made possible with the advent of modern vegetable oil-seed processing. This ratio also increased from the concomitant decline in omega-3 fatty acid intake over that same time period because of a notable drop in fish consumption—abundant in n-3 fatty acids—in addition to the heavier use of animal grain feed, rich in omega-6 fats. Instead of allowing livestock to graze on omega-3-rich grass, as was the custom back in the 19th century and earlier, the practice of feeding cattle grains led to omega-6 rich meats (Cordain et al., 2005; Kris-Etherton et al., 2000; Simopoulos, 1999). Some have argued that since between the mid-1980s and 1990s the ratio has subsequently fallen from 12.4:1 to 10.6:1 because of a shift towards ingesting more vegetable oils with higher omega-3 content such as soy bean, canola, and flaxseed (Kris-Etherton et al., 2000). This shift took place in response to research findings that linked excessive

intakes of omega-6 fatty acids to the promotion of cardiovascular disease, cancer, inflammatory and autoimmune disorders (Simopoulos, 2002). Still, even an omega-6 to omega-3 ratio of 10:1 is considered too elevated because of the nefarious effects this proportion of n-6 fatty acids has on health. In contrast the WHO recommends a ratio of 5-10:1, whereas Sweden has fixed the goal at 5:1, and Japan at between 4–2:1 (Kris-Etherton et al., 2000), which are ratios more associated with lower mortality rates in heart disease patients, decreased risk of breast cancer, less inflammation in rheumatoid arthritis, and decreased asthma symptoms (Simopoulos, 2002). Moreover, it is generally agreed that health risks tend to be more elevated when total polyunsaturated fats (PUFAs) exceed 10% of DRI calories; the preference is to aim for PUFAs to remain around 7% of calories in order to minimize the synthesis of the pro-inflammatory compounds—prostaglandins, thromboxanes, leukotrienes—that are metabolic end products of omega-6 fatty acid metabolism (Kris-Etherton et al., 2000). And despite the recognition of omega-3 fatty acids as beneficial in reducing the risk of chronic disease, the prospect of being able to decrease the ratio back to even the 1930s levels of 8.4:1 is remote. This is because modern agricultural practices have diminished the omega-3 fatty acid content of foods such as meats, eggs, leafy vegetables, and cultured fish, once considered to be good sources of this fat (Simopoulos, 1999). Moreover, the hydrogenation process that solidifies oils to produce margarines that emulate butter-like consistency was created in 1897. This process unfortunately introduced into the diet very atherogenic trans-fatty acids, now estimated to represent 7.4% total fatty acid intake (Cordain et al., 2005).

While the Neolithic period did introduce greater abundance of total fat with animal husbandry and the planting of seed-yielding oils, it is more the Industrial Revolution and its mechanized processing of food that flooded the market with unusually large amounts of soybean and corn oil, high in omega-6 fatty acids, that have possibly created the greatest damage to human health.

Macronutrient Composition—It has been advanced by some, in the academic fields of nutrition and archeology, that the macronutrient distribution of contemporary societies has shifted in significant ways from the dietary profile of hunter-gatherer

Table 1.2

Recommended Macronutrient Proportions by Age

Ranges of Age Groups	Carbohydrate	Protein	fat
Young children (1–3 years)	45–65%	5–20%	30–40%
Older children and adolescents (4–18 years)	45–65%	10–30%	25–35%
Adults (19 years and older)	45–65%	10–35%	20–35%

Source: Institute of Medicine. Dietary Reference Intakes for Energy, Carbohydrate, Fiber, Fat, Fatty Acids, Cholesterol, Protein, and Amino Acids. Washington (DC): The National Academies Press; 2002.

tribes in that protein intake would have declined from 25% of calories—more reflective of the Paleolithic era—to 15.4% of caloric needs—typically seen in today's modern era (Cordain et al., 2005). Dietary Reference Intakes (DRIs), established by the Institute of Medicine (I.O.M., 2002), recommends, for adult Americans 19 years and older, carbohydrate intakes between 45–65% of DRI calories; fat ingestion between 20–35% of DRI calories, and protein consumption within the range of 10–35% of DRI calories. These Acceptable Macronutrient Distribution Ranges (AMDR) are associated with diminished risks of diseases in a population (I.O.M., 2002). (Institute of Medicine, 2002) (Table 1.2). The WHO (2002) recommends a more conservative 15% of calories as an ideal protein intake for most normally active humans on the planet, which equals about 0.75g/kg body weight. This last recommendation is based on intricate nitrogen balance studies that measure true bodily requirements for nitrogen, as established from nitrogen consumed, and nitrogen excreted in the form of urea nitrogen and some fecal matter. Those supporting the Paleolithic diet contend that protein ingestion would have varied between 15–35% (Lindeberg, 2005) or 19–35% of energy needs (Cordain et al., 2005) with a much lower carbohydrates intake range of 22–40% of calories (Cordain et al., 2005). These protein and carbohydrate estimates infer a potential fat intake varying between 25%–59% of energy needs, a value considered much higher than the 21% estimated by the Kris-Etherton group (2000). Conclusions about the Paleo diet appear equivocal at this time as others have estimated that the Paleolithic societies did not consume a low carbohydrate diet (Lindeberg, 2005) but certainly one containing carbohydrates (44–64%

of calories) that are consistent with the Healthy Eating Guidelines for Americans 2015 (Table-2).

Recent work has shown that protein, consumed as 23% of caloric needs, causes a clinically significant drop in blood lipid profiles suggesting a clear health benefit that is protective against heart disease. Studies are also demonstrating that the current mean U.S. population protein intake—around 15% of calories—may be suboptimal and could afford to be higher and more consistent with the Paleolithic hypothesis (Cordain et al., 2005). However, in contrast with the notion that such high meat intake is consistent with our evolutionary genome and therefore beneficial to health, Marion Nestle (1999) advances that the proposal that man is genetically geared towards a high protein intake is easily refuted on the basis that most primates today are actually vegetarians, and not carnivores. Moreover, Dr. David Jenkin's research team out of the University of Toronto (Wong et al., 2012) advances that the vegetarian diet, high in soluble fiber, is critical at maintaining a healthy gut microbiota and is able to lower serum cholesterol levels. And although there have been publications promoting high protein and low calorie diets as more effective in weight loss than high carbohydrates and low fat diets, at least on the short term, there are several long-term follow-up studies that claim high protein diets are not capable of sustaining weight loss; in fact most put on significant weight after dieting (Mann et al., 2007). It just might be premature to throw out those vegetables, fruits, and grains.

Micronutrient Density—The hominid of the Neolithic era had an agricultural-based diet that greatly reduced his access to the broad assortment of plants, and plant-based nutrients, typical of the nomadic Paleolithic hunter-gatherer's diet. In that sense, the Neolithic diet was lower in nutrient density (mg of nutrients per kilocalorie) compared to the Paleolithic diet, but likely did not contribute to a surge in chronic disease prevalence similar to what is seen today. It was not until technologically-advanced food processing began to introduce large amounts of refined sugar, and foods made with refined sugar, in addition to processed oils—making up 36.2% of the calories of a typical U.S. diet—that the risk of poor nutrition and health may have truly begun (USDA, 1997; Cordain et al., 2005). Indeed, survey data from 1994–1996 revealed that about 50% of Americans did not meet the Recommended Dietary Allowance (RDA) for vitamin B-6, vitamin A, magnesium, calcium, and zinc, and that as many as 33% did not meet folate requirements (Cordain et al., 2005). What is striking is the progressive decline in the nutritional quality of the U.S. diet over the last 50–75 years, concomitantly with the sharp decrease in vegetables, seafood, and lean unprocessed meat consumption nationwide. During the 1930s and 40s these foods were replaced by bleached non-enriched flour—mechanically-milled to remove the nutrient-rich bran and wheat germ—which quickly became the United States' flour of choice, furnishing up to 50% of calories for a majority of Americans, and consequently peppering the American landscape with significant clusters of malnutrition (Bobrow-Strain, 2003, 2007). Even today, despite the enrichment of flour and grains with thiamin, riboflavin, niacin, folate and iron—a countering safeguard against nutrient-deficiency disease—Loren Cordain and her colleagues (2005) advance that heightening population intakes of grains, breads and cereals, which are mostly processed, at the expense of vegetables, fruits, and lean meats, can lead to an important lowering of the nutrient density of the food supply and increase the risk of disease and infections in the population (Cordain et al., 2005). The problem had become so visibly alarming that the Surgeon General's 1988 report on nutrition and health emphasized the consumption of fruits, vegetables, whole grains, lean meats, and low fat dairy as a strategy to quell the noticeable jump in the prevalence of chronic diseases (Davis & Saltos, 1999).

Acid-Base Balance—The principle that the acid-base balance of the diet could so easily affect human health is grounded in the biochemical reality that foods, once ingested, digested and absorbed, generate either bicarbonate or acids that flow systemically into the body (Sebastian et al., 2002; Frasetto et al., 1998). The current North American diet, because of its preponderance of acid-yielding foods such as dairy products (especially hard cheeses), cereal grains, salt (because of the chloride ion), meats, fish, shellfish, and eggs, generate a low grade metabolic acidosis that is sufficient to precipitate important losses of bone calcium (Carrera-Bastos, et al., 2011). By contrast, Cordain and colleagues (2005) argue that the Paleolithic diet would have been abundant in base yielding fresh fruit, vegetables, tubers, roots, and nuts, and that the Neolithic era in addition to the age of industrialization would have effectively displaced base-yielding fruit and vegetables out of the regular diet.

Sodium-Potassium Ratio—The American public consumes on average roughly 3300 mg of sodium/day whereas potassium (K) intake is much lower at 2600 mg/day, resulting in sodium to potassium ratio (Na: K) that is greater than 1. The transition of the Paleolithic hominid from the nomadic hunter-gatherer society to the agricultural-based society would have caused somewhat of a downward shift in potassium consumption, a process facilitated by the displacement of fruits and vegetables, by grains and milk—vegetables contain four times the K found in grains and milk. However, technological processing of food in addition to transitioning to the Neolithic diet would have specifically caused an overall 400% drop in potassium intake and a simultaneous 400% jump in dietary sodium content (Cordain et al., 2005). It appears that a chronically high Na: K ratio could increase the risk of developing chronic illnesses, including hypertension, cardiovascular disease, osteoporosis, and some intestinal cancers to name but a few (Cordain et al., 2005; Jansson, 1996; Tryns, 1988, Antonios & MacGregor, 1996).

Fiber—Because of the preponderance of sugar, dairy, alcohol and vegetable oils in the American diet, all of which contain no fiber but still makeup 48.2% of the U.S. diet, it is not surprising that mean daily fiber intake of 17g/day is much lower than the recommended 25-38g (A.N.D 2015) needed for good gastrointestinal health. In fact, no more than 5% of the US population meet Adequate Intake recommendations (A.N.D., 2015). The problem of suboptimal fiber intake in our modern culture is further exacerbated by the fact that 85% of wheat consumed in the United States is refined and processed, and therefore depleted of fiber (Krauss et al., 2000). Hunter-gatherers, by contrast, would have regularly consumed in the vicinity of 42.5g of a mixture of soluble and insoluble fiber because of the noticeable absence of milk, oil, grains, sugar, and processed foods, which have been responsible for a significant proportional decrease in the dietary fiber content of the modern Western diet (Cordain et al., 2005). Meeting dietary fiber requirements is important in reducing the risks of type-2 diabetes, cardiovascular disease, coronary heart disease, and specifically colorectal and stomach cancers (A.N.D, 2015).

Physical Inactivity—Hunter-gatherer populations and those cultures not yet disturbed by modern-day food habits, typically seen in industrialized countries (Carrera-Bastos et al., 2011), are characteristically endowed with superior markers of health, physical fitness, and lean body composition. Indeed, blood pressures (BPs) measured in horticulturalists and hunter-gatherer societies, like the Yanomamo, an indigenous people, still living in the Amazonian rain forest, varied between 104/65 and 113/71 in men, and between 102/62 and 121/71 in women. These are values that are significantly below the 120/80 cut-off used as an optimal guidepost for health in Western society (Carrera-Bastos, et al., 2011).

Consequently, greater disease rates have often been blamed by the substantive decline in physical activity which took place with the disappearance of the nomadic tradition. Carrera-Bastos and colleagues (2011), in their review of the literature, advance that there is convincing evidence linking physical inactivity to the appearance of insulin resistance, dyslipidemia, obesity, hypertension, type-2 diabetes, coronary artery disease, angina, myocardial infarction, congestive heart failure, stroke, intermittent claudication, gallstones, various types of cancer, age-related cognitive dysfunction, sarcopenia, and osteopenia.

Paleolithic communities appear to be protected from these debilitating degenerative diseases because they tended to have lower body mass indexes (BMIs), and small waist circumferences compared to the modern North American. Additionally, in Paraguay, the hunter-gatherer Kitava and Ache Indians tend to have lower fasting blood leptin and blood sugars compared to the residents of most Western countries (Carrera-Bastos et al., 2011). Visual acuity and aerobic capacity, measured using VO2max, tend also to be superior in hunter-gatherer tribes living in Amazonian territories compared again to Westerners. Consistent with higher activity levels, hunter-gatherer communities also have good bone health markers in addition to lower fracture rates (Carrera-Bastos et al., 2011).

It does appear that the modernization of the diet in the last 150 years, in combination with a less physically active society, have greatly contributed to the many chronic diseases of our time. Interestingly, most if not all of the causes appear to be preventable, yet populations are not motivated to move in unison on matters of health. However, despite some malnutrition having affected various populations over specific timelines, famines and plagues have been the most significant and remarkable causes of widespread malnutrition, human misery and death throughout history (Nikiforuk, 1996). In the end we can talk nutrient density and optimal nutrition all we want, the truth of the matter is that, in human history, it is the lack of food, rather than food of poor quality, that has defined the great sorrowful historical tragedies of humankind.

1.2 MALNUTRITION AND FAMINES: THEIR IMPACTS ON SOCIETY

1.2.1 Introduction to the Impacts of Plagues and Famines

It was the famines that catalysed human misery, at unprecedented levels, through hunger and deficiency diseases. This is certainly supported by the roughly 1800 famines that would have swept across the British Isles and China between the years 100 BC and AD 1910 (Brothwell & Brothwell, 1969). But it was specifically the devastating famines that ploughed through Europe from 1308 to 1332 that Western historians long remember because the hunger not only caused indelible and horrifying levels of human suffering in the minds of the European people, but the very scarcity of food drove, through mass hysteria, the population to seek food at all cost; some, for instance, came to rely on dogs, cats, excrement and even children to fill their cooking pots (Kishlansky, 1991). Physically weakened, the population subsequently became vulnerable to the scourge of pneumonic and bubonic plagues, which visited the European continent, first between 1351 and 1358, wiping out roughly 24 million people, second in 1362, and again in 1369, when it killed primarily children (Nikiforuk, 1996).

© DEA/G. DAGLI ORTI/Getty Images

Figure 1.1 *Michel Serre (1658–1733),* The Plague in Marseilles in 1721.

The plague revisited Europe afterwards, in several waves, but with less virulence, before its final retreat from Europe in 1720, hitting Marseille and killing 80,000 people (Figure 1.1). It also hit Venice in 1575 and in 1630, killing an estimated 13% of every new generation (Nikiforuk, 1996).

European society was able to begin to strongly recover from the devastation left by the plague only around the 15th century. Coincidentally, the resilience of the population was further fuelled by the Renaissance, also known as the rebirth of European society. And so it was that humanity was celebrating and exalting itself in a rebirth that translated into numerous wars gradually ending, and unemployment rates dropping to their lowest in recent memory—the consequence of a small post-plague population. Throughout the 15th century, the marketplace became diversified in an unprecedented way: meat and dairy products were abundantly and frequently part of the diet. Pork and lamb consumption of this magnitude would not be seen again

until the 19th century. Revitalizing the economy was nevertheless no small task as epidemics and plagues continued to decimate the population every six years, between 1350 and 1450. Consequently, the economy remained stagnant until the end of the 15th century (Nikiforuk, 1996). However, in the early 16th century, the economy prospered once the population began to grow again. Moreover, as agricultural production began to intensify at the start of the 17th century, and further diversify, yielding specialty crops like sugar, saffron, fruits, and wines, and as imported exotic goods from the Far East spilled over into the marketplace (Kishlansky, 1991), the population suddenly had access to greater food availability. Both an improved economy and diet contributed most significantly to population health. This was facilitated by better transportation and communication systems, in addition to an agricultural surplus of grains. The population's access to more nutritious, affordable, and varied foods invariably led to an improved life expectancy (Kishlansky, 1991). Cities grew in both number and size, and even though they were made of dark and narrow streets that stunk from raw sewage, rotting foodstuff, and slaughterhouses, the marketplace, still nevertheless became the epicenter of human activity.

1.2.2 Malnutrition during the 18th-Century Agricultural Revolution

At the beginning of the 18th century, Louis XIV drew France into a financial crisis of epic proportion, beginning in 1701 with his participation in the war of Spanish Succession, which was to last until 1714. The war became too costly to manage over time, leading to a debt so great the monarch never recovered from it (Rowlands, 2009). It precipitated a financial crisis that destabilized the country's economy and military power; food prices significantly rose, causing wheat to accumulate in the numerous grain warehouses spread throughout the country. Louis XIV resisted the imposition of price ceilings on wheat, and grain didn't reach the cities where human misery was growing quickly. Then in January 1709 record low temperatures of –15C° engulfed France for several weeks, precipitating the famous famine of 1709 represented in this earlier period lithograph (Figure 1.2) (Miller, 1999; Rowlands, 2009).

© *Morphart Creation/Shutterstock.com.*

Figure 1.2 Relief soup, in Paris, during the famine of 1709. *Vintage engraved illustration. Magasin Pittoresque 1875.*

However, by 1740, better housing and a greater availability of food—the result of the Agricultural Revolution, which is considered one of the great turning points in human history (Kishlansky, 1991)—favored a sizable increase in the population. It transformed single-estate subsistence farms that produced small but diversified crop yields, into large commercial farming plantations that became dedicated to single-crop production. This led to the buyout of the middling-sized landholders and an eventual increase in the landless agrarian labor force that roamed the countryside in search of work and food (Kishlansky, 1991). Paradoxically, it was specifically the population growth, fostered by a decline in death rates resulting from the retreat of both wars and plagues (Kishlansky, 1991), that drove prices skyrocketing because of greater demand, but also precipitated a downward adjustment of wages during the second half of the 18th century; this, in the end, limited the consumer's purchasing power, and made the plight of the poor, living in the cities, much more acute. And while widespread famines no longer swept through country sides, villages, towns, and countries as they did back in the 14th century, there was still a persistent low-grade starvation and undernutrition that kept 10% and 15% of most 18th century European societies—roughly 20 million

people, most of whom were urbanites—in unrelenting states of hunger and misery as portrayed in the hungry child with bread (Figure 3.1). Paradoxically, the Agricultural Revolution, despite increasing crop yields would have generated a prominence of hunger and of poor-quality diets that were more rampant at the end of the 18th century than at the beginning. In fact, Robert Vial (1989) submits that the nutritional quality of the diet, at that time, may have been the poorest in European history. Mark Kishlansky (1991), in his book *Civilization in the West*, describes a diet consisting mostly of bread baked from a mix of rye, barley, and wheat that was dipped into a cooking pot filled with vegetable soup made from the following ingredients: small peas and cabbage during the summer and turnips, celery, and pumpkin during the winter. Meat and potatoes were added to the cauldron once per week if the father was lucky enough to find work (Kishlansky, 1991). Food scarcity still nevertheless persisted in clusters up until the end of the 18th century. In particular, the French, who were still caught in the turmoil of the French Revolution, were without bread, meat, butter, and vegetables during the winter of 1793–94.

1.2.3 Malnutrition and Disease during the 19th-Century Industrial Revolution

As the Industrial Revolution took hold by the early to mid-19th century, large populations, in search of the higher-paying factory jobs, migrated from the rural countryside to the large urban centers, where complex monumental factories were bellowing out plumes of smoke, the grim and dirty iconic image of an industrialized age. In England, the seat of the first industrial society, the percentage of the population residing in cities exploded between the end of the 18th century, when no more than 30% of the English were urbanites, to an astounding 50% by 1841 (Morley, 2007). This significant urban expansion, which took place in cities such as London, Birmingham, Manchester, and Liverpool, began to erode agricultural fields that were too close to the city limits, and, at the same time, increased the prevalence of the urban poor who were relegated to live in indescribable squalor (Morley, 2007). The great social urban experiment created a hellish situation in which an unholy mix of pauperism, crime, dirt, disease, deprivation, and death gravely tainted the age of the great cities of Europe (Morley, 2007). Like a petri dish, the densely populated cities became a common breeding ground for whooping cough, scarlet fever, small pox, typhus, tuberculosis, and influenza; it was an environment of disease with high enough death rates that life expectancy was seriously shortened to 29 years of age, for instance, in districts such as East London (Morley, 2007).

Moreover, access to nutritious foods was rather limited as the new urbanites had transitioned from a rural reliance on garden produce to a dependency on the grocer's rather narrow inventory which, by early winter, had depleted reserves of cabbage, leeks, and onions—high in vitamin C or ascorbic acid. Consequently, the urbanite, unlike the rural farmer, was limited to a sparse diet of starch, bread, some tinned foods, and meat until the spring, at which point, scurvy outbreaks began to primarily sweep through the cities' poorer districts (Carpenter, 1986). Medical interventions were powerless at preventing or containing the scourge of scurvy that swept through the dark crowded streets of many European cities. The sparse diets and the frequent hunger that devastated France during the French Revolution, from 1789 to 1795, caused many nutritional diseases that could not be prevented by the field of medicine (Kishlansky, 1991), but also heightened the vulnerability of the population to many infectious diseases like smallpox, and tuberculosis that rampantly moved through English cities (Morley, 2007).

© NinaMalyna/Shutterstock.com.

Figure 1.3 *A portrait of a poor beggar child with a piece of bread in her hands.*

It was, however, the emergence of the cholera epidemic in the early 19th century that brought man once again to his knees. The field of medicine remained powerless in halting the spread of cholera, which began in the Orient between 1816 and 1823, and eventually struck terror throughout Europe starting in both Sunderland in Britain in 1831, and Paris in 1832, eventually striking the London district of Soho in 1854 where it sickened as many as 14,000 souls and caused 618 deaths (Summers, 1989). A new generation was now terror-stricken, as it watched doctors struggle in vain to contain the scourge that had far too many resemblances to the plague from long ago. No medication, no therapeutic cleansing, no elixir from ages past could abate its terrorizing advance; it killed quickly and agonizingly. By 1826 it had reached over the Atlantic, where it sickened and killed many Americans in cities like Boston, New York, New Orleans, and Philadelphia; it revisited the United States in many waves up until 1873 (Pyle, 1969). Remarkably the solution to containing the epidemic came from the relentless investigative work of the English anesthetist John Snow in 1849 (Pyle, 1969). He found that cholera infected a leaking cesspool that leached into the drinking water at the Broad Street water pump in the Soho district of London (Summers, 1989); from there, it spread throughout the city. Dr. Snow contented that it was infected water rather than foul-smelling air—which was the main tenet of the popular miasmic theory (Halliday, 2001) of disease—that was the primary vector for the spread of cholera (Halliday, 2001). Snow's theory was not well accepted because the dominant miasmic theory had entrenched most into believing that foul putrid-smelling air was responsible for illness. However, it was English reformer, Sir Edwin Chadwick, who was responsible for instigating public health reforms in England that eventually contained the spread of cholera (Halliday, 2001). He almost single-handedly convinced the English Parliament with his 1842 report: *"The Sanitary Conditions of the Laboring Population"* that public reforms were necessary; he had managed to draw, through statistical analysis, a strong corollary between the poor living and working conditions of the laboring class and the higher disease rates. His report, dubbed the *Chadwick report*, strongly advocated for economic growth and social order for the working class; the understanding was that higher wages could improve nutrition, living conditions, and the overall health of families (Morley, 2007). His report also discussed the importance of civil engineering rather than medicine in the promulgation of the public's health in the cities (Bump, 2015); he was convinced that cleaning up the dung heaps on the streets and better management of the street drains and sewers would invariably lead to cleaner air and ultimately to the improved health of the laborer (Bump, 2015; Morley, 2007). His report eventually inspired the creation of the Public Health Act of 1948, which galvanized public and government support to repair and clean up the urban environment (Halliday, 2001). The civil engineer, Joseph Bazalgette was eventually hired to build a sophisticated system of intercepting sewers between 1859 and 1875. Once implemented, the new re-engineered sewers did in fact sharply cut death rates, and prevented further spread of the epidemic (Summers, 1989). In addition, a system of drains and piped-in fresh water that did not cross with the sewer, was structurally set-up for private dwellings (Morley, 2007).

Part of Chadwick's legacy, after he died in 1890, was the implementation of a public health service in Britain by 1848, which led to the free school meals for needy children with the passing of the Provision of Meals Act of 1905 (Gunderson, 2014), and the National Insurance Act (1911). These reforms eventually led to full social security in Britain by 1948 with the National Health Service (Bump, 2015).

The cholera epidemic ended both because of dramatic improvements in public hygiene and because of the lower class' greater purchasing power. The labor class now worked long hours in factories and brought home larger incomes. It was, in truth, the overall improved living conditions of the people that caused disease and death rates to plummet, and not any single medical intervention (Summers, 1989; Margotta, 1996). The greater incomes meant that complete families had greater access to milk, potatoes, and meats for consumption. In fact, between 1834 and the launching of the National Health Service in 1948, the gross domestic product, expressed per capita, rose 3.5 times in the United Kingdom (Bump, 2015). The improved availability of food ensured that a broader population base was well fed and resistant to infections, consequently leading to a harder-working labor force (Morley, 2007; Margotta, 1996). As the 19th century came to a close, there was a period of economic prosperity that took place, especially between 1850 right

up to World-War-I. This was a time when London and U.S. cities such as Brooklyn and Chicago were revamping their waterworks and sewer systems, bringing unemployment to low levels and ridding themselves of any new waves of the deadly cholera (Bump, 2015; Goldman, 1997). However, as if by turning the page on this troublesomely dark period of the new industrialized societies, a brighter and healthier future would open before the people of this modern age, it became evident that this would not be the case. Indeed, the ever growing population flowing to the great cities created logistical problems with clear health implications that needed to be solved. The first was the disposal of human sewage, which we just explored; the second was the problem of feeding growing populations now congregating in large urban centers.

1.3 FOOD IMPURITY, MALNUTRITION AND POISONING IN THE 20TH CENTURY

The technological advancements that fuelled the Industrial Revolution permitted large-scale urban manufacturing to take root, and revolutionize the labor force and the economy with higher wages near the end of the 19th century. All this was promoted by public health reforms in England that were championed by political reformers like Edwin Chadwick (Morley, 2007). And so food production became intertwined with the innovative hydraulics, automated conveyor belts, and mechanized milling in order to meet the increased demand of a growing urban population (Peterson, 1965). Unfortunately, because the food industry was more interested in large volume food production and distribution, there was initially little interest in quality and safety. Historians like Gabriella Petrick, an associate professor in the department of nutrition and food studies and the department of history and art history at George Mason University, agree that mechanization of grain harvesting, flour milling, bread baking, and meat slaughtering changed the way Americans ate, and by the early 20th century launched industrialized food production (Petrick, 2012). Consequently, because of the numerous small food producers, as well as the vendors and merchants that lined the city streets who were not regulated in any way, the incidence of food poisonings jumped significantly (Petrick, 2012). The U.S. food industry had created what Gabriella Petrick (2012) refers to as *"Hell with the lid taken off."* There was a growing public unease around food purchased and consumed between the Civil War and World War-I because of the putrefaction of meat from poorly regulated slaughterhouses, and general widespread unsanitary conditions throughout the food industry (Harvey Young, 1989). Petrick, writes, *"The urbanizing process made acquiring and consuming all manners of food (from meat to milk to apples, flour and canned goods) an anxiety-provoking process, especially for the women who were largely responsible for purchasing and cooking the family's meals"* (Petrick, 2011).

The young and the elderly, because of their more vulnerable immune systems, would commonly succumb to food-borne illnesses. Eating became a dangerous endeavor as food preparation standards were sorrowfully missing between the late 19th and the start of the 20th centuries.

However, through an Act of Congress in 1862, President Abraham Lincoln created the U.S. Department of Agriculture (USDA), which was the foundational government body that would be needed for U.S. federal regulation of the food industry to take place later on. The Division of Chemistry was created soon after, and placed under the leadership of Charles M. Whetherill. It was subsequently renamed the **Bureau of Chemistry** in 1901 (USDA, 2012), with Harvey Wiley appointed as chief chemist (Wiley, 1929). His preoccupation with the safety of food is noteworthy, as he was convinced that the food, more than drugs, represented a greater risk to human health (Swann, 2005). Wiley's efforts to ensure the safety of food was a welcomed involvement, since pieces of metal, sand, rock, and organic material—such as bugs and rotting and diseased meat—were frequently found in food products throughout the 1800s. However, the desire to legislate controls and standards on the food industry was squelched in great part by the U.S. Board of Trade, who wanted to facilitate commerce and not tie food companies up with regulatory controls (Spiekermann, 2011).

An interventionist role for government in food manufacturing and processing became more relevant, however, with the scandalous unsanitary and dangerous environments of the U.S. meat packing and slaughtering plants. The work was so repugnant that the industry had trouble hiring American-born workers who refused to submit to such austere and unsafe working conditions (Figure 1.4). Instead, foreign-born workers mostly made up of Slavs, Poles and Germans (Commons, 1904), desperate for work, were promptly hired as they were much less likely to complain about the harsh and inhuman environment. However, in 1906, author Upton Sinclair (Sinclair, 1906) gave a scathing depiction of the meatpacking industry, as it existed in the United States, in his best-selling novel, *The Jungle*. In it, Sinclair refers to the plant workers as paid slave laborers, who worked excessively long hours in despicable filthy conditions. The novel shocked the U.S. public with its vivid description of horrific scenes, in which workers, who had accidently fell into meat grinders, had their remains incorporated into meat products, only to be shipped to stores and sold. The public outcry was so great, that President Theodore Roosevelt was forced to inquire about the veracity of the novel's depictions. He sent trusted Labor Commissioner, Charles P. Neill, and social worker, James Bronson Reynolds, to conduct surprise audits of the American meatpacking industry. The Neil-Reynold's report to the president confirmed that Upton Sinclair had indeed written an accurate portrayal of the industry (Petrick, 2011). It was this novel that was responsible for generating a public outcry that was so momentous that President Roosevelt had little difficulty having Congress enact the **Federal Meat Inspection Act (FMIA)** and the **Pure Food and Drug Act** in 1906 (USDA, 2012). This was the legislation that was instrumental at kick-starting the cleanup of the American food industry by preventing food adulteration at the national level. In the background, it was the USDA's Bureau of Chemistry—under the leadership of chief chemist of Dr. Harvey W. Wiley—that was the true driving force behind the **Pure Food & Drug Act** of 1906. His involvement was, in fact, so well recognized that the legislation was often referred to as the Wiley Act (Wiley, 1929). Finally, a pure food supply was becoming more of an achievable reality.

However, the Act of 1906 was worded in such a way that additives and substitute ingredients were still acceptable in the government's definition of "pure food." This was a bit of conundrum because on the one hand, the chemical advances of the late 18th and 19th centuries were providing compounds that could stabilize as well as enhance the appearance and taste of a wider assortment of cheaper foods, while on the other hand, the processing of food in clean and sophisticated plants, made the food in the United States safe to eat without fear of sickness. The question was being asked: how safe were these compounds added to food?

In England, the problem of chemical food adulteration had also become an outrage and an embarrassment which was finally brought to light with the publication of Thomas Accum's 1820 book titled *Treatise on the Adulteration of Foods and Culinary Poisons* (Accum, 1820). In it, the German chemist described industrial food practices that shocked the nation. Accum's training as a chemist enabled him to accurately detect the presence and describe the action of chemicals that had been found in foods, beverages, and alcohol. He described the existence of lead in olive oil that had originated from the pressing plates, and significant residues of copper coming from one of the processing steps in the manufacturing of catsup. Alarmingly, he described the way the manufacturing of cheap confectionaries resulted in the use of red coloring contaminated with lead, in addition to white confits made from sugar, starch, and white pipe clay. Accum also investigated the distribution and selling practices of milk by common merchants. He noted the rather deceitful practice of diluting milk with water to yield large volumes, and the disreputable procedure of thickening cream by mixing portions of chalk, milk, and cream together. Also cheeses, colored with anetto, could contain red lead in concentrations deemed to be sufficient to make individuals seriously sick (Accum, 1820). His description of the popular use of alum in wheat flour, in addition to lead and copper salts in beer brewing, made the English furious. But most scandalous to the London authorities was the counterfeiting of coffee with substitutes such as burnt peas, beans, or other grains, a practice viewed as indefensible (Accum, 1820). Because food industry leaders managed to ruin his reputation, forcing him out of London and eventually England for his scathing description of the food industry, deviant food adulteration practices continued, unabated for another 30 years in England (RSC, 2015).

Back in the United States, around the middle of the 19th century, scandals of food adulteration and chemical contaminations frequently made newspaper headlines. In the background was the 19th-century Health Reform Movement which, by 1830, decried the modernization of the food supply. Sylvester Graham, in his *Treatise on Bread and Bread-Making*, encouraged individual households, in a time of vanishing self-sufficiency, to purchase the best unrefined flour for baking homemade fresh bread (Nissenbaum, 1980). Graham was calling, much like a prophet in the desert, the American public to return to traditional bread-making; but similar to the prophets of times past, his pleas fell pretty much on deaf ears. The American household was transitioning from being a production unit, whereby 85% of manufactured goods in the United States were generated from the household in 1800, to a purchasing unit by 1830. This meant that household goods such as furniture, clothes, and food had to be primarily bought outside the home. This significant loss in household self-sufficiency translated into the U.S. home becoming more commercially dependent on food to feed the family. Bobrow-Strain (2007), in *Kills the Body Twelve Ways*, writes that between 1850 and 1900, the number of commercial bakeries increased 700%, while homemade bread dropped, by 1920, from 80% to a mere 6% of all bread produced in the United States (Bobrow-Strain, 2007). The stores and shops were selling more ready-made white wheat-raised breads, along with pastries and cakes that looked fresh and delicious. The truth of the matter was that these pretty white cakes and breads were stabilized with preservatives such as alum, ammonia, sulphate of zinc, and even sulphate of copper (Nissenbaum, 1980). What was appealing to the American public was that the white sliced bread, purchased from the bakery shelves saved valuable time, was shelf-stable, and was safe. Bobrow-Strain writes: *"In an age obsessed with concerns about purity, hygiene, and sanitation, the new loaves were engineered to appear streamlined, sparkling clean, and whiter than white. After decades of enduring a reputation for filth, contamination, and foot dragging around pure-food legislation, commercial bakers had turned purity into their greatest selling point"* (Bobrow-Strain, 2007).

Other commercial foods were being made more attractive and shelf-stable with the use of other additives. For instance, adding small doses of sodium benzoate to food extended the holding time of vegetables significantly after harvest; this allowed year-round canning to take place. Harvey Wiley, the chief chemist at the USDA's Bureau of Chemistry, had uncovered that sodium benzoate, even in small doses, caused gastrointestinal distress in human volunteers (Wiley, 1929). Also, there was a heightened risk of lead poisoning occurring from the lead solder in canned tomatoes. The erosive strength of the tomatoes' acidity caused the lead to leach into the tomatoes (Wiley, 1929). Although the incidence of food poisonings was plummeting after the passage of the 1906 Pure Food Act, there was a delayed awakening to the reality that a pure food supply, as defined by the U.S. Congress, could not be the complete answer to population health as food poisonings were still reported in the United States and internationally (Spiekermann, 2009).

© Oleg Golovnev/Shutterstock.com.

Figure 1.4 Central slaughterhouse in Chicago. *Engraving was by Maynar, from picture by painter Taylor. Published in magazine Niva, publishing house A.F. Marx, St. Petersburg, Russia, 1893*

However, it was the discovery of vitamins in the late 19th to 20th centuries that redefined human nutrition from more scientific and medical perspectives, and along with the technological innovations of that time—refrigeration, transportation, milling, extrusion and packaging—and dietary guidelines, the pathway was set towards a more **industrial**

diet in the United States between 1880 and 1930 (Leveinstein, 1988; Petrick, 2012). Petrick defines the industrial diet as made of "...*foods that are mass produced in a factory setting and require no or very little cooking to make them edible. These foods are also packaged which make them highly portable. Examples of industrial foods are commercially canned goods; frozen foods; ice cream; breads, cakes, and pies purchased at bakeries and/or groceries and supermarkets; cake mixes; hot and cold cereals; instant mashed potatoes; pastry/pie shell mixes; and jams and jellies.*"

The discovery of vitamins changed food in three distinct ways: First, there was now a scientific dimension attributed to food that involved the micronutrients, the proteins, carbohydrates, and fats; second the business of manufacturing and marketing foods was now weaving itself around the nutrition theme. Suddenly foods were nutritious in specific ways as it was defined by vitamin content; and third, politically, foods could now be regulated by laws, codes, labeling standards and so on. In Europe, between 1880 and 1914, the food supply and food production were undergoing important changes that were driven by the nutrient paradigm and the hope for safe food (Spiekermann, 2009). Government regulatory systems were organized to ensure the health of the people, and to prevent fraudulent practices in labeling and content management (Peterson, 1965). The nutrient paradigm propelled efforts toward nutrient-based standardizations—using the Codex Alimentarius—and regaining the consumer's trust, which had been lost since the food adulteration scandals of the early 1900s (Spiekermann, 2009).

1.4 NUTRITIONAL GUIDANCE IN THE 20TH AND 21ST CENTURIES

1.4.1 The Prevalence of Chronic Disease in the United States

The importance and urgency of providing nutritional guidance and standards to the U.S. population, in the new millennium, stems from the worrisome rise in the prevalence of chronic disease most especially since the early 1980s. The Centers for Disease

Control and Prevention (CDC) estimates that between 1980 and 2017 the United States' national health expenditure grew from $256 billion to an astounding $3.5 Trillion. This 1267% increase in healthcare costs, spread over close to a forty year period, is so extraordinarily large that the burden on the country's healthcare financial system has created substantive shockwaves (OSG, 2001; CDC, 2011 Martin et al., 2018). This jump has saddled the population with a cumbersome debt that represents 16.4% of the U.S. national income. More than 50% of this total expenditure comes from hospital care and the clinical services of a physician. The reason is not that America is afflicted with coughs and twisted ankles, but rather from chronic debilitating and degenerative conditions like obesity, type-2 diabetes, cancer, and cardiovascular disease (Martin, 2012). Obesity is, in fact, the root cause of conditions like hypertension, atherosclerosis, gallbladder disease, sleep apnea, type-2 diabetes, some cancers and many cases of depression, and it most certainly carries a powerful fiscal punch; in the year 2000 the total cost to manage obesity was $117 billion/year (OSG, 2001). The CDC now estimates that as much as 75% of the total health care costs are tied specifically to chronic diseases (CMMS, 2012). About 15 years ago, the Office of the Surgeon General (OSG) of the United States identified obesity as a public health problem for which new public health strategies needed to be implemented (OSG, 2001). Yet since that time, only 3.2% of the national health expenditure has been tagged for government-sponsored public health. There is some concern that few of the strategies aimed at changing the dietary habits of Americans will be successful. And yet, there is very little debate around whether those habits and sedentary lifestyles are at the heart of the obesity and chronic disease crisis now afflicting the United States (OSG, 2001). Indeed, between 1994 and 1996 only 3% of the U.S. population actually consumed four of the five food pyramid food groups (USDA, 1998). The deplorable amount of vegetables consumed by the population is what incited a 5-A-DAY campaign which was managed by the USDA, in concert with the National Cancer Institute, the

Produce for Better Health Foundation, CDC, and the American Cancer Society in 1991 (Figure 1.5).

Figure 1.5 *The Eat 5 a Day nutrition campaign.*

Interest in nutrition, in the earlier part of the 20th century, was quite high, but for much different reasons than today. Diseases once thought to be infectious—inspired by Louis Pasteur's important work—were now being reclassified as nutritional deficiency diseases (CDC, 1999; Rosenfeld, 1997). Nutritional deficiencies such as pellagra, goiter, and rickets were, by the 1920s and 30s, prevalent problems that were being treated by wide scale public health initiatives in the United States. For instance, the 1921–1929 **Maternal and Infancy Act** ensured the use of nutritionists in helping to favorably change pregnancy outcomes and decrease infant and mother mortality rates through prenatal care and nutrition programs. Additionally, the USDA published its first food guide for young children in 1916 (Figure 1.6) and then a set of dietary recommendations in 1917 for the general public using a five food group model; in the 1930s the federal government instituted school feeding and nutrition education programs and began nationwide nutrition surveys to assess the nutritional health of the population. Also by 1924, the iodization of salt had begun in order to quell the risk of goiter and cretinism in the population (CDC, 1999).

Figure 1.6 *Food for Young Children by Caroline L. Hunt. United States Department of Agriculture Farmers' Bulletin 717*

The story in Canada did not look much better. The British Columbian and Saskatchewan provincial governments conducted a nutritional survey in 1946 that found that 21% of children had at least one sign of clinical vitamin A deficiency and there was evidence of past rickets in about 50% of school children (CPHA, 2014).

The 1917 dietary recommendations were intended to be nutritional standards for good health in the United States. Those recommendations, based on five food groups, were adapted to a first food guide for weekly food purchases for the average American family in 1921 (Davis & Saltos, 1999; Welsh et al., 1993). A 1923 version quickly came out afterwards for educators and extension workers who were specifically training housekeepers (Welsh et al., 1993), and to assist the nontraditional families with greater than five members (Davis & Saltos, 1999). The harsh economic realities of the 1929 crash translated into hardship and difficulties accessing good, reliable, and nutritious foods for many hungry unemployed men and their families. In fact, prices had significantly skyrocketed, which made it very difficult for the average worker to afford many of the basic protective foods such as milk, butter, tomatoes, citrus fruits, leafy, green and yellow vegetables, and eggs. The USDA's home economist, Hazel Stiebeling (1939), estimated at the time that Americans

were only consuming 80% of their requirement for milk, 85% of butter needs, 65% of their ideal intake for eggs, only 30% of their requirement for tomatoes and citrus, and close to 0% of their vegetable needs. The American diet had to have been sufficiently inadequate in the 1930s for home economist Margaret Reid to refer to *"a hidden hunger that threatens to lower the zest for living and to sap the productive capacity of workers and the stamina of the armed forces"* (Reid, 1943).

It was the malnourished unemployed workers during the Great Depression who inspired Hazel Stiebeling, a USDA food economist, to establish a new food guide (1933-1942), that would serve as a benchmark for weekly purchases of families based on 12 food groups (milk; potatoes and sweet potatoes; dry beans, peas and nuts; tomatoes and citrus fruits; leafy green and yellow vegetables; other vegetables and fruits; eggs; lean meats, poultry and fish; flour and cereals; butter; other fats; and sugars (Welsh et al., 1993). The guide was also organized into four cost levels to facilitate more economic but still wise food purchases by the consumers, who, in times of war rationing, needed to know about alternative foods of equal nutritional value (Stiebeling, and Ward, 1933). The 1933 guide had, however, one very particular feature that may have misdirected the American population to liberally consume processed cereals and bleached flours that were devoid of nutrient content. Whereas the 1916 food guide recommended that 20% of consumed calories come from cereals and other starchy foods, the 1933 food guide encouraged unlimited or as desired intakes of bread, cereals, and flour to no doubt increase the ingestion of cheap calories (Davis & Saltos, 1999).

The processing of the American food supply had become so extensive between 1900 and 1940 that there were reported cases of malnutrition even among U.S army recruits around 1935. This was a time when nutritional risk was at an all-time high because of the historical food rationing policies of WWI, and the economic collapse of the Great Depression of 1929, which hit the American public in a second wave around 1934. These crises created food restrictive habits that carried forward into the mid-1930s. Dietary selection had become narrower—the consequence of cheap food budgeting—with 50% of calories consumed as white bread by the 1930s (Bobrow-Strain, 2013). This had serious implications since the love affair Americans had with white bread—which was at that point highly processed and unenriched—was making many nutritionally ill. Indeed, one-third of military recruits were rejected for active duty because they were malnourished. Epidemiologists had unearthed by the late 1930s and early 1940s that a surprising prevalence of malnutrition was peppering a variety of low-income sectors of the population including low-income high school kids. In 1938, for instance, a New York City community health center had detected malnutrition in 37% of low income high school students. Similarly, throughout the 1930s, prevalence of 75% riboflavin deficiency, 65% scurvy or near scurvy, and 54% pre-clinical vitamin A deficiency had peppered the U.S. landscape (Bobrow-Strain, 2013).

In response, the National Nutrition Conference for Defense was organized in 1941 by the Food and Nutrition Board of the National Academy of Sciences. The goal of the conference was to examine potential public health strategies that could contain the malnutrition, and develop healthy eating principles capable of galvanizing support for a major shift in eating practices. This conference was nevertheless memorable for having released the United States' first Recommended Dietary Allowances (RDAs) for calories, protein, iron, calcium, vitamins A, C and D, and for thiamin, riboflavin, and niacin (Davis & Saltos, 1999). However, public health nutrition education programs and advertising could not get the masses to abandon their white impoverished bread in favor of the more nutritionally rich whole wheat bread. Americans would not abandon their beloved white bread for they appeared to hold on, "like a shipwrecked mariner to its buoy" (Bissonnette, 2013).

Nutritionally impoverished by the use of mechanized roller mills and bleach treatments, the white flour used in the industrial production of white bread had very few nutrients left. Harvey W. Wiley, the head of the Food and Drug Administration (FDA) by 1910, was critical of the practice of bleaching flour using **nitrogen trichloride** (Wiley, 1929). Paradoxically, despite a Supreme Court decision in and around 1911 to ban the practice of bleaching flour, the practice still continued right up to 1948, but only after Dr. Wiley was ousted of his position in 1912, and an overriding executive decision was issued from the White House. Dr. Wiley, in a 1914

issue of *Good Housekeeping*, characterized the nutritionally empty bleached flour as "white and waxy as the face of a corpse" (Wiley, 1929). The practice of using nitrogen trichloride to bleach flour ceased after well-controlled dog experiments, conducted by British nutritionist, Lord Mellanby, revealed that the animals suffered from running fits of epilepsy. Similar experiments repeated here at home by American scientists confirmed identical worrisome outcomes in four different animal species. It is perplexing that the nitrogen trichloride ban by the FDA occurred after close to 40 years of use by the industry. More surprising still is the fact that, soon after, the FDA approved the use of **chlorine dioxide** for bleaching flour, and this, despite protests from U.S. army nutritionists (Bobrow-Strain, 2013). Meanwhile numerous cases of malnutrition were popping up everywhere as the United States reliance on bleached white bread continued to grow (Bobrow-Strain, 2013).

The FDA in the United States and Health and Welfare in Canada began proposing a number of bills that intended to force the food industry to add some of those nutrients back, to "enrich" the foods they were producing. The bill was defeated in the United States, but U.S. producers began enriching flour and cereals voluntarily after World War II anyway, in order to get government contracts to cater to the military foodservice, which did require enriched flour (Bobrow-Strain, 2013). In Canada, regulatory policies for the enrichment of processed flour were first passed in 1964, requiring that all flour be enriched with thiamin, riboflavin, niacin, and iron. Folic acid was added to the requirement later on. Right now the Canadian government considers food fortification as a legal requirement for the food industry, and as a public health strategy to combat nutritional deficiency disease (Canadian Food Inspection Agency, 2014).

There is no doubt that America was confounded by the most severe after-effects of Industrial Food Production: the health decline of its population. The National Nutrition Conference for Defense, concerned that it might not have soldiers healthy enough to support ally efforts in Europe, set the ground work for the USDA to release, in 1943, the **National Wartime Nutrition Guide** (Figure 1.7) leaflet (Bobrow-Strain, 2013). It downgraded the liberal recommendation for white bread as a caloric buffer, and consisted of seven food groups:

group-1: green and yellow vegetables; group-2: oranges, tomatoes and grapefruit; group-3: potatoes and other vegetables and fruits; group-4: milk and milk products; group-5: meat, poultry, fish and eggs, and dried peas and beans; group-6: bread, flour and cereals; and finally, group-7: butter and fortified margarines (Welsh et al.,1993).

Source: USDA

Figure 1.7 *The USDA's 1943 National Wartime Nutrition Chart.*

The food guide, although represented for the first time in chart format, had several limitations that made it necessary to revise it by 1946. To start, the guide's overall goal was to assist the public to eat well during the wartime food restrictions. Second, it was meant as a foundational diet for the American public, and was intended to address about 80% of the nutrient needs (Welsh, et al., 1993). The third problem was that the guide provided next to no guidance for butter and sugar intake (David & Saltos, 1999). Admittedly, obesity and type-2 diabetes were not the big epidemics they are today and therefore the authors of the guide could easily be forgiven this transgression. The 1946 version of the guide was more popular and useful in that it did propose food group servings, but neglected to specify portion sizes—something the public and educators increasingly desired. Surprisingly, this guide must have still

met some important educational need since it was used for close to a decade (Davis & Saltos, 1999).

In 1956 the USDA issued a more simplified food guide that became popularly known as "**The Basic Four**" (Figure 1.8) which referred to four basic food groups: Milk, Meat, Fruits and Vegetables, and Grain Products. In contrast with other food guides, this one made minimum recommendations of foods to be consumed from each food group in order to meet nutrient needs. It was intended no longer to be used as guide to only make up a foundational diet. As an educational tool this food guide hit the mark and remained in use up until 1979 (Davis and Saltos, 1999).

Source: USDA

Figure 1.8 *The USDA's 1956 Food Guide known as the Basic Four.*

It was in the 1970s that scientific evidence was emerging in support of the notion that Americans were increasing their risk of heart disease by overconsuming total fat, saturated fat, dietary cholesterol, and sodium. The **Senate Select Committee on Nutrition and Human Needs**, which was headed by Senator George McGovern, established the 1977 **Dietary Goals for the United States** (Figure 1.9). For the first time, it set quantitative goals for the overconsumption of fatty acids, cholesterol, protein, carbohydrates, sodium, and sugar. This Dietary Goal report was less concerned about meeting nutritional needs of the population as it was about steering people away from the dietary excesses which had been tied to chronic disease (David & Saltos, 1999).

Using the Senate Select Committee's report as a guidepost, the USDA created a new 1979 food guide (Figure 1.9) that targeted the three big bad boys of American eating: **fats**, **sugars** and **sodium** (Moss, 2014), which were included in the USDA's 1979 publication titled: *"Food,"* because of their indisputable tie to chronic disease. The food guide also targeted fats, sweets, and alcoholic beverages as a fifth food group pegged for moderation in the diet. Protein was mysteriously left out of the USDAs guide, because of the Senate Select Committee's rather drastic recommendation to restrict protein at 12% of calories by decreasing meat consumption. This was not only significantly less than the 16% ingested by the average American at the time, but also not well supported by the scientific evidence (Welsh, et al., 1993; Gori, 1975). However, there were nevertheless some good studies published by the mid-1970s that attributed a protective role against colon cancer (Phillips, 1975) to the lacto-ovo-vegetarian diet of Seventh Day Adventists; the research was not pointing directly at meat consumption as being cancer-causing, but the committee's reading of the literature suggested that a cautious approach would justify recommending a reduction in meat intake. In his review of the literature of that time period, Roland Phillips concluded, *"that the relatively low intake of protein and fat by members of this religious group may favorably alter the body's response to chemical carcinogens"* (Phillips, 1975). More notable still in this discussion was the concern that both the meat and egg industries would be negatively affected; this was sufficient to send very powerful lobbyists to Washington in defense of the United Egg Producers and the National Cattlemen's Association with the clear task of sanitizing the USDA's guide (Nestle, 2002).

They did exactly what they set out to accomplish and a little more: First, the recommendation to decrease meat consumption, that was in the original draft of the Select Committee's Report, got modified to *"decrease consumption of animal fat, and choose*

meats, poultry and fish which will reduce saturated fat intake" (Nestle, 2002). Second, they made sure that Senator McGovern would lose his senate seat in the next election, and that Congress would be left with a strong message from the meat industry never to challenge meat consumption in the United States again (Nestle, 2002). Marion Nestle (2002), author of *Food Politics*, commented that the pressure to amend the wording in order to shed a more positive light on meat consumption was significant. This was most certainly viewed, in some nutrition circles, as a travesty since the link between diet and cancer was certainly emerging. In fact, as early as the 1980s, publications linking 30% of cancers in Western countries to diet were already in circulation (Doll et al., 1981).

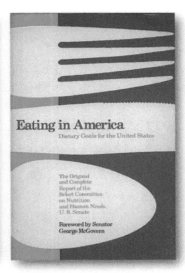

Source: USDA

Figure 1.9 *The 1979 USDA Food Guide, which included a fifth food group pegged for moderation.*

Around 1979, the findings of a study, sponsored by the American Society for Clinical Nutrition, that looked at dietary practices as they related to health outcomes, were included in *Healthy People: The Surgeon General's Report on Health Promotion and Disease Prevention*. This report also recommended that excess intakes of calories, fat and cholesterol, salt, and sugar be avoided. Based on the findings of this report, both the Department of Health & Human Services (DHHS) and the USDA formulated a set of seven principles to healthy eating which was published in 1980 as the first edition of *Nutrition and*

Your Health: Dietary Guidelines for Americans (David & Saltos, 1999; Welsh et al., 1993):

1 Eat a variety of foods
2 Maintain a healthy weight
3 Choose a diet low in saturated fat and cholesterol
4 Choose a diet with plenty of vegetables, fruits and grain products
5 Use sugar in moderation
6 Use salt and sodium only in moderation
7 If you drink alcohol beverages, do so in moderation

Although these early guidelines were more qualitative rather than quantitative in their directives to reduce intakes of fat, saturated fat, cholesterol, and sodium, they still ruffled food industry feathers. Since 1980, there have been a total of seven revisions of the Dietary Guidelines for Americans, which have been published every five years: 1985, 1990, 1995, 2000, 2005, 2010, and 2015 (Davis & Saltos, 1999).

In 1985 Dietary Guidelines for Americans were issued, but this time with very little protest from the medical community and the food industry, despite not having changed from the 1980 guidelines. It was just untenable for the food industry to continue opposing what the scientific and medical communities had been upholding as truth: that high red meat and saturated fat intakes were unhealthy. Additionally, the guidelines discouraged following unsafe restrictive diets, ingesting large vitamin doses, and drinking all forms of alcohol during pregnancy (Davis and Saltos, 1999).

By 1984 the next Food Guide titled: *A Pattern for Daily Food Choices* (Figure 1.10) was developed by the USDA in cooperation with the American Red Cross as a "food wheel." Unlike previous dietary guides that focused on establishing a foundational diet, this one was now attempting to assist Americans in meeting nutrient objectives by recommending specific numbers of servings while at the same time counseling on moderation (Davis & Saltos, 1999).

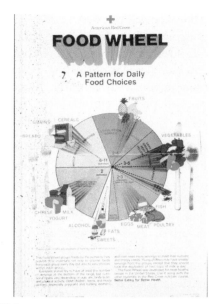

Source: USDA

Figure 1.10 *The USDA 1984 Food Wheel Guide: A Pattern for Daily Food Choices.*

This food wheel guide contained a total of five food groups (group-1: bread, cereal, rice, and pasta group; group-2: the vegetable group; group-3: the fruit group; group-4: the milk, yogurt, and cheese group; group-5: the meat, poultry, and fish, dry beans, eggs, and nuts). There was a sixth group consisting of fats, oils, and sweets that needed to be consumed in moderation. Although there was a more practical side to the guide, it virtually went unknown by the general public (Davis &Saltos, 1999). Consequently, in 1988 work was underway to revise the 1984 food guide and make it graphically more visible, while promoting the concepts of variety, proportionality, and moderation, all of which got integrated into a pyramid design (Figure 1.11), which was published in 1992 (Davis & Saltos, 1999).

In 1989 the DHHS formed an advisory committee with the intent of reviewing the 1985 Healthy Eating Guidelines. The committee relied on two important reports: first, the Surgeon General's Report on Nutrition and Health, and second, the National Research Council's 1989 report called *Diet and Health: Implications for Reducing Chronic Disease Risk*, to formulate its guidelines. While the Surgeon General's Report emphasized eating a variety of fruits, vegetables and whole grains in addition to lean selections of meat and fish, the National Research Council's Report identified fat and saturated fat as the most significant determinants of chronic disease in American society. The Council's Food and Nutrition Board even formulated quantitative cutoffs: total fat: no more than 30% of total calories; saturated fat: less than 10% of calories; and cholesterol: less than 300 mg (Davis & Saltos, 1999). This led to incorporating, in the **1990 edition of the Dietary Guidelines for Americans**, numerical cut-offs on total fat (≤30% of calories) and saturated fat (<10% of calories).

Strategically, the **Nutrition Labeling and Education Act** (**NLEA**) was passed in 1990—in preparation for the release of the 1992 food guide—in an attempt to slowly groom the public for a greater awareness of good health nutrition standards. This Act enabled the consumer to wisely shop for food using the Nutrition Facts Panel, located on the back or the side of packaged food. Now the shopper could determine whether the product they were purchasing was a **good source** (≥10% of the daily value (DV)) or an **excellent source** (≥20% of the DV) of a given nutrient; the consumer, concerned about health risks, could decide if the product was high (≥ 20% of the DV) in sodium, saturated fat, cholesterol or total fat or if it was low (≤5% of DV) in fat and sodium for instance (FDA, 2004).

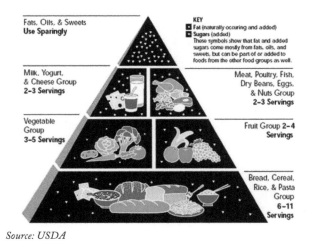

Source: USDA

Figure 1.11 *USDA & DHHS 1992 Food Pyramid.*

The 1992 Food Guide was specifically revised in order to cater to the needs of those groups that were nutritionally at risk such as children, and low income adults with low literacy skills. In this 1992 food guide, the notion of moderation was reflected by fatty and sugary food products being relegated to the peak of the pyramid; the visual impact of situating this group at the pyramid's peak was very powerful. The 32-page booklet that accompanied the food guide provided additional guidance pertinent to selecting foods low in fat, saturated fat, cholesterol, added sugars, or sodium within each food group. The graphic pyramid design of the food guide heightened its use by health professional, educators, media and the food industry, and successfully facilitated the wide dissemination of nutritional guidelines (Davis & Saltos, 1999). The food industry was however quick to criticize it on the grounds that it gave hierarchical importance to certain food groups, or in other words, some foods were encouraged to be eaten more often and in greater quantities than other foods. It was specifically the meat and dairy industries that were upset with their narrow place on the third level of the pyramid. No food group should be called good or bad was the industry's position (Nestle, 2002). Health professionals were also upset that grains and cereals were located at the base of the pyramid; they felt the guide contributed to the obesity crisis by promoting the ingestion of too many grains and cereals (Nestle, 2011). Nevertheless, the 1992 Food Guide did manage to cause a downward swing in the public's love for red meat and butter consumption, which in turn led to a decline in saturated fat intake; contrariwise, poultry and fish intake did increase. Consequently, epidemiologists and dietitians were expecting a proportional decrease in the incidence of heart disease at the population level. The paradox was that the nefarious trans-fats, generated from all the margarines and shortenings that had flooded the marketplace since the late 1960s, were actually increasing heart disease risk. Indeed, this did not become evident until 13 years later when Walter Willett and his colleagues (1993) from Harvard confirmed in 1993 that trans fats were affecting cardiovascular health in important ways: first, LDL cholesterol rose; second, HDL cholesterol (good cholesterol) dropped; and third, inflammatory markers increased.

The last noteworthy event of 1990 was the passing of the **1990 National Nutrition Monitoring and Related Research Act** which made it mandatory for the USDA and the DHHS to issue Healthy Eating Guidelines at least every five years. The 1995 Dietary Guidelines for Americans were, in fact, the first to have been mandated by statute (Davis & Santos, 1999). It also introduced specific fat guidelines for children—toddlers between 2 to 5 years should consume no more than 30% of calories as fat. They also gave greater prominence to recommendations for cereals, fruits, and vegetables.

The publication of the 2005 Dietary Guidelines for Americans were however more helpful; they incorporated the Institute of Medicine's acceptable macronutrient distribution ranges (AMDR) for protein (10–35% of DRI calories), fat (20–35% of DRI calories) and carbohydrates (45–65% of DRI calories), fiber (21–38g), polyunsaturated linoleic omega-6 fatty acids (5–10% of DRI calories) and the alpha-linolenic omega-3 polyunsaturated fats (0.6–1.2% of DRI calories) (Institute of Medicine, 2002). These DRIs were important quantitative guidelines that reflected the scientific investigations of the role of diet in reducing health risks.

Leading up, however, to the 2005 publication of the pyramid, the 1997 joint review by the World Cancer Research Fund (WCRF) and American Institute for Cancer Research (AICR), only somewhat of a strong association between red meat and colorectal cancer could be found. The authors of the Research Fund report concluded: *"A substantial amount of data from cohort and case control studies showed a dose–response relationship, supported by evidence for plausible mechanisms operating in humans. Red meat is a convincing cause of colorectal cancer."* The overall data at that time did not convince the Food Guide Committee, but it was sufficient for the joint investigative bodies to conclude that red meat intake should be less than 3 oz-wt per day. Links between red and processed meats, and cancer in general, however, were not very conclusive (World Cancer Research Fund & American Institute for Cancer Research, 1997). Finding a consensus was difficult as there were studies like that of Maureen Murtaugh (2004) that could only establish modest relationships between meat and colorectal cancer. The authors write: *"Our results suggest a modest, non-significant increase in the risk of rectal cancer with consumption of well-done meat and white meat cooked at high temperatures (fried, baked,*

broiled, or barbecued) among men." From the research it is difficult to conclude if it was the meat itself or, in particular, animal fat, the heterocyclic amines or the processing of meat that were tied to rectal cancer.

It was specifically the large-scale prospective Nurses' Health and U.S. Professional Men's cohorts that began to generate convincing evidence that cancer was indeed associated with red meat consumption. Walter Willett, a researcher from Harvard, in the early to mid-1990s showed that the relationship between colon cancer and red meat were worrisome and difficult to contest (Giovannucci et al., 1994; Willett et al., 1990).

There was however some complexity surrounding the role of meat in the etiology of colon and rectal cancers. In fact, by the new millennium, some of the evidence linking meat directly to cancer was equivocal (Trustwell, 2002). It would seem that the carcinogenicity of meat was more related to how often meat was consumed, the actual quantities ingested, and on whether the meat was lean or fatty. Others have insisted that cancer risk may actually be related to the cooking method, and doneness of meat (Murtaugh, 2004).

Before the food guide changed again, Americans would have to wait for one more Healthy Eating Guidelines report that was issued in 2000, and the 2002 Dietary Reference Intakes (DRIs). And so in 2005, the USDA and DHHS published the more abstract colored pyramid, which has often been represented without food models (Figure 1.12). This colorful designer pyramid created some confusion and was disliked and criticized almost immediately. In the design, the stripes for grains, milk, and vegetables look almost identical in size. The government appeared to have successfully deflected any negative recommendations or advisories away from meat and the meat industry by creating a purple strip that was only slightly smaller in width to that of vegetables; also, the proportionality that had been conveyed in the previous more traditional pyramid, appeared to have been changed in this newer model so as to not intimate preference for one food group more than another (Nestle, 2005). This version of the guide wanted to communicate a message of balance between food and exercise. The man walking over the pyramid however caused some problems; it was interpreted by some to give credence to the idea that with exercise one could simply walk right over the need for dietary guidance (Bissonnette, 2013). The other limitation was that the public could only learn about the serving sizes for each of the food groups by accessing the www.mypyramid.com website. Again the pyramid fell short of instructing the public about healthy fats and whole grain options (Nestle, 2005), and it did not differentiate fatty red meats from lean red meat, poultry, fish, or beans (Johnson, 2005). The pressure was on to rethink the food guide design once again, with the goal of conveying a simpler nutrition message that most could understand.

Source: USDA

Figure 1.12 *The new USDA & DHHS 2005 Food Pyramid.*

The now familiar www.chooseMyplate.gov food guide (Figure 1.13) was introduced in 2010, after many years of harsh criticisms of the MyPyramid Food Guide, concomitantly, with the newly revised Healthy Eating Guidelines for Americans 2010. They were lauded as an effort that greatly simplified the nutrition message to the youth because of the familiar plate design, but unfortunately, besides conveying that fruits and vegetables needed to make up half of the plate, many felt that the guide fell short of providing any serious guidance with respect to the importance of whole grains, lean meats, and quality vegetables. However, a notable change was that the Meat and Beans category was now renamed as protein. It was a subtle change that likely went unnoticed by the public but not by nutritionists and dietitians. It appeared that the scientific data finally allowed researchers and the Food Guide Committee to disapprovingly wave an accusatory finger at processed and unprocessed red meats. This may have been enough to allow the USDA to emphasize protein foods rather than meat in the MyPlate design.

The findings now coming out of the long term prospective studies demonstrate significant risk of diabetes, cardiovascular disease, and cancers with red meat consumption (Pan et al., 2012). In fact, both the Health Professionals Follow-up Study (HPFS) and the Nurses' Health Study (NHS), that followed 38,000 men and 83,000 women respectively, showed greater overall mortality in cohorts consuming processed and unprocessed red meat intake. Interestingly, when fish, nuts, poultry, legumes, and low-fat dairy replaced red meat in the diet, then the risk of mortality noticeably declined (Pan et al., 2012).

In addition to its colorful and logically intuitive display, the MyPlate food guide (Figure 1.13) has a website (https://www.choosemyplate.gov/) aimed at instructing the public about food portions and variety. Click the www.ChooseMyPlate.gov website, and you will notice at the top of the page the DIETARY GUIDELINES FOR AMERICANS. The student can click on the featured guidelines title, and scroll down to the section called: "Dietary Guidelines Resources for Professionals." Right under, the student can click on "2015-2020 Dietary Guidelines for Americans" in the box below. The current guidelines, jointly formulated by Health & Human Services and the USDA, reflect the reality that half of adult Americans have one or more chronic diseases that can be prevented with proper diet management (Dietary Guidelines for Americans, 2015). Here below are the highlights of the five key points that make up the 2015-2020 dietary guidelines:

1 Throughout the lifespan, Americans must comply with a healthy eating pattern in order to regulate appropriate caloric intakes so as to manage healthy body weights, support the selection of nutrient-rich foods, and reduce the risk of developing chronic diseases.

2 Americans must choose a variety of nutrient-dense foods from all four food groups in amounts recommended for their caloric requirements.

3 Americans must limit added sugars and saturated fats to less than 10% of DRI calories, and reduce sodium intake to less than 2300 mg/day.

4 Americans must make healthier beverage choices, by preferentially selecting nutrient-dense beverages that use ingredients from some or all of the food groups.

5 Americans must support healthy eating principles in home, school, work and communities (USD HHS & USDA, 2015).

Returning back to the home page of ChooseMyplate.gov, the student will notice that each of the five sections of the MyPlate food guide can be clicked with the mouse. This provides the opportunity to learn the standard serving size equivalents of various foods found in each group. For instance, clicking on FRUIT features the option: EXPLORE FOOD GALLERY. Click on that option then click on: "Learn more about the Fruit Group" which is located at the top of the page. Scroll down until the second blue banner titled: CUP OF FRUIT TABLE is reached. Click on that banner, and the student should see what one fruit cup equivalent is equal to. For instance, the student should understand that if your client eats the following:

> 1 cup of applesauce
> 1 large banana
> 1 small apple
> 1/2 cup of dried raisins

it can be concluded that the patient has consumed a total of 4 fruit cup equivalents. Similar exercises can be conducted for the vegetable, protein, grains and dairy groups. Students need to rehearse taking down and compiling the cup or ounce equivalents consumed by fictitious clients. This exercise helps students better assess the quality of the diet consumed by their patients or clients. This is a basic skill that every health professional should acquire. More exercises of this kind can be found at the end of the chapter.

By contrast, Harvard's School of Public Health created its own plate design (Figure 1.14) that had a clear and simple nutrition education message integrated within the graphic image itself. This effort was in response to the criticisms made against the USDA's MyPlate design on the basis that it lacked important readily accessible and meaningful dietary guidance. In truth, as a public health tool, the Harvard model does not refrain from revealing the salient points that the public needs to grasp:

1 Potatoes and French fries don't count as valid vegetables
2 Avoid sugary drinks (excess juices and all sodas)
3 Avoid bacon, cold cuts, and other processed meats
4 Give preference to fish, poultry and beans, and limit the intake of red meat and cheese.
5 Liberally consume varied vegetables and in generous amounts
6 It encourages the intake of healthy oils; limits butter and instructs to avoid trans-fats.

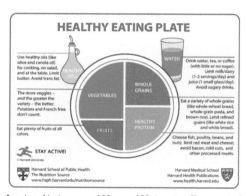

Credit: As printed in image and Harvard University. For more information visit: www.health.harvard.edu. NOTE: Harvard Health Publications does not endorse any products or medical procedures.

Figure 1.14 *Harvard School of Public Health's version of the Myplate Food Guide.*

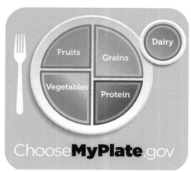

Source: USDA

Figure 1.13 *The USDA & DHHS ChooseMyPlate 2010 Food Guide.*

DIETARY ASSESSMENT EXERCISE

This diet assessment exercise intends to introduce the student to the Three-Day Food Record, which is considered, after the Weighted Food Record, one of the most accurate diet assessment methods.

1 The first step consists of documenting the approximate volume (cups, pints, gallons) and weight (oz-wt) of food consumed over three days (2 week-days and one weekend), indicating the place and the time the food was consumed.

2 In the second step, the student is asked to enter the ingested food in the website below: https://sparkpeople.com Once you are in the website, you are prompted to enter your name, date of birth, weight, height. Specify that your goal is "weight maintenance." Then select the FREE TRIAL.

3 Now you are ready to begin entering the foods you consumed and assigning them to breakfast, Lunch, Dinner or Snacks. After having entered a complete day of food consumed, scroll down to REPORTS and click on TODAY'S FULL REPORT. This will give the day's average intake for the various nutrients. Enter these averages into the DAY-1 column in a table, similar to the one found below. After entering food for three days, calculate the average for the three days and enter those averages in the last column at the right of the table.

4 Determine the serving equivalents of PROTEIN, GRAINS, VEGS, FRUITS & DAIRY using the chooseMyPlate.gov website and following the instructions provided on page 30 near the end of this chapter.

NUTRIENTS/KCALS	DAY-1	DAY-2	DAY-3	AVERAGE
CALORIES/DAY				
TOTAL FAT (grams)				
CHOLESTEROL(Milligrams)				
SODIUM (Milligrams)				
PROTEIN oz-equivalent				
IRON (Milligrams)				
GRAINS oz-equivalent				
VEGS Cups equivalent				
FRUITS Cups equivalent				
DAIRY Cups equivalent				

CHAPTER 1 PRACTICE QUESTIONS

1 Identify the century and the years when the most virulent waves of bubonic and pneumonic plagues swept through Europe killing upwards of 24 million souls.

2 Describe the impact(s) the two plagues (bubonic and pneumonic) had on the people of Europe.

3 Identify the 2017 US health care expenditure and its reflection of the current dietary habits of Americans.

4 Explain how the prevalence of disease in Western societies significantly rose with the adoption of key dietary changes.

5 What exactly do historians attribute to the increased vulnerability of Europe to the great plagues of the Middle Ages?

6 How did the 19th century Industrial Revolution contribute to the rise in malnutrition and disease in Europe?

7 Identify the key government regulatory agencies and regulations intended to control food impurities and food poisonings in the US at the start of the 20th century.

REFERENCES

1 Accum, F. (1820). *Adulteration of foods & culinary poisons: Exhibiting the fraudulent sophistications of bread, beer, wine, spirituous liquors, tea and coffee.* London: Joseph Mallett Printing, 360.

2 Aeillo, L. C., & Wheeler, P. (1995). The expensive tissue hypothesis. *Current Anthropology 36*, 199-221.

3 (A.N.D) Academy of Nutrition & Dietetics(2015). Position of the Academy of Nutrition and Dietetics: Health Implications of Dietary Fiber. J. Acad. of Nutr. & Diet; 115(11): 1861-1870

4 American Cancer Society (ACS). (2017). Cancer Facts & Figures 2017. URL: https://www.cancer.org/research/cancer-facts-statistics/all-cancer-facts-figures/cancer-facts-figures-2017.html

5 American Cancer Society (ACS). (2015). Cancer Facts & Figures 2015. URL: https://www.cancer.org/research/cancer-facts-statistics/all-cancer-facts-figures/cancer-facts-figures-2015.html

6 American Cancer Society (ACS). (2010). *Cancer facts & figures 2010.* Retrieved from http://www.cancer.org/research/cancerfactsstatistics/cancerfactsfigures2010/index

7 American Cancer Society (ACS) (2008). *Cancer facts & figures 2008.* Retrieved from http://www.cancer.org/acs/groups/content/@nho/documents/document/2008cafffinalsecuredpdf.pdf

8 American Cancer Society (ACS). (2004). *Cancer facts & figures 2004.* Retrieved from http://www.pink-ribbon-pins.com/CancerRates2004.pdf

9 American Cancer Society (ACS). (2002). *Cancer prevention and early detection, facts and figures 2002.* Available at http://www.cancer.org/downloads/STT/CPED2002.pdf

10 American Society of Clinical Nutrition. (1979). Task Force: The evidence relating six dietary factors to the nation's health. *American Journal of Clinical Nutrition* (Supplement) *32*, 2621-2748.

11 Anand, P. et al. (2008). Cancer is a preventable disease that requires major lifestyle changes. *Pharmaceutical Research 25* (9), 2097–2116.

12 Antonios, T.F., & MacGregor, G.A. (1996). Salt—more adverse effects. *Lancet, 348*, 250–1

13 Bissonnette. D.J. (2013). *It's all about nutrition: Saving the health of Americans.* New York: University Press of America, 220 pp.

14 Boaz, N.T. (2002). *Evolving health: The origins of illness and how the modern world is making us sick.* New York: Wiley & Sons, Inc.

15 Bobrow-Strain, A. (2013). *White bread: A social history of the store-bought loaf.* Boston: Beacon Press, 272.

16 Bobrow-Strain, A. (2007). Kills a body twelve ways: Bread fears and the politics of what to eat. *Gastronomica: The Journal of Food and Culture 7*; 7(3): 45-52. Retrieved from http://comenius.susqu.edu/biol/312/killsabodytwelveways.pdf

17 Brothwell, D., & Brothwell, B. (1998). *Food in antiquity: A survey of the diet of early peoples. expanded edition.* Baltimore: Johns Hopkins University Press, 283.

[18] Bump, J.B. (2015). *The long road to universal health coverage health systems & reform: Historical analysis of early decisions in Germany, the United Kingdom and the United States* 1(1), 28–38.

[19] Canadian Food Inspection Agency. (2014). *Prohibition against the sale of unenriched white flour and products containing unenriched flour.* Retrieved from http://www.inspection.gc.ca/food/labelling/food-labelling-for-industry/grain-and-bakery-products/unenriched-flour/eng/1415915977878/1415915979471

[20] Canadian Public Health Association (CPHA). *Food fortification.* Retrieved from http://www.cpha.ca/en/programs/history/achievements/09-shf/fortification.aspx

[21] Carpenter, K.J. (ed). (1986). *The history of scurvy and vitamin C.* Cambridge: Cambridge University Press, 228.

[22] Carrera-Bastos, P., Fontes-Villalba, M., O'Keefe, J. H., Lindeberg, S., & Cordain, L. (2011). The westernized diet, and lifestyle and diseases of civilization. *Research Reports in Clinical Cardiology:2*, 15–35.

[23] Carter, J. C. (2006). *Discovering the Greek Countryside at Metaponto.* Thomas Spencer Jerome Lectures, 23rd series. Ann Arbor: The University of Michigan Press.

[24] Cartwright, C. *Origins and history of homeopathy.* Available at: http://www.oxford-omeopathy.org.uk/homeopathy-origins-history.htm

[25] CDC. (2013). *National Health Expenditure 2013 Highlights.* Retrieved from http://www.cms.gov/Research-Statistics-Data-and-Systems/Statistics-Trends-and-Reports/NationalHealthExpendData/downloads/highlights.pdf

[26] CDC (1999). Achievements in Public Health 1900-1999. Safer and Healthier Foods. *MMWR Weekly 48(40)*, 905-913. Retrieved from http://www.cdc.gov/mmwr/preview/mmwrhtml/mm4840a1.htm

[27] Centers for Medicare and Medicaid Services (CMMS). (January 2012). Office of the Actuary, National Statistical Group. National Health Care Expenditure Data.

[28] Commons, JR., (1904). Labor Conditions in Meat Packing and the Recent Strike. The Quarterly Journal of Economics; 19 (1): 1-32

[29] Cordain, L.S., Eaton, B., Sebastian, A., Mann, N., Lindeberg, S., Watkins, B. A., O'Keefe, J. H., & Brand-Miller, J. (2005). Origins and evolution of the Western diet: health implications for the 21st century. *American Journal of Clinical Nutrition 81*, 341–54.

[30] Davis, C., & Saltos, E. (1999). Dietary recommendations and how they have changed over time in: *America's Eating Habits: Changes and Consequences* Frazao, E (Ed) USDA: Economic Research Service Washington, DC. USDA. Agriculture Information Bulletin No. (AIB-750), 33-50.

[31] Del Prato, S., Leonetti, F., Simonson, D.C., Sheehan, P., Matsuda, M., & De-Fronzo, R.A. (1994). Effect of sustained physiologic hyperinsulinaemia and hyperglycaemia on insulin secretion and insulin sensitivity in man. *Diabetologia 37*, 1025–35.

[32] Doll, R., & Peto, R. (1981). The causes of cancer: quantitative estimates of avoidable risks of cancer in the United States today. *Journal National Cancer Institute. 5 66*, 1191–308.

[33] Food & Drug Administration. (2004). How to understand the use of the nutrition facts panel. Retrieved from http://www.fda.gov/Food/IngredientsPackagingLabeling/LabelingNutrition/ucm274593.htm#overview

[34] Foster-Powell, K., Holt, SHA., & Brand-Miller, J.C. (2002). International table of glycemic index and glycemic load values 2002. *American Journal of Clinical Nutrition 76*, 5-56.

[35] Frazao, E. (1999). *America's eating habits: Changes and consequences.* USDA Economic Research Service. USDA. Agriculture Information Bulletin No. (AIB-750), 494. Retrieved from http://www.ers.usda.gov/publications/aib-agricultural-information-bulletin/aib750.aspx

36 Frassetto L.A., Todd, K.M., Morris, R.C., & Sebastian, A. (1998). Estimation of net endogenous noncarbonic acid production in humans from diet potassium and protein contents. *American Journal of Clinical Nutrition 68*, 576–83.

37 Frericks, R.R. Broad street pump outbreak. *UCLA Department of Epidemiology, School of Public Health website.* Available at http://www.ph.ucla.edu/epi/snow/broadstreetpump.html

38 Fryar, C.D., Carroll, M.D., & Ogden, C.L. (2012). Prevalence of overweight, obesity, and extreme obesity among adults: United States, Trends 1960–1962 Through 2009–2010 *National Center for Health Statistics.* CDC. Retrieved from http://www.cdc.gov/nchs/data/hestat/obesity_adult_09_10/obesity_adult_09_10.pdf

39 Fryar, CD., Carroll, MD., and Ogden, CL. (2018). Prevalence of Overweight, Obesity, and Severe Obesity Among Adults Aged 20 and Over: United States, 1960–1962 Through 2015–2016. NCHS September. URL: https://www.cdc.gov/nchs/data/hestat/obesity_adult_15_16/obesity_adult_15_16.pdf

40 Fryar CD, Carroll MD, Ogden CL (2016). Prevalence of overweight and obesity among children and adolescents aged 2–19 years: United States, 1963–1965 through 2013–2014. National Center for Health Statistics Data, Health E-Stats. Available at: https://www.cdc.gov/nchs/data/hestat/obesity_child_13_14/obesity_child_13_14.htm

41 Giovannucci E., Rimm, E.B., Stampfer, M.J., Colditz, G.A., Ascherio, A. & Willett W.C. (1994). Intake of fat, meat and fiber in relation to risk of colon cancer in men. *Cancer Res. 54*, 2390 – 2397.

42 Goldman, J.A. (1997). *Building New York's sewers: developing mechanisms of urban management.* West Lafayette: Purdue University Press, 235.

43 Gori, G.B. (1975). The diet, nutrition, and cancer program of the NCI national cancer program. *Cancer Research 3*, 3545-3547.

44 Gould S.J. (2002). *The structure of evolutionary theory.* Cambridge, MA: Harvard University Press.

45 Gunderson, G.W. (2014). *National school lunch program (nslp): background and development in Europe. USDA.* Retrieved from http://www.fns.usda.gov/nslp/history_1#england

46 Hales, CM., Carroll, MD., Fryar, CD., and Ogden, CL. (2017). Prevalence of Obesity Among Adults and Youth: United States, 2015–2016. NCHS Data Brief No. 288, October. URL: https://www.cdc.gov/nchs/products/databriefs/db288.htm

47 Halliday, S. (2001). Death and miasma in Victorian London: A persistent belief. *BMJ* 323,1469–71.

48 Harvey Young, J. (1989). *Pure food: Securing the Pure Food and Drugs Act of 1906* Princeton, NJ: Princeton University Press.

49 Heron, M. (2013). Death Rates. Deaths: Leading Causes for (2010. *U.S. Census Bureau, CDC/NCHS. National Vital Statistics Report 62* (6), 2-96.

50 Holesh, JE., and Martin, A. (2018). Physiology, carbohydrates. StatPearls Publishing; 2018 Jan-. URL: https://www.ncbi.nlm.nih.gov/books/NBK459280/

51 Institute of Medicine. (2002). *Dietary reference intakes for energy, carbohydrate, fiber, fat, fatty acids, cholesterol, protein, and amino acids.* Washington D.C.: The National Academies Press. Retrieved from https://www.iom.edu/~/media/Files/Activity%20Files/Nutrition/DRIs/DRI_Macronutrients.pdf

52 Jansson, B. (1986). Geographic cancer risk and intracellular potassium/sodium ratios. *Cancer Detect Prev 9*, 171-9.

53 Jenkins, DJ., Wolever, TM., Taylor, RH. et al., (1981). Glycemic index of foods: a physiological basis for carbohydrate exchange. Am.J.Clin. Nutr; 34(3):362-6. URL: https://academic.oup.com/ajcn/article-abstract/34/3/362/4692881?redirectedFrom=fulltext

[54] Johnson, C.S. (2005). Uncle Sam's diet sensation: MyPyramid: An overview and commentary. *Med. Gen. Med, 793*, 78.

[55] Kishlansky, M., Geary, P., & O'Brien, P. (1991). *Civilization in the West*. New York: Harper-Collins, 1021.

[56] Krauss, R.M., Eckel, R.H., Howard, B. et al. (2000). AHA dietary guidelines: revision (2000: A statement for healthcare professionals from the *Nutrition Committee of the American Heart Association, 102*, 2284-99.

[57] Kris-Etherton, P.M. et al. (2000). Polyunsaturated fats in the food chain in the United States. *American Journal of Clinical Nutrition* 71(suppl), 179S–88S.

[58] Lindebeg, S. (2005). The Palaeolithic diet-(The Stone-Age diet). *Scandinavian Journal of Nutrition, 49* (2),75-77.

[59] Mann, T. et al. (2007). Medicare's search for effective obesity treatments: Diets are not the answer. *Am Psychol Apr 62*(3), 220-33.

[60] Margotta, R. (1996). *The Hamlyn history of medicine*, ed. Paul Lewis. London: Institute of Neurology.

[61] Martin, AB., Hartman, M., Washington, B., Catlin, A., et al. (2018). National Health Care Spending In 2017: Growth Slows To Post–Great Recession Rates; Share Of GDP Stabilizes. Health Affairs; 38(1). URL: https://www.healthaffairs.org/doi/full/10.1377/hlthaff.2018.05085

[62] Martin, AB., Lassman, D., Washington, B., and Catlin, A. (2012). Growth In US Health Spending Remained Slow In 2010; Health Share Of Gross Domestic Product Was Unchanged From 2009. Health Affairs; 31 (1). URL: https://www.healthaffairs.org/doi/10.1377/hlthaff.2011.1135

[63] Murtaugh, M.A., Ma, K.N., Sweeney, C., Caan, B.J., & Slattery, M.L. (2004). Meat consumption patterns and preparation, genetic variants of metabolic enzymes, and their association with rectal cancer in men and women. *J Nutr.;134* (4), 776–784.

[64] May, A.L., Freedman, D., Sherry, B., & Blanck, H.M. (2013). Obesity —United States, 1999–2010. Center for Disease Control and Prevention (CDC). *Morbidity and Mortality Weekly Report (MMWR)* 62(03), 120-128. Retrieved from http://www.cdc.gov/mmwr/preview/mmwrhtml/su6203a20.htm

[65] Miller, Judith A. (1999). *Mastering the market the state and the grain-trade in Northern France, 1700–1860*. Cambridge, UK: The Press Syndicate of the University of Cambridge.

[66] Milner, J. A. (2000). Functional foods: The U.S. perspective. *American Journal of Clinical Nutrition* 71(6), 1654s–1659s.

[67] Morley, I. (2007). City, chaos, contagion, Chadwick and social justice. *Yale Journal of Biology and Medicine* 80, 61-72.

[68] Moss, M. (2014). *Salt, sugar and fat: How the food giants hooked us*. New York: Random House, 423.

[69] Murtaugh, M.A. (2004). Meat consumption and the risk of colon and rectal cancer Current Medical Literature: *Clinical Nutrition* Vol. 13 Issue 4, 61.

[70] Nesse, R.M, & Williams, G.C. (1994). *Why we get sick. The new science of Darwinian medicine*. New York: Times Books.

[71] Nestle, M. (1999). Animal versus plant foods in human diets & health: Is the historical record unequivocal? *Proc. Nutrition Society* 58, 211-218.

[72] Nestle, M. (2002). *Food politics: How the food industry influences nutrition & health*. Berkeley, CA: University of California Press, 457.

[73] Nestle, M. (May 31, 2011). Goodbye food pyramid: The USDA to announce a new food icon. *The Atlantic*. Retrieved from http://www.theatlantic.com/health/archive/2011/05/goodbye-food-pyramid-usda-to-announce-a-new-food-icon/239645/

[74] Nikiforuk, A. (1996). *The fourth horseman: A short history of plagues, scourges and emerging viruses*. Toronto: Penguin Group.

75 Nissenbaum, S. (1980). *Sex, diet, and debility in Jacksonian America*. Chicago: The Dorsey Press. American Society and Culture: The Dorsey Collection, 198.

76 Office of the Surgeon General (OSG) of the United States (2001). *The Surgeon General's Call To Action To Prevent and Decrease Overweight and Obesity*. NIH. Retrieved from http://www.ncbi.nlm.nih.gov/books/NBK44206/

77 Ogden, C.L., Carroll, M.D., Kit, B.K., Flegal, K.M. (2014) *Prevalence of childhood and adult obesity in the United States*, 2011–2012 JAMA; 311(8):806–814

78 Pan, A., Sun, Q., Bernstein, A.M., Schulze, M.B., Manson, J.E., Stampfer, M.J., Willett W.C., & Hu, F.B. (2012). Red meat consumption and mortality: results from 2 prospective cohort studies. *Arch Intern Med* 172, 555-563.

79 Pang, G., Xie, J., Chen, Q., & Hu, Z. (2014). Energy intake, metabolic homeostasis, and human health. *Food Science and Human Wellness* 3, 89–103.

80 Peterson, M. S. (1965). Establishing a modern food industry: The resources of the technical literature. In: *Food Technology the World Over*. Vol 2, ed. M. S. Peterson and D. K. Tressler. Westport, CT: AVI Publishing, 3–37.

81 Petrick, G.M. (2012). Industrial Food. In: *The Oxford handbook of food history*, Pilcher, JM ed. Oxford University Press. Retrieved from http://www.oxfordhandbooks.com/view/10.1093/oxfordhb/9780199729937.001.0001/oxfordhb-9780199729937-e-15

82 Petrick, G. M. (2011). "Purity as life": H.J. Heinz, religious sentiment, and the beginning of the industrial diet. *History and Technology* 27(1), 37–64.

83 Phillips, R.L. (1975). Role of life-style and dietary habits in risk of cancer among Seventh-Day Adventists. *Cancer Research*, 35, 3513-3522.

84 Plato/ (2005). *Critias & Timeus*. Chicago: Achron Press

85 Popkin, B., & Nielson, A. (2003). The world's increased intake of sugar. *Nutrition Research Newsletter* 22 (12), 7.

86 Pyle, G.F. (1969).The diffusion of cholera in the United States in the nineteenth century. *Geographic Analysis* 1 (1), 59-75. Retrieved from http://onlinelibrary.wiley.com/doi/10.1111/j.1538-4632.1969.tb00605.x/epdf

87 Reid, M.G. (1943). *Food for the people*. New York: John Wiley & Sons, 653.

88 Rensberger, B. (November 26, 1992). Was golden age of ancient Greece tarnished? Research: Scientists were stunned when they examined skeletons from a Greek colony and found widespread disease and malnutrition. *L.A. Times*.

89 Rosenfeld, L. (1997). Vitamine—vitamin. The early years of discovery. *Clinical Chemistry* 43(4): 680-685. Retrieved from http://www.clinchem.org/content/43/4/680.full

90 (RSC) Royal Society of Chemistry. (2015). *The fight against food adulteration*. Retrieved from http://www.rsc.org/education/eic/issues/2005Mar/Thefightagainstfoodadulteration.asp

91 Rowlands, G. (2009). France 1709: Le Crunch. *History Today* 59(2). Available at http://www.historytoday.com/guy-rowlands/france-1709–le-crunch.

92 Sebastian A., Frassetto, L.A., Sellmeyer, D.E., Merriam R.L., & Morris R.C. (2002). Estimation of the net acid load of the diet of ancestral preagricultural *Homo sapiens* and their hominid ancestors. *American Journal of Clinical Nutrition* 76, 1308–16.

93 Simopoulos, A.P. October (2002).The importance of the ratio of omega-6/omega-3 essential fatty acids. *Biomed Pharmacother* 56(8), 365-79.

94 Simopoulos, A.P. (1999). Essential fatty acids in health and chronic disease. *American Journal of Clinical Nutrition* 70(3 Suppl), 560S-569S.

95 Sinclair, U. (1906). The Jungle. New York: Doubleday, Page & Company

96 Spiekermann, U. (2011). Redefining food: The standardization of products and production in Europe and the United States 1880-1914. *History and Technology*, 27(1), 11-36.

97 Spiekermann, U. (2009).Twentieth-century product innovations in the German food industry *The Business History Review*; 83(2) A Special Issue on Food and Innovation: Published by: The President and Fellows of Harvard College, 291-315. Retrieved from http://www.jstor.org/stable/40538844

98 Stiebeling, H.K. (1939). *Better nutrition as a national goal: The problem*. Year Book of Agriculture, 380.

99 Stiebeling, H.K. & Ward, M. (1933). *Diets at four levels of nutrition content and cost*. U.S. Department of Agriculture, Circ. No. 296, 59.

100 Summers, Judith. (1989). *Soho—A history of London's most colourful neighborhood*. London: Bloomsbury, 113-117.

101 Suzuki, N. (2010). Popular health movement and diet reform in 19th century America. *The Japanese Journal of American Studies* 21,111–137

102 Swann, J. (2005). 100 years of the 1906 food and drugs act. The Formation and Early Work of the Drug Laboratory USDA Bureau of Chemistry. *Apothecary's Cabinet*, Fall; 9, 1-9.

103 Svizzero, S. (2014. Pre-Neolithic economy. *History of Economic Ideas* -3, 1-17.

104 Thomas, L.H., Jones, P.R., Winter, J.A., & Smith, H. (1981). Hydrogenated oils and fats: the presence of chemically-modified. *The American Journal of Clinical Nutrition* 34:877-886.

105 Tuyns, A. J. (1988). Salt and gastrointestinal cancer. *Nutr Cancer* 11, 229 -32.

106 USDA & USDHHS. (2015). Scientific report of the 2015 Dietary Guidelines Advisory Committee. Retrieved from http://health.gov/dietaryguidelines/2015-scientific-report/15-appendix-e3/e3-1-a4.asp

107 USDA. (2012). *FSIS history*. Retrieved from http://www.fsis.usda.gov/wps/portal/informational/aboutfsis/history/history

108 USDA (U.S. Department of Agriculture) and U.S. DHHS (U.S. Department of Health and Human Services). (December 2010). *Dietary Guidelines for Americans, 2010*. 7th Edition, Washington, DC: U.S. Government Printing Office.

109 USDA. (1998). *USDA continuing survey of food intakes by individuals, 1994–96*.

110 USDA (U.S. Department of Agriculture). (1997). Agricultural Research Service. *Data tables: results from USDA's 1994-96 Continuing Survey of Food Intakes by Individuals and 1994-96 Diet and Health Knowledge Survey*. ARS Food Surveys Research Group. Retrieved from http://www.barc.usda.gov/bhnrc/ foodsurvey/home.htm

111 US DHHS & USDA (2015). Dietary Guidelines for Americans 2015-2020. Executive Summary. URL: https://health.gov/dietaryguidelines/2015/guidelines/executive-summary/#guidelines

112 Trustwell, A.S. (2002). Meat consumption and cancer of the large bowel. *European Journal of Clinical Nutrition* 56, Suppl 1, S19–S24.

113 U.S. Senate Select Committee on Nutrition and Human Needs. (1977). *Dietary goals for the United States, 2nd ed*. Washington, DC: U.S. Government Printing Office.

114 USDA Food Safety & Inspection Service. *FSIS history*. Available at http://www.fsis.usda.gov/wps/portal/informational/aboutfsis/history

115 Vial, R. (1989). *Moeurs, santé et maladies en 1789*. Societe des editions Londreys, Paris.

116 Warburton, DER., Nicol, CW., Gatto, SN., and Bredin, SSD. (2007). Cardiovascular disease and osteoporosis: Balancing risk management. Vascular Health and Risk Management:3(5) 673–689

[117] Webster's New World Medical Dictionary 3rd edition (2008). *Humoralism*. Hoboken, NJ: Wiley Publishing, Inc., 204.

[118] White, MC., et al., (2014). Age and Cancer Risk: A Potentially Modifiable Relationship. Am J Prev Med; 46(301): S7–15. doi: 10.1016/j.amepre.2013.10.029

[119] Welsh, S.O., Davis, C., & Shaw, A. (1993). *USDA's food guide: background and development*. Hyattsville, MD: Nutrition Education Division USDA Publication # 1514. Retrieved from http://www.cnpp.usda.gov/sites/default/files/archived_projects/FGPBackgroundAndDevelopment.pdf

[120] WHO Technical Report Series 935. (2002). *Protein and amino acid requirement in human nutrition. Report of a joint WHO/FAO/UNU Expert consultation*. Retrieved from http://apps.who.int/iris/bitstream/10665/43411/1/WHO_TRS_935_eng.pdf?ua=1

[121] Wiley, H.W. (1929). *The history of a crime against the food law*. Milwaukee, WI. Lee Foundation for Nutritional Research, 413.

[122] Willett. W.C. (2000). Diet and cancer. *The Oncologist* 5, 393-404.

[123] Willett, W.C., Stampfer, M.J., Manson JE., et al. (1993). Intake of trans fatty acids and risk of coronary heart disease among women. *Lancet* 351, 581-5.

[124] Willett W.C., Stampfer, M.J., Colditz, G.A., Rosner, B.A. & Speizer, F.E. (1990). Relation of meat, fat and fiber intake to the risk of colon cancer in a prospective study among women. *New England Journal of Medicine* 232, 1664–1672.

[125] Wong, J.M.W. et al. (2012). Microbiota diet and heart disease. *Journal of AOAC International* 95 (1), 24-30.

[126] World Health Organization. (2001). *Cancer Strategy*. Retrieved from http://www.who.int/ncd/cancer/strategy.htm

[127] Wynder, E. L., and Gori, G. B. (1977). Contributions of the environment to cancer incidence: an epidemiologic exercise. *J Natl Cancer Inst* 58, 825–32.

CHAPTER 1 ANSWERS

1 Identify the century and the years when the most virulent wave of bubonic and pneumonic plagues swept through Europe killing upwards of 24 million souls.
ANSWER: The 14th century between 1351-1358

2 Describe the impact(s) the two plagues (bubonic and pneumonic) had on the people of Europe.
ANSWER: In wiping out such a large fragment of the population, it took up until the 15th century for the European economy to move from stagnant to vibrant and diversified by the end of the 15th century.

3 Identify the 2017 US health care expenditure and its reflection on the current dietary habits of Americans.
ANSWER: By 2017 the US health expenditure rose to $3.5 Trillion/year and was a reflection of the obesity crisis which accounts for the majority of chronic diseases. It is estimated that 75% of health care costs are tied to chronic diseases like hypertension, cardiovascular disease, and type-2 diabetes.

4 Explain how the prevalence of disease in Western societies significantly rose with the adoption of key dietary changes.
ANSWER: the modernization of the food supply led to a rise in the glycemic index of food; there was a change in the fatty acid distribution which led to a significant drop in the omega-3 to omega-6 fatty acid ratio; the sodium: potassium ratio rose thereby leading to a greater prevalence of chronic diseases such as osteoporosis and hypertension; the micronutrient density of food would have significantly declined with the processing of food resulting in widespread malnutrition especially in the US by the beginning of the 20th century; the macronutrient distribution of the diet changed to include large amounts of refined carbohydrates, and larger amounts of total fat and saturated fat; the acid-base balance would have significantly changed with more of a Neolithic diet consisting of greater consumption of cereals, dairy and meats at the expense of less base foods such as fruits and vegetables. This important change would have made the skeletal structure of man more vulnerable; inactivity rose in the neolithic population compared to the paleolithic, but it is more importantly seen in the modern man of the 21st century where the computer age has made the human species true couch potatoes. The resulting inactivity has increased the prevalence of cancers, obesity, type-2 diabetes and heart disease; and finally the low fiber content of the 19th and 20th centuries, resulting from mechanized milling and a fundamental dislike of fruits and vegetables, increased risks of type-2 diabetes, cardiovascular disease, coronary heart disease, stomach and colorectal cancers.

5 What exactly do historians attribute to the increased vulnerability of Europe to the great plagues of the Middle Ages?
ANSWER: The many significant famines that devastated Europe at the beginning of the 14th century made malnutrition and hunger rampant throughout Europe. This made the population vulnerable to the devastating sweep of the plagues.

6 How did the 19th century Industrial Revolution contribute to the rise in malnutrition and disease in Europe?
ANSWER: The sudden rise in urban population density that occurred as homeless agricultural families migrated from the rural setting to the cities, created year around demand for food which the cities were not prepared to accommodate. The lack of grocery stores and safe methods of food distribution resulted in both problems of malnutrition such as scurvy and food poisonings.

7 Identify the key government regulatory agencies and regulations intended to control food impurities and food poisonings in the US at the start of the 20th century.
ANSWER: USDA, the Bureau of Chemistry, the FDA, the Pure Food and Drug Act of 1906, and the Federal Meat Inspection Act.

CHAPTER 2
Key Nutrition Concepts and Calculations

Ditary cut off recomendatozt

dealins with money

anything dealins with a percentage of people - it is affecting

© Syda Productions/Shutterstock.com

2.1 PRINCIPLES OF HEALTHY EATING

2.1.1 Population Dietary Guidelines to Achieving Health

Nutrition and medical research, consisting of long-term prospective studies often lasting several decades, have concluded that nutrition plays a key role in the prevention of chronic diseases. In fact, it is currently believed that dietary and lifestyle modifications can prevent or at least minimize the development of chronic diseases derived from being obese or overweight (Willett et al., 2006), which, according to 2008 statistics, cost $147 billion per year to manage (Finkelstein et al., 2009). This is because obesity leads to a vast array of costly chronic conditions that significantly affect quality of life, notably

(How much money is spent on trying to mange chronic dicuses caused by obesity

cardiovascular disease, hypertension, type-2 diabetes, sleep apnea, gastrointestinal diseases (diverticulosis, gallbladder), degenerative disorders (arthritis), asthma, and some cancers (NIEHS, 2018; CDC 2018). Therefore early intervention programs are encouraged in obesity and overweight prevention, as dietary preferences and habits are more strongly established during infancy and childhood. In the last 10 years type-2 diabetes has become a worrisome epidemic, now affecting 8% of adult Americans; if the current trend is not changed, type-2 diabetes is forecasted to afflict 33% of adult Americans by 2050 (CDC, 2010).

Type 2 diabetes prediction

It is somewhat reassuring to note that changes in lifestyle do wield a tremendous impact in the prevention of some cancers. Although overall cancer incidence has declined in recent years, cancer nevertheless claimed more lives than heart disease in individuals younger than 85 years old (Pathak 2016). In

43

fact between 14% and 20% of all cancer deaths are tied to overweight and obesity (Calle et al., 2003). The overall dietary trend to reduce total fat intake has shown some benefit, notably a 40% reduction in the incidence of ovarian cancer measured in 50,000 women over an eight year period (NIH, 2007). Mazzetti and colleagues (1998) advance that 33% of breast cancers could be averted by decreasing alcohol consumption, and increasing the consumption of fruits, vegetables and vegetable oil, along with heightening the frequency of exercise.

In the year 2000, the U.S. Department of Health and Human Services (DHHS) put forth the Healthy People 2010 guidelines to help people reduce the risk of lifestyle-related disease. Unfortunately, it made very little progress toward this goal. So here we are again with the Healthy People 2020 trying to decrease chronic disease caused by diet and overweight. Healthy People 2020 guidelines recommend these key goals to reduce death rates from the most significant threats:

1 Attaining high-quality, longer lives free of preventable disease, disability, injury, and premature death.

2 Achieving health equity, eliminating disparities, and improving the health of all groups.

3 Creating social and physical environments that promote good health for all.

4 Promoting quality of life, healthy development, and healthy behaviors across all life stages. (CDC, 2015)

These new recommendations recognize the role of not only diet and exercise but also the policies and environments in schools, work sites, health care organizations, and communities that encourage or discourage healthy behaviors. All these environments need to have policies and practices that are influential in managing healthy body weights in the population (CDC, 2015). In fact, nutrition and weight status are among the top 42 topics that are addressed in Healthy People 2020.

The Healthy People 2020 define a healthy diet as respecting these three precepts:

1 Consume a variety of nutrient-dense foods within and across the food groups, especially

whole grains, fruits, vegetables, low-fat or fat-free milk or milk products, and lean meats and other protein sources.

2 Limit the intake of saturated and trans fats, cholesterol, added sugars, sodium (salt), and alcohol.

3 Limit caloric intake to meet caloric needs. (DHHS, 2015)

The *Dietary Guidelines for Americans* (DGAs), formulated every five years by the USDA and DHHS, are meant to identify the key dietary and lifestyle issues that need to be addressed for population disease reduction. They represent the practical ways of achieving part of the Healthy People goals. The 2015–2020 DGAs revolve around two major concepts: The first is that a healthy eating pattern needs to be maintained in order to ensure that healthy weights and good health are achieved over the long term. The second is that nutrient-dense foods and beverages need to be regularly consumed as part of a healthy eating pattern in order to optimize health in the population. The DGAs are based on three main eating patterns: first, the USDAs MyPlate food model; second, the healthy vegetarian eating pattern, and third, the healthy Mediterranean style of eating pattern (DHHS, 2015). There are five main recommendations proposed in the 2015–2020 Dietary Guidelines for Americans to help the U.S. population achieve overall health and prevent chronic diseases (DHHS, 2015).

1 Americans are encouraged to achieve and maintain a healthy weight by consuming adequate daily caloric intakes and judiciously making wise food and beverage choices that are nutrient-dense and favorable to reducing the risk of chronic diseases.

2 Americans are encouraged to limit their caloric intakes while choosing nutrient-dense foods from across all the food groups and in amounts consistent with the Myplate recommendations.

3 Americans need to put a limit on calories coming specifically from added sugar in addition to limiting intakes of saturated fats and sodium by making better food and beverage choices that are consistent with healthy eating patterns.

4 Americans must shift their food and beverage choices away from less healthy options and more in the direction of personal and cultural preferences that are healthy and derived from all food groups in order to ensure successful and enduring dietary shifts.

5 Americans are also encouraged to become active in supporting and promoting healthy eating in multiple public settings whether in schools, workplaces, churches, and community centers (DHHS, 2015).

Additionally, the DGAs make very specific key recommendations that are consistent with the DASH (Dietary Approach to Stop Hypertension) diet (NIH, 2015). Indeed, they recommend a variety of dark green, red and orange vegetables, legumes, starch and non-starchy vegetables; grains are also an important recommendation—about 50% should be whole grains. Fruits of all kinds, dairy foods, and finally protein foods, consisting not only of lean meat, but fish, poultry, eggs, in addition to legumes, nuts, seeds and and soy, should be part of a varied diet. Oil get a singular mention as they are important sources of essential fatty acids and are richly found in canola, corn, olive, peanut, safflower, soybean, and sunflower oils. Palm, palm-kernel and coconut oil are not part of a recommendation for oil as they are elevated in saturated fats. Trans-fats, artificially produced by hydrogenating oils in the creation of margarines snack foods, prepared desserts, and shortenings, increase the risk of cardiovascular disease, and therefore need to be minimally consumed in the diet (DHHS, 2015). Despite attempts by the food industry at reducing trans-fats in the diet, they still remain prominent in some margarines, shortenings, desserts, microwave popcorn and artificial coffee creamers (DHHS, 2015). The importance of regular exercise cannot be overstated in these public health goals, as it is now recognized that regular vigorous exercises are associated with a 30-40% decline in colon cancers (NCI, 2009). Currently, a mere 20% of adults in the US (17% of women and 24% of men) meet the minimal Physical Activity Guidelines for Americans 2008 (DHHS, 2008). In fact, overall physical outputs associated with transportation, work and home are also declining. Research has identified excessive electronic screen time as the main cause for increased sedentary activities in the population (DHHS, 2015).

There are four key recommendations that quantify the dietary cut-offs regarded as important to contain the risk of heart disease and weight gain in the population:

1 < 10% of calories/day should be consumed as added sugar.

2 < 10 percent of calories/day should be consumed from saturated fats.

3 <2300 milligrams (mg)/day of sodium should be consumed.

4 Moderate alcohol consumption should be encouraged for women (up to 1 drink/day)and men (up to 2 drinks/day)of legal drinking age (DHHS, 2015).

weight management

There is good evidence to suggest that weight management practices should revolve around consuming the recommended macronutrient distribution ranges for the three macronutrients. Maintaining low total fat intake and relatively high carbohydrate intake is one of the key strategies to ensure modest weight loss over time (Wing & Phelan, 2005). The more efficacious strategies for significant weight reduction always include a notable investment in moderate to strenuous exercise on a regular basis integrated with lifestyle modification programs that include everything from low calorie diets, personal trainers, lifestyle coaches all the way to doctor-prescribed appetite suppressant drugs to bariatric surgery (Montesi et al., 2016). But first, the focus of this discussion will be on the main macronutrients.

Low Fat high Carb excess low calories

2.1.2 Carbohydrates

Carbohydrates can be structurally organized into three main categories: sugars, oligosaccharides and polysaccharides (Cummings and Stephen, 2007).

1. **Simple sugars** consist of monosaccharides (glucose, fructose, galactose), disaccharides (sucrose, lactose, maltose), trioses (glycerose), tetroses (erythrose), and pentoses (ribose). Each disaccharide consists of two monosaccharides linked together by a glycosidic bond (Figure 2.1). The chemical structure in Figure 2.1 illustrates how glucose linked to fructose, through a glycosidic bond, creates sucrose, otherwise known as table sugar. Similarly, when galactose combines with glucose there is a formation of lactose, which is the main sugar in

Added sugar since 1970s ↓ decline in density

milk. And when two glucose monosaccharides are linked, maltose is formed; maltose and maltodextrins are used extensively by the food industry as an additive to beverages, beer, cereals, pasta, and a variety of other processed food products requiring slight sweetening (Hofman et al., 2016). In addition, there are more complex carbohydrates called oligosaccharides consisting of 3 to 10 monosaccharides (maltodextrins and raffinose), or polysaccharides (amylose, cellulose or glycogen) entailing more than 10 monosaccharides (Gropper & Smith, 2013; Cummings and Stephen, 2007). Sugar, naturally present in food and added to food play an important role in flavor enhancement (Murphy and Johnson, 2003), but since the 1970s, added sugar has become significantly more prominent in the US diet with the marketplace dominance of processed foods and sweetened beverages (Chun et al., 2010). This significant rise in added sugar intake has led to a visible decline in the nutrient density of the diet (Murphy and Johnson, 2003).

↓ death rates ↑ fiber diet

2. Starches: Most of the carbohydrate intake of North Americans consists of 60% starches, whereas 30% is made up of sucrose and 10% lactose (Keim et al., 2006). The Academy of Nutrition and Dietetics' 2015 position paper update on fiber, reports on some large scale cohort studies that show overall lower mortality rates in people that consume high fiber diets (A.N.D, 2015). Starches are divided into either **amylose** or **amylopectin** (Figure 2.2). Amylose consists of unbranched glucose molecules linearly connected by glycosidic α (1-4) bonds. Only about 21% of starches consist of amylose, whereas between 75% and 83% of starches are made up of amylopectin (Hofman et al., 2016; Keim et al., 2006). Indeed, potato, rice, and wheat, which are abundantly consumed in the United States are elevated in amylopectin (Keim et al., 2006)., whereas the foods elevated in amylose tend to resemble **resistant starches**. Foods such as starchy fruits (banana) and vegetables (parsnips), beans, and legumes (soybeans, kidney beans, navy beans, lentils) tend to be elevated in the starch called amylose. Amylopectin is a branched starch consisting of both the linear glycosidic α (1-4) and the branched α (1-6) bonds (Figure 2.2). Because of the extensive branching, it is easier for enzymes to digest the amylopectin, thus leading to a greater glucose release into the blood compared with amylose, which has no branching

Amylose + Amylopectin

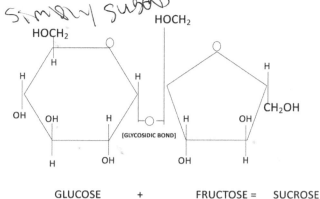

GLUCOSE   +   FRUCTOSE =   SUCROSE

Figure 2.1 *Chemical structure of sucrose.*

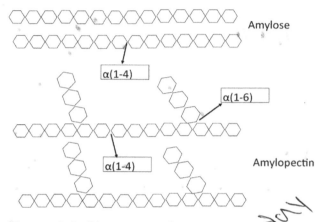

Figure 2.2 *Dietary starches.*

grams of carbs per day

(Hofman et al., 2016) and decreased glucose tolerance (Byrnes et al., 1995). The Recommended Dietary Allowance (RDA) for carbohydrates is 130 g per day for adults and is derived from the smallest amount that is required for adequate brain nourishment and to prevent ketosis (Keim et al., 2006). Ketone production—resulting in ketosis or rise of ketones in the blood—occurs from an incomplete metabolism of fat because of inadequate carbohydrate intake.

fiber, non digestable

3. Fiber: Total fiber, found in food, is classified, according to the Institute of Medicine (IOM), into either Dietary Fiber or Functional fiber (A.N.D., 2015; IOM, 2005). Dietary fibers are made up mostly of non-digestible carbohydrates—known also as resistant starches (Birt et al., 2013)—which are naturally present in the food (A.N.D., 2015). The non-digestible components, found in plants and fruits, include carbohydrates like cellulose, hemicellulose and pectin (Holesh and Martin, 2018). These

Non disable components in Plants

[Handwritten margin notes: "Fiber can nourish but because it is water repellant" / "Probiotics are fibers but all fibers don't have prebiotics" / "Dietary Fiber" (left margin) / "Functional Protein" / "Prebiotic Probiotics" (left margin) / "of fiber is being consumed" (right margin) / "Cellulose" (right margin)]

are fibers, resistant to gastrointestinal (GI) digestive enzymes, and therefore, cannot be hydrolyzed and absorbed. This non-digestible class of fiber also encompasses "lignin," which does not fall under the broad category of carbohydrate (Turner and Lupton, 2011). Fibers, because they are resistant to digestive enzymes, can nourish the colonic bacteria and engender significant proliferation of healthy microbiota or microbial culture, in the gut, in addition to softening the stool and ensuring bulk for easier defecation (Holesh and Martin, 2018). Dietary fibers are traditionally classified as either "water soluble" or "water insoluble" and thus will exercise different mechanical effects depending on their osmotic capacity to bind to water. A fiber is deemed water soluble when it binds to water as is the case of pectins, thereby forming gel-like consistency that softens the texture of the stool. Water insoluble refers to bran fibers, for instance, which repel water and do not undergo gelatinization. Bran fibers, however, can cause a bulk effects on stool, therefore leading to a shortened transit time through the GI tract--less constipation--aided by the flushing water effect in the GI tract (Lupton, 2006; Keim et al., 2006). Excellent sources of dietary fiber are primarily identified as grains, vegetables, legumes (all types of beans and lentils), nuts, seeds and fruits (Turner and Lupton, 2011).

Functional fibers are also non-digestible oligosaccharides—large carbohydrate structures—that have been extracted from popular foods such as leeks, asparagus, chicory, Jerusalem artichokes, garlic, onions, wheat, oats, and soybeans (Slavin, 2013). They are also synthesized, and then added to food, but their common impact is that they have specific physiological health benefit such as overall better GI health, lower risks of obesity, type-2 diabetes, and colon cancer (A.N.D., 2015). Probiotics are often advocated for good GI function and long term health and popularly consumed as Lactobacillus or Bifidobacterium in different foods like yogurts and kefir. However, the FDA has not yet approved any probiotics for any prevention or treatments of disease (NIH, 2016); the most popular functional fibers with clear benefits are referred to as prebiotics—consisting exclusively of non-digestible carbohydrates—that are subject to gut fermentation, resulting in the proliferation of microbiota that synthesize short chain fatty acids (SCFAs) such acetate, propionate and butyrate (A.N.D., 2015; Slavin, 2013; Birt, et al.,

2013:). Put simply, all prebiotics can be classified as fibers, but not all fibers have that fermentable prebiotic characteristics (Slavin, 2013). The SCFAs tend to form gases (Eswaran, et al., 2013) which positively influence the pH in the GI tract, thus creating a more acidic environment, conducive to increased mineral absorption and diminished pathogenic bacterial growth, healthy microbiota and ultimately offering protection against systemic inflammation (A.N.D, 2015). By contrast, when there is a disruption of the gut microbiota—also known as dysbiosis—there are heightened risks of type-2 diabetes, inflammatory bowel disease, obesity and colorectal cancer (Birt, et al., 2013). The best known functional fibers are wheat dextrin, acacia gum, psyllium, banana, whole grain wheat, and whole grain corn (Slavin, 2013). The North American diet is considered impoverished in overall total fiber content; NHANES survey data, collected between 2009 and 2010, confirmed a mean 17g/day of total fiber intake by the US population (Reicks, et al., 2014), or in other words, about 50% of the recommended amount (A.N.D., 2008). A Recommended Dietary Allowance (RDA) for fiber has not been established, however an Adequate Intake (AI) based on energy needs (14g/1000 kcals consumed) has been determined to be a reliable recommendation for decreased cardiovascular risks (IOM, 2005). This means, in practical terms, that a woman whose DRI calorie needs are 1800 kcals/day would require 25g of fiber per day, whereas a man needing 2714 kcals/day would have an AI equal to 38g of fiber per day (Lupton & Trumbo, 2006). Moreover, populations that consume adequate amounts of fiber—between 25 and 40g/day—do not experience as much gastrointestinal distresses such as constipation, heartburn, bloating, diarrhea, nausea and abdominal discomforts as frequently as those with low fiber intakes (A.N.D., 2015). Cellulose is an indigestible plant starch made up of glucose molecules linked together by ß (1-4) bonds that are non-hydrolysable by the amylase enzyme; this is because the amylase enzyme can only hydrolyze α (1-4) glycosidic bonds. Cellulose is most abundantly found in legumes, which represent an excellent source of fiber.

The **Acceptable Macronutrient Distribution Ranges** (AMDR) were published by the Food and Nutrition Board of the Institute of Medicine, National Academy of Sciences (NAS, 2002c) as part of a series of reports on Dietary Reference Intakes

(DRI) in order to give guidance for dietary planning for three specific purposes: (1) to ensure a low prevalence of chronic disease in the population, (2) to ensure the adequate intake of essential nutrients by the population, and (3) to encourage adequate energy intake to sustain physical activity and weight maintenance (NAS, 2002c). The premise of these recommendations is grounded in the understanding that any significant deviance in the proportion of macronutrients consumed regularly by a population can lead to a higher prevalence of chronic disease. Consequently, epidemiologists have concluded that the AMDR for carbohydrates needs to be between 45% and 65% of energy needs in order to ensure adequate fiber, sugar, and complex starch intake and energy. In practical terms this translates into between 225 g and 325 g of carbohydrates on a 2,000 kcal diet.

4. Sugars: It has been shown that when **added sugar** represents more than 25% of total calories required, there is a concomitant decline in the nutrient quality of the diet. Indeed, studies have shown that a mean added sugar intake of 26.7% of total energy leads to lower intakes of vitamins A, C, B_{12}, folate, calcium, phosphorus, magnesium, and iron (NAS, 2005b). An ideal recommended amount of added sugar has not been established, but the Institute of Medicine recommends limiting added sugar to a maximal amount of 25% of calories (Murphy and Johnson, 2003; Institute of Medicine, 2002). Healthy Eating Guidelines for Americans-2015 recommend no more than 10% of calories as added sugar (DHHS, 2015). Consequently, <10% of DRI calories will be the added sugar limit used in this textbook. Added sugar has been identified as the sugar added to food during processing, and includes glucose, dextrose, sucrose, fructose, high fructose corn syrup, corn syrup, molasses, syrups, maltose, and lactose, representing upwards of 13% of calories consumed per day by Americans (DHHS, 2015). Similarly, when **total sugar** is <20% of Dietary Reference Intake (DRI) (See section 2.2) calories, there is no apparent reduction of any nutrients in the diet (NAS, 2005b), and is therefore recommended in this textbook as the maximal allowed in the diet. As a guide to help students visualize the quantity of sugar that can be contained in a food product, consider that 1 teaspoon of sugar weighs 4 grams. This means the next time you read on the nutrition facts panel on the back of a food product that there are 28 grams

of sugar per serving, you can now translate that into seven teaspoons of sugar which can be calculated by dividing 28g by 4g because there are 4g of sugar in 1 teaspoon.

2.1.3 Proteins

Proteins make up the structural components of cells, hormones, and enzymes. They consist of amino acids—there are 20 amino acids in all—which are made up of an amino-N group (NH2), a carboxyl-carbon group (COOH), and a side chain (R), responsible for the distinct identity of each amino acid (Gropper & Smith, 2013). (See Figure 2.3.)

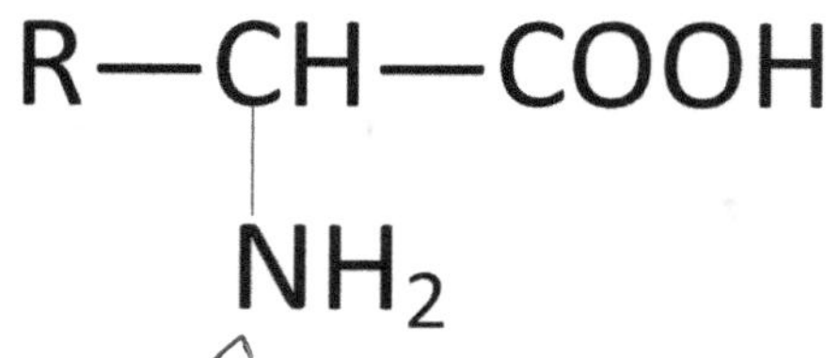

$$R-CH-COOH$$
$$NH_2$$

Figure 2.3 Chemical structure of an alpha-amino acid.

It is the nitrogen specifically that distinguishes proteins from the other macronutrients. Amino acids are categorized as indispensable, dispensable, or conditionally indispensable. There are a total of nine indispensable amino acids, represented in Table 2.1. **Indispensable** means that all of the nine amino acids must be contained in the dietary protein in order to be used in the structural synthesis of body proteins in the form of muscle, collagen, and various organs. **Conditionally indispensable** means that the amino acids are indispensable only in certain individuals, like premature infants or individuals with certain conditions like metabolic abnormalities resulting from trauma or disease. In neonates, for instance, the transformative action of enzymes may be subdued or compromised enough to slow the synthesis of cysteine from methionine, thus making cysteine conditionally indispensable. In catabolic states, glutamine synthesis may also be limited, thus necessitating the inclusion of glutamine in the nutritional support of ICU patients. The **dispensable** amino acids (alanine, aspartic acid, asparagine, glutamic acid, and serine) can be endogenously synthesized and are not required from the diet (Matthews, 2006).

Table 2.1

The Dispensable and Indispensable Amino Acids

Indispensable	Conditionally Indispensable	Dispensable
Leucine	Arginine	Alanine
Isoleucine	Cysteine	Aspartic Acid
Valine	Glutamine	Asparagine
Threonine	Glycine	Glutamic acid
Lysine	Proline	Serine
Histidine	Tyrosine	
Methionine		
Phenylalanine		
Tryptophane		

(Adapted by author from Matthews, 2006, and from Gropper & Smith, 2013)

Proteins come in various lengths and complexity. Two amino acids linked together by a peptide bond is called a dipeptide; three amino acids linked together by peptide bonds is referred to as a tripeptide; and more than three amino acids linked together are identified as a polypeptide. The skeletal muscle, representing 40% of the total protein in the body, and 43% of the total body mass, is the most abundant protein structure. Skin and blood combined, represent 35% of total protein, while visceral protein, found in the liver, heart, diaphragm, kidney and spleen, account for 25% of total protein (NAS, 2005d; Gropper & Smith, 2013). After fats, proteins are the second largest energy reserve in the entire body. In malnutrition, it is specifically the non-collagen proteins that become vulnerable to catabolism resulting in protein erosion (Matthews et al., 2006).

Proteins of **high biological value** come from animals and contain all nine indispensable amino acids. Proteins of lower biological value, originating from plants, are limited in some indispensable amino acids. For instance, the protein in bread, pasta, and rice is of poor biological value and cannot be used to synthesize bodily protein structures such as muscle. Vegetable protein, as a rule, is considered protein of lower biological value. This means that vegans, who only consume vegetables, legumes, and grains in their diet, must apply the vegetarian principle of **protein complementarity** in order to consume all

the nine essential amino acids in sufficient amounts to allow protein synthesis to take place in the body. Lysine is the amino acid that is limited in grains whereas methionine is the one limited in legumes. When both legumes and grains are combined together they complement each other's limiting amino acid, thus providing all nine essential amino acids (Johnston & Sabate, 2006).

While qualitatively, the amino acid makeup of the diet is important, the quantity of protein consumed plays a paramount role in meeting the nutritional needs of individuals. Consequently, protein requirements can be established very accurately using the body weight or, less accurately, using caloric requirements. Body weight serves as a reliable standard, as it better reflects individual needs. Reliable nitrogen balance studies have confirmed the RDA for the adult body equals 0.8 g per kg body weight (BWT) of protein for normal maintenance (Matthews et al., 2006); for a 70-kg person requiring 2,500 kcal per day this represents 56 g or 9% of DRI calories. The WHO reports (WHO, 2007; 2002; 1985) that 97.5% of the population 18 years and older appears to require 0.83 g protein per kg body weight per day for maintenance (WHO, 1985), while the dietary reference intakes (DRIs) in the US conclude similarly that adult men and women ages 19 to 70 years require 0.80 g/kg/d (Table 2.2). However, the DRIs for protein do reflect the varying needs of individuals depending on their stages of life (Table 2.2). The Institute of Medicine recommends protein intakes using the Acceptable Macronutrient Range Distribution (AMDR) of 10%-35% of DRI calories (Geisler et al., 2017; NAS, 2005d). Establishing protein requirements, based on body weight, is an alternate method, used in medicine, because of its accuracy. However, protein, unlike fat and carbohydrates, represents a specific body burden associated with nitrogen from protein being excreted from the kidney as urea. Hence the more protein consumed the greater the kidney's glomerular filtration rate (GFR) (Tuttle et al., 2002). It is based on the idea of an overtaxed GFR that long term protein intakes exceeding 2.2 g/kg/d are not recommended. The lower limit of the AMDR for protein (10%) coincides with the minimal DRI of 0.8 g/kg/d, whereas the upper limit of the AMDR for protein (35%) is tagged to 3.0 g/kg/d (Geisler et al., 2017) for an individual weighing 80 Kg who requires 2742 kcals/d--an amount deemed excessive based on body weight. The International Society of Sports Nutrition recognizes that most physically active individuals require protein intakes between 1.4-2.0 g/kg/d (Cambell, et. al., 2007). In order to achieve the maximal anabolic effect of protein, Schoenfeld and Aragon (2018) advance that total protein intakes of 1.6-2.2 g/kg/d should be consumed over 4 meals at a rate of 0.4 to 0.55 g/kg/meal. Other investigators (Antonio et al, 2014) found no changes in body composition with protein intakes of 4.4g/kg/d over 8 weeks, but this same group did find, in a follow up study, lean mass accretion with a protein intake of 3.4 g/kg/d (Antonio et al., 2015). Work done by Geisler and colleagues (2017) suggests that protein DRIs for healthy adults and elderly, who are mildly active, may be inadequate, suggesting that body composition measures of lean mass (LM) may provide a more accurate estimation of needs. They report, in their review of the literature, that meeting the DRI of 0.8g/kg/d was associated with a decline in LM over time. Others (Morais et al., 2006) achieved nitrogen balance in the elderly with protein intakes varying between 1.0 and 1.3 g/kg/d. High protein intakes (>2.0g/kg/d) should be viewed with caution as calcium excretion from the kidney rises significantly, when measured above this cut-off for 1 week; moreover, exceeding this cutoff has also been tied to bone resorption or decalcification (Kok et al., 1990). Furthermore, an elevated animal protein to vegetable protein intake heightened the risk of greater bone resorption and of post-menopausal bone fractures (Sellmeyer et al., 2001). Considering the long term negative effects of high protein intakes

Table 2.2

RDAs and AIs*for protein at different stages of life.

Life Situation	RDA for protein in g/kg body weight/day
Babies 0-6 months *	1.52 g/kg/d
Infants 7-12 months	1.0 g/kg/d
Children 1-13 years of age	
1-3 years of age	1.05 g/kg/d
4-13 years of age	0.95 g/kg/d
Adolescent boys and girls	0.85 g/kg/d
Adult men & women 19-70 years of age	0.80 g/kg/d
Pregnancies	1.1 g/kg/d
Lactation	1.3 g/kg/d

Adapted by author from data collected from: Institute of Medicine 2005. Dietary Reference Intakes for Energy, Carbohydrate, Fiber, Fat, Fatty Acids, Cholesterol, Protein, and Amino Acids. *Washington, DC: The National Academies Press.*
https://doi.org/10.17226/10490

on bone in concert with ideal protein ingestion for beneficial growth in lean mass, it would seem that for a healthy adult population (>18 years of age) that a maximal protein intake of no greater than 2.0 g/kg/d should be followed over the long term (Wu, 2016; Kok et al., 1990; Cambell et al., 2007). The WHO more cautiously advances that no significant benefits can be achieved with protein intakes exceeding 1.5 g per kg BWT (WHO, 2002, 1985). This amount represents 16.8% of DRI calories for a 70-kg person requiring 2,500 kcal/day. Most adults, according to the WHO, will likely meet their protein requirements, even if they do exercise, by consuming between 10% and 15% of DRI calories. A consensus position statement was jointly formulated in 2009 by the Academy of Nutrition and Dietetics (A.N.D), Dietitians of Canada (D.C) and the American College of Sports Medicine (ACSM) for endurance and resistance training (ACSM, 2009). Protein turnover and accretion is significantly greater than the RDA when muscles are taxed by rigorous training. The position statement that all sports management professionals should follow is 1.2-1.7 g/kg/d for resistance training depending on frequency and intensity, whereas endurance training, not geared towards increasing muscle mass, but consisting of continuous hours of endurance training over several days should be between 1.2-1.4 g/kg/d (ACSM, et al., 2009).

2.1.4 Lipids

Lipids encompass a broad assortment of compounds that include triglycerides, phospholipids, and sterols, all playing roles in the structure of cells and the makeup of hormones. Fats, in the form of triglycerides, represent 95% of all lipids consumed in the diet, and they are a significant source of energy for the body. Structurally, 90% of the triglyceride consists of fatty acids, and the other 10% is made up of glycerol, which is the 3-carbon backbone to the triglyceride (see Figure 2.4). A fatty acid attaches to each of the hydroxyl (OH) ends of the glycerol molecule to form a triglyceride.

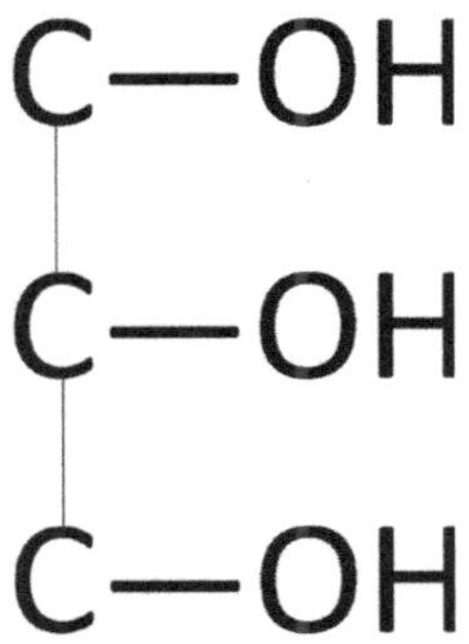

$$C—OH$$
$$C—OH$$
$$C—OH$$

Figure 2.4 *Glycerol molecule—the backbone of the triglyceride molecule.*

Fatty acids are carbon chains of varied lengths ranging between 4 and 26 carbons, all recognizable by the methyl end (CH3-) at one end and the carboxyl group (-COOH) at the other end of the chain (Jones & Kubow, 2006).

$$CH_3\text{-}CH=CH=CH\text{-}COOH$$

These fatty acids can be in the form of saturated fatty acids, cis-polyunsaturated (n-6 or n-3) fatty acids, cis-monounsaturated (n-9) fatty acids, or trans fatty acids (Gropper & Smith, 2013).

Saturated: $CH_3\text{-}CH_2\text{-}CH_2\text{-}CH_2\text{-}COOH$

Polyunsaturated: $CH_3\text{-}CH=CH=CH\text{-}COOH$

Monosaturated: $CH_3\text{-}CH_2\text{-}CH=CH\text{-}COOH$

Structurally, the polyunsaturated fats have two or more double bonds; they tend to be of vegetable origin and in a liquid state at room temperature. The two exceptions are coconut and palm oils, which are saturated despite being of vegetable origin (Figure 2.5). Saturated fats have no double bonds and are a solid consistency at room temperature. All these fatty acids are the main substrates for the absorption of fat-soluble vitamins (A, D, E, and K). In other words, without fats, humans and mammals in general would not be able to absorb fat-soluble vitamins (Gropper & Smith, 2013; NAS, 2005e).

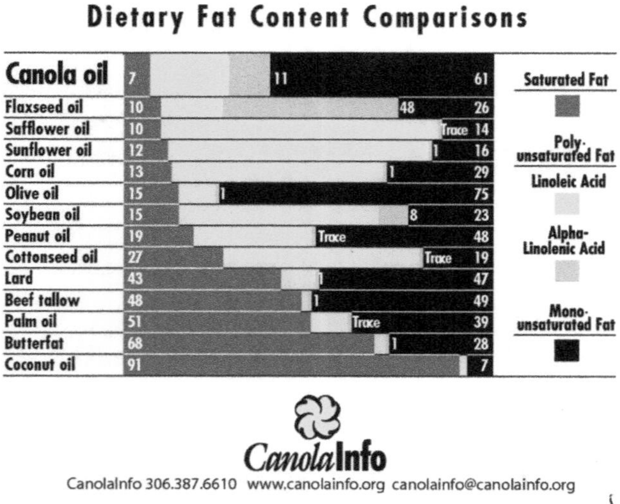

Dietary Fat Content Comparisons

Oil	Saturated Fat	Poly-unsaturated Fat / Linoleic Acid	Alpha-Linolenic Acid	Mono-unsaturated Fat
Canola oil	7	11		61
Flaxseed oil	10	48		26
Safflower oil	10	Trace		14
Sunflower oil	12	1		16
Corn oil	13	1		29
Olive oil	15	1		75
Soybean oil	15	8		23
Peanut oil	19	Trace		48
Cottonseed oil	27	Trace		19
Lard	43	1		47
Beef tallow	48	1		49
Palm oil	51	Trace		39
Butterfat	68	1		28
Coconut oil	91			7

CanolaInfo

CanolaInfo 306.387.6610 www.canolainfo.org canolainfo@canolainfo.org

Credit Copyright © Canolainfo.org. Reprinted by permission.

Figure 2.5 Dietary fat content comparisons of different types of oils. Used with permission from the Canola Council of Canada.

Each gram of fat (fatty acid) contains 9 kcal, or more than twice the energy found in either protein or carbohydrates. There is no RDA or AI for fat, nor is there a tolerable upper intake level (UL) because of insufficient data. There is, however, an AMDR for the healthy consumption of fat that varies between 20% and 35% of DRI calories. And while in a diet-crazed society total fat intake appears to be the main concern for weight loss purposes, the quality of the fat holds an equal if not superior position of importance. Studies have shown that fat intakes varying between 10 and 50% of calories, show on the short term, no detrimental effect on health (NAS, 2005e). Additionally, recent longitudinal cohorts have also failed to link total fat intake with risk of coronary disease (Willett, 2012; Hu et al, 1997).

The idea that fat played a critical role in animal growth and development was proposed by German nutritional scientist H. Aron in 1918. It wasn't clear whether it was the absence of fatty acids or of the vitamins solubilized in them that was responsible for compromised growth. It took until 1929 before George and Mildred Burr—two nutritional biochemists from the Department of Botany at the University of Minnesota—showed that fats were essential for the normal growth of rats, independent of vitamin content (Burr & Burr, 1929). When fed a fat-free diet, rats began showing symptoms of scaly skin, tail necrosis, impaired growth and fertility, and increased death rates. However, one of the rat groups was treated with a 20% lard diet, which reversed the symptoms; the lard consisted of 10% linoleic acid. It was this work and other studies that confirmed the notion of essential fatty acid deficiencies. Other studies demonstrated that it was specifically the **linoleic** (C18:2n-6) and **α-linolenic acids** (C18:3n-3) that were finally recognized as essential. This meant that individuals had to consume fatty acids via the diet in order to acquire their nutritional and physiological benefits. This was confirmed in 1958 when infant formula lacking fatty acids led to essential fatty acid deficiency in human infants.

There is currently not enough data to develop an RDA for the fatty acids. Consequently an AI was derived from the mean intake of a community that showed no signs of deficiency (NAS, 2005e). The AI for linoleic acid was determined to be 17 g per day for young men and 12 g per day for young women. The AMDR for linoleic acid is 5% to 10% of DRI calories. The AI for α-linolenic (n-3) acid is 1.6 g per day for men and 1.1 g per day for women. There is also an AMDR for α-linolenic acid: 0.6%–1.2% of DRI calories. Most of the oils consumed in the United States are polyunsaturated oils such corn, soy, and sunflower seed oils (Figure 2.5). They are mostly composed of linoleic acid. Maintaining the intake of linoleic within 5% to 10% of DRI calories is a worthy objective, as there is some concern that exceeding the 10% cut-off may create a pro-oxidant and pro-inflammatory environment that could dispose the body to develop chronic diseases such as cardiovascular disease and cancer. The DGAs caution the population to consume less than 10% (<10%) of DRI calories in the form of saturated fat. This is because excess saturated fat in the diet has been associated with increased risk of heart disease (NAS, 2005b).

Monounsaturated fats (MUFAs) are of the omega-9 (n-9) classification, chemically represented by no more than one unsaturated bond:

$$CH_3\text{-}CH_2\text{-}CH=CH\text{-}CH_2\text{-}CH_2\text{-}COOH$$

Focus Box 2.1

Exercise 1: This focus box is meant to remind students to learn the macronutrient ranges that have been presented in this section. It is important to memorize the macronutrient percent ranges in the [% Dietary Standard] column in the table below, as they have been found to be consistent with healthy eating principles. They are displayed below:

Carbohydrates: 45–65% of DRI calories

Protein: 10–35% of DRi calories

Fat: 20–35% of DRI calories

Polyunsaturated fats: 5–10% of DRI calories

Saturated fats: <10% of DRI calories

Monounsaturated fat: ≥11% of DRI calories

Knowing these cut-offs allows students to establish an individual's dietary standards for a specific total energy expenditure (TEE). If a man's TEE= 3476 kcal/day, then his recommendation for the above mentioned macronutrients would be indicated in the column: [Standard in Grams]

Nutrient	% Dietary Standard	Standards in Grams	Actual Gram Intake
Carbohydrates	45–65%	391–565 g	483 g
Protein	10–35%	87–304 g	95 g
Total Fat	20–35%	77–135 g	157 g
Saturated fat	<10%	<39 g	22 g
Polyunsaturated fat	5–10%	19–39 g	11 g
Monounsaturated fat	≥11%	≥42 g	28 g

The table can assist the student in visualizing the way in which macronutrient ranges are set up as part of an individual's standard. The carbohydrate ranges, for instance, were calculated by multiplying 3476 kcals by 0.45 and then again 0.65. The values were then divided by 4kcal/g.

(3476kcals x 0.45)/4kcals/g = 391 g and then the same calculation for the upper limit:

(3476kcals x 0.65)/4kcals/g = 564.85 g ~565 g.

Repeat the same steps for protein (4kcal/g) and then for fat (9kcals/g).

It is then possible to enter the patient's actual intakes, likely analyzed by computer, into the actual intake column. At this point it is possible to observe if the intakes fall below, within or above the nutritional standards. In the example above the monounsaturated and polyunsaturated fat intakes were **suboptimal**. The carbohydrates, proteins and saturated fats are all considered **adequate**, whereas the total fat is most certainly **excessive**.

monoglyceride

Although not considered essential in the diet, MUFAs have been found to decrease the risk of heart disease (Willett, 2012; Hu et al., 1997). Current intakes of MUFAs in the United States are estimated to be between 12% and 13% of energy intake, and roughly 50% comes from animal meat fat such as beef tallow and lard (Figure 2.5). Clinical trials have shown that ingesting 17%–33% of calories as MUFAs reduced risk factors; individuals who experienced therapeutic benefits ingested even 33%–50% of total energy as MUFAs (NAS, 2005b). The protective role of MUFAs was originally reported in the 1986 (Keys et al, 1986) follow up to the 1956 Seven Countries study (Keys et al., 1980). It showed that with higher intakes of monounsaturated fats, there was a significant decline in mortality rates from coronary heart disease (NAS, 2005b). A meta-analysis conducted on several feeding trials has concluded that overall MUFAs appear to modestly decrease LDLs and increase HDLs. A number of studies published since the late 1990s also report that monounsaturated fat intake—oleic acid specifically—offers good protection against cancers of the breast, colon, and possibly the prostate. Although some study findings have been equivocal about oleic acid's protective role against cancer, there is convincing evidence that olive oil consumption—rich in oleic acid—protects against breast cancer specifically. It is unclear at this time if it is the fatty acid specifically or components of the oils such as squalene, antioxidants, or phenolic compounds that are providing protection (NAS, 2005b).

Taking these studies into account, from a minimalist approach it can be argued that a healthy diet should not contain less than 11% of DRI calories as MUFAs, even though no official RDA, AI, or AMDR for MUFAs currently exists. Here is the basic rationale: Given that saturated fats should be <10% of DRI calories, and that polyunsaturated fats (mostly made of omega-6 linoleic acid) should remain between 5% and 10% of DRI calories, this leaves 11% of DRI calories coming from the omega-9 MUFAS in order to makeup no more than 30% of calories, assuming maximal allowances are met for saturated and polyunsaturated fats. If MUFA intake is suboptimal (<11% DRI calories), then, in order to meet 30% of energy in the form of fat, the rest of the fatty acids must be supplied from either saturated fats, polyunsaturated fats, or both. This is not desirable given the importance of

keeping the pro-oxidant n-6 fats between 5% and 10% of DRI calories (NAS, 2005b). The oils with the highest content of MUFA fats are olive, peanut, and canola oils (Figure 2.5).

2.2 DETERMINING THE DIETARY REFERENCE INTAKES (DRIs)

In the United States, the Institute of Medicine (IOM), one of the arms of the National Academy of Sciences, works to establish dietary guidelines. Specifically, the IOM's Food and Nutrition Board (FNB) has established specific dietary reference intakes (DRIs) for macronutrients in order to ensure long-term population health. The DRIs consist of a set of recommended intakes for various nutrients that fused together the U.S. Recommended Dietary Allowance and the Canadian Recommended Nutrient Intakes (RNIs). The joint effort was coordinated by the Standing Committee on the Scientific Evaluation of Dietary Reference Intakes (DRIs) of the FNB in collaboration with Health Canada. (See Figure 2.6.)

DIETARY REFERENCE INTAKES (DRIs)

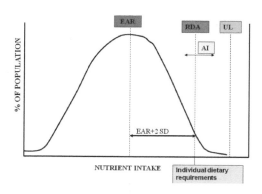

Figure 2.6 *Dietary reference intakes (DRIs).*

To determine the DRIs, the FNB gathered together several key nutritional markers: the Recommended Dietary Allowances (RDAs), the adequate intakes (AIs), the estimated average requirements (EARs), and the tolerable upper intake levels (ULs). Each of these levels represents a different type of nutritional measurement, which will be defined in the following sections (NAS, 2005a).

Establishing the RDA—The Recommended Dietary Allowance (RDA) refers to dietary nutrient intake levels that need to be ingested by the individual to achieve an adequate intake of the specific nutrient. In that sense, a nutrient's RDA is the minimum intake goal deemed necessary over a prolonged period, to meet the nutritional needs of an individual for that nutrient; it is not an optimal level to attain but rather the minimal intake for good health for most people. The FNB defines the RDA as *"the average daily dietary nutrient intake level sufficient to meet the nutrient requirement of nearly all (97–98%) healthy individuals in a particular life stage and gender group"* (NAS, 2005a).

The RDA is determined first by establishing the EAR of that nutrient. The variability of nutrient needs is determined between individuals and then a standard deviation is calculated. The RDA is then established by adding 2 standard deviations to the EAR as indicated in equation 2.1:

$$(2.1)\ RDA = EAR + (2 \times SD\ \text{requirement})$$

If the data are insufficient to calculate a standard deviation, then a standard 10% coefficient of variability (CV) is determined. In this case the RDA would be established using equation (2.2):

$$(2.2)\ RDA = EAR + 2\,(0.1 \times EAR)$$
$$= 1.2 \times EAR$$

Establishing the EAR—The estimated average requirement (EAR) is defined by the FNB as *"the average daily nutrient intake level estimated to meet the requirement of half (50%) the healthy individuals in a particular life stage and gender group"* (NAS, 2005a). From a practical perspective, the EAR does not represent the nutrient needs of an individual and thus cannot be used as a specific goal to be achieved by an individual. Rather, the EAR is intended to estimate the nutrient needs of a population, and in that sense any randomly selected individual would have a 50:50 chance that the EAR matches their true requirement of a specific nutrient. The EAR can only be used as a standard to which a mean population intake could be compared to. Similarly, it can be used in order to plan the diet of a group. A government can use the EAR to establish agricultural

policies for a nation or determine food relief strategies for a population affected by famine. Also, defining the size and makeup of a food relief basket, for those on social assistance, would be done using the EAR.

Establishing the AI—Adequate intake levels (AIs) are defined by the FNB as *"the recommended average daily intake level based on observed or experimentally determined approximations or estimates of nutrient intake by a group (or groups) of apparently healthy people that are assumed to be adequate—used when an RDA cannot be determined"* (NAS, 2005a). The RDA sometimes cannot be determined because of limitations in scientific methodology; therefore estimations are made based on sound observations. Researchers will identify a healthy population in which no underlying nutritional deficiency diseases are observable. Next, they conduct a random dietary assessment of a large sample of the population in order to measure the median nutrient intake. The FNB affirms that the AI is expected to meet or surpass the amount deemed necessary for normal growth, the maintenance of good health, and adequate concentrations of blood circulating nutrients. However, because the AI is much less accurately derived than the RDA, there is the possibility that the AI may overshoot an individual's true RDA. Hence, when using AIs in individual counseling, much more caution must be used.

Establishing the UL—The tolerable upper intake level (UL) is the highest cut-off below which the majority of the population runs no risk of experiencing nutrient toxicity. It is noteworthy that the risk of toxicity increases exponentially the more a person exceeds the UL. The need to establish a UL arose with the extensive food fortification that has taken place since the 1990s and the widespread use of nutrient supplements (NAS, 2005a).

2.3 MEANINGFUL CALCULATION CONCEPTS

When making nutritional calculations, there are several definitions to keep in mind. First, there are two broad categories of nutrients: **Macronutrients** consist of carbohydrates, protein, and fat, and **micronutrients** consist of vitamins, minerals, and microminerals. A third nutrient category is water,

Focus Box 2.2

Exercise 1: It's important to be able to convert units from one measurement system to another accurately and with ease. The goal for students is to study Table 2.3 and then test their abilities. If a patient weighs 198 lb and his height is 5 feet 10 inches, determine his weight in kilograms and his height in centimeters.

Exercise 2: If a person consumes 3 cups of milk in a day, how many milliliters does he consume?

Table 2.3

Metric Conversion Table

US Customary Units	Metric Units
1 lb (16 oz weight)	454 g (0.454 kg)
1 oz (weight)	28 g
1 oz (fluid measure)	30 ml
2.2 lb	1 kg
1 inch	2.54 cm = 0.0254 m
1 measuring cup	240 ml
1 tablespoon	15 ml
1 foot = 12 inches	30.48 cm

which must be consumed in amounts sufficient to maintain body water content between 55%, in the elderly, and 75% of total body weight in infants (Nicolaidis, 1998).

There is, in addition, a very distinct category called the **non-nutrient components** of food. These components are not considered essential for life since their absence from the diet does not cause specific deficiency symptoms. However, these non-nutrients include a broad spectrum of phytochemicals (flavonoids, phenolic acids and caretonoids to name a few) found in plant foods such vegetables, fruits and grains, and some teas (Dillard et al, 2000) that shield the biological system from known chronic diseases like many types of cancers heart disease in addition to several neurodegenerative conditions (Probst et al., 2017; Leitzmann, 2016). It is not surprising, then, that simple diets consisting of varied fruits, vegetables, breads, and cereal products, which contain these non-nutrients, consumed in abundance with dairy and little processed meats, are consistent with good health (Gropper & Smith, 2013). In

support of eating significant plant foods in the diet, NHANES data, collected in 2012 and analyzed by a research team out of Tufts University, found that close to 50 percent of cardiometabolic deaths that year were attributed to poor eating habits (Penalvo et al, 2017).

Completing nutritional calculations also requires familiarity with measurement units. Measuring food intake, body energy requirements, and body composition are key to determining levels of macro- and micronutrients in a population. In the United States, we use the English-based "customary units" of pounds, ounces, feet, and so on. Researchers outside the United States (and sometimes in the United States as well) present these levels in metric measurements. Table 2.3 presents the important metric conversions that are necessary to convert customary units into metric units.

Accuracy in conversion is crucial in making key assessments of food intake, body energy requirements, and body composition. Many of the formulas in the nutritional and medical sciences use metric

Table 2.4

Activity Factors for men and women that can be used with the Mifflin St. Jeor equation for the determination of TEEs

ACTIVITY LEVELS	MALE & FEMALE	MEAN
No physical activity	1.27	1.27
Light/sedentary activity level	1.40–1.69	1.53
Active/moderate activity level	1.70–1.99	1.76
Vigorous /heavy activity level	2.00–2.40	2.25

WHO (1985). Energy and protein requirements: Report of a joint FAO/WHO/UNU; FAO (2001), Energy Requirements of Adults, In: Human Energy Requirements, Food and Nutrition Technical Report series# 1 Report of a Joint FAO/WHO/UNU

weights in kilograms, height in either meters or centimeters, and fluid measurements in milliliters and liters. This becomes relevant when estimating food and fluid intake and prescribing infusion rates of medicines and nutrients in the area of nutritional support and critical care medicine. For instance, protein prescriptions can be given according to body weight. A patient weighing 175 lbs who is not obese can be prescribed protein as 1.2 g per kg body weight, also expressed as 1.2 g/kg BWT. How many grams can this patient receive? First, the person's body weight must be converted to kilograms. How is that done? Table 2.3 indicates that 1 lb = 0.454 kg. So multiply the weight in pounds by 0.454 kg: the patient weighs 79.45 kg. If you are prescribing 1.2 g protein per kg body weight, then his target protein intake will be calculated as follows: 79.45 kg x 1.2 g = 95.34 g or (rounded down) 95 g of protein.

Another important calculation is the estimation of resting energy needs and total energy needs (this includes physical activities). These energy requirements are estimated using height in centimeters or meters and weight in kilograms. Hence, if a 35-year-old male, 5 feet 10 inches tall and weighing 250 lb, is seen in outpatient clinic for weight loss, the dietitian will have to calculate the patient's energy needs—at his current weight—in order to determine how many calories he normally requires for weight maintenance. In the initial consultation, the goal is to assess the patient's current dietary practices and compare the estimated caloric or energy intake with the recommended intake. The patient's weight will need to be converted to kilograms (250 lb × 0.454 kg/lb

= 113.5 kg). His height in centimeters will need to be established (70 inches × 2.54 cm/inch = 177.8 cm). In order to determine the resting energy expenditure (REE), these values are then inserted into a gender-specific formula, along with his age, in order to determine REE. This is the amount of calories needed to maintain a stable weight while lying in the supine (laying-down) position. The preferred formula for non-hospitalized patients is the Mifflin St. Jeor equation (Mifflin, 1990):

$$REE \text{ for Men} = [10 \times (\text{weight in kg}) + 6.25 \times (\text{height in cm})] - [(5 \times A\,(\text{age}) - 5)]$$

$$REE \text{ for Women} = [10 \times (\text{weight in kg}) + 6.25 \times (\text{height in cm})] - [(5 \times A\,(\text{age}) + 161)]$$

In order to establish this man's REE, it would be necessary to enter his weight in kilograms (113.5 kg), his height in centimeters (177.8 cm), and his age in years (35 years) into the formula above in order to generate the following REE:

$$REE = [(10 \times 113.5 \text{ kg}) + (6.25 \times 177.8 \text{ cm})] - [(5 \times 35) - 5] = (1135 + 1111.25) - 170 = 2{,}076 \text{ kcal}$$

The patient's REE would be documented as 2076 kcal per day. This resting energy level normally represents 60%–75% of total energy expenditure (TEE). The thermic effect of food equals 10% of TEE, and exercise generally ranges between 15% and 30% of TEE (McArdle et al., 2013). A person

Exercise 1: Students should practice using both the Mifflin St. Jeor and Gerrior equations in esti-mating the total energy expenditure (TEE) of a subject. Knowing the patient's TEE it will then be possible to assess the patient's diet based on the healthy eating standards (Focus Box 2.1) set up using the TEE. So then to begin, try your hand out with this mini case: Rosie is a 33-year-old female patient whose weight= 257 lbs; height=5 feet 4 inches and who has a mean light activity factor (AF=1.53). Calculate this patient's TEE using the Mifflin St. Jeor equation and an AF.

Exercise 2: How would you assess the total sugar intake of a patient who has a DRI energy requirement of 2600 kcals/day, and who consumes 135 g of total sugar per day?

Table 2.5

Activity Factors (AF) for Different Levels of Activity for the Determination of Total Energy Expenditure (TEE) using the Gerrior Equation

Activity Level	Activity Factor Male	Activity Factor Female
Sedentary	1.00	1.00
Mildly active	1.12	1.14
Active	1.27	1.27
Very active	1.54	1.45
Extremely active	2.20	2.00

Gerrior, S. et al., (2006).

who exercises above the norm would be closer to an REE equal to 60% of the TEE, whereas one with exercise levels below the norm would have an REE closer to 75% of the TEE. The next step would involve multiplying the REE by an activity factor (AF) in order to calculate the TEE. The AF is based on whether the patient is generally (a) not active (AF=1.27); (b) lightly active (AF=1.53); moder-ately active (AF=1.76); (c) heavily active (AF=2.25). So then, using the Mifflin St. Jeor equation, this 35-year-old male weighing 113.5 kg who is moderately active (AF=1.76) would have a total energy expenditure (TEE) equal to: 3653.76 or 3654 kcals/day (2076 kcals x 1.76) (WHO, 1985). Please consult Table 2.3 for activity factors that can be used with the Mifflin equation for the calculation of TEEs. For consistency, please use the MEAN values found in table 2.4.

Shirley Gerrior and colleagues propose two sets of formulas based on gender that can help establish the TEE without having to first establish the REE. The Gerrior equation (Gerrior, 2006), seen below, has a physical activity (PA) factor imbedded within the formula (Table 2.5). The result is an estimation of the patient's TEE. This equation does not permit a calculation of only the REE.

For men:

[handwritten: 407.16]

$$\text{TEE} = [864 - (9.72 \times \text{age}_{years})] + [PA \times ((14.2 \times \text{wt}_{kg}) + (503 \times \text{ht}_{meters}))]$$

For women:

[handwritten: 175.44   211.56]

[handwritten: 28]

$$\text{TEE} = [387 - (7.31 \times \text{age}_{years})] + [PA \times ((10.9 \times \text{wt}_{kg}) + (660.7 \times \text{ht}_{meters}))]$$

[handwritten: 1.12   242   167.64 cm]
[handwritten: 109.868 Kg   1036 t]

[handwritten: 2373]

Focus Box 2.4

The concept, introduced here, pertains to calculating energy expenditure from exercise. Walking at a pace of 3 mph, for instance, can expend 0.026 kcal for every pound of body weight and for every minute of walking. It is consequently expressed as: 0.026 kcal/lb/min.

Exercise 1: How many kcals would a man, weighing 250 lbs, expend, while walking 3 mph?

Exercise 2: If running a 6 minute mile expends 0.115 kcal/lb/min, then how many kcals would a 189 lbs man expend weekly, if he ran 45 minutes at a frequency of 3 times per week.

Exercise 3: What would be this person's average daily caloric expenditure from running?

Using the previous case of the 35-year-old, 250-lb man, it would now be possible to estimate his total energy expenditure if we assign an activity level of "active." The completed equation would then be expressed as follows:

$$TEE = [864 - (9.72 \times 35)] + [1.27 \times ((14.2 \times 113.5 \text{ kg}) + (503 \times 1.78 \text{ m}))]$$

It is possible to simplify the expression of the above equation:

$$TEE = [523.8] + [1.27 \times (1612 + 895)]$$

$$TEE = 524 + 3183.94 = 3707.74 \sim 3708 \text{ kcal/day}$$

Thus 3708 kcal represents the total energy expenditure (TEE) of the 250-lb, 35-year-old active male; students should take notice of the degree to which both estimations, using very distinct activity factors come very close to one another (3654 kcal $_{(Mifflin \times AF)}$ versus 3708 kcals $_{(Gerrior)}$.

2.4 ORGANIZING NUTRIENTS

Table 2.5 classifies nutrients into: macronutrients, micronutrients, and water. Note that the caloric value of food comes only from the macronutrients and alcohol.

Carbohydrates: 4 kcal/g
Protein: 4 kcal/g
Fat: 9 kcal/g
Alcohol: 7 kcal/g

Dietitians need to be able to competently convert grams (g) of macronutrients into calories (kcal). For example, a patient who is prescribed 300 g of carbohydrates will be ingesting 1,200 carbohydrate kcal (300 g × 4 kcal/g). In a similar fashion, the intake of 100 g of protein is equivalent to 400 kcal of protein (100 g × 4 kcal/g). Finally, a patient who consumes 65 g of fat daily is taking in a total of 585 kcal of fat (65 g x 9 kcal/g).

2.4.1 Principle of a Diet Prescription

Using the patient's total energy requirements, a dietitian can assign a specific percent of those calories to carbohydrates, protein, and fat, as long as those percentages are consistent with Healthy Eating Guidelines for Americans and the IOM's AMNRs (IOM, 2002). (see Focus Box 2.1). Afterward, the goal is to convert those calories to grams of carbohydrates, protein, and fat. The final step is to assign servings of foods that match up with the macronutrient assignment.

Let's look at an example. Mr. Johnson's DRI for calories is 3,545 kcal per day. The dietitian assigns a percent of the total calories to carbohydrates, consistent with the AMDR of 45% to 65%. She decides to calculate 60% of calories as carbohydrates; this means about 532 g of carbohydrates (3,545 kcal × 0.60, divided by 4 kcal/g). Similarly, she prescribes 15% of DRI calories to protein, which is consistent with the recommended AMDR for protein (10%–35% of DRI calories); this translates into 133 g of protein per day (3,545 kcal × 0.15, divided by 4 kcal/g). And finally, the dietitian assigns 25% of the calories to fat. The dietitian recommends that one-quarter of all daily energy intakes come from fat, which is consistent with the AMDR of 20%–35% of DRI calories. This means the patient would consume a total of 98.5 g of fat (3545 kcal × 0.25, divided by 9kcal/g). It is important that the percent values add up to 100% (60% + 15% + 25%). In summary then, the patient's complete dietary prescription is outlined here:

Carbohydrates: 532 g
Protein: 133 g
Fat: 99 g

Table 2.6 provides a broad understanding of the requirements for nutrients. Water-soluble vitamins are needed on daily basis because they are not stored extensively in the body. Fat-soluble vitamin requirements, on the other hand, are based on monthly needs, as the body reserve for these vitamins tends to be more significant since they are stored in organs—most notably the liver—and adipose tissue (Gropper & Smith, 2013).

The importance of water cannot be overstated as it is directly tied to blood volume and blood pressure. Insufficient volume of fluid consumed translates into less blood volume and pressure and consequently a lower rate of oxygen reaching the tissue. Lower oxygen rates can lead to dizziness and fatigue. This makes sense if you consider that water makes up between 45% and 75% of a normal body weight and about 70–75% of muscle mass and 10-40% of fat mass (Jéquier and Constant, 2010; I.O.M, 2005b). The body water reserve is divided between the extracellular and intracellular fluids, and it therefore plays a critical role in facilitating the movement of anions and cations in and out of the cells (Gropper & Smith, 2013). Fluid requirements are based on total fluid losses from the skin, digestive system, kidneys and lungs (I.O.M, 2005b). In a temperate environment, a healthy individual will experience insensible losses (sweat and natural evaporation from skin) equal to 450 ml/d. This value obviously increases with exercise especially in high temperature environments. Respiratory losses from the lungs are generally about 300 ml/day, while urinary excretion average 1600 ml/d. Fluid lost in the stool totals about 200 ml. In total, fluid losses from a typical North American adult living in a temperate climate will lose between 1500 ml to 3100 ml/d in fluid. The mean fluid loss of 2550 ml/d is frequently used as a reference point for practical calculations (Riebl and Davy, 2013). Additionally, fluid need is tied to whether the environment is temperature-controlled or not. There are no RDAs for fluid intake but the US and Germany use AIs based on the IOF (2005b) data on fluid and electrolytes. Popkin and colleagues (2010) recommend establishing fluid recommendations based on the ratio of AI fluid recommendations by age and gender/Estimated Energy Requirements (EER), and found ratios that varied between 0.93 ml/kcal for toddlers ages 2-3 all the way up to 1.5 ml/lcal for women ages 51 or more. Using the table from the Popkin group (2010) two mean fluid requirements could be established for each gender: Females: 1.0 ml/kcal and males: 1.3 ml/kcal (Popkin et al., 2010). In practical terms, this means that a male living in a temperate zone, and who requires 3,400 kcal per day, may need to ingest a total daily fluid load of up to 4.42 liters (3,400 kcal × 1.3 ml/kcal = 5,100 ml). The general understanding is that 26% of that fluid requirement will come from foods especially if ample fruits and vegetables are part of the diet. Total fluid ingestion from water and other fluids (milk, juices and other) will represent 62% of total fluid needs, while fluid derived from metabolic processes will total 300 ml/d or roughly 12% of total needs (Riebl and Davy, 2013). In practical terms the average adult should consume about 7 cups of fluid/d.

Table 2.6

Macronutrients and Micronutrients

Nutrient Class	Definition	Function
1.0 MACRO-NUTRIENTS	**Large molecular structures of carbon, oxygen, and hydrogen**	**They provide energy.**
Carbohydrates	Complex starches, simple sugars, and fibers, which are non-digestible and therefore unable to provide calories.	Complex carbohydrates and sugars provide a rapid source of calories: 4 kcal/g; they are the only source of fiber with recommended intake of 14 g/1,000 kcal.
Proteins	Molecularly made up of amino acids, which consist of nitrogen, oxygen, carbon, and hydrogen	They are essential for building muscle and cell structures linked to organs and vascular network; they provide energy: 4 kcal/g.
Fats	A broad category of lipids consisting of triglycerides, phospholipids, and sterols	They ensure neurological development and absorption of fat-soluble vitamins; provide 9 kcal/g and essential fatty acids: linolenic (omega-3) and linoleic (omega-6) fatty acids.
2.0 MICRO-NUTRIENTS	**Small organic compounds**	**They are required from the diet in small amounts in order to ensure proper biological functions.**
Fat-soluble vitamins	Vitamins A, E, D, K	They require fat for absorption and storage; requirements are given in monthly amounts.
Water-soluble vitamins	Vitamins making up B complex and C	They require an aqueous environment for absorption and are not stored; requirements are given in daily amounts.
Major minerals	Ca, P, Mg, Na, K	Requirements are given in daily amounts.
Microminerals	Fe, Cu, Cr, Zn, F	Requirements are given in daily amounts.
3.0 WATER	**1.0–1.5 ml/kcal**	**50–70% of the body is made up of water.**

Source: Gropper & Smith, 2013.

REFERENCES

[1] A.C.S.M (American College of Sports Medicine et al., (2009). Nutrition and athletic performance. Med Sci Sports Exerc;41(3):709-31. doi: 10.1249/MSS.0b013e31890eb86.

[2] A.N.D. (Academy of Nutrition and Dietetics) (2015). Position paper of the Academy of Nutrition and Dietetics: Health Implications of Dietary Fibers. J. of the Academ. Nutr & Diet; 115 (11): 1861-1870

[3] A.N.D. (Academy of Nutrition and Dietetics) (2013). Position Paper of the Academy of Nutrition and Dietetics: The Role of Nutrition in Health Promotion and Chronic Disease Prevention. *J Acad Nutr Diet*. 113, 972–979. Available at http://www.eatright.org/About/Content.aspx?id=8381

[4] A.N.D. Academy of Nutrition and Dietetics. (2008). Position Paper of the Academy of Nutrition and Dietetics—Health Implications of Dietary Fiber. *JADA* 108(10):1716–1731. Available at http://www.eatright.org/About/Content.aspx?id=8355

[5] Antonio, J., et al. (2015). A high protein diet (3.4 g/kg/d) combined with a heavy resistance training program improves body composition in healthy trained men and women – a follow-up investigation. J Int Soc Sports Nutr; 12: 39. doi: 10.1186/s12970-015-0100-0

[6] Antonio, J., Peacock, CA., Ellerbroek, A., Fromhoff, B., and Silver, T. (2014). The effects of consuming a high protein diet (4.4 g/kg/d) on body composition in resistance-trained individuals. J Int Soc Sports Nutr; 11: 19. doi: 10.1186/1550-2783-11-19

[7] Birt, DF., et al., (2013). Resistant Starch: Promise for Improving Human Health Adv Nutr; 4(6): 587–601. doi: HYPERLINK "https://dx.doi.org/10.3945%2Fan.113.004325"10.3945/an.113.004325

[8] Bissonnette, D.J. (2014). *It's All About Nutrition: Saving the Health of Americans.* Lanham, MD: University Press of America.

[9] Burr, G.O., Burr, M.M. (1929). A new deficiency disease produced by the rigid exclusion of fat from the diet. *J Biol Chem.* 82, 345–367.

[10] Byrnes, SE., Miller, JC., and Denyer, GS. (1995). Amylopectin starch promotes the development of insulin resistance in rats. J Nutr;125(6):1430-7.

[11] Calle EE, Rodriguez C, Walker-Thurmond K, Thun MJ (2003). Overweight, obesity, and mortality from cancer in a prospectively studied cohort of U.S. adults. The New England Journal of Medicine;348(17):1625–1638. URL: https://www.ncbi.nlm.nih.gov/pubmed/12711737

[12] Campbell, B., Kreider, R.B., Ziegenfuss, T., La Bounty, P., Roberts, M., Burke, D., Landis, J., Lopez, H., and Antonio, J. (2007). International Society of Sports Nutrition position stand: protein and exercise. *Journal of the International Society of Sports Nutrition*; 4 (8): 1–7 DOI: 10.1186/1550-2783-4-8

[13] CDC (2018). Adult Obesity: Causes and Consequences. Taken from the Center for Disease Control and Prevention website: URL: https://www.cdc.gov/obesity/adult/causes.html

[14] CDC. (2010). *Number of Americans with diabetes projected to double or triple by 2050*. Retrieved from the Center of Disease and Control Website: http://www.cdc.gov/media/pressrel/2010/r101022.html

[15] Chun, OK., Chung, CE., Wang, Y., Padgitt, A., and Song, WO., (2010). Changes in Intakes of Total and Added Sugar and their Contribution to Energy Intake in the U.S. Nutrients; 2(8): 834–854. doi: 10.3390/nu2080834

[16] Cummings, JH., and Stepen, AM. (2007). Carbohydrate terminology and classification. Eur J Clin Nutr;61 Suppl 1:S5-18. URL: https://www.ncbi.nlm.nih.gov/pubmed/17992187

[17] DHHS (2015). U.S. Department of Health and Human Services and U.S. Department of Agriculture. 2015–2020 *Dietary guidelines for Americans. 8th Edition.* December 2015. Available at http://health.gov/dietaryguidelines/2015/guidelines/.

[18] DHHS (2008). U.S. Department of Health and Human Services. *Physical activity guidelines for Americans.* Washington (DC): U.S. Department of Health and Human Services; 2008. ODPHP Publication No. U0036. Available at: http://www.health.gov/paguidelines. Accessed Feb, 2016.

[19] Eswaran S, Muir J, Chey WD. (2013) Fiber and functional gastrointestinal disorders. Am J Gastroenterol;108(5):718-727

[20] *FAO (2001). Energy Requirements of Adults* In: Human Energy Requirements, Food and Nutrition Technical Report series# 1 Report of a Joint FAO/WHO/UNU Expert Consultation, 35-52 Retrieved from http://www.fao.org/docrep/007/y5686e/y5686e07.htm#TopOfPage

[21] Finkelstein EA, Trogdon JG, Cohen JW, Dietz W. (2009) Annual medical spending attributable to obesity: payer-and service-specific estimates. Health Affairs (Millwood). ;28(5):w822-31. doi: 10.1377/hlthaff.28.5.w822.

[22] Gerrior, S. et al., (2006). An easy approach to calculate estimated energy requirements. *Prev Chronic Dis.* [serial online] 3(4), 1–4. Available at http://www.cdc.gov/pcd/issues/2006/oct/06_0034.htm

[23] Gropper, S.S. and Smith J.L. (2013). *Advanced Nutrition and Human Metabolism, 6th edition.* Belmont, CA: Wadsworth, 586 pp

[24] Hofman, DL., Van Bull, VJ., and Brouns, FJPH. (2016). Nutrition, Health, and Regulatory Aspects of Digestible Maltodextrins. Crit Rev Food Sci Nutr; 56(12): 2091–2100.

[25] Hu, F.B., Stampfer, M.J., Manson, J.E., Rimm, E., Colditz, G.A., Rosner, B.A., Hennekens, C.H., and Willett, W.C. (1997). Dietary Fat Intake and the Risk of Coronary Heart Disease in Women. New Engl. J. Med; 337:1491–1499

[26] I.O.M (Institute of Medicine, Food Nutrition Board).(2005). Dietary Reference Intakes for Energy, Carbohydrates, Fiber, Fat, Fatty acids, Cholesterol, Protein, and Amino Acids. Washington, DC: The National Academies Press.

[27] I.O.M (Institute of Medicine of the National Academies). (2005b) Water. Dietary Reference Intakes for Water, Sodium, Chloride, Potassium and Sulfate. Washington, D.C: National Academy Press. pp. 73–185.

[28] Institute of Medicine (2002). *Dietary reference intakes for energy, carbohydrate, fiber, fat, fatty acids, cholesterol, protein, and amino acids.* Retrieved from https://www.iom.edu/Reports/2002/Dietary-Reference-Intakes-for-Energy-Carbohydrate-Fiber-Fat-Fatty-Acids-Cholesterol-Protein-and-Amino-Acids.aspx

[29] Jaggers JR, Sui X, Hooker SP, et al. (2009) Metabolic syndrome and risk of cancer mortality in men. European Journal of Cancer;45(10):1831–1838.

[30] Jéquier E, Constant F. (2010). Water as an essential nutrient: the physiological basis of hydration. Eur J Clin Nutr; 64(2):115-23.

[31] Jones, P.J.H., & Kubow, S. (2006). Lipids, sterols and their metabolites. In Ibid., 92–135.

[32] Keim, N.L., Levin, R.J., & Havel, P.J. (2006). Carbohydrates. In Ibid., 62–82.

[33] Keys, A., Aravanis, C. H. Blackburn, H., Buzina, R. et al., (1980). Seven countries. A multivariate analysis of death and coronary heart disease. Cambridge: Harvard University Press.

[34] Keys A, Menotti A, Karvonen MJ, Aravanis C, Blackburn H, Buzina R, Djordjevic´BS, Dontas AS, Fidanza F, Keys MH. (1986). The diet and 15-year death rate in the Seven Countries Study. Am J Epidemiol 124:903–915.

[35] Kok DJ, Iestra JA, Doorenbos CJ, Papapoulos SE. (1990). The effects of dietary excesses in animal protein and in sodium on the composition and the crystallization kinetics of calcium oxalate monohydrate in urines of healthy men. Journal of Clinical Endocrinology and Metabolism;71(4):861–867.

[36] Leitzman, C. (2016). Characteristics and Health Benefits of Phytochemicals. Forsch Komplementmed;23(2):69-74. doi: 10.1159/000444063

[37] Matthews, D.E. (2006). Proteins and amino acids. In Ibid., 23–61.

[38] Mezzetti M., La Vecchia C., Decarli A., Boyle P., Talamini R., Franceschi S. (1998) J Natl Cancer Inst; 90(5):389-94.

[39] Mifflin, M.D. et al. (1990). A new predictive equation for resting energy expenditure in healthy individuals. *Am J Clin Nutr.* 51, 241–247.

[40] Montesi, L., et al., (2016). Long-term weight loss maintenance for obesity: a multidisciplinary approach. Diabetes Metab Syndr Obes; 9: 37–46. Published online: doi: 10.2147/DMSO.S89836

[41] Morais JA, Chevalier S, Gougeon R. (2006). Protein turnover and requirements in the healthy and frail elderly. J Nutr Health Aging. 2006; 10(4):272-83.

[42] Murphy, SP., and Johnson, RK., (2003). The scientific basis of recent US guidance on sugars intake. Am J Clin Nutr. ;78(4):827S-833S. URL: https://www.ncbi.nlm.nih.gov/pubmed/14522746/

[43] National Academy of Sciences (NAS), Institute of Medicine, Food and Nutrition Board. (2005a). *Dietary reference intakes for energy, carbohydrate, fiber, fat, fatty acids, cholesterol, protein, and amino acids (macronutrients). Chapter 1: Introduction to dietary reference intakes.* Available at \http://www.nap.edu/catalog/10490/dietary-reference-intakes-for-energy-carbohydrate-fiber-fat-fatty-acids-cholesterol-protein-and-amino-acids-macronutrients

[44] National Academy of Sciences (NAS), Institute of Medicine, Food and Nutrition Board. (2005b). *Dietary reference intakes for energy, carbohydrate, fiber, fat, fatty acids, cholesterol, protein, and amino acids (macronutrients). Chapter 11: Macronutrients and healthful diets.* Available at http://www.nap.edu/catalog/10490/dietary-reference-intakes-for-energy-carbohydrate-fiber-fat-fatty-acids-cholesterol-protein-and-amino-acids-macronutrients

[45] National Academy of Sciences (NAS), Institute of Medicine, Food and Nutrition Board. (2005c). *Dietary reference intakes for energy, carbohydrate, fiber, fat, fatty acids, cholesterol, protein, and amino acids (macronutrients). Chapter 13: Applications of dietary reference intakes for macronutrients.* Available at \http://www.nap.edu/catalog/10490/dietary-reference-intakes-for-energy-carbohydrate-fiber-fat-fatty-acids-cholesterol-protein-and-amino-acids-macronutrients

[46] National Academy of Sciences (NAS), Institute of Medicine, Food and Nutrition Board. (2005d). **Dietary** *reference intakes for energy, carbohydrate, fiber, fat, fatty acids, cholesterol, protein, and amino acids (macronutrients). Chapter 10: Proteins and amino acids.* Available at http://www.nap.edu/catalog/10490/dietary-reference-intakes-for-energy-carbohydrate-fiber-fat-fatty-acids-cholesterol-protein-and-amino-acids-macronutrients

[47] National Academy of Sciences (NAS), Institute of Medicine, Food and Nutrition Board. (2005e). *Dietary reference intakes for energy, carbohydrate, fiber, fat, fatty acids, cholesterol, protein, and amino acids (macronutrients). Chapter 8: Dietary fat: Total fat & fatty acids.* Available at http://www.nap.edu/catalog/10490/dietary-reference-intakes-for-energy-carbohydrate-fiber-fat-fatty-acids-cholesterol-protein-and-amino-acids-macronutrients

[48] NCI (National Cancer Institute). (2009). *Physical activity and cancer.* Retrieved February 22, 2016 from: http://www.cancer.gov/about-cancer/causes-prevention/risk/obesity/physical-activity-fact-sheet

[49] Nicolaidis S.(1998). Physiology of thirst. In: Arnaud MJ, editor. Hydration Throughout Life. Montrouge: John Libbey Eurotext; p. 247.

[50] NIEHS (2018). Health Education-Obesity. Taken from the NIH's National Institute of Environmental Health Science. URL: https://www.niehs.nih.gov/health/topics/conditions/obesity/index.cfm

[51] NIH (2016). Probiotics in depth. Taken from the NIH's National Center for Complementary and Integrative health. URL: https://nccih.nih.gov/health/probiotics/introduction.htm#hed2

[52] NIH (2015). *Description of the DASH eating plan.* Taken from the National Heart, Lung and Blood Institute website on February 22, 2016: http://www.nhlbi.nih.gov/health/health-topics/topics/dash

[53] NIH (2007). Low fat diet may cut ovarian cancer risks. Taken from the National Institutes of Health (NIH) website: https://www.nih.gov/news-events/nih-research-matters/low-fat-diet-may-cut-ovarian-cancer-risk

[54] Pathak, EB. (2016). Is Heart Disease or Cancer the Leading Cause of Death in United States Women? Womens Health Issues;26(6):589-594. doi: 10.1016/j.whi.2016.08.002

[55] Penalvo, MR., Cudhea F, Imamura F, Rehm CD, Mozaffarian D. (2017). Association Between Dietary Factors and Mortality From Heart Disease, Stroke, and Type 2 Diabetes in the United States. JAMA. 7;317(9):912-924. doi: 10.1001/jama.2017.0947. PMID: 28267855.

[56] Popkin, Bm., D'Anci, KE., and Rosenberg, IH., (2010). Water, hydration and health. Nutr Rev; 68(8): 439–458. doi: 10.1111/j.1753-4887.2010.00304.x

[57] Reicks M, Jonnalagadda S, Albertson AM, Joshi N. (2014). Total dietary fiber intakes in the US population are related to whole grain consumption: Results from the national health and nutrition examination survey 2009 to 2010. Nutr Res;34(3):226-234.

[58] Riebl, SK., and Davy, BM., (2013). The Hydration Equation: Update on Water Balance and Cognitive Performance. ACSMs Health Fit J. 17(6): 21–28. doi: 10.1249/FIT.0b013e3182a9570f

[59] Schoenfeld, BJ., and Aragon, AA. (2018). How much protein can the body use in a single meal for muscle-building? Implications for daily protein distribution. J Int Soc Sports Nutr. 2018; 15: 10. doi: 10.1186/s12970-018-0215-1

[60] Sellmeyer DE, Stone KL, Sebastian A, Cummings SR. (2001). A high ratio of dietary animal to vegetable protein increases the rate of bone loss and the risk of fracture in postmenopausal women. American Journal of Clinical Nutrition;73(1):118–122.

[61] Turner, NC., and Upton, JR. (2011). Dietary Fiber. Adv Nutr; 2(2): 151–152. URL: https://www.ncbi.nlm.nih.gov/pmc/articles/PMC3065764/

[62] Tuttle KR, Puhlman ME, Cooney SK, Short RA. (2002). Effects of amino acids and glucagon on renal hemodynamics in type 1 diabetes. Am J Physiol Renal Physiol; 282(1):F103-12.

63 U.S. Department of Agriculture, U.S. Department of Health and Human Services. (2010). *Dietary Guidelines for Americans, 2010*, 7th ed. Washington, DC: U.S. Government Printing Office.

64 U.S. Department of Health and Human Services. *HealthyPeople.gov*. Available at http://www.healthypeople.gov/2020/default.aspx

65 U.S. Department of Health and Human Services (DHHS) and U.S. Department of Agriculture (USDA). (2005). *Dietary guidelines for Americans*, 6th ed. Washington, DC: U.S. Government Printing Office.

66 WHO. (2016). *Dietary recommendations/nutritional requirements*. Available at http://www.who.int/nutrition/topics/nutrecomm/en/

67 (WHO, 2007) World Health Organisation Dietary Reference Intakes for Energy, Carbohydrate, Fibre, Fat, Fatty Acids, Cholesterol, Protein and Amino Acids (Macronutrients) World Health Organisation (WHO); Geneva, Switzerland: (WHO Technical Report Series 935)

68 WHO. (2002). *WHO Technical Report Series 935. Protein and amino acid requirements in human nutrition*. Report of a Joint WHO/FAO/UNU Expert Consultation. Geneva: United Nations University.

69 WHO. (1985). *Energy and protein requirements: Report of a joint FAO/WHO/UNU expert consultation*. WHO Technical Report Series No. 724. Geneva. Retrieved on May 4th, 2015 from: http://whqlibdoc.who.int/trs/who_trs_935_eng.pdf

70 Willett WC. (2012) Dietary fats and coronary heart disease (Review). J Intern Med; 272: 13–24.

71 Willett, WC., Koplan, JP., Nugent, R., Dusenbury, C., Puska, P., Gaziano, TA., (2006). Chapter: 44: Prevention of Chronic Disease by Means of Diet and Lifestyle Changes. In: Disease Control Priorities in Developing Countries. 2nd edition (Jamison DT, Breman JG, Measham AR, et al., editors.) Washington (DC): The International Bank for Reconstruction and Development / The World Bank; New York: Oxford University Press.

72 Wing RR, Phelan S (2005). Long-term weight loss maintenance. Am J Clin Nutr;82(1 Suppl):222S–225S.

73 Wu, G (2016). Dietary protein intake and human health. Food Funct; 7(3): 1251-65. doi: 10.1039/c5fo01530h

CHAPTER 2 ANSWERS

FOCUS BOX 2.2

1 Weight in kilograms = 198 lb × 0.454 kg/lb = 89.89 kg.
Height in centimeters = 5 feet 10 inches = 70 inches. 70 inches × 2.54 cm/inch = 177.8 cm or 1.78 m.

2 Since 1 cup=240 ml then 3 cups will equal 720 ml (3 x 240 ml) or 0.72 Liter.

FOUCS BOX 2.3

1 Convert her weight into kilograms (257 lbs x 0.454 = 116.68 kg) and then her height into centimeters (64 inches x 2.54 cm/inch = 162.56 cm). Plug these values along with her age into the Mifflin St. Jeor equation and then multiply that value by 1.53 to generate the TEE.

REE = [(10 × kg) + (6.25 × cm)] − [(5 × Age) +161] x AF

REE = {[10 x 116.68 Kg) + (6.25 x 162.56 cm)] − [(5 x 33years) + 161]} x 1.53

REE = {[1166.8 + 1016] − [165+161]} x 1.53

REE = {2182.8 − 326} x 1.53

REE = 1856.8 x 1.53 = 2840.90 kcals ~2841 kcals/day

2 First, determine the patient's upper cut-off for total sugar (<20% of DRI calories). The calculation is: 2600 kcals x 0.20 / 4 kcal/g = <130 g/day. If he is ingesting 135 g/day, his intake is excessive.

FOCUS BOX 2.4

1 6.5 kcal/min (250 lbs x 0.026 kcal/lb/min). So then, if 60 minutes of walking is prescribed 7 days per week, he would expend 390 kcal/day (6.5 kcal/min x 60 minutes). He would also be expending 2730 kcal/week from walking regularly at that pace (390 kcal/day x 7 days).

2 189 lbs x 0.115 kcal/lb/min = 21.74 kcal/min. Since he runs 45 minutes for a typical run, then in total, he would expend 978 kcal/RUN (21.74 kcal/min x 45 min). Since he runs 3 times per week, his weekly expenditure = 2934 kcal/week (978 kcal/run x 3 runs).

3 Since his weekly expenditure equals 2934 kcal, then it can be concluded that his average daily expenditure from exercise is: 2934 kcals divided by 7 days = 419 kcal/day.

CHAPTER 3

The Problem of Obesity

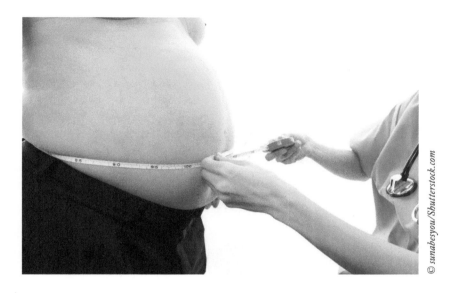

© sunabesyou/Shutterstock.com

3.1 THE PREVALENCE OF OBESITY IN THE UNITED STATES

Percent obese Percent (handwritten note)

The prevalence of obesity is central to the discussion of public health in the United States because of the numerous secondary diseases that arise from it. Moreover, obesity is an epidemic in this country and has attained pandemic status worldwide (Meldrum et al., 2017). NHANES data from 2015–2016 confirms that overweight and obese prevalence in the US has gone from 67% in 2005 to 71.2% of US adult men and women in 2016 (Fryar et al., 2018). The data further confirms that as many as 39.8% are obese, up from 34% (Hales et al., 2017). Most concerning is that as many as 33.4 % of children, ages 2 to 19, were in 2014, either overweight (16.2%) or obese (17.2%) (Fryar et al, 2016; Ogden et al., 2006). Epidemiologists predict that, if left unchecked, the obesity prevalence will grow to 47% of the U.S. adult population by 2030 (Kelly et al., 2008). More troubling were the findings that 31.7% of children and adolescents (2–19 years old) were also overweight or obese, and that the fastest growing obesity segment is the severely obese (AND, 2009). When these data are stratified, disturbing statistics begin to emerge that carry dire repercussions at a national level. Indeed, between 1988 and 2008 the prevalence of obesity in children (6–11 years old) jumped an astounding 400%—going from 4% to 20% in three decades (Roger et al., 2012)—which is the cause of much alarm sociologically as well as medically. Invariably, this prevalence jump among the youth has translated into a dramatic surge in health care problems throughout the United States. According to the CDC, national health expenditure between 1980 and 2010 grew from $256 billion to $2.6 trillion per year, and subsequently climbed to $3.5 Trillion by 2017 (Martin et al 2018). a jump that is so extraordinarily large that it defies the imagination.

The obesity problem is not limited to the United States but has insidiously begun to infiltrate countries like China that have rapidly succumb to the industrialized world of materialism, fast food, greater food availability, and low physical activity.

At this stage, while the prevalence of obesity in China is but a mere 2.9%, public health alarm bells are ringing because 18.6% of Chinese adults are now overweight (Popkin, 2006). Combining the overweight and obese adults together shows that between 1992 and 2002, the combined prevalence went from 14.6% to 21.8% (Popkin, 2006)

In the United States the problem of obesity continues to cause concern as healthcare professionals are uncertain they will be able to tackle the onslaught of secondary chronic disease coming from adults, adolescents and children. One particular area of worry is the effect of diet and obesity on pregnancy. The National Health and Nutrition Examination Survey (NHANES) (Ogden et al., 2006) found that between 1999 and 2002, 26% of women of reproductive age considered themselves overweight, and 29% claimed to be obese. In total then, 55% of adult women between the ages of 18 and 40 were potentially beginning their pregnancy already suffering from a weight management problem that could directly impact the fetus (Ogden et al., 2006). Indeed, it is now well established that obese pregnant mothers put their fetus at greater medical risk, most notably for neural tube defects (Rasmussen et al. 2008), fetal macrosomia, stillbirth, congenital abnormalities, and future risk of obesity and type-2 diabetes later in life. The mothers become highly susceptible to gestational diabetes, cesarian delivery, gestational diabetes and type-2 diabetes later in life (Leddy et al., 2008). Moreover, central obesity, characterized by increased abdominal fat accumulation, produces more atherogenic lipoproteins (Nieves, et al., 2003), and adipocytokines that have inflammatory properties that could threaten the integrity of the vascular lining and cells (Rasouli & Kern, 2008). During pregnancy it is unclear to what extent these nefarious byproducts of obesity make their way past the placenta and affect the baby directly. We do know that medical practitioners are increasingly treating mothers who begin their pregnancies overweight or obese. They must manage these women by prescribing calorie-controlled diets aimed at limiting the total weight gain, in addition to the rate of weight gain over the duration of the pregnancy.

3.2 THE CAUSES OF OBESITY

The Harvard School of Public Health identifies three leading factors that are fueling the obesity crisis worldwide (Harvard School of Public Health, 2012): first, the food environment; second, the built environment; and third, new technologies.

3.2.1 The Food Environment

Countries that are stricken with economic hardship, unemployment, and poverty experience decreased food availability. In developing countries, land is often owned by large agribusiness companies and used to produce cash crops like sugar destined for export rather than food crops intended to sustain the local population. A dedication to large-scale production of cash crops, in addition to lowering the quantity and quality of the food supply available to local farmers, makes crops like sugar very cheap for nations that import them. This translates into a big shift away from sustainable agricultural production, which could feed a population, to greater importation and consumption of foods such as soft drinks, vegetable oils, meats, and dairy products according to Barry Popkin (2007). This greater importation of processed foods has increased caloric density of the world's diet, and is most certainly responsible for important increases in obesity, specifically in countries like Mexico, China, and India.

3.2.2 The Built Environment and New Technologies

The urbanization of America has led to the disappearance of agricultural communities and their replacement by malls and other retail and residential spaces. As rural farm workers gravitated to the urban centers for better-paying factory jobs, they required cars to shop and work. This has led to a decrease in overall energy expenditure. Walking has become less of a necessity of daily living, and demanding physical labor has been replaced by desk work in the financial, service, and information markets.

The global effect of built environments on weight was documented in a Chinese obesity study. Sara Bleich, a research scientist with the Harvard Initiative for Global Health, in attempting to comprehend the complex issues involved in worldwide obesity, reported that "Results indicate that the increase in caloric intake is associated with technological innovations such as reduced food prices, as well as changing socio-demographic factors, such as increased urbanization and increased female labor force participation" (Bleich et al., 2007).

3.2.3 Genetic Issues

Genetic and epigenetic changes and metabolic anomalies can also contribute to obesity. Metabolic abnormalities or chromosomal defects can alter the basal energy levels of the body, change the propensity to store fat, or even affect the satiety signals that control appetite. These conditions together affect only 1% of the population, and therefore cannot be considered as influential in the current U.S. obesity epidemic.

There are several genetic abnormalities responsible for unusual weight gain and fat deposits, but for the sake of keeping the text relevant to an introductory course in nutrition, only four will be mentioned. The first is called **Prader-Willi Syndrome** (**PWS**). This is a rare congenital condition that originates from a defect in the father's chromosome, causing mental retardation, hypogonadism, hypotonic muscles, short stature, and an insatiable appetite leading to obesity early in life. Patients with PWS have an average height that varies between 4 feet 11 inches and 5 feet 1 inch. These children, if left unsupervised, can eat constantly and gain frightful amounts of weight. This form of chromosomal abnormality, which occurs at a frequency of 1 in every 15,000 to 30,000 births, causes these children to eat and store fat more readily because of a disturbance in the signals sent to the satiety center of the brain. The average weight for people with PWS is 176 lb for females and 216 lb for males. A variation of PWS, in which the chromosomal anomaly occurs on a specific maternal chromosome, is called Angleman's syndrome, and is characterized by a more severe mental retardation but without any obesity.

The second genetically-based obesity condition is **Bardet-Biedl syndrome.** It is recognizable by the symptoms of retinal degeneration, mental retardation, obesity, polydactyly (additional fingers), and hypogenitalism.

The third genetic abnormality that leads to obesity is called **Alstrom-Hallgren syndrome**. This third condition bears many similarities to Bardet-Biedl syndrome in that it is also characteristically identified by obesity and blindness. To help distinguish the two, additional symptoms have been tagged to Alstrom-Hallgren syndrome: deafness, diabetes mellitus, and the absence of mental retardation (Bray, 1998).

Finally, the fourth genetic condition, which was identified by Friedman in 1994 in the obese ob/ob mouse and subsequently observed in obese cousins of Pakistani descent in 1997, has been identified as **leptin deficiency** (Farooqi & O'Rahilly, 2009). In leptin deficiency, mutations to the gene responsible for encoding leptin leads to hyperphagia (overeating), a severe form of obesity (morbid obesity), hypogonadism, and a compromised immune system. Obese individuals who lack leptin, an adipose tissue-derived protein, are unable to utilize the body's normal homeostatic mechanism that recognizes increasing adipose tissue as feedback to shut off the hunger signal. Therefore leptin-deficient patients have a persistent uncontrollable appetite that causes them to eat insatiably without experiencing the soothing effects of being full. When patients with this disorder are treated with leptin, their appetites normalize and they lose weight (Farooqi & O'Rahilly, 2009).

The genetic disposition for obesity (apart from specific disorders) began to be studied seriously in the 18th and 19th centuries. As genetics evolved during the 20th century, with the important discoveries of Francis H. C. Crick (1916–2004) and James D. Watson (1928–), the notion of a single obesity gene—known as a Mendelian transmission—came into the discussion. Dr. Claude Bouchard, while he was professor at Laval University in Quebec, did phenomenal work in the 1988 Quebec Family Study. His team tracked family ties to obesity and was successful in differentiating between the impact of the environment and genetics (Bouchard et al., 1988; Bouchard, 1997). In reviewing the 1991 Norway and 1998 Quebec studies, he was able to quantify the heritability of obesity to between 25% and 40% of inter-individual differences in BMI and body fat. Bouchard concludes: "Thus the genetic heritability of the obesity phenotypes accounts for 25–40% of the age- and gender-adjusted phenotypic variances."

In other words, family ties appear to increase the risk of a young child becoming obese.

Other studies have confirmed the correlation between obese children and obese parents. One study of obese children showed that 30% had two obese parents (though Bouchard clarifies that between 25% and 35% of obese individuals came from families with normal weight parents). Other research from the 1990s calculate that the risk of becoming obese increases two- to threefold if there is obesity in the family and that the risk increases further with the severity of the obesity (Bouchard, 1997).

What is unclear, however, is whether this is because of an "obesity gene" or simply family culture in terms of eating and exercise habits. No studies so far have been able to confirm a Mendelian transmission that could explain familial obesity. The Bouchard studies were able to quantify that 60%–75% of obesity variances between individuals were not genetically based but rather were tied to the environment in a broad sense. This signified that everything from accessibility to fast foods, grocery stores, and fresh and affordable produce to single-parent families with low incomes and poor eating habits, right down to individual and family food preferences, in addition to low physical activities, caused weight gain. In other words, it appears that the genes load the gun, but that it is the environment that pulls the trigger.

3.2.4 Satiety Mechanisms

The cause of obesity does appear to be greatly influenced by the calories we consume versus the calories we expend in physical activity. Given that we live in an environment that has conditioned us to lower physical activity (Bleich et al., 2007), the question really boils down to why our satiety mechanism does not kick in to preserve us from overeating. In order to answer this question, it is best to review the two main mechanisms involved in appetite regulation.

First, there is the **homeostatic mechanism** that is centrally regulated by the arcuate nucleus located in the hypothalamus. This central nervous system regulatory mechanism depends on a long-term signaling system involving insulin and leptin and on a short-term episodic signaling involving ghrelin, peptide YY, cholecystokinin, and glucagon-like peptide. The interaction of these two systems informs the brain about energy stores and the variance in the flow of

nutrients in relations to eating. In practical terms this means that when body fat reserves go down, leptin—a hormone secreted from adipocytes—also declines in the blood, thus stimulating the hypothalamus' appetite center. In contrast, when leptin increases from a greater number or size of adipocytes the appetite center is less stimulated, and the desire for food decreases. Insulin is a hormone secreted in response to the ingestion of carbohydrates and protein. When excess carbohydrates are consumed, the ß cells of the pancreas secrete more insulin, thereby facilitating greater absorption of glucose into the cells and possibly greater fat synthesis in the case of excess glucose. With greater adiposity there is a tendency toward insulin insensitivity, leading to a metabolic condition called **insulin resistance**, which is usually seen as high circulating insulin, or hyperinsulinemia. Insulin concentrations in this condition remain elevated but lose their effectiveness in facilitating glucose access to cells. Consequently, blood glucose remains elevated (hyperglycemia), and so does blood insulin. Interestingly, in normal weight individuals, when insulin is maintained low—normally seen in response to low carbohydrate intake—there is a heightened signaling for the breakdown of fat (lipolysis). However, in insulin resistance, the persistence in elevated insulin may actually prevent the lipolysis or the breakdown of fat. This could be responsible for trapping individuals in chronic obesity or fatness. Also it is believed that in the **adipo-insular axis**, insulin stimulates the release of leptin from white adipose tissue, thus controlling appetite (Perry & Wang, 2012).

This signaling process maintains body reserves of fat relatively constant and, in theory, at a healthy level. In situations of chronic obesity, it is not clear whether the body develops a new homeostasis that is set at a higher weight and at a greater adiposity. If this is the case, then understandably the body's homeostatic mechanism would work in favor of maintaining this new normal, albeit at a greater weight and with more body fat.

The short-term episodic signaling system responds to the short-term consumption of food. Hence, when the stomach is empty, the ghrelin hormone is secreted from the stomach to alert the brain that it needs to eat; hunger is thus great when ghrelin levels in the blood are elevated. Cholecystokinin is the first gut hormone to be released from the GI tract. Within 15 minutes of initiating the ingestion of a meal, this hormone acts by reducing the appetite (Perry & Wang, 2012). Similarly, glucagon-like peptide (GLP-1) is also released from both the small intestine and the colon in response to number of calories ingested. The peripheral administration of GLP-1 or GLP-1 receptor agonists has clear anorexigenic effects, or suppression of appetite. Their action appears to reduce gastric acid secretion and gastric emptying. There is growing evidence that in obese individuals there is a delay in the release of GLP-1, which in turn delays appetite suppression after ingesting food. **Oxyntomodulin** is the more recently discovered gut hormone capable of suppressing the appetite. With a similar precursor as GLP-1, this hormone is secreted concomitantly with GLP-1 in proportion to the calories consumed at a meal (Perry & Wang, 2012).

The second process of appetite regulation comes from a cortico-limbic neural network that stimulates the hedonic center of the brain, otherwise known as the pleasure center, located in the frontal lobe (AND, 2009). The neural network receives signals from endocannabinoids, serotonin, and dopamine. This is where the pleasantness, the liking, and the wanting of a food get tagged to food palatability. It is a strong driving force behind our desire to eat certain foods, and it can lead to significant weight gain if there is an inappropriate sensitization of the hedonic system to unhealthy foods (AND, 2009). It is well recognized that the draw to consuming specific foods is linked to our desire to experience the pleasurable sensations of that food. How often have we claimed, at the end of a gargantuan Thanksgiving meal, that we simply could not eat another bite, but changed our mind quickly when the pumpkin pie was served? Our memory of how delicious that pie is and our desire for pleasure become strong motivators to eat, even though we may have an abundance of adipose tissue; in this case the desire for pleasure overrides the long-term homeostatic mechanism involving leptin. Researchers are now using terminology like "addiction" to describe this kind of relationship to food, principally because of a **dopaminergic dysfunction** evidenced by a notable decline in the number of dopamine receptors in the striatum of the brain (Merlo et al., 2009). The relationship with obesity is such that the more obese an individual, the lower the number of dopamine receptors.

There are two hypotheses that have been postulated to explain this anomaly: First, those addicted to foods experience a high degree of pleasure from food because of abundant release of dopamine associated with specific highly flavorful foods. Second, normal amounts of food do not provide enough rewards to the hedonic system because of the lower number of receptors. The need for pleasure rewards therefore incentivizes greater food intake (Yarnell et al., 2013).

3.3 ASSESSMENT OF OBESITY

It is crucial to establish a prognosis when assessing a patient for a treatment of weight loss and attendant health problems. A poor prognosis would be given if the patient had a high risk of complications or a low probability of complying with medical or dietetic directives. By contrast, a good prognosis signifies a reasonable expectation of compliance and weight loss success accompanied by an improvement or recovery from secondary diseases such as insulin resistance and hypertension. In the treatment of obesity, a good prognosis would be assigned to an obese patient who is motivated to lose weight, and who, in all likelihood, will successfully lose at least 10% of the initial body weight; this is sufficient to decrease several risk factors secondary to obesity such as hypertension, hyperlipidemia, and hyperglycemia (AND, 2009). A prognosis can best be formulated by interviewing the patient and documenting key relevant issues in the body composition, dietary assessment, medical history, psychological profile, and nutritional information (AND, 2009).

3.3.1 Body Composition Assessment

The first step in assessing an obese patient is to gather pertinent clinical information that is considered useful in formulating a diagnosis, prognosis and establishing a care plan. The first meaningful step in establishing a comprehensive care plan involves determining the patient's body composition using **anthropometric** measurements. There are five anthropometric measures that are frequently used: height, weight, body mass index (BMI), and waist circumference and skinfold measurement. These tools help the clinician or dietitian determine if the body is disproportionally large or small relative to a standard. The first measurement is intuitive: it is the body weight. The practitioner should measure the patient's current body weight with shoes and heavy clothing taken off; and then can inquire about the patient's weight history, and the family's history of obesity; the weight status of the patient's mother and father is relevant to the long term prognosis and to understanding the severity of the weight struggle. A percent weight increase should be determined if at all possible:

$$[(current\ weight - past\ weight)\ /\ past\ weight] \times 100 = percent\ weight\ increase$$

An acute increase in body weight over a relatively short period like three to six months can suggest that significant events were likely affecting the patient and could have led to overeating and rapid weight gain. A slower weight gain over six months to one year intimates a change in lifestyle such as less walking, or loss of membership at the health club or even injury that limits exertion, leading to a drop in energy expenditure and inevitable weight gain in most cases.

The intention in inquiring about the patient's weight history is to look for a vacillating pattern of weight gain and weight loss that can reflect a struggle with binge eating and/or chronic dieting followed by rebound weight gain. This informs the clinician about the prognosis for successful long term weight loss.

The assessment methods used on a patient should inform the clinician about the risk of disease. An elevated body weight or body fat should be linked to risk of morbidity. The body mass index (BMI) is one such measurement.

The BMI is calculated by dividing the weight in kilograms by the height in meters squared. As an example, a 6 feet 1 inch man weighing 278 lbs would have a BMI indicating he suffers from Obesity class-2:

$$BMI = (278\ lbs \times 0.454kg/lb)\ /\ (73\ inches \times 0.0254)^2$$

$$BMI = 126.21\ Kg\ /\ (1.85\ meters)^2$$

$$BMI = 36.88$$

The BMI has been stratified to more objectively identify those who are overweight or obese. This identification is not based on appearance but rather on disease risk. A BMI <18.5 tends to be linked to higher morbidity because of thinness, whereas a BMI of 25–29.9 refers to overweight; a BMI of 30–34.9 classifies a patient as obesity class-1; a BMI of 35–39.9 indicates obesity class-2; a BMI of 40–49.9 infers morbid obesity, and a BMI equal or greater than 50 is termed super obesity (National Institutes of Health [NIH], 2000; Sturm and Hattori, 2013). The higher the BMIs above the normal range of 18.5–24.9, the greater the health risks (Després, 2012; AND, 2009).

The BMI, also known as the Quetelet index, measures body weight relative to height, and does appear to correlate with body fat mass in middle-aged adults, although it must be made clear that the BMI does not measure fat directly, nor does it in anyway distinguish between fat mass and lean body mass (Willett et al., 1999). Its usefulness as a predictor of morbidity remains relatively good (AND, 2009). Next, is the breakdown of the BMIs as they relate to a healthy weight, overweight, obese, or severely obese status:

BMI tracker

BMI: < 18.5 underweight	
BMI: 18.5-24.9: healthy weight	
BMI: 25-29.9: overweight	Obesity class-I: 30-34.9
BMI: 30-39.9: obesity	Obesity class-II: 35-39.9
BMI: ≥40: Extreme obesity class-III	

National Institutes of Health/National Heart Lung and Blood Institute/North American Association for the Study of Obesity (NHLB) (2000); Obesity Education Initiative. The Practical Guide Identification; Evaluation, and Treatment of Overweight and Obesity in Adults. NIH Publication Number 00-4084

In research, **hydro-densitometry** (water displacement) and **dual X-ray absorptiometry** have been used with great accuracy in measuring body fat, however they are impractical at the clinical level (Willett et al., 1999). There are other indirect methods that can be used in the clinical setting to measure body fat or fatness such as **skinfold measurements**, **bioelectrical impedance**, and **waist circumference**. The goal is to measure the percentage of body fat and then compare the percentage to a gender-specific standard in order to establish if the person is over fat. Even though total body fat does logically present as a very valuable and accurate risk assessor, there was little data before 2000 linking body fat to health risks. Gallagher and colleagues (2000) successfully linked BMIs to body fat percentages. Establishing percentage of body fat in patients is important because someone could be overweight or obese as determined by an elevated BMI, but yet have an increased muscle mass and a healthy fat mass. On the other hand, if the patient has a percentage of body fat greater than the norm, as determined by skinfold measurements, bioelectrical impedance measurement, or BodPod, then he is truly classified as over fat. Both Gallagher and colleagues and the U.S. Army Body Composition Program (2013; AR 600-9) identified healthy body fat levels of roughly 8%–23% for most men and 20%–35% for most women. The body fat cut off above which health risk increases for man is >21% and for women is >32%. The body fat only becomes one marker of risk that can be measured over time; a loss or gain in body fat can help better understand the upward or downward shifts in total body weight.

It has been made clear in recent years that the assessment should not be limited to total body fat only, but also to a measurement of intra-abdominal fat (visceral fat), which has been shown to be associated with a higher atherogenic risk (Willett et al. 1999).

Indeed, ever since 1956, when the French physician, Dr. Jean Vague, published his findings linking cardiovascular disease in men, with abdominal fat, has body fat distribution been on the radar of physicians. Dr. Vague called the visceral fat accumulation, he observed in men, a male-type or **android** obesity. In contrast, the female-type obesity called **gynoid** obesity, in which fat accumulates in the thighs rather than the abdomen, was not associated with cardiovascular risk (Després, 2012). It was Jean-Pierre Després and his research team at Laval University, in Quebec, Canada who, back in the 1990s, brought the total body fat paradox to the forefront once again. He showed that cardiovascular risk was significantly different in two overweight or obese individuals with identical percent body fat (Després, 2012). He identified that the metabolic realities that were linked specifically to visceral fat, such as insulin resistance, cholesterol atherogenic dyslipidemias, high triglycerides, and low high density lipoproteins (HDL), were heightening the risk of morbidities. In contrast, patients with subcutaneous fat deposits and very little visceral fat had normal metabolic profiles, and much lower cardiovascular risks (Despres et al., 1990).

The **waist circumference** is a fast method to predict whether a patient is at risk of metabolic syndrome, because it increases with abdominal and waistline fat deposits. If the waist circumference is greater than 40 inches and 35 inches, for men and women respectively, there is a high risk of morbidities (NAS, 2005) (hypertension, type-2 diabetes, and hyperlipidemias) and mortality independent of the BMI measurement (AND, 2009; NIH, 2000). The NIH's Heart, Blood, and Lung Institute's method of determining waist circumference consists of placing the measuring tape at the superior border of the iliac crest and wrapping it around the waist. The problem with the circumference measurement is that it is

Table 3.1
Healthy Body Fat Percent in Whites, African Americans, and Asians

	Healthy BMI	% Body Fat
Men	18.5–24.9	8–23%
Women	18.5–24.9	20–35%

Gallagher et al., 2000

unable to distinguish between true abdominal and subcutaneous fat. Després does argue that both the serum triglycerides in concert with the waist circumference can be a much better predictor of visceral fat. He writes: "More than a decade ago, we proposed that the simultaneous presence of fasting hypertriglyceridemia and of an enlarged waistline would be predictive of excess visceral adiposity, a clinical phenotype that we first described as **hypertriglyceridemic waist**" (Després, 2012).

3.3.2 Medical History

The third step in determining a prognosis is the medical history. Medical history is vital for ascertaining if there are any endocrine, neurological, or genetic causes of obesity. Here it would be pertinent to identify the age of onset of the obesity and the family weight history specific to both parents and grandparents. Also pertinent is the history of medications used and their purposes. Next it would be useful to document the obesity-related disorders that have been flagged such as hypertension, hyperlipidemias, sleep apnea, and gallbladder disease. The metabolic and degenerative characteristics of obesity should also be noted using the blood biochemistry and monitoring fasting blood glucose, and blood lipoprotein values such as LDL, HDL and triglycerides (TG). The BP should be held at less than 120/80 to maintain low health risk. Consider that a pre-hypertensive condition can be diagnosed with a BP = 120-139/80-89 (Krause & Escott-Stump, 2008); however, recent American Heart Association 2013-guidelines recommend that the initiation of medical treatments for hypertension begin at a BP > 140/90 (AHA, 2013). It would be useful to document the severity of the obesity based on BMI, percent body fat, anatomical traits, secondary diseases, degenerative features, and the extent of physical disabilities linked to the obesity in addition to any neoplastic complications (AND, 2009).

3.3.3 Psychological Evaluation

The fourth step in determining a prognosis is a psychological evaluation. The clinician should interview the patient and also look for medical signs of any of the following issues: suicidal ideation, drug use such as psychotropic medications, binge eating,

bulimia, depression, post-traumatic stress disorder, or any kind of addictive behavior (AND, 2009).

3.3.4 Nutritional Evaluation

The final step in determining a prognosis and a nutrition care strategy is a nutritional evaluation. At this step it is important to consider the patient's weight history by documenting the age of onset of obesity, the maximal weight maintained as an adult, the lowest weight achieved, the duration of weight loss, any weight regain, and the specific weight loss methods that have been followed. It would be pertinent to note the various weight loss diets followed as a teenager and as an adult. There are several that can be identified: fasting, very low calorie diets, low calorie diets, dieting in combination with exercise, appetite suppressant medication, bariatric surgery, behavior modification, psychiatric counseling, and liposuction.

The goal here is to understand to what extent the patient has had a history of yo-yo dieting and whether he or she has engaged in abusive dieting practices. Abusive practices, especially when the patient is young, can predispose the patient to compulsive food behaviors that endure into adulthood and future weight gain (Mann et al., 2007). It would be relevant for the dietitian or clinician to identify any behaviors symptomatic of disordered eating. At this point the primary care physician would need to be alerted so that a psychological consult could be issued.

3.3.4.1 Assessment of Dietary Habits and Lifestyle

The next step involves an assessment of the patient's dietary patterns. Using a **24-hour recall, usual food intake,** or **food frequency questionnaire (FFQ)**, the dietitian can document the patient's usual daily meal patterns by looking for skipped meals and preferred foods, determining snacking practices, and establishing the largest and smallest meals consumed daily. Using the usual food intake measure, the dietitian can get an idea of the nutritional quality of the diet and approximate total calories consumed. It is vital that the clinician know the approximate calories consumed on a daily basis in order to compare it to the patient's estimated total energy expenditure (TEE).

Burke: Diet History Components. 3-components.

An assessment of the patient's dietary patterns of eating is an important step in identifying key risk factors in the way a person eats. The dietitian can conduct a **diet history** with the goal of assessing the patient's usual food intake. It usually involves three distinct components according to the model developed by Bertha Burke in 1947 (Burke, 1947): The first step is a 24-hour recall followed by the collection of additional general information pertaining to the patient's usual food choices. A typical question could be: What is the first thing you eat or drink upon waking up? The second step pertains to cross-checking the information gathered from the 24-hour recall and the usual food choices using a **Food Frequency Questionnaire**; this method measures the frequency at which specific foods listed on a standardized questionnaire are consumed. It is a cross-check of the quality of the patient's diet. In the third step the dietitian asks the patient to keep a **Daily Food Record** (Figure 3.1) (Gibson, 1990); the latter assesses the intake of food over a 3-day period; the mean of the 3-days tends to more accurately represent usual food eating patterns as shown in the frequency of meals and snacks consumed per day (see Figure 3.1). The Food Record also documents the location of where the food was eaten, in addition to the estimated portion of food consumed. The dietitian can generate an estimated mean caloric intake and can get a more or less accurate sense of the patient's nutrient profile. Sometimes just a **24-hour recall** is conducted to get a quick determination of the patient's dietary selections over the last 24-hour period, assuming it more or less reflects a usual pattern of eating; this method is sometimes preferred because there is a more accurate recall of foods, snacks and portion sizes.

Once a reasonably accurate assessment of the patient's usual food intake is documented, the dietitian can then proceed to establishing the patients resting energy expenditure (REE) using the Mifflin-St-Jeor equation previously explained in Chapter 2 and reproduced below for convenience:

Men: [(10 x weight in kilograms) + (6.25 x height in centimeters)]–[(5 x age in years) -5]

Women: [(10 x weight in kilograms) + (6.25 x height in centimeters)]– [(5 x age in years) + 161].

This equation is regarded as the most accurate and recommended for use in an obese or overweight American population (AND, 1990). This REE then should be multiplied by an activity factor (AF) reflective of the patient's activity of daily living in combination with some kind of physical exercise schedule (see Table 2.3). For consistency, it is preferable to use the MEAN value specific to an activity level. In the US, the average DRI calories for active men (>18 years of age) is estimated at 3067 kcals/day, whereas it is 2403 kcals/day for adult women (NAS, 2005).

Activity Factor

Using the food record, the dietitian can establish a more accurate **nutrient intake analysis** (NIA) in which calories, macronutrients and micronutrients are determined using anyone of an array of nutrient analysis softwares and then transcribed on to a Nutrient Intake Analysis Form (Figure 3.2). In the DRI column, the Acceptable Macronutrient Distribution Ranges (AMDR) established by the USDA are calculated out as grams based on the DRI calories, and compared to the actual gram intake calculated by the nutrient analysis software. For instance, the AMDR for carbohydrates is 45-65% of DRI calories. If a patient's energy requirement is 2450 kcal/day then the patient's recommended carbohydrate range for healthy eating would be 276–398 g (2450 kcal x 0.45/4 and 2450 kcal x 0.65/4). If the patient overconsumes carbohydrates above 398 g then his intake is classified as "**excessive**;" if he consumes under the 276 g cut off then his intake is "**suboptimal**" whereas, an intake within the range is considered "**adequate**" (NAS, 2005). Similarly, non-severe moderate malnutrition can be diagnosed when energy intake is <75% of DRI calories for a period exceeding 7 days (White et al., 2012). Excessive calories can be concluded when intakes are chronically >25% of DRI calories, based on the understanding that the expected intra-individual variability in caloric intake is ± 23% (NAS, 2005). (See Figure 3.2 for example). Micronutrients such as fat-soluble and water-soluble vitamins in addition to minerals and micro-mineral intakes are compared to the DRIs in Figure 3.2. A micronutrient intake that is less than the cut-off of

USDA

Mal Nutro

54% of DRIs is regarded as being at a high probability (P=1) of being consistently deficient in the diet; a nutrient that is ≤ 66% of the DRI is at a 93% probability rate of being deficient; this is based on Dr. George Beaton's probability model of deficient nutrient intakes (Gibson, 1990—Table 8.5). So then if a male patient consumes 585 mcg of retinol (vitamin A) his intake would be assessed at 65% of DRI of 900 mcg/day; this could be interpreted as having a high probability (P=0.93) of being chronically deficient in the diet (see Figure 3.2). In similar fashion, other micronutrients can be assessed; for the sake of consistency, the cut-off for high risk of dietary micronutrient deficiency will be ≤ 66%. There are of course micronutrients for which it is recommended to be less than the cut-off provided here or in Figure 3.2. For instance, it is advisable for saturated fat intake to remain <10% of DRI calories and likewise, it is best for sodium to remain under the UL cut-off of 2400 mg, and for total sugar and dietary cholesterol to be <20% of DRI calories and 300 mg respectively. Review Figure 3.2 and attempt to duplicate the DRIs for the macronutrients based on the DRI calories. Micronutrient excesses can be determined only when the dietary intake exceeds the ULs for a specific vitamin or mineral (NAS, 2005). Please consult the ULs located at the end of chapter-3. If a nutrient does not have a UL, then it cannot be assessed as excessive as in the cases of thiamin and riboflavin.

In an overweight or obese patient, the clinician should expect to see both frequent and infrequent eating practices. Indeed, erratic eating patterns can lead often to poor food choices often selected from vending machines or snack bars. It often implies skipping breakfast, which threatens the patient's ability to meet daily calcium and fiber requirements, but also increases the risk of developing obesity (AND, 2009). The quality of the meals and snacks need to also be evaluated, in a subsequent step, by assessing the environmental factors that may induce or encourage specific eating behaviors. The dietitian will attempt to determine the degree to which meals are eaten together at home as a family, or in isolation. Next, she needs to inquire if the patient's eating habits are guided by any ethnic food preferences and whether lifestyle factors characterized by tight schedules and finances, dictate the necessity to frequently eat fast-food and restaurant meals.

The patient's exercise history also becomes relevant to the assessment, as energy expenditure through exercise is an important determinant in successful weight management (AND, 2009). The idea here is to determine if the patient has a strong and significant history of exercise and sports, as it strengthens the likelihood that the patient will be willing to engage in regular exercise. When integrated within a weekly routine, heightened activities of daily living and structured exercise can increase total daily energy expenditure and help manage body weight. Although weight loss through exercise alone has not been found to be substantive, benefits from exercise have been associated with lower co-morbidities and overall death rates (AND, 2009). Determining the barriers to exercise and the patient's familiarity with disciplined exercise helps the clinician ascertain the patient's readiness to change his or her lifestyle. Additionally, the dietitian should try to define what exactly motivates the patient to want to lose weight, and identify the current life stressors and support system that may motivate him or her to want to readily make the needed lifestyle changes (AND, 2009). So then to summarize, a clinician or dietitian while assessing dietary and lifestyle factors needs to specifically consider the following:

Total caloric and macronutrient intake

- Nutrient and caloric densities of foods
- Dietary patterns/eating frequency
- Quality of the meals and snacks
- Exercise history and current routines
- Readiness to change

FFQ = quality

The FFQ is an excellent method of assessing the quality and variety of food consumed on a regular basis. For instance, the FFQ can help answer the question: Does my patient consume enough fruits and vegetable? The dietitian will document, for instance, the weekly frequency with which the patient consumed vegetables from the cruciferous family (broccoli, cabbage, Brussels sprouts, cauliflower, broccoflower, turnip, kale). This class of vegetable is a good source of **vitamin C**, **soluble fiber**, and **phytochemicals** that are protective against heart disease and many types of cancers. A computer-generated nutrient profile, similar to Figure 3.2, indicating elevated vitamin A content, is considered an excellent surrogate for a rich and colorful vegetable intake. This is

veggies

	DAY-1 FOOD RECORD		
	DAY/DATE: _____		
MEAL	**LOCATION**	**FOODS CONSUMED**	**QUANTITY**
Breakfast	Home	Kellogg's raisin bran cereal Milk 2%	1 ½ cups ¾ cup
Am snack	Quick-trip	Debby Cake	1(56g)
Lunch	Office Lunch room	Turkey sandwich (2 slices of White bread + 1 pat of butter + 1 Tbsp of reg. mayonnaise + 1 slice of processed Kraft cheese	2
Pm snack	Work break room	Yoplait yogurt (Vanilla) Coke (Reg)	½ cup 12 Fl-oz
Dinner	Home	Spaghetti pasta Meat sauce Mozzarella cheese (Shredded) French crusty bread Salad (Mixed greens, carrot shavings, cucumbers, tomatoes) Balsamic vinegar dressing	3 cups 1.5 cups ½ cup 3 slices(70g) 2 cups 2 Tbsp
Evening snack	Home	Regular Popcorn Butter	6 cups ½ cup

Figure 3.1 *Example of a Food Record Used in 3-Day Food Intake Assessments*

because **ß-carotene,** a carotenoid abundantly found in orange and dark green vegetables, is a precursor to **vitamin A.** It also is an antioxidant that plays a protective role against oxidative stress (Gropper & Smith, 2013).

In the North American context, there are a select number of nutrients that are medically pertinent in obesity cases, as they tend to be either suboptimal in the diet or excessive and thus affect health in an important way. Those nutrients that are excessive and significantly increase the risk of cardiovascular disease (CVD) and metabolic syndrome are saturated fats and trans-fatty acids. They need to be replaced by monounsaturated fats and omega-3 fats (Willett et al., 2006). Paradoxically, despite the abundant calories consumed by obese and overweight patients, some nutrients have clearly become suboptimal in their diets primarily because of the over-consumption of high calorically dense foods of poor

nutritional quality; it is estimated that 27%–30% of calories consumed by American children and adults are nutritionally impoverished processed foods, and that sweeteners and desserts contribute 18%–24% of those total calories (Willett, et al., 2006).

Studies have also identified eating patterns in the obese population that need to be flagged: Generally, as nutrient-poor processed foods increase in the diet, nutrient-dense food intake proportionally declines. For instance, when fat intake is greater than 30% of total calories, there is a tendency to observe a decline in the dietary intake of vitamins A, C, and folate (NAS, 2005). It is additionally concerning that as sweetened beverages increase in the diet, milk consumption decreases, thus causing calcium and vitamin D intakes to plummet. Fat-soluble vitamins and antioxidants tend to be unusually low in the morbidly obese, most notably vitamin A, ß-carotene and α-tocopherol (vitamin E). Baseline iron deficiency

Nutrient/calories	Quantity	DRI	% DRI	Deficient	Adequate	Excessive
CALORIES (Kcals)	1820 kcals	2450 (1837–3063 kcals)	74.28%	X		
PROTEIN (g)[1]	75g	61–214g	123%–35%		X	
FAT (g)	63g	54–95g	117%–66%		X	
CARBO (g)	252g	276–398g	91.3–63.3%	X		
SUGAR (g) < 20% DRI calories		<123 g				
DIETARY FIBER (g)		30g				
SATUR FAT (g) (<10% of DRI kcals)		≤27g				
MONO FAT (g) (11–20% of DRI kcals)		30–54g				
POLY FAT (g) (5–10% of DRI kcals)		14–27g				
CHOLESTEROL(mg)		<300mg				
VITAMINS						
RETINOL [VIT A] mcg (RAE)	585	700–900	83.57–65%	X		
VIT D (mcg)	11	15	73.3%		X	
VIT E (a-Tocoph) mg		15				
VIT K (mcg)		75–120				
THIAMIN [VIT B1] (mg)		1.1–1.2				
RIBOFLAVIN [VIT B2] (mg)		1.1–1.3				
NIACIN (B3) (mg)		14–16				
PYRIDOXIN [VIT B6] (mg)		1.3				
FOLATE DFE (mcg) *		400				
COBALAMIN [VIT B12] (mcg)		2.4				
ASCORBIC ACID [VIT C] (mg)		75–90				
MINERALS						
CALCIUM (mg)		1000				
SODIUM (mg)		<2400				
MAGNESIUM (mg)*		310–420				
POTASSIUM (mg)		4700				
IRON (mg)		8–18				
ZINC (mg)		8–11				

Micronutrient DRIs values were taken from the DRI tables of Mahan, K.L. And Escott-Stump, S Krause's Food and Nutrition Therapy 2008, St-Louis MO: Saunders-Elsevier 1352.

DRIs for Calcium and Vitamin D 2010 updated values from: Institute of Medicine of the National Academy. Retrieved from http://www.iom.edu/Reports/2010/Dietary-Reference-Intakes-for-Calcium-and-Vitamin-D/DRI-Values.aspx

YELLOW SHADE: Fat-soluble vitamins; require dietary fat for proper absorption

BLUE SHADE: Water soluble vitamins; solubilized in water for easy absorption

NOTE: Saturated fat should be < 10% of total calories, while monounsaturated fats (MUFAs) should ideally be at least ≥11% of DRI calories; polyunsaturated fats need to be between 5–10% DRI calories. Convert the percentage associated with saturated, polyunsaturated and monounsaturated fats into grams (% x (DRI kcal/d) /9)

Consult the table below for UL levels specific to some nutrients. This will allow you to determine if your intakes are excessive. For DRIs, consult your profile report that has your specific DRI for each micronutrient.

The ULs for Mg, and Niacin are used to assess excessive intakes, only when these nutrients are taken in supplement forms. If the Mg and Niacin is strictly consumed from non-fortified foods or supplements then do not consider their intakes greater than UL as excessive.

VITAMIN A: The use of carrots contributes significant amounts of retinol equivalents in computer analysis. So if vitamin A appears over the UL, verify whether most of the vitamin A is coming from carrots or another carotenoid, because carotenoids do not cause retinol (vitamin A) toxicity. Only animal products containing vitamin A (Retinol) can be excessive if exceeding the UL.

FOLATE: Folate is regarded as excessive if taken as a supplement or in the form of foods fortified with folic acid. So consult the "source analysis" report and determine what foods are mostly contributing folate. If the foods are fruits and vegetables: NOT EXCESSIVE because the folate is inactive. If the folate is coming from fortified breads and cereals then it is EXCESSIVE if > 1000 mg/day.

[1] Protein assessments need to consider also the body weight expressed as g/kg/day intake (0.8–2.0g/kg/day is considered adequate)

Figure 3.2 *Example of a mean Nutrient Intake Analysis Form*

anemia has been reported in 44% of adults prior to undergoing gastric bypass surgery. Vitamin D deficiency is more widespread in the general population than previously thought and besides impairing calcium absorption, vitamin D deficiency is suspected to affect the immune system, thereby increasing the body's susceptibility to cancers, diabetes mellitus, autoimmune diseases, and cardiovascular disease (Xanthakos, 2009).

Willet. Folate, occur Fiber

Clinicians should also question patients about their intake of nutrient supplements. Willett and colleagues identified folate as a nutrient at risk in developing countries that are westernizing and has recommended the fortification of the food supply with folic acid in order to decrease the incidence of neural tube defects. Fiber intake is also a concern as chronically low intakes are responsible for constipation, which greatly impacts gastrointestinal disease (Willett et al., 2006).

Environmental factors have possibly the most significant impact on the way people eat and may explain in part why obesity is a disease that afflicts the poor and immigrants with modest financial reserves. Indeed, fast food restaurants abound in low-income urban areas whereas grocery stores are fewer. One-parent families may tend to eat in cheap restaurants or fast food chains outside the home because of tight schedules, financial constraints, and work obligations that make home cooking challenging.

But it is not only the poor who are becoming obese. Professionals bound to their desks for long hours are prone to significant weight gain. Accountants, financial analysts, and customer service representatives are all glued to their seats, some of them for long hours. The prospect of making a meal at home is not likely as there is simply not enough time. On the way home, having dinner at the restaurant with a client is far more likely than sitting down to a full cooked meal with the family. Eating out frequently is indeed tied to excess caloric intake because restaurant food is loaded with salt, sugar, and fat. Tie in the larger portions and alcohol consumption, and it is far more likely to exceed caloric needs at a restaurant than at the home dinner table.

To round out a prognosis, ask the patient about exercise. In this environment of financial stress,

poverty, and tight schedules, the ability to include regular exercise is also difficult. Sedentary jobs that occupy long hours can cause employees to expend far few calories than they did in previous decades. The opportunity to exercise in a gym after work is less likely for single parents with children at home or for professionals with long work hours. Ask about the patient's exercise history. Here the clinician is attempting to uncover if the patient did sports as a child, an adolescent, and as a young adult. This is relevant because if physical activity was introduced, early on in a person's life, then it is more likely that they will be more receptive to a prescription of physical activity. Those growing up with very little exposure to the persevering spirit developed with training are less inclined to believe that sports or exercise can benefit their health or wellbeing (AND, 2009).

It is necessary, in the final stages of the interview, to establish a weight-loss goal and to clarify the reasons for wanting to lose weight. This helps the dietitian ascertain the subject's readiness to make important lifestyle changes and thus to formulate a positive prognosis. *end of prognosis gathering*

3.4. OBESITY TREATMENTS

3.4.1 Weight Loss Management Strategies

The Academy of Nutrition and Dietetic's (AND) 2009 position paper on weight loss recognizes that there can be different goals for weight management interventions that may not always be consistent with actual loss of body weight:

- Prevention of weight gain or stopping weight gain in an individual who has been seeing a steady increase in his or her weight
- Varying degrees of improvements in physical and emotional health
- Small maintainable weight losses or more extensive weight losses achieved through modified eating and exercise behaviors
- Improvements in eating, exercise, and other behaviors." (AND, 2009)

Environmental Factors. Poor isn't the only ones getting Fat

3.4.2 Popular Weight Loss Methods

Diet Restrictions—The most popular form of obesity treatment is dietary restriction. The rationale is founded on the principle that if calories or energy is restricted, then body weight will decline at a rate that is proportional to the degree that energy is limited. The classic and generally accepted approach is to prescribe a low-fat diet that restricts calories by 500–1,000 kcal per day in order to cause 1–2 lb weight loss per week. Medically, there are significant improvements in heart disease risk factors with as little as 5%–10% weight loss (AND, 2009).

Since the 1970s numerous weight loss diets have come in and out of vogue. Very low calorie diets (VLCDs), popular for their rapid rate of weight loss, consisted of only 300–800 kcal per day fortified with a complete arsenal of micronutrient supplements containing 100% of the RDA. This kind of diet usually contains less than 50g of carbohydrates (Paoli et al., 2013) and is not generally consistent with long-term health, as energy is too restrictive to accommodate normal and sustainable eating behavior. VLCDs afforded 3–5 lb of weight loss per week, but a high likelihood of regaining most of the weight (Mann et al, 2007). VLCDs are not advised for people with BMIs <30 but are now frequently prescribed for patients preparing to undergo gastric bypass surgery.

There were also low calorie diets (LCDs) that recommended 1000–1,600 kcal per day. These diets generally offered adequate nutrition quality but insufficient energy for some individuals (Weight Control Information Network, 2014). Many recent diets (Atkins, Pritikin, Scarsdale, Weight Watchers) are LCDs and offer meal plans that contained specified amount of calories. However, overall, these diets have not been successful in maintaining weight loss over the long term (1–5 years). Often the weight regain surpassed the amount of weight that was initially lost, and the dieter ended up heavier than before. Tracy Mann and colleagues (2007) found that between 33% and 67% regained more weight than lost.

The documentary *Obesity in America: A National Crisis* (Bissonnette, 2011) does a complete review of diet restrictions as a treatment modality. In addition,

Ma et al. (2007) did a comprehensive review of the most popular diets since the 1970s. They rated diets based on their overall nutritional content and ability to lead to long-term, sustainable weight reduction, measured on a scale they called the alternative healthy eating index. Dean Ornish and Weight Watchers were diets that achieved high diet quality scores of 92.3% and 82% respectively. The other diets investigated in the review were classified as suboptimal since they extensively manipulated macronutrients and did not propose reasonable and healthy ways of eating that were sustainable. The problem with many diets is that they restrict calories too far below the normal energy needs for weight maintenance. It is not uncommon for an obese individual requiring 3,800 kcal per day to be placed on a low-carbohydrate diet of 1,500 kcal per day with only 20 g per day of carbohydrates. The patient will indeed lose weight along with body protein in the initial phase of the diet because he is experiencing the equivalent of starvation.

The type of dietary strategy that is fixated on extensive caloric restriction is in clear opposition with the position paper of the Academy of Nutrition and Dietetics (2009) on weight management. The AND's position clearly states the importance of long-term sustainable weight loss, healthful eating practices that are enduring, and physical activity: "successful weight management to improve overall health for adults require[s] a lifelong commitment to healthful lifestyle behaviors emphasizing sustainable and enjoyable eating practices and daily physical activity."

Physiologically and biochemically, there are a few things that happen to the body when it is placed on very restrictive or very low calorie diets (VLCD) or an LCD that restricts carbohydrates. First, glycogen reserves in the liver—used for glucose homeostasis in the blood— begin to decrease through the biochemical process of **glycogenolysis** initiated with the secretion of **glucagon** from the alpha cells of the pancreas in response to low blood sugars (Berg et al., 2002). Glycogen becomes almost completely depleted after 24 hours of fasting (Newsholme & Leech, 1983). Depending on how low the carbohydrates are in the diet—<50g/day is considered a ketogenic diet—it will take between 24-64 hours to deplete most of the glycogen (Newholme & Leech, 1983), which is broken down to glucose-6-phosphate and then in turn is dephosphorylated to glucose through the action of the hepatic enzyme **glucose-6 phosphatase**. This enzyme is found only in liver and not in muscle, therefore explaining why muscle glycogen cannot synthesize glucose for the maintenance of homeostatic blood glucose (Harris, 1997).

Fasting — What happens in body

Already by day one of a fast, there is a 13-fold increase in the total levels of blood ketones (Figure 3.3),—improperly metabolized fats—but the most extensive is the 226-fold jump in serum ketones by the seventh day of the fast compared to the well-fed sate; afterwards, the ketones incrementally rise at a slower pace right up to the 42nd day of fasting (Newsholme & Leech, 1983). Though not considered a complete fast, the use of a VLCD will produce very similar results to the metabolic adaptations described above. The ketone bodies can cross the blood-brain barrier and continue to supply the brain with a vital substrate for energy, despite the low glucose availability. The ketones also have an anorexic effect, thus cutting the appetite and helping the dieter to more easily control food intake, at least in the short term (Paoli et al., 2013). It is important to comprehend at this stage why a low carbohydrate or fasting state increasingly produces ketone bodies.

Fat burning

It would appear that carbohydrates play an important role in ensuring continued oxidation of fats during weight loss. One of the key concepts of fat metabolism is that **fat burns in the flame of carbohydrate metabolism** (Paoli et al., 2013). In other words, carbohydrates that are processed down the glycolytic cycle eventually form pyruvate. The latter is transferred from the cytoplasm to the mitochondria where it is converted to Acetyl CoA, which ultimately is necessary to initiate the first reaction of the TCA cycle involving the condensation of both oxaloacetate and Acetyl CoA through the action of citrate synthase (Olson, 1997). The continued abundant supply of **oxaloacetate** is important for the continued function of the TCA cycle, located in the mitochondria of the cell; this is the site of fat, protein, and carbohydrate oxidation. The TCA cycle along with the electron-transport chain, located in the mitochondrial membrane, are the main sites of ATP production (Olson, 1997). While following a VLCD, a subject should experience a decline in the glycolytic generation of pyruvate, leading ultimately to a slowdown of the TCA cycle. It all begins when

carbohydrates and calories are no longer consumed in any notable amount; from that point, there ensues a drop in liver glycogen in response to the secretion of glucagon from the alpha-cells of the pancreas in an effort to normalize the blood glucose via the pathway of glycogenolysis (Harris, 1997). High circulating glucagon will also inhibit the biochemical synthesis of fatty acids by causing a decline in the production of pyruvate and of the activity of Acetyl CoA carboxylase—which catalyzes the reaction Acetyl CoA → fatty acids. Additionally, glucagon will also stimulate gluconeogenesis in the liver (Berg, et al., 2002), which also generates glucose from pyruvate, lactate, oxaloacetate, and numerous glucogenic amino acids. So then the TCA cycle is slowed during VLCDs or fasting because of the gluconeogenetic reaction which depletes the **oxaloacetate** for its conversion to phosphoenolpyruvate (PEP) and then eventually to glucose (Figure 3.3). This fall in the concentration of oxaloacetate plays a critical role in limiting the entry of Acetyl CoA into the TCA cycle and ultimately slowing oxidative metabolism (Berg et al., 2002). The consequence is the conversion of Acetyl CoA to ketone bodies such as acetoacetate and β-hydroxybutyrate (Olson, 1997), which are preferentially utilized by muscle and heart early on in the fast in order to spare glucose for the brain until about the second day of fasting. In a prolonged fast, lasting 24-48 hours, or low carbohydrate diets, ketones begin to cross the blood brain barrier in order to supply the brain with a substrate that replaces the brain's reliance on glucose (Newsholme & Leech, 1983). By this time, lipolysis is so extensive, that the TCA cycle, having slowed considerably (see the explanation above) is unable to fully oxidize fat, redirecting the Acetyl CoA—the end-metabolite prior to oxidation in the TCA cycle—in the direction of ketone body production (McGary, 1997). To overturn the process of ketosis, it is therefore advised to begin supplying the patient with a minimum of 130 g/day of carbohydrates for an average size person, in order to ensure sufficient amounts of oxaloacetate is available for the normal functioning of the TCA cycle (IMNA, 2005).

The second thing that happens in this kind of highly restrictive caloric diet is that the body attempts to recapture the lost weight as part of a survival mechanism aimed at maintaining homeostasis. It does this by causing an increase in appetite. Leptin, a

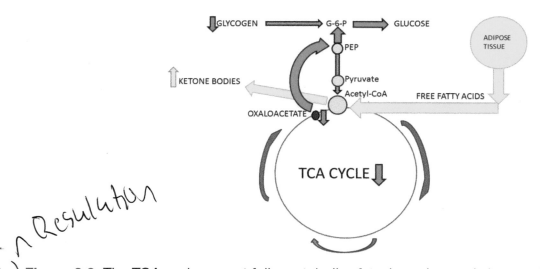

Figure 3.3 *The TCA cycle cannot fully metabolize fat when glucose is less available, therefore leading to the synthesis of ketone bodies (acetoacetate and β-hydroxybutyrate).*

Leptin Regulation

hormone generated from the fat cells of the body, signals the hypothalamus about the body fat reserves. When body fat reserves have declined, circulating leptin concentrations will also be low, thus signaling an appetite response from the hypothalamus and a recovery of lost body fat. Similarly, when adipose tissue is abundant, circulating leptin will be more elevated, thus producing a loss of appetite. Also, as part of the homeostatic mechanism, ghrelin, a stomach hormone that lets the brain know that it needs food when it is empty, encourages the dieter to seek food to satisfy his hunger. The combined effect of low leptin and elevated ghrelin, during dieting, can make binging difficult to resist. This is why these highly restrictive calorie diets often lead to ravenous appetites, uncontrollable eating, and significant weight regain (AND, 2009).

hedonic center

The third thing that happens when a person is on a VLCD is that the dieter experiences cravings because of the habituation of the brain's hedonic center (AND, 2009) to high taste sensations through chronic consumption of fast foods and snack foods high in salt, sugar, and fat. This becomes an even greater problem in obese children who have been brought up on highly processed foods with highly addictive flavors. The more subtle taste of fresh fruits and vegetables cannot compete with the sensational flavors and aromas that have been developed in processed foods. How can an apple compete with a hamburger, a banana split, or a milkshake? The answer is that it cannot. The child remains attached

to an impoverished food supply that stimulates high taste sensations while providing virtually no nutritional quality.

This is an inappropriate sensitization of the hedonic system that can have dire consequences for the child brought up on highly processed foods. It explains how teenagers can consume up to 1,000 kcal per day in soft drinks (Bissonnette, 2009). This kind of deviant food consumption displaces nutritious foods such as milk, vegetables, and fruits out of the daily menu. Here then lies the problem: An obese patient will not have any kind of ability to appreciate the nutritious menu proposed by a dietitian in an outpatient weight loss clinic. Although children do not understand the importance of achieving and maintaining a healthy weight, teenagers do. Yet an obese teenager's taste habituation, formed from modeling both parents and peers (Merlo, et al, 2009), enslaves him into repeat acquisition behavior and overeating from which he cannot escape; the consequence is a lifetime psychological and behavioral problems linked to obesity and binge eating (Merlo et al., 2009), in addition to depression and aggression (Hasler et al, 2004). Research done in the late 90s and early 2000s described an American pediatric population that had become so obese—200-400% increase since the mid 1990s (Ogden, 2004)—that 89% of overweight teenagers suffered from at least one risk factor for cardiovascular disease (Cook et al., 2003). The problem is that once an obese teenager has been conditioned to eat a certain way, the evidence appears to

obesity in 90's

intimate that he knows what he likes, and what he likes can quite often supplant what is healthy. The reality is that compliance to healthy eating standards will not take place because of addiction (Merlo et al., 2009). Regardless of whether the notion of food addiction is accepted, the research confirms an entrenched eating behavior in adulthood that was formed in childhood (Merlo et al. 2009). A recent review of childhood eating behaviors (Birch, 2007) reported that the typical daily diet of between 18 to 33% of US infants and toddlers contained no vegetable serving of any kind except for French fries. The review further confirmed that poor eating habits formed as toddlers tend to become much worse as they transition into adolescents (Birch, 20007) and to persist long into adulthood (Merlo et al., 2009).

Pharmacotherapy—The use of anorectic agents to suppress appetite became a popular treatment modality in the late 1990s and early in the 2000s.

Appetite was viewed as the enemy, and therapies tried to eliminate or limit the appetite so that the struggle to keep calories in check was more manageable. Sibutramine and Orlistat were two drugs that received FDA approval for long-term clinical management of obesity in the early 2000s. Studies were done in both adults and children, and the results were predictable: While the subjects took the drugs daily, weight loss was regular and significant. When the drugs were discontinued, weight regain was observed in almost all of the subjects. A meta-analysis by Haddock and colleagues, (2002). demonstrated that no one medication showed clear superiority in treatment effect over another. Interestingly, prolonged therapy after six months did not coincide with continued or greater weight loss. In fact, more of a plateau appears to occur at the six-month mark, with no evidence of benefit occurring afterward.

Sibutramine—a mixed serotonin, norepinephrine, and dopamine reuptake inhibitor—was banned by the FDA in 2010 because of concerns it led to higher risks of stroke and cardiovascular events (Yarnell et al., 2013). Orlistat is the only remaining drug that has been approved to treat obesity for up to one year. It works by inhibiting fat absorption and has only been able to afford a mean 6.5 lbs of weight loss at the end of a year. The Yarnell team (2013), after reviewing the overall effectiveness of drug therapy in weight loss, concluded that "*Despite their use, these pharmaceuticals for obesity have failed to produce significant, enduring weight loss and at best have provided only modest, short-term benefit.*" They argued that because food addiction is now being discussed as meaningful player in the obesity crisis, "*the role of behavior modification can be highlighted in conjunction with pharmacological interventions, for the treatment of food addictions.*"

3.4.3 The Most Effective Obesity Treatments

Exercise—While the longstanding strategies of weight loss diets have not produced the desired results in the majority of the population, research still shows that total daily or weekly caloric deficits are necessary for weight loss. Studies have shown that long-term weight loss is achieved with programs that include physical activity.

Very few studies have included sufficient amounts of exercise to even permit a 5% loss of body weight from exercise alone (AND, 2009). The time commitment to physical activity must be quite large in order to cause substantive weight loss by increasing energy expenditure alone. Using doubly labeled water, Schoeller and colleagues (1997) demonstrated that in order to maintain weight loss, individuals need to commit to expending between 11 and 12 kcal per kg per day in physical activity beyond normal daily expenditure. This represents a surprisingly elevated amount of energy that few people have the time to commit to. For instance, a 183-lb (83-kg) individual would have to expend approximately 955 kcal per day, 7 days per week, in order to maintain weight loss. This represents a 2.5-hour commitment at the gym every day. Realistically, few would be able to free up that much time in a day.

The National Weight Loss Registry currently tracks 10,000 people—80% of participants are women—who have lost on average 66 lb and kept it off for a mean of 5.5 years. On average, Registry members report expending 2,684 kcal per week from exercise alone—the equivalent of walking four miles per day seven days a week (AND, 2009). A more recent visit to the Registry's website shows that about 90% of the subjects participate in at least one hour of daily exercise—the most popular activity being walking.

This would equate to expending 1,800–2,100 kcal per week or roughly 300 kcal per day for just this additional walking. In addition, 62% of participants watched less than 10 hours of TV per week. The point here is that the commitment to physical activity must be significant in order to derive any clear benefits, but so must be the decision to minimize sedentary activities involving computers, television, and gaming.

The current 2015 *Dietary Guidelines for Americans* also includes the Federal Physical Activity Guidelines for Americans (FPAGA) that were issued in late 2008 (US DHHS, 2008). They recommend between 150 to 300 minutes per week of moderate to vigorous aerobic exercise for adults in order to maintain healthy weights (NAS, 2005). This translates into 60 minutes of moderately intense exercise five days per week, or 30 minutes of vigorous exercise fives day per week (US DHHS, 2008). Many individuals require much more than that, but 150–300 minutes is certainly a good place to start.

Behavioral Intervention—Behavior modification was an approach that became popular in the late 1980s. Now it is more aptly called cognitive behavioral therapy, and its goal is to identify cues that set off or trigger inappropriate eating habits. The principle is based on the notion that small but consistent changes in behavior are more enduring than large and dramatic shifts. This approach utilizes food and exercise monitoring, extensive record keeping, problem solving, and nutrition education in an attempt to restructure the individual's knowledge base, way of thinking, and ultimately behavior. It strongly advocates going beyond weight scales and weight losses and instead emphasizes that health and fitness come with changes in lifestyles anchored in behavioral modification (AND, 2009).

The AND's Nutrition Counseling work group had been, for several years, monitoring the effectiveness of self-monitoring for weight loss in the adult population. Right now the evidence is limited that behavioral modification and behavioral therapy are effective; results over the long term show that weight loss is modest and weight regain occurs frequently. The PREMIER Diabetes Prevention Program, Finnish Diabetes Prevention, and Look-AHEAD studies have shown significant changes in body weight and in risk indicators of heart disease and cardiovascular disease in those groups subject to

lifestyle modification strategies (AND, 2009). The Diabetes Prevention Program, in particular, demonstrated that behavioral modification was even more efficacious at causing weight loss over the long term than general recommendations and pharmacotherapy. Yarnell et al. (2013) recognize that psychotherapy can be helpful in managing co-morbid psychiatric disorders such as depression, anxiety, loneliness, boredom, anger, and interpersonal conflict that lead to dysfunctional eating such as binging and to significant weight gain and obesity.

Bariatric Surgeries—There is a class of obesity called morbid obesity that has grown a startling 400% between 1983 and 2000. Morbid obesity refers to individuals who are at least 100 lb over their healthy weight and who carry a high degree of morbidity or sickness that is far more serious than plain obesity. Morbid obesity is diagnosed when the body mass index (BMI) is ≥40 but less than 50. Remarkably the rate of increase of those who were super obese, defined as having a BMI ≥50, during that same time interval was 500%. Using data from the Behavioral Risk Factor Surveillance System, Sturm and Hattori (2013) measured a 70% increase in the prevalence of morbid obesity between 2000 and 2010, with the rate of increase slowing down since 2005. As it stands right now, 6.6% of the adult population or about 15.5 million people are classified as morbidly obese (Sturm & Hattori, 2013). Bariatric surgical interventions have been traditionally reserved for individuals with BMIs ≥40 who have not been successful in trying less invasive weight loss methods. The surgery has also been performed on individuals with BMIs between 35 and 40 if they also suffer from diabetes, hypertension, or sleep apnea. Bariatric surgeries have been shown to be the most effective therapy in terms of initiating significant and sustainable weight loss. There are a number of types of bariatric surgery: gastric bypass, adjustable gastric band, gastroplasty, biliopancreatic diversion, and gastric sleeve. These procedures have been successful in facilitating between 47.5 and 70% weight loss (AND, 2009).

There are, however, problems with bariatric surgery. Although on average, bariatric surgery causes an overall mean initial weight loss of 88 lb, between 20% and 30% of patients experience complications that are responsible for nutrient deficiencies and long-term health problems reported upon follow-up. Moreover, there is a troubling regain of lost weight in about 20%–34% of surgeries (Yarnell et al., 2013). Results remain more impressive than weight loss diets, but surgery doesn't address the fact that compulsive eating is a behavioral problem that is not completely solved with a smaller stomach pouch. Patients who have become morbidly obese have chronically consumed calories that have significantly exceeded their body's requirements. If a person puts on 25 extra pounds at the end of a year, but does nothing to attempt to lose this weight, this person risks becoming morbidly obese after four to five years. On a daily basis, this translates into an extra 240 kcal per day above the normal requirement. Add in a noticeable drop in physical activity, and additional pounds are added on more quickly.

The human cost associated with this form of gigantic bodily distortion goes beyond measure. At this point, the propensity to fall and fracture limbs increases, and the motivation to do exercise drops dramatically;

fatigue and chronic pain become prominent complaints. Hence patients are not likely to comply with new healthy dietary directives, nor are they prone to initiate exercise regimes that are rigorous enough to cause significant energy expenditure. Surgery, then, is seen as a life-saving intervention.

3.5 OBESITY CASE STUDY: CASE 3.1: GRADUAL WEIGHT GAIN OVER 3 YEARS IN A 27-YEAR-OLD WOMAN

3.5.1 Presentation

A 27-year-old woman on medical assistance weighing 230 lb (height: 5'10") presents with elevated LDL cholesterol, borderline hyperglycemia, high blood pressure (BP), and some anxiety. The patient's

Table 3.2
Patient Chart Information

Marla C. CHART INFORMATION	
Age: 27	
Weight: 230 lb	
Height: 5 feet 10 inches	
Patient lost boyfriend and job. Has been on social assistance for three years and gained 55 lb.	
She has a sedentary activity level	
ACTUALS	**STANDARDS**
FPG: 120 mg/dl	80–100 mg/dl
BP: 150/110	≤120/80
BMI: 32.96	18.5–24.9
% Body fat: 39%	20%–35%
Waist circumference: 44 in	<35 in
Kcals consumed: 2515 kcal	2844 kcal
A1C: 5.9%	<6.5%

American Diabetes Association (2011) Standards of Medical Care in Diabetes—2012. Diabetes Care. Suppl. 1, S11–63.
FPG: fasting plasma glucose.

Table 3.3

Usual Food Intake Record

PATIENT NAME: Marla C. 24-HR FOOD INTAKE RECALL		
FOODS CONSUMED	QUANTITY CONSUMED	PLACE
BREAKFAST:		
Orange Tang or orange drink (beverage)	2 cups	Kitchen
Kraft white bread, toasted	2 pieces	
Butter (salted)	1 tablespoon	
AM SNACK		
Chocolate bar (Snickers) reg. size	52.7 g (1.9 oz wt)	Work lounge
Coca Cola (reg.)	12 fl oz (355 ml can)	
LUNCH		
Coca Cola (reg.)	12 fl oz (355 ml can)	Work lounge
Bologna sandwich	2 slices (44 g)	
Mayonnaise (Hellman's)	2 Tbsp	
Lay's Salt & Vinegar Potato Chips	1 oz bag	
PM SNACK		
Coca-Cola (reg.)	12 fl oz (355 ml can)	Work lounge
Gummy bears	19 pieces	
DINNER		
Stouffer's Lasagna Italiano	7.67 oz wt (215 g)	TV room in the house
Beer (Dos Equis)	1 bottle	
Italian bread	3 (1 oz wt)	
Butter (salted)	3 pats	
Homemade mixed green salad	2 cups	
Bottled Italian salad dressing	3 Tablespoons	
EVENING SNACK		
No snacks recorded		

© Kletr/Shutterstock.com.

Figure 3.4 *Obese and depressed woman*

primary care physician reports that she gained 55 lb over the last three years because of depression. He recommends a consultation with the clinic's registered dietitian in order to ensure a healthy weight loss diet. The goal is a minimal 5–10% weight loss in order to positively affect blood lipids, blood glucose, and BP and ultimately avoid any BP and diabetes medication.

3.5.2 Body Composition Assessment

The clinician starts by measuring the patient's BMI (kg/m^2) to establish if she is overweight, obese, or morbidly obese. Taking her weight in pounds (230 lb) and multiplying it by 0.454 will provide a metric weight of 104.42 kg. Taking her height (70 in) and multiplying it by 0.0254 provides a height in meters of 1.78 m. The BMI can now be determined:

$$BMI = 104.24 \text{ kg}/(1.78 \text{ meters})^2$$

$$BMI = 32.96$$

She is classified as obesity class-1.

Next her body fat needs to be determined using one of three methods:

1 **Skinfold measurements** can be used to estimate the full body percent fat.

2 **Bioelectrical impedance assessment (BIA)** can calculate whole body percentage of fat using the impedance of a light electrical flow through the body. The greater the fat content the greater the impedance of the mild electrical current, and the lower the fat the lower the impedance, or the greater the conduction of the current.

3 **Plethysmography**, otherwise known as the BodPod measurement, can very reliably and accurately determine the total body fat through air displacement in an enclosed chamber.

The clinician uses BIA to determine the patient's total body fat of 39%. The waist circumference using a measurement tape position on the top of the iliac crest equals 44 inches.

3.5.3 Dietary Assessment

The dietitian at this point assesses the patient's dietary habits using a **Usual Food Record** and a food frequency questionnaire (FFQ) (AND, 2009). The dietitian asks questions like "in the morning when you wake up, when is the first time that you consume or eat something?" From the usual food record, the dietitian will plug foods, typically ingested on a normal day, into the diet analysis software. It will determine the total calories, macronutrients and micronutrients usually ingested. The FFQ does not establish the quantity consumed but rather the quality of the food consumed (AND, 2009) in that it attempts to determine the frequency at which nutritious and non-nutritious foods are regularly ingested. At this point it would be relevant to determine the patient's DRI for calories using the Mifflin St. Jeor equation and an appropriate activity factor reflective of her sedentary activity. The equation is below:

$$\text{Women: } [(10 \times \text{weight in kilograms}) + (6.25 \times \text{height in centimeters})] - [(5 \times \text{age in years}) + 161].$$

$$REE = [(10 \times 104.42 \text{ kg}) + (6.25 \times 177.8 \text{ cm})] - [(5 \times 27) + 161]$$

$$REE = [1044.2 + 1111.25] - 296 = 1859.45 \sim 1859 \text{ Kcal}$$

Consulting Table 2.3 will enable the student to select an activity factor (AF). The mean value for a light /sedentary activity is 1.53. So now the patient's total energy expenditure (TEE) or in other words her DRI calories equal:

$$1859 \text{ kcal} \times 1.53 = 2844 \text{ kcals/day}$$

3.5.4 Nutritional Interpretation of the Diet

To help interpret the ingested calories and macronutrients, the dietitian refers to the Acceptable Macronutrient Distribution Range (AMDR) reviewed in the previous chapter. She uses the preferred macronutrient ranges for carbohydrates (45%–65%), protein (10%–35%, with the usual requirement set at 15%), and fat (20%–35%), with the maximal cut-off usually set at 30%.

The patient (Table 3.3) is under her daily caloric goal by 12%. She is within her carbohydrate and fat goals, but falls beneath her healthy protein range. Based on her body weight, she only consumed 0.37g/kg body weight of protein, which is far below her physiological requirement of 0.8 g/kg. Total sugar refers to sugars consumed through fruits, vegetables, and milk in addition to sugars added to processed foods (added sugar). The patient's total sugar intake of 218 g exceeds her maximal allowance by 53.3% because of the soft drinks and Tang she usually consumes caused her total sugar intake to exceed 20% of her DRI calories. Her excessive sodium intake is not surprising given that she eats a lot of foods that are very processed, notably the lasagna and the salad dressing.

3.5.5 Interpretation of Medical Indices

The dietitian considers the key medical symptoms of blood sugars, hemoglobin (Hb) A1C, and blood pressure. In 2009, the American Diabetes Association, the International Diabetes Federation (IDF), and the European Association for the Study of Diabetes (EASD) formed an International Expert Committee that recommended the use of a Hb A1C cut-off of ≥6.5% in diagnosing a patient with diabetes mellitus. Pre-diabetes could be reasonably diagnosed with an Hb A1C between 5.7% and 6.4%. This means the patient is at an elevated risk of developing diabetes in the future. Similarly the fasting plasma glucose (FPG) value falls within the range of 100–125 mg/dl and confirms pre-diabetes. Also a random blood glucose ≥200 mg/dl signifies hyperglycemia. This patient's A1C at 5.9% and fasting plasma glucose of 120 mg/dl confirms that this patient is at a high risk of becoming diabetic. The

Table 3.3
Nutrient Breakdown of Usual Food Intake vs. Recommended Intake

Nutrient	Recommended Daily Intake	Actual Daily Intake
Kcal (Miffin St-Jeor)	2,844 kcals	2,515 kcals
Carbohydrates	427 g (60% DRI kcal) (320–462 g)	385 g
Protein	108 g (15% DRI kcal) (71–249 g)	39 g
Fat	79 g (25% DRI kcal) (63–111 g)	91 g
Total sugar	<142 g (20% DRI kcal)	218 g
Total salt	<2,400 mg	3008 mg

Calories measured using the www.myfitnesspal.com website.

blood pressure is above the normal range established for normotensive patients (>120/80) and can decidedly be interpreted as hypertension.

3.5.6 Dietary Recommendations

As is the case so often in patients who have gained weight, there tends to be an under reporting of the patient's true food intake. Nevertheless, based on the quality of her food intake there are only a few dietary aberrations that need to change to significantly cut back on her empty calories consumed. In this case removing Coca-Cola and Tang from the menu would eliminate 560 kcal from her intake. Additionally, it would be a good idea to drop the chocolate bar and the gummy bears. In total, the empty calories coming from snacks and sweetened beverages at lunch and breakfast total 950 kcal in a typical day. In the next step the patient should be prescribed a 2844 kcal/day diet for weight maintenance and the prevention of further weight gain and consisting of 427g of carbohydrates, 108g of protein and 79g of fat (Table 3.3).

The clinician would want to ensure that the patient can maintain weight stability and refrain from further weight gain for about two to four weeks, during which healthy foods and eating habits can be instigated. Once this is achieved, the clinician helps the patient develop a diet for mild to moderate weight loss using both caloric restrictions and regular exercise. To do this, she recommends some food exchanges. First, white bread should be changed to a whole wheat bread. Second, the Tang at breakfast needs to be replaced by a 4 fl-oz pure orange juice and one to two fruit servings (for example, one small banana and half a grapefruit). Third, a high fiber cereal should be included such a Raisin Bran, Grape Nut Original, Bran Buds, Bran Flakes, All Bran, Fiber One, or Kashi Original. There are others but these are all considered excellent sources of fiber as they contain at least 5 g per serving. Fiber is all too often suboptimal in the diet because of the highly processed food consumed by North Americans. Unless a high fiber cereal is consumed in the morning, it is very difficult to meet fiber requirements by the end of the day (AND, 2009). Fourth, a minimum of three vegetable servings need to be added throughout the day. Perhaps one vegetable at lunch and two at dinner could be selected such as corn, green beans, broccoli, Brussels sprouts, cabbage (or coleslaw), turnips, carrots, or sweet potato (yams). Emphasis should be placed on keeping her total sugar and sodium below cut-offs.

3.5.7 Determining the Goal Body Weight

The clinician then sets a weight goal for the patient. Using the two compartment model of body composition, it is possible to determine the patient's fat free mass (FFM): total body weight (TBW) = body fat (BF) + fat free mass (FFM). Since the clinician knows the total body weight (230 lb) and the percent body fat (39%), it can be calculated that the FFM equals 61% of the total body weight (100% − 39% = 61%). This means that 39% fat mass equals 89.7 lb (0.39 × 230 lb) and that FFM equals 140.3 lb (230 lb − 89.7 lb). The equations are written below:

$$(3.1)\ FFM = TBW \times 0.61$$

$$(3.2)\ FFM = 230\ lb \times 0.61 = 140.3\ lb$$

Now it is possible to more precisely determine a weight goal with the understanding that the patient's FFM must NOT decline with weight loss, but rather the body fat must undergo a decrease. Consequently, if the dietitian establishes a 25% body fat as a goal then the following equation can be set up in order to calculate the goal weight (GWT). This is a healthy goal to aim for as it is within the healthy range of 20%–35% for women. It is now possible to write the following two equations:

$$(3.3)\ (100 - 25\%) \times GWT = 140.3\ lb = FFM$$

$$(3.4)\ GWT = 140.3/0.75 = 187\ lb$$

The healthy weight or GWT that this patient should aim for is therefore 187 lb, which would represent a 43-lb weight loss.

Next, the clinician decides upon the rate of weight loss. Traditionally, 1–2 lb per week has been advised by the frontline providers and the dietitians. This is achieved by subtracting 500–1,000 kcal from her current maintenance diet (AND, 2009).

In practice, this approach would advocate for a daily energy intake of 1844–2344 kcal per day while maintaining her current sedentary lifestyle. The prognosis for this type of approach is not very good. Most patients, while capable of dropping excess weight rapidly, tend to regain significant weight within a year of achieving their goal if their energy expenditure does not increase (Mann, 2007). Therefore the clinician should prescribe weekly exercise in order to complement the caloric restriction needed to achieve this rate of weight loss. By adding a brisk walk (3.5 miles per hour which equals an expenditure of 0.0287 kcal/lb/min) lasting 75 minutes every day to her routine, the patient can burn an additional 495 kcal per day or 3465 kcals/week (0.0287 kcals/lb/min x 230 lb x 75 minutes x 7 days). In total, then, with a 500 kcal/day restriction, in combination with the exercise routine, she should experience an overall daily energy deficit equal to 995 kcal/day.

It would be possible to predict the rate of weight loss knowing that a 3,500 kcal deficit causes 1 lb of weight loss. Assuming the patient could maintain this regime, she would be experiencing a weekly caloric deficit of 6965 kcal. This can be translated in pounds lost by dividing 6965 kcals by 3,500, which equals 1.99 lbs or 2 lbs of weight loss per week. Given that her goal is to drop 43 lb, she should expect to take almost 21.5 weeks to achieve her final goals. The primary care physician should be satisfied with

a weight loss of 11–23 lb, which represents a 5–10% weight loss and therefore sufficient to cause a medical improvement in BP and FPG (AND, 2009).

In recent years, the 3500 kcal deficit model for weight loss was no longer recommended by scientific bodies like the American Society for Nutrition and the International Life Sciences Institute (Webb, 2014). The main limitation is that the rate of weight loss gradually decreases until it plateaus roughly after 6 months of dieting (Webb, 2014). Both the Pennington Biomedical Research Center and the NIH have developed predictive equations that forecast a much slower rate of weight loss over the long term. For instance, a 33 year old woman with a body weight of 230 lbs and a height of 5 feet 5 inches, who has a light activity, and caloric requirement for weight maintenance of 2626 kcals/day would need to follow a restrictive diet of 1808 in order to lose 43 lbs at a rate of 1 lb/week. Using the 3500 kcal/day model, a 500 kcal/day restriction (2126 kcal/day) would predict reaching the goal weight of 187 lbs within within 43 weeks. However, the revised formula recommends 1808 kcals/day in order to achieve that extent of weight loss, thereby representing a 818 kcal/day deficit. To lose at a rate of 2 lb/week, the patient would need to ingest 1236 kcal/day or experience a 1390 kcal/day deficit over 151 days (21.5 weeks), whereas the 3500 kcal/day model, would forecast that extent of weekly weight loss with the ingestion 1626 kcal/day. For now, it is sufficient to understand the process of weight loss using the linear 3500 kcal/day model. The non-linear model will, however, be discussed in future chapters.

CHAPTER 3 PRACTICE QUESTIONS

1 Calculate the BMI of a man weighing 256 lbs with a height equal to 5 feet 9 inches.

2 If a man has a height of 5 feet 10 inches how much should he weigh in order to have a healthy BMI of 24?

3 A woman weighing 198 lbs has 47% body fat. Determine the goal weight she should expect to achieve if the goal is for your patient to achieve 23% body fat.

4 If a 255 lbs patient needs to lose 67 lbs and the clinician prescribes an exercise routine that involves walking at 3.5 miles/hr (0.03 kcal/lb/min) for 60 minutes three times per week, how long will it take the patient to reach her goal following a straight linear calculation model?

5 If a 24 year-old female patient weighing 228 lbs with a height of 5 feet 5 inches has a sedentary activity level, calculate her total energy expenditure (TEE) using the Mifflin St. Jeor equation and the appropriate mean activity factor.

6 If a 24 year-old female patient weighing 228 lbs with a height of 5 feet 5 inches has a mild activity level, calculate her total energy expenditure (TEE) using the Gerrior equation and the appropriate activity factor.

7 Assuming you reviewed and understood the process of ketogenesis during fasting or very low carbohydrate diets, explain the strategy that would be most effective in normalizing the ketone levels in the blood.

8 Complete a nutritional assessment form, similar to the one described in Figure 3.2 by first calculating your personal DRI calories using the Mifflin equation multiplied by an appropriate activity factor (see Table 2.3 in chapter 2). Type in the DRI calories into the first box under the DRI column. Next, establish DRI ranges for carbodydrate, protein, total fat, polyunsaturated, monounsaturated and saturated fat using the DRI calories. All of the micronutrient DRIs remain the same as indicated in Figure 3.2.Then, using the three day dietary record completed at the end of chapter-1, enter the macronutrients and micronutrients that were analyzed into the "quantity" column of your assessment form. Finally, determine whether the nutrient intakes are "suboptimal, adequate, or excessive." Remember that only the DRI calories are used for calculating the DRIs for the macronutrients.

APPENDIX-I

DIETARY REFERENCE INTAKES (DRIs): TOLERABLE UPPER INTAKE LEVELS (ULs), FOR MICRONUTRIENTS IN ADULTS AGES 19–70

Vitamin A	3000 mcg/day
Vitamin C	2000 mg/day
Vitamin D	50 mcg/day
Vitamin E	1000 mg/day
Folate	1000 mcg/day
Pyridoxine (B6)	100 mg/day
Niacin (B3)	35 mg/day
Calcium	2500 mg/day
Copper	10,000 mcg/day
Zinc	40 mg/day
Fluoride	10 mg/day
Iodine	1,100 mcg/day
Iron	45 mg/day
Magnesium	350 mg/day
Phosphorus	4000 mg/day
Sodium	2300 mg/day

Source: National Academy of Science (NAS), 2005b.

The ULs for vitamin E, niacin, and folate pertain to synthetic forms found in supplements, fortified foods, or a combination of the two. The UL for vitamin A pertains to the active retinol form.

REFERENCES

[1] ADA (American Diabetes Association) (2011). Standards of medical care in diabetes—2012. *Diabetes Care*. 35 Suppl. 1, S11–63.

[2] AND (Academy of Nutrition and Dietetics). (2009). Position paper on weight management. *J Am Diet Assoc*. 109, 330–346.

[3] AHA. (2013). *American Heart Association backs current BP treatments*. Retrieved from http://www.heart.org/HEARTORG/Conditions/HighBloodPressure/PreventionTreatmentofHighBloodPressure/American-Heart-Association-backs-current-BP-treatments_UCM_459129_Article.jsp

[4] Astrup, A. et al. (2004). Atkin's and other low carbohydrate diets: Hoax or an effective tool for weight loss. *The Lancet* 364(9437), 897–899.

[5] Berg, J.M., Tymoczko, J.L., & Stryer, L. (2002). Section: 30.3: 3 *Food Intake and Starvation Induce Metabolic Changes. Biochemistry*, 5th edition. New York: W.H.Freeman.

[6] Birch, L. (2007). Influences on the development of children's eating behaviours: From infancy to adolescents. *Can J Diet Pract Res*; 68(1): s1–s56

[7] Bissonnette, D. (2013) *It's all about nutrition: Saving the health of Americans*. Lanham, MD: University Press of America.

[8] Bissonnette, D.J. (2009). *Obesity in America: A National Crisis*. DVD. Mankato MN: St. Jude Nutrition Medical Communications. New York: Films for the Humanities and Sciences.

[9] Bleich, S. et al. (2007). *Why is the developed world obese?* NBER Working Paper 12954. Cambridge, MA: National Bureau of Economic Research (NBER), 43.

[10] Bouchard, C. (1997). Genetics of human obesity: Recent results from linkage studies. *J Nutr*. 127(9), 1887S–1890S.

[11] Bouchard, C. et al. (1988). Inheritance of the amount and distribution of human body fat. *Int J Obes*. 12, 205–215.

[12] Burke, B.S. (1947). The dietary history as a tool in research. *Journal of the American Dietetic Association* 23, 1041-1046.

[13] Cook S., Weitzman M., Auinger P, Nguyen M, Dietz W.H. (2003). Prevalence of a metabolic syndrome phenotype in adolescents: Findings from the third National Health and Nutrition Examination Survey, 1988–1994. *Arch Pediatr Adolesc Med*;157:821–7.

[14] Després, J.P. (2012). Body fat distribution and risk of cardiovascular disease: Update. *Circulation* 126, 1301-1313.

[15] Farooqi, S., O'Rahilly, S. (2009). Leptin: A pivotal regulator of human energy homeostasis. *Am J Clin Nutr*. 89 Suppl., 980S–984S.

[16] Fryar, CD., Carroll, MD., and Ogden, CL. (2018). Prevalence of Overweight, Obesity, and Severe Obesity Among Adults Aged 20 and Over: United States, 1960–1962 Through 2015–2016. NCHS September. URL: https://www.cdc.gov/nchs/data/hestat/obesity_adult_15_16/obesity_adult_15_16.pdf

[17] Fryar CD, Carroll MD, Ogden CL. (2016) Prevalence of overweight and obesity among children and adolescents aged 2–19 years: United States, 1963–1965 through 2013–2014. National Center for Health Statistics Data, Health E-Stats. Available at: https://www.cdc.gov/nchs/data/hestat/obesity_child_13_14/obesity_child_13_14.htm

[18] Gallaghe, D. et al. (2000). Healthy percentage body fat ranges: An approach for developing guidelines based on body mass index. *Am J Clin Nutr.* 72(3), 694–701.

[19] Gropper, S.S. and Smith J.L. (2013). Advanced Nutrition and Human Metabolism, 6th edition. Belmont, CA: Wadsworth, 586 pp

[20] Gibson, R.S. (1990). *Principles of nutritional assessment.* New York: Oxford University Press, 691.

[21] Haddock, C.K. et al. (2002). Pharmacotherapy for obesity: A quantitative analysis of four decades of published randomized clinical trials. *Int J Obes.* 26(2), 262–273.

[22] Hales, CM., Carroll, MD., Fryar, CD., and Ogden, CL. (2017). Prevalence of Obesity Among Adults and Youth: United States, 2015–2016. NCHS Data Brief No. 288, October. URL: https://www.cdc.gov/nchs/products/databriefs/db288.htm

[23] Harris, R.A. (1997). Carbohydrate metabolism: Major metabolic pathways and their control. In: *Textbook of biochemistry with clinical correlations* (Thomas M. Delvin, Ed). New York: Wiley-Liss, 267-333.

[24] Harvard School of Public Health. (2012). The obesity prevention. *Globalization.* Available at: http://www.hsph.harvard.edu/obesity-prevention-source/obesity-causes/globalization-and-obesity/

[25] Hasler, G., Buysse, D.J., Klaghofer, R., et al. (2004). The association between short sleep duration and obesity in young adults: A 13-year prospective study. *Sleep*;27:661–6.

[26] Institute of Medicine of the National Academies (IMNA). (2005). *Dietary reference intakes (DRIs) for Energy, carbohydrates, fiber, fat, fatty acids, cholesterol, protein and amino acids.* Washington DC: National Academic Press. Retrieved from http://www.nal.usda.gov/fnic/DRI/DRI_Energy/energy_full_report.pdf

[27] Kelly, T., Yang, W., Chen, C.S., Reynolds, K., & He, J. (2008) Global burden of obesity in 2005 and projections to 2030. *Inter J Obesity (Lond)* 32, 1431–1437.

[28] Leddy, M.A., Power, M.L. & Schulkin, J. (2008). The impact of maternal obesity on maternal and fetal health. *Rev Obstet Gynecol.*; 1(4): 170–178.

[29] Ma, Y. et al. (2007) A dietary comparison of popular weight loss plans. *JADA* 107(10), 1786–1791.

[30] Mann, T. et al. (2007) Medicare's search for effective obesity treatments. *American Psychologists* 62(3), 220–233.

[31] Martin, AB., Hartman, M., Washington, B., Catlin, A., et al. (2018). National Health Care Spending In 2017: Growth Slows To Post–Great Recession Rates; Share Of GDP Stabilizes. Health Affairs; 38(1). URL: https://www.healthaffairs.org/doi/full/10.1377/hlthaff.2018.05085

[32] Meldrum, DR., et al. (2017). Obesity pandemic: causes, consequences, and solutions-but do we have the will? Fertil Steril.;107(4):833-839. doi: 10.1016/j.fertnstert.2017.02.104. Epub 2017 Mar 11

[33] Merlo ,L.J., Klingman, C., Malasanos, T.H., & Silverstein, J.H. (2009). Exploration of food addiction in pediatric patients: A preliminary investigation. *J Addict Med*; 3(1): 26–32.

[34] McGary, J.D. (1997). Lipid metabolism I: utilization and storage of energy in lipid form. In: *Textbook of biochemistry with clinical correlations* (Thomas M. Delvin, Ed). New York: Wiley-Liss, 361-393.

35 National Academy of Sciences (NAS), Institute of Medicine, Food and Nutrition Board. (2005). *Dietary reference intakes for energy, carbohydrate, fiber, fat, fatty acids, cholesterol, protein, and amino acids (macronutrients). Chapter 11: Macronutrients and healthful diets.* Available at http://www.nap.edu/catalog/10490/dietary-reference-intakes-for-energy-carbohydrate-fiber-fat-fatty-acids-cholesterol-protein-and-amino-acids-macronutrients

36 National Academy of Sciences (NAS), Institute of Medicine, Food and Nutrition Board. (2005b). *Dietary reference intakes for energy, carbohydrate, fiber, fat, fatty acids, cholesterol, protein, and amino acids (macronutrients).* Appendix-D: Dietary Intake Data from the Third National Health and Nutrition Examination Survey (NHANES III), 1988–1994 Available at: http://www.nap.edu/catalog/10490/dietary-reference-intakes-for-energy-carbohydrate-fiber-fat-fatty-acids-cholesterol-protein-and-amino-acids-macronutrients

37 National Institute of Diabetes and Digestive and Kidney Disease (NIDDKD). (2014). *Weight Control Information Network.* Retrieved from http://www.win.niddk.nih.gov/publications/low_calorie.htm#lcd

38 National Institutes of Health/National Heart Lung and Blood Institute/North American Association for the Study of Obesity (NHLB). (2000). Obesity Education Initiative. *The practical guide identification, evaluation, and treatment of overweight and obesity in adults.* NIH Publication Number 00-4084. Available at http://www.nhlbi.nih.gov/guidelines/obesity/prctgd_c.pdf

39 Newsholme, E.A., & Leech, A.R. (1983). *Biochemistry for the medical sciences.* New York: John Wiley & Sons, 952.

40 Nieves, D.J., Cnop, M., Retzlaff, B., Walden, C.E., Brunzell, J.D., Knopp, R.H., & Kahn, S.E. (2003). The atherogenic lipoprotein profile associated with obesity and insulin resistance is largely attributable to intra-abdominal fat. *Diabetes*; 52 (1): 172–179

41 Ogden C.L. et al. (2006). Prevalence of overweight and obesity in the United States, 1999–2004. *JAMA.* 295, 1549–1555.

42 Ogden, C.L. (2004). Defining overweight in children using growth charts. *Md Med*;5:19–21.

43 Olsen, M.S. (1997). Bioenergetics and oxidative metabolism. In: *Textbook of biochemistry with clinical correlations.* Thomas M. Delvin, ed. New York: Wiley-Liss, 217-266.

44 Perry, B., & Wang, Y. (2012). Appetite regulation and weight control: the role of gut hormones. *Nutrition and Diabetes.* 2, e26; doi: 10.1038. Retrieved from http://www.nature.com/nutd/journal/v2/n1/full/nutd201121a.html

45 Popkin, B.M. (2006). Global nutrition dynamics: the world is shifting rapidly toward a diet linked non-communicable diseases. *American Journal of Clinical Nutrition* 84, 289-98.

46 Popkin, B.M. (2007). The world is fat. *Scientific American*, September; 88–95.

47 Rasmussen, S.A., Chu, S.Y., Kim, S.Y., Schmid, C.H., & Lau J. (2008). Maternal obesity and risk of neural tube defects: a meta-analysis. *Am J Obstet Gynecol.* 2008;198(6):611–9

48 Roger, V.L. et al. (2012). AHA statistical update: heart disease and stroke statistics 2012. *Circulation* 125, e2–e220.

49 Rasouli, N., & Kern, P.A. (2008). Adipocytokines and the metabolic complications of obesity. *J Clin Endocrinol Metab*; 93(11 Suppl 1): S64–S73.

50 Schoeller, D.A., Shay, K., & Kushner, R.F. (1997) How much physical activity is needed to minimize weight gain in previously obese women? *American Journal Clinical Nutrition* 66, 551–556.

51 Sturm, R., & Hattori, A. (2013). Morbid obesity rates continue to rise rapidly in the United States *Int J Obes (Lond).* 37(6), 889–891. Available at http://www.ncbi.nlm.nih.gov/pmc/articles/PMC3527647/

[52] Sturm, R. (2007). Increases in morbid obesity in the USA: 2000–2005. *Public Health* 121, 492–496.

[53] U.S. Army. Army Regulation 600-9 (revised June 28, 2013). *The Army Body Composition Program*. Available at http://www.apd.army.mil/jw2/xmldemo/r600_9/main.asp

[54] U.S. DHHS (Department of Health and Human Services).(2008) Physical Activity Guidelines for Americans. Washington (DC): U.S. Department of Health and Human Services; 2008. ODPHP Publication No. U0036. Available at: http://www.health.gov/paguidelines.

[55] Webb, D., (2014). Farewell to the 3,500-Calorie Rule. Today's Dietitian; 26 (11): 36 retrieved on July 5, 2016 from: http://www.todaysdietitian.com/newarchives/111114p36.shtml

[56] White, J.V., Guenter, P., Jensen, G., Malone, A., Schofield, M., et. al., (2012). Consensus Statement: Academy of Nutrition and Dieteticsand American Society for Parenteral and Enteral Nutrition: Characteristics Recommended for the Identification and Documentation of Adult Malnutrition (Undernutrition). JPEN (J Parenter Enteral Nutr) ;36:275-283

[57] Willett, W.C. et al. (2006) Prevention of chronic disease by means of diet and lifestyle changes. In: Jamison D.T., ed. *Disease Control Priorities in Developing Countries*. 2nd ed. Washington, DC: World Bank.

[58] Willett, W.C., Dietz, W.H., & Colditz, G.A. (1999). Guidelines for Healthy Weight. *New England Journal of Medicine* 341, 427-434.

[59] Xanthakos, S.A. (2009). Nutritional deficiencies in obesity and after bariatric surgery. *Pediat Clin North Amer.* 58(5), 1105–1121. Retrieved from http://www.ncbi.nlm.nih.gov/pmc/articles/PMC2784422/

[60] Yarnell, S. et al. (2013). Pharmacotherapies for overeating and obesity. *J Genet Syndrome and Gene Therapy*. 4(3), 131. Retrieved from http://www.ncbi.nlm.nih.gov/pmc/articles/PMC3697760/

CHAPTER 3 ANSWERS

1 37.95—class-2 obesity

2 24 = Kg / (1.78 meters)^2 So now the unknown variable (Kg) can be algebraically formulated as follows: Kg = 24 x (1.78 m)^2 = 76.04 Kg or 167 lbs

3 136 lbs

4 3.27 years

5 2732 Kcals

6 2740 Kcals

7 Raise carbohydrates to a minimum of 130g /day

CHAPTER 4

The Problem of Cardiovascular Disease

© lola1960/Shutterstock.com

4.1 THE PREVALENCE OF CARDIOVASCULAR DISEASE (CVD)

The obesity epidemic carries serious long term health implications because of the increased morbidity associated with being overweight and obese (Whitlock et al., 2009). There is a tendency towards heightened risk factors and a greater incidence of diabetes mellitus as well as cardiovascular disease (CVD) endpoints such as coronary heart disease, stroke, and heart failure. In addition, degenerative joint disease, asthma, and cancer are intimately tied to obesity. Cardiovascular disease refers to people suffering from hypertension, heart disease (HD), stroke, peripheral artery disease (PAD), and diseases of the veins. It is the most prevalent medical disorder in the United States with a total of 82.6 million Americans who have one or more types of CVD, representing about 24% of the U.S. popula-

tion. It is not surprising then that as many as 76.4 million suffer from hypertension. As of 2008 both CVD and stroke alone carried a price tag of $297.7 billion in direct and indirect costs. It is also responsible for the greatest mortality in the United States, representing 810,810 deaths in 2008 or 32.8% of all reported deaths in the United States that year. By contrast, cancers and benign neoplasms cost $228 billion in direct and indirect medical expenses (Roger et al., 2012). Although the death rates from CVD have declined in the U.S. by 30.6% between 1998 and 2008, it rose 25% worldwide between 1999 and 2010 according to the Global Burden of Disease study (Lozano et al., 2012). Despite the recent decline in U.S. death rates, CVD still remains a significant health burden. This is especially true when specific metrics of good cardiovascular health are measured in the population. It is estimated that 63% of adult whites, and 71% of adult African and Mexican Americans have only three or fewer ideal metrics of good health out of seven (Roger et al., 2012).

Globally, between 62% and 63% of all deaths from the combined impact of cardiovascular disease, chronic kidney disease and diabetes were attributed to 4 risk factors: elevated BMI, blood pressure, blood glucose and serum cholesterol (Danaei, et al., 2014). However, in recent years, the importance of BMI and blood glucose values have significantly increased globally, and their relevance as risk predictors of overall population mortality have likewise done the same (Danaei et al., 2011). It is, however, important to understand that 75% to 76% of hypertensive heart disease deaths in women and men respectively, are nevertheless attributed to a combination of the 4 risk factors, whereas of the four, hypertension and BMI were the most important determinants. By contrast, high blood pressure predicted 48% of ischemic heart disease cases whereas high cholesterol was a distant second risk factor in 23% of patients (Danaei et al., 2009)

4.2 THE CAUSES OF CARDIOVASCULAR DISEASE

4.2.1 Poor Diet and Lifestyle Habits

There are four basic behaviors that are considered healthy and conducive to keeping CVD in check in the population. First, moderate to high levels of physical activity need to be included on a daily basis; daily commitments of 60 minutes/week day or 300 minutes per week of moderate to strenuous aerobic exercise greatly contribute to managing stable body weights in addition to increasing the HDL cholesterol, known as the good cholesterol (US DHHS, 2008; NAS, 2005). Moreover, including vigorous sports into the weekly schedule, or becoming moderately fit, through daily 60–90 minute exercise commitments—optimal for the most significant risk reduction—reduced mortality rates by between 23% to 46% (NAS, 2005). It is concerning that in 2013, only 27% of high school students, in the US, admitted participating in at least 60 minutes per day of physical activity in the previous 7 days. Moreover, a mere 29% participated in daily physical education classes at school (CDC, 2015). Second, the decision not to smoke sizably decreases a person's risk of

developing heart disease. Approximately 23% of Americans adults are smokers in the United States; third, maintaining a BMI<25 has been clearly associated with lower risks of CVD; however, as many as 31.8% of US children and adolescents and 70.7% of US adults fail to meet healthy weight standards (CDC, 2014); fourth, meeting five healthy dietary practices can substantially decrease CVD risks, notably selecting first, a diet rich in fruits and vegetables, second, whole grains and high fiber foods, third, 8 oz-wt of oily fish per week, fourth, limit the intake of both saturated and trans fats, and fifth, minimize or eliminate beverages and foods sweetened with added sugar (AHA, 2006).

The American Heart Association Diet & Lifestyle Recommendations (AHA, 2015; 2006) affirm the importance of 1) consuming ≥4 to 5 servings/day of fruits and vegetables; 2) a minimum of two 4.0 oz-wt servings/week of oily fish such as salmon, mackerel, herring, albacore tuna, lake trout or sardines; 3) maintaining sodium intake to around 1500 mg/day is ideal for lowering BP; 4) keeping added sugar intake to <100g/day for women and <150g/day in men; 5) ensuring the consumption of 6-8 oz-equivalent of grain foods/day of which at least 3 oz-wt/day should be whole grains; 6) select fat-free, one-percent-fat and low-fat dairy products; 7) limiting red meats and specifically processed meats high in saturated fats and sodium; and 8) saturated fat intake should be kept at <7% of calories, preferably no more than 5-6% of total calories and trans-fats <1% of calories and cut back on the use of hydrogenated vegetable oils (AHA, 2015; 2006).

The NHANES 2009–2010 (CDC, 2014b) survey data measured a number of cardiovascular health risks in the U.S. population, and the findings are setting off alarms at the national level. In the 12–19 year old age group there are a number of dietary and lifestyle practices that heighten this age group's risk of developing CVD early on in their lives (**Figure 4.1**). At a most fundamental level, impoverished eating habits are now forcibly making this crisis alarmingly dangerous. This concern is supported by national nutrition surveys that have shown that as many as 28.5% of high school students consume <1 fruit serving/day, whereas 32.2% consume <1 vegetable/day (CDC, 2011). More recent NHANEs 2009–2010 data (CDC, 2014b) suggests that the quality of the vegetable consumed are also questionable. Indeed, as many as 89.9% of teenagers do not consume dark green vegetables, and 25.1% do not include red and orange vegetables in their daily selection of produce. The quality of fruit consumption does not fare any better; approximately 78.4% of adolescents do not include melons, citrus or berries into their diet (CDC, 2014b).

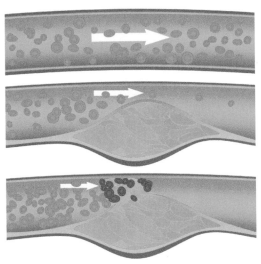

Credit © Monkey Business /Shutterstock.com

Figure 4.1 *Atherosclerosis in the arteries.*

And it is the quality of the fats that are consumed specifically that impact the vascular system. Atherosclerosis is defined as a chronic inflammatory disease that generally culminates in athero-thrombotic complications, after several decades of silent development. A gradual thickening of the arterial walls by an atheroma (Figure 4.1) causes a slowed circulation because of a narrowing of the artery leading gradually to obstruction. The end point is acute coronary syndromes, which often occur as a heart attack or stroke (NHLBI, 2014b). Indeed, arterial obstruction prevents the oxygen-rich blood from reaching specific tissues. A heart attack occurs when a specific region of the heart muscle receives inadequate oxygen; a stroke is when regions of the brain are deprived of blood because of a vascular obstruction (Figure 4.1). Cardiovascular risk factors such as hypercholesterolemia, hypertension, smoking, or diabetes are often at the source of the inflammation. There are other circumstances however, when inflammation precedes atherosclerotic alterations.

One of the theories behind atheroma formation begins with an arterial wall injury resulting from elevated BP. Damage to the inner wall of the artery called the endothelium, initiates an inflammatory response, which causes a convergence of free and esterified cholesterol, monocytes, and macrophages, which form a foam-like substances that attempts to heal the injury through fibrosis and calcification. It is precisely at the location of arterial lesions that platelets begin to aggregate and stick to the injury site, leading often times to the formation of blood clots and to an eventual obstruction to blood flow (Figure 4.1), resulting in a heart attack (Balanescu et al., 2010; Grundy, 2006). The diet can protect against the formation of an atheroma and heart attack most notably through the consumption of omega-3 fatty acids, abundantly found in oily fish. These fish are particularly rich in EPA and DHA, which are known fatty acids that protect against strokes and cardiovascular events. Sadly, only 9.2% of teenagers and 18.3% of adults over 20 years of age consume ≥2-3.5oz-wt of oily fish servings/week. The sodium content of food tends to be elevated with greater processing. The ingestion of sodium needs to be controlled because of its tie to hypertension. Here again there are concerns at the population level as less than 1% of teenagers and adults maintain their sodium intake <1500mg/day. The NHANES 2005–2006 survey revealed that 90.4% of adult Americans do in fact exceed their maximal daily allowance of 2400 mg.

Sugary beverages are being ingested in larger volumes at an earlier age. In fact, 68% of teenagers fail to drink ≤450 kcal/week, and as many as 48% of adults fail to keep soft drinks and other sugary beverages in check. When a composite of four to five healthy eating behaviors were monitored in the NHANES 2007–2008 survey, none of the teenagers and a mere 0.3% of the adults met four to five out of the eight recommended healthy eating practices. Is there any wonder that CVD risk factors still remain elevated?

4.2.2 Abnormal Lipid Metabolism

Although serum cholesterol has been used since the 1960s as a screening tool for detecting patients at high risk of CVD, it is paradoxical that only 32%

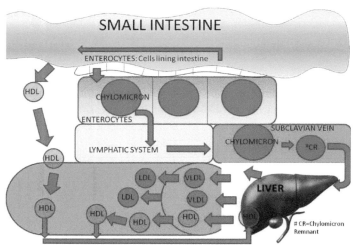

SMALL INTESTINE

ENTEROCYTES: Cells lining intestine

CHYLOMICRON

ENTEROCYTES

LYMPHATIC SYSTEM

SUBCLAVIAN VEIN

CHYLOMICRON → #CR

LIVER

LDL   VLDL
LDL   VLDL
HDL   HDL   HDL
HDL

CR=Chylomicron Remnant

Image courtesy of David Bissonnette

Figure 4.2 *Lipoprotein metabolism.*

of patients with CVD in the 1960s actually had hypercholesterolemia. Since that time, the percent of CVD patients with elevated cholesterol has dropped to between 20.8 and 22.5% of CVD patients between 1988 and 2000 (Sachdeva et al., 2009). Sachdeva and colleagues (2009) found that close to 50% of patients with cardiovascular disease who were admitted to hospital for treatment had LDLs less than 100 mg/dl on admission, whereas it was specifically the HDL that posed a much greater risk to most of the patients. Indeed, they identified over 50% of CVD patients with HDLs less than 40, and fewer than 10% who had reached the ideal HDL levels of ≥60 mg/dl. Understanding how lipoproteins are formed and work within the scheme of lipid metabolism is critical for understanding the diagnosis of heart disease risks as well as the treatments. It begins with fat ingestion in our diet and the absorption of that fat from the lumen of the intestine into the blood and then to the various tissues either for deposition or energy production. The ideal model would be that all the fat ingested at a meal would be taken up by the individual cells and oxidized in the Tricarboxilic Acid (TCA) cycle to ATP. In this way there would be no surplus fat to deposit in any of the adipocytes. Obesity would not be a problem in this context. Unfortunately, obesity and heart disease are two of the main epidemics currently afflicting American society. The main dietary deviances that are causing these problems are the excess total and saturated fats consumed regularly by the population.

Once fat is ingested, the bile, secreted from the gallbladder, emulsifies the fat into dispersed droplets, called micelles, which are then easily hydrolyzed principally by the "lipase" enzyme secreted by the pancreas. Pancreatic lipase is considered the most important fat digestive enzyme. It cleaves the fatty acids from the glycerol backbone thus resulting in free fatty acids. The latter are absorbed into the enterocytes—the cells lining the small intestine—where they are encapsulated into a large lipoprotein called a **chylomicron**. Inside this lipoprotein are long and some medium chain fatty acids, glycerol, phospholipids, proteins and cholesterol. These chylomicrons are released into the circulation first via the **lymphatic system**, which eventually connects with the subclavian vein (superior vena cava) (Figure 4.2). As the chylomicron circulates in the blood leading to the liver, it deposits its main cargo of triglycerides into muscle cells, where the fatty acids are eventually oxidized, and into the adipocytes for storage. Afterwards, having lost most of the triglycerides, the chylomicron becomes a **chylomicron remnant** (**CR**), containing significantly less triglycerides and proportionally more cholesterol which it deposits in the liver. From there, very low-density lipoproteins (VLDLs) are released from the liver into circulation with the objective of redistributing the triglycerides into lean tissue and adipose tissue (Hegele, 2009).

As this lipoprotein makes its deposits, it becomes first an intermediary density lipoprotein (IDL) and finally a low-density lipoprotein (LDL) containing mostly cholesterol. It is this lipoprotein that accumulates in the blood of patients with high cholesterol. The high density lipoproteins (HDLs), by contrast, are considered cholesterol scavengers; they are generated from peripheral tissues like the intestines, and from the liver (Figure 4.1). They scavenge the cholesterol from the vascular epithelium and return it to the liver to be repackaged again as VLDLs and recirculated in the blood or utilized for the synthesis of bile by the liver. The clinician, looking over a patient's lipid profile, wants to see elevated HDLs, low LDLs and triglycerides (TG) (See Table 4.2 for lipid standards). The primary targets of lipid-lowering therapy are the LDLs according to the National Cholesterol Education Program (NCEP).

4.3 ASSESSMENT OF CARDIOVASCULAR DISEASE

An important and valuable tool used in the assessment of CVD is **metabolic syndrome**. The NHANES 2003–2006 survey data confirmed that 34% of adult Americans suffer from metabolic syndrome. A cluster of risk factors for CVD and diabetes are used by the frontline clinicians to screen for patients with metabolic syndrome. These are patients with three or more of five risk factors:

1 Fasting blood glucose >110 mg/dl

2 HDL cholesterol <40 mg/dl in men and <50 mg/dl in women, or who are receiving pharmacotherapy for low HDLs

3 Serum triglycerides ≥150mg/dl or receiving medication for hypertriglyceridemia

4 Waist circumference ≥40 inches in men, and ≥35 inches in women

5 BP with a systolic value ≥130 mm Hg and a diastolic ≥85mm Hg or a patient treated with antihypertensive drugs who has a history of hypertension (AHA, 2014; NHLBI, 2001).

While most patients with diabetes have metabolic syndrome, some prefer to stratify these patients into a distinct risk category because of the diabetes. Nevertheless, the criteria used to screen patients with metabolic syndrome is consistently used in the healthcare field and so must be well known by dietitians, nurses, and other health care professionals.

4.4 STRATEGIES TO CONTROL CVD

The American Heart Association's (AHA) 2020 goal is to improve cardiovascular health by 20% in the U.S population. The AHA defines "ideal cardiovascular health" as the absence of any of the clinical symptoms of CVD, and of the presence of seven health behaviors such as increased lean body mass—this intimates a low but healthy percentage of body fat,—avoidance of smoking, heightened and regular physical activity [PA], and healthy dietary intake practices that are consistent with the standards of the **Dietary Approaches to Stop Hypertension [DASH]** (Table 4.1). In addition, the AHA recommends reaching and maintaining these blood markers: i-untreated total cholesterol <200 mg/dl; ii-untreated BP <120/<80 mm Hg; and, iii- fasting blood glucose <100 mg/dl. Achieving these health behaviors may prove to be more challenging than most people think (AHA, 2006). The diagnosis of high blood pressure should begin once the BP is equal or greater than 140/90, whereas a person is pre-hypertensive with a BP 120–139/80–89 mmHg (AHA, 2014b).

Strategies for complying with the DASH Diet— The DASH diet encompasses strict dietary guidelines that are healthy but stringent enough to reduce the risks of heart disease in the population if followed closely. The guidelines overlap with the U.S. Food Guide and the Healthy Eating Guidelines for Americans. In many ways the DASH diet is more stringent and therapeutic in decreasing BP. The DASH diet is generated from extensively studying the dietary factors that are most protective against hypertension. Historically, sodium and salt were thought to be the most influential factors in the etiology of hypertension. The DASH diet still encourages a target sodium intake of no more than 1500 mg per day, but now recognizes the importance of calcium, magnesium, potassium, and fiber in maintaining BP in a healthy zone. The goal is to achieve the nutrient intakes recommended in Table 4.1. NHLBI (2014).

Dietary Recommendations of the DASH Diet— Respecting the DASH diet guidelines means eating four to five servings of vegetables per day, an amount most of the American public is not likely to consume. Nevertheless, the standard DASH diet recommends vegetables that are rich in magnesium and potassium such as tomatoes, carrots, broccoli, sweet potatoes, and include greens of various types like spinach, kale, and cabbage, all good sources of fiber. One serving of leafy greens is 1 cup and so is ½ cup of cooked or raw vegetables. The idea is to creatively decrease meat portions by increasing the proportion of vegetables in a dish, for instance.

Fruits servings need to increase to four to five servings/day. One serving is understood to be 1 medium size fruit, ½ cup of fresh, frozen or canned (with no syrup or added sugar), or ½ cup of juice. Fruits need very little preparation, and so can be eaten on the run, as a dessert, or as a flavorful snack any time of the day. The snacking industry in the United States is controlled by large multinational corporations that flood the grocery stores with cheap non-nutritious snack foods; their goal is not to feed the population but to make a lot of money. Hence massive snacking publicity campaigns flood the media and the market place, whether on billboards, TV, Internet commercials, or magazines. The ads encouraging the consumption of soft drinks, candies, cakes, pastries, and chips are everywhere. The catastrophic consequences of these expensive campaigns is that the desire to eat fruit instead has gone down considerably since the 1980s.

Dairy intake needs to represent two to three servings a day as this is a major source of calcium, vitamin D, and protein. Indeed, three servings of milk contain 24 g of high quality protein, 900 to 1100 mg of calcium, and 120 to 300 IU of vitamin D. Milk is fortified in the United States following the standard of 40-100 IU/100 Kcals. One serving of dairy equates to 1 cup of milk (skim or 1%) and 1.5 oz-wt of cheese. Plain yogurt can be incorporated in the diet with much greater ease than sweetened yogurts.

Table 4.1
Daily Nutrient Goals Achieved by Following the DASH Diet

Prevent Hypertension

Total fat	≤27% of calories
Saturated fat	≤6% calories
Cholesterol	<150 mg/day
Protein	18% of calories
Carbohydrate	55% of calories
Std. Na DASH limit	<2300 mg/day
Low Na DASH diet	1500 mg/day
Potassium	4700 mg/day
Magnesium	500 mg/day
Calcium	1,250 mg/day
Fiber	30 g/day
Vegetables	4-5 servings/day
Fruits	4-5 servings/day
Whole grains	6-8 servings/day
Nuts, seeds, legumes	4-5 servings/day
Lean meats, poultry, fish	<6oz-wt/day

Source: AHA, 2006; NHLBI's Guidelines (2014) retrieved from https://www.nhlbi.nih.gov/health/health-topics/topics/dash/

For desserts, it is a good idea to mix frozen unsweetened berry blend fruit mixes into plain yogurt; this strategy maximizes dairy and fruit consumption without including any added sugar (**Figure 4.5**).

Grains need to be included to the tune of six to eight servings/day. One serving consists of ½ cup of cooked cereal, pasta or rice; it will also include 1 oz-wt of dry cereal, or 1 oz-wt of bread. The goal is to select whole grain products that are elevated in fiber. For instance, brown rice, whole grain pasta, and a high fiber cereal containing at least 5 g per serving are excellent choices for reaching the fiber intake goal of 30 g per day.

Lean meats, poultry, and oily fish are encouraged. The goal is to consume six or less servings per day. One serving has been defined as 1 oz-wt of meat or 1 egg. Eating enough protein in the diet has not been a problem for the American public in recent years because of the abundant meat consumed in the United States. However, the quality of that protein needs to be scrutinized more closely. As a rule the United States is not a great consumer of fish and seafood, but yet, history and research informs us that the omega-3 fats found in salmon, herring, and tuna, are highly protective against heart disease. Otherwise, leaner cuts of poultry and red meats need to be purchased more frequently. The goal here is to decrease saturated fat to ≤6% of calories (DASH diet standard).

Nuts, seeds, and legumes should be consumed more frequently and in greater abundance. The goal is to reach four to five servings per week. One serving is characteristically 1/3 cup of nuts, 2 tablespoons of seeds, or ½ cup of cooked legumes like lentils,

Table 4.2
ATP III Classification of Blood Cholesterol and Triglycerides

Bio measures	Goals mg/dl	Interpretations
LDL Cholesterol (mg/dl)	<100	Optimal
	100-129	Near optimal
	130-159	Borderline High
	160-189	High
	≥190	Very high
TTL Cholesterol (mg/dl)	<200	Desirable
	200-239	Borderline High
	≥240	High
HDL Cholesterol (mg/dl)	≥40	desired for men
	≥50	desired for women
	≥60	Ideal / protective against heart disease
Triglycerides (TG) (mg/dl)	<150	Desirable
	150-199	Borderline High
	200-499	High
	≥500	Very high

Source: Shils, M.E, 2006, p: 1896; AHA, 2006; NHLBI, 2005, 2001

Romano beans, kidney beans, navy beans, or soy beans. These are excellent sources of vegetable protein which, when complemented with grains in the diet, form complete proteins. These foods are rich in healthy oils that contain omega-3 and monounsaturated fatty acids. Legumes are also rich in magnesium and potassium, not to mention soluble fibers that help regulate serum cholesterol and decrease the risk of some cancers (Mayo Clinic, 2014; NAS, 2005b).

Fats and oils are valuable in regulating cardiovascular risks. The vilification of fats in recent years has led to the adoption of low fat weight loss diets by many individuals, and to a significant decline in healthy fat intakes. The DASH diet encourages consuming no more than 27% of calories as fat, and giving preference to monounsaturated fats. In order to maintain saturated fats to <6% of calories, it is imperative that individuals limit their intakes of meat, butter, cheese, whole milk, cream, and eggs, in addition to lard, solid shortenings, palm and coconut oils. There is also intent to restrict the trans fats by avoiding baked goods, crackers, and fried foods made from shortenings and hard margarines (NAS, 2005b).

To help the patient maintain a healthy weight, the recommendation is to consume five or fewer servings of sweets/week. This includes limiting the ingestion of regular soft drinks, candies, and pastries of various types.

Therapeutic Lifestyle Change (TLC)—The Third Report of the Expert Panel on Detection, Evaluation, and Treatment of High Blood Cholesterol in Adults (Adult Treatment Panel III or ATPIII) has updated a set of guidelines for interpreting blood cholesterol values (Table 4.2). These parameters have been adopted by the National Cholesterol Education Program (NCEP) as clinical guidelines that can help clinicians understand the severity of the hypercholesterolemia and better interpret the dietary and lifestyle guidelines the patients might have to follow in order to significantly alter the clinical risks.

The TLC has specific therapeutic dietary recommendations that can assist the patient in significantly reducing blood lipid values without medications. A minimal 5-10% weight reduction has been shown to be minimally needed to induce cardiovascular and type-2 diabetes risk reduction

Table 4.3
Nutrient Composition of the TLC Diet

Therapeutic Lifestyle Change

NUTRIENTS	RECOMMENDED INTAKE
Saturated Fat	<7% calories
Polyunsatured fat	Up to 10% calories
Monounsaturated fat	Up to 20% calories
Total fat	25-35% calories
Carbohydrates	50-60% calories
Fiber	20-30g/day
Protein	~15% calories
Cholesterol	<200mg/day
Grains	7 servings/day
Vegetables	5 servings/day
Fruits	4 servings/day
Lean meats, poultry, fish	≤5 oz-wt/day

Shils, M.E. et. al. (2006) p: 1898; AHA, 2006

(Wing et al., 2011) in combination with regular physical activity will benefit a patient if minimal dietary adjustments are made: saturated fat should be kept <7% of total kcals, total dietary cholesterol <200 mg per day, 2 g per day of plant stanols/sterols can be taken in combination with viscous soluble fibers (10-25g/day). The recommendations in Table 4.3 are the complete TLC dietary guidelines (Shils, et al., 2006).

4.5 CVD CASE STUDY-4.1: A 54-YEAR-OLD MALE WITH HYPERLIPIDEMIA

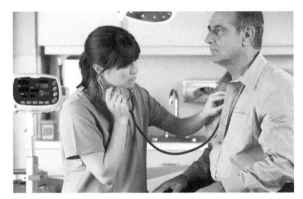

Credit © Monkey Business /Shutterstock.com

Figure 4.3 *A 54-year-old male being treated for hyperlipidemia.*

4.5.1 Presentation

John B. is a 54-year-old male business executive who came for his yearly checkup. He presented with no specific complaints and has maintained a clean bill of health for all of his life. The yearly review documented early hypertension, and hypercholesterolemia. His current weight: 183 lbs; his height: 5 feet 9 inches. Patient admits gaining 20 lbs over the last year because of excessive work-related travel. Consequently he has not been able to maintain his normal YMCA exercise commitment of 1 hour and 30 minutes at a frequency of 3 times a week.

4.5.2 Diet Assessment

His dietary habits changed slightly in that he has been eating out more because of traveling and business meetings. He is also drinking more beer and wine at meals compared to previous years. Otherwise his meals are balanced according to the MyPlate food guide.

4.5.3 Body Composition Assessment *usual*

Patient's BMI of 24 has been maintained stable for many years, which is within the healthy range of 18.5 to 24.9. His current 20 lb weight gain in the last year now results in a BMI equal to 27 which *current*

Table 4.4
Results of Medical Tests

TESTS	ACTUAL	GOAL
Glucose (mg/dl)	85	≤100
LDL Cholesterol (mg/dl)	135	<100
HDL Cholesterol (mg/dl)	38	≥60
BP mmHg	138/87	<120/80
Triglycerides (TG) (mg/dl)	179	<150
Total Cholesterol (mg/dl)	223	<200

Source: NCEP 2001 report JAMA 16 (285): 2486- 97

places him in the overweight category as he is situated within the range of 25 to 29.9. His waist circumference equals 41 inches. Because the circumference measure is >40 inches, he is at risk from mild visceral fat accumulation.

4.5.4 Medical Assessment

His blood biochemistry and general medical exam results are displayed in Table 4.4 above.

The profile indicates that John B. has hypertension, that blood glucose are normal, but that both LDL and total cholesterol are borderline elevated; HDL is too low, and triglycerides are borderline elevated and he is pre-hypertensive. This is an ideal candidate for diet therapy and lifestyle modification to help bring risk factors down.

4.5.5 Recommendations— Exercise Prescription

First, weight loss is the primary goal; losing 20 lbs over the next 40 weeks should bring his BP down. Aiming for slow but regular weight loss is possibly the ideal way to lose weight as it decreases the chances of weight regain after dieting. In addition, including an exercise schedule could possibly accomplish two things: first, accelerate the weight loss from heightened energy expenditure; second, exercise is known to increase HDL cholesterol in the blood. According to the *2008 Physical Activity Guidelines for Americans*, adults should minimally complete 150 minutes/week of moderate intensity aerobic exercise (2 hours 30 minutes) or 75 minutes/week of vigorous aerobic exercise (1 hour 15 minutes). Spread over five days that works out to be 30 minutes/day of moderate intensity exercise or 15 minutes/day of vigorous exercise. The patient should additionally dedicate two days or more/week to muscle strengthening exercise. This would help the patient lose the weight or at the very least prevent further weight gain (US DHHS, 2008). Physical activity can be increased, for improved health benefits, to 300 minutes/week of moderate intensity exercise or 150 minutes/week of vigorous aerobic exercise (US DHHS, 2008).

Diet Prescription: A restrictive diet would not be recommended as the patient only recently gained weight because of excess alcohol intake and more meals eaten in restaurants while traveling. The patient should simply be advised to drink only one alcoholic beverage with meals, and to consistently eat only 50-75% of the portion of food served at a restaurant; this will decrease total fat, saturated fat, and sodium in amounts sufficient to bring down LDLs and TGs. The rationale here is simply that larger portions are generally served in restaurants, and often the entrées are cooked in oil and salt to enhance the taste. It is a successful approach used to increase sales and repeat food acquisition behaviors. Otherwise, recommend that the patient continue to eat normally.

4.6 CVD CASE STUDY-4.2: A 38-YEAR-OLD MALE WHO SUFFERED A HEART ATTACK

Credit © Luis Louro /Shutterstock.com

Figure 4.4 *A 38-year-old heart attack victim.*

4.6.1 Presentation

Ryan V. is a 38-year-old pharmaceutical sales representative with a family history of heart disease. He suffered a heart attack about five weekends ago while doing home repairs. He underwent bypass surgery two weeks ago and is now stable.

4.6.2 Medical Assessment

The BMI reveals that Ryan is obese. There is a family history of heart disease and obesity; both his father and mother are obese. Prior to the heart attack his weight was 305 lbs; since the surgery he has lost 49 lbs resulting from a loss of appetite. Since the heart attack he stopped eating snacks, drinking beer and barely eats his regular meals. He admits experiencing a fear of eating as he perceived most of his dietary selections as being responsible for his heart attack. His chart information is described in Table 4.5.

This patient has serious hypertension that will require medication. His LDL cholesterol is high and will need to be managed by diet and statins (Stone et al., 2013). His total cholesterol is also high. The low levels of HDLs represent a second risk factor that can be related to smoking, elevated trans-fatty acid intake, low exercise, excessive weight, or consuming a lot of refined foods. The patient should be questioned about these possibilities (Harvard Publications, 2010). Mildly elevated triglycerides usually indicate abundant sugar consumption in the form of sucrose or fructose. Being overweight, smoking and consuming alcohol can also contribute to rising serum triglycerides (Malloy, 2007). Very elevated triglycerides tend to be the result of diabetes. The patient's TG levels are in the high risk range of 200 to 499 mg/dl. Considering his elevated fasting glucose (178 mg/dl) it would be reasonable to suspect type-2 diabetes mellitus. Weight loss will still be recommended in order to avoid having to prescribe oral hypoglycemic agents to control the blood sugars.

Table 4.5
Patient Chart Information

Ryan V... CHART INFORMATION		
Age: 38		
Current Weight: 256 lbs		
Usual Weight: 305 lbs		
Height: 5 feet 11 inches		
Patient lost 49 lbs since suffering a heart attack and going through bypass surgery		
TESTS	**ACTUAL**	**GOAL**
*Glucose (mg/dl)	178	≤100
LDL Cholesterol (mg/dl)	165	<100
HDL Cholesterol (mg/dl)	36	≥60
BP mmHg	162/92	<120/80
Triglycerides (mg/dl)	221	<150
Total Cholesterol (mg/dl)	309	<200

Source: NCEP 2001 report JAMA 16 (285), 2486- 97; American Diabetes Association (2011) Standards of Medical Care in Diabetes—2012 Diabetes Care. Suppl. 1, S11-63. * Fasting plasma glucose

4.6.3 Body Composition Assessment

The dietitian used skinfold calipers to determine the percent body fat using a four site approach: Biceps, triceps, subscapular and supra-iliac. Using specific tables, a total fat of 47% was established.

Waist circumference = 56 inches

His weight: 256 lbs; height 5 feet 11 inches; BMI= 256 lbs × 0.454 lbs/kg / $(71 \text{ inches} \times 0.0254 \text{ meters/inch})^2$

The BMI= 116.22 kg/ $(1.803 \text{ meters})^2$ = 35.75 He is therefore classified as "obese Class-2."

This assessment indicates that the patient is over fat, and has an overabundance of highly atherogenic visceral fat, as indicated by the waist circumference greater than 40 inches.

4.6.4 Lifestyle Assessment

A review of the patient's chart reveals that the patient works long hours and is often traveling nationally. He covers a large territory and so admits to being in motels and hotels most of the time. He refers to his lifestyle as stressful as he is unable to partake in leisurely exercise except on weekends when he is home with his wife and two children. He reports going out to eat in the restaurant to give his wife a break when he is home on weekends. He rates his activity level as low.

Dietary Assessment—The dietitian sat down with the patient and questioned him about his regular eating habits prior to the heart attack. She used a Usual Food Intake assessment in order to evaluate his usual caloric consumption (Table-4.6), and a Food Frequency Questionnaire (FFQ) to ascertain the quality of his diet. The dietitian also assessed the patient's caloric requirements based on his initial reported weight prior to the heart attack (305 lbs). She used the Gerrior equation for total energy expenditure:

For men:

$$TEE = [864 - (9.72 \times \text{Age-years})] + [PA \times ((14.2 \times \text{wt.kg}) + (503 \times \text{ht. meters}))]$$

$$TEE = [864 - (9.72 \times 38))] + [1.12 \times (14.2 \times 138.47 \text{ Kg}) + (503 \times 1.803 \text{ meters}).$$

$$TEE = [864 - 369.36] + [1.12 \times (1966.27 + 906.91)]$$

$$TEE = [494.64] + 1.12 (2873.18)$$

$$TEE = 3712.60 \sim 3713 \text{ kcals}$$

Table 4.6

Usual Food Intake Record

PATIENT NAME: Ryan V USUAL FOOD INTAKE		
FOODS CONSUMED	QUANTITY CONSUMED	PLACE
BREAKFAST: TIME		
Never consumes breakfast		
Coffee (Starbucks Grande + cream)	3 cups (900 ml) or 30fl-oz	Kitchen & car

AM SNACKS TIME:		
Chocolate bar (Snickers®) Reg. size	105.4g (3.76 oz-wt)	Office/car
Pepsi Cola(Reg.)	12fl-oz (355 ml can)	
Donut (Dunkin donut jelly-filled)	3	
LUNCH TIME:		
Pepsi Cola® (Reg.)	12fl-oz (355 ml can)	restaurants
French Fries (McDonald's®)	Large	
Lay's plain® Potato Chips (bag)	5oz bag	
PM SNACK TIME:		
Pepsi Cola® (Reg.)	12 fl-oz (355 ml can)	McDonald's
Big Mac®	1(7.6oz-wt)	
DINNER TIME:		
Sirloin Steak (Logan's Roadhouse®)	16 oz-wt (448g)	restaurant
Beer--Indian Pale Ale (IPA)	20 fl-oz	
Baked Potato (Logan's Roadhouse®)	1 whole	
Butter (salted)	4 pats	
Pasta salad	2 cups	
ENEVING SNACK TIME:		
Orville Reddenbacher...butter popcorn	9 cups popped	
Pepsi Cola® (Reg)	20 fl-oz (591 ml)	

NUTRIENT BREAKDOWN OF USUAL FOOD INTAKE

Kcals recommended: 3713 kcal/day (3342–4084 Kcals/day)	Kcals eaten: **6700 kcals**
Carbohydrates recommended: 557 g/day (60% DRI Kcals) (418–603 g)	Carbohydrates eaten: **770 g**
Protein recommended: 139 g/day (15% DRI Kcals) (93–325 g)	Protein eaten: **185 g**
Fat recommended: 103 g (25% DRI Kcals) (83–144 g)	Fat eaten: **320 g**
Total Maximal Sugar: <186 g (20% DRI Kcals)	Total Sugar eaten: **272 g**
Total Maximal Sodium: <2400 mg/day	Sodium eaten: **5505 mg**

Calories measured using the www.myfitnesspal.com website.

The usual food intake record (Table 4.6) reveals that prior to the heart attack the patient usually consumed 6700 Kcal/day or 80.4% in excess of his DRI calories. This amount of calories could justifiably cause significant weight gain.

Of particular interest was the alarming amount of fat regularly consumed, representing 44.3% of his caloric intake, an amount that far exceeded the recommended macronutrient range of 25 to 35%, proposed by the TLC diet. Also carbohydrate intake far exceeded his recommended healthy range of (418–603 g). His protein intake was acceptable, but his total sugar intake—most of which was added sugar—exceeded his maximal allowance of 186g/day. Since maximal added sugar is <10% of calories, or 93 g, his actual intake can therefore be considered alarmingly elevated. This elevated sucrose intake can, in part, explain the elevated triglycerides (Mallow, 2007). Fiber intake was 45 g/day which on the surface appears to meet the daily requirement of 30 g. However, when broken down per 1000 kcals to be consistent with AND guidelines, the patient is actually consuming 6.92 g/1000 Kcals, which is far less than the recommended 14 g/1000 kcals. It can be concluded therefore, that the patient's diet is poor in fiber content.

4.6.5 Diet Prescription

He has been referred to a dietitian who is a member of cardiac rehabilitation services; she will be reviewing his usual diet and teaching him the DASH diet. The first step consists of prescribing a weight maintenance diet that will first stabilize his weight at his current weight of 256 lbs, while taking into account his low activity factor. Since the heart attack the patient has lost a lot of weight through a fear of eating and poor appetite. It is important at this point to introduce him to healthy eating, reassuring him that it is safe to eat. Once his weight has stabilized, then a more thoughtful plan for slow and gradual weight reduction in combination with increased physical activity may be introduced. Again, the dietitian used the previous TEE equation to assess his daily caloric needs at his current weight of 256 lbs:

For men:

$$TEE = [864 - (9.72 \times \text{Age-years})] + [PA \times ((14.2 \times \text{wt.kg}) + (503 \times \text{ht. meters}))]$$

$$TEE = [864 - (9.72 \times 38)] + [1.12 \times (14.2 \times 116.22 \text{ Kg}) + (503 \times 1.803 \text{ meters}).$$

Table 4.7
Diet Prescription for Weight Maintenance

Macronutrients	Diet prescribed	Goal
Carbohydrates	462g (1847 Kcals)	55%
Protein	151g (605 Kcals)	18%
Fat	101g (907 Kcals)	27%
Total Calories	3359 Kcals	3359 Kcals
Saturated fat	<22g	<22g
cholesterol	<150mg	<150mg
Sodium	<2300 mg	<2300 mg

$$TEE = [864 - 369.36] + [1.12 \times (1650.32 + 906.91)]$$

$$TEE = [494.64] + 1.12 (2557.23)$$

$$TEE = 3358.74 \sim 3359 \text{ kcals}$$

So then, the total daily calories necessary to maintain this patient's weight at 256 lbs for a short transition period and assuming a low activity factor is: 3359 kcals/day. The goal is to prescribe a low fat and a high carbohydrate intake rich in complex starches that are high in fiber and consistent with DASH dietary standards.

Using the Acceptable Macronutrient Distribution Range (AMDR) established by the Institute of Medicine (I.O.M) and the DASH diet guidelines as guideposts the dietitian prescribed 55% of calories as carbohydrates, 18% as protein, and 27% as fat. Her intent was to maintain saturated fat <6% of calories and dietary cholesterol <150 mg/day. Taking into account the elevated BP, the dietitian recommended keeping sodium intake to <1500 mg/day. Consistent with the full rationale governing the DASH diet, the dietitian also recommends a diet rich in foods abundant in fiber, magnesium (Mg), potassium (K), and calcium (Ca) as they are helpful in controlling BP.

The dietitian's diet prescription for weight maintenance is found in Table 4.7.

There are a number of foods that will need to disappear from his usual menu while he is on the maintenance diet. This means that the food items are non-negotiable; he needs to eliminate them from his normal fare in order to break away from the addictive nature of these foods: soft drinks (regular and diet), fast food, and unhealthy snack foods (chips, donuts, chocolate bars). These foods are important contributors of total and saturated fats, and therefore need to be removed from the menu, and replaced by a broad variety of fruits. Here, innovative approaches will need to be taken into account to get these fruits consumed. This will be rather difficult in the beginning because of the patient's taste preference for foods high in sugar, salt, and fat.

Innovative strategies involve the use of plain yogurt, high fiber breakfast cereals, and food carvings. Here are some suggestions:

1 Plain low fat yogurt added to frozen berry blend fruits that have no added sugar. Spoon out 1/3 cup of berry blend fruit into a small plastic container, top with ½ cup of plain yogurt, sprinkle 1 tablespoon of granola, and then seal the lid and store in the refrigerator. These are quick snacks that can be easily accessed. This will increase the patient's calcium and antioxidant intake (Figure 4.5).

2 For breakfast, 1 cup of high fiber cereal consisting of 1/3 cup of Kellogg's Brand Buds®, 1/3 cup of old fashioned whole oats, 1/3 cup of dried fruits (raisins, dates, cranberries, and apricots). Serve with skim milk or yogurt.

3 A smoothie can also be a creative method of consuming vitamin and mineral-rich foods. Mix together in a blender ½ cup of yogurt (low fat), 1 medium banana, and ½ cup of thawed frozen berries (blackberry, strawberry and cherry mix). Blenderize until smooth, pour in a container that can be sealed and refrigerated.

Credit © Africa Studio /Shutterstock.com

Figure 4.5 *Fresh & frozen fruits mixed with yogurt.*

Image courtesy of David Bissonnette

Figure 4.6 *Carved melon swan with fresh fruit.*

4 Carve out the center of a watermelon with your children—get them to participate even minimally in the process—and fill it with chunks of pineapple, apples, grapefruit, oranges, cantaloupe, strawberries, and blueberries. Mix in about 1/2 cup of pure orange juice. Their involvement will entice them to want to eat what they participated in creating. Gardening with the children also produces increased interest in consuming vegetables. Serve at meal time so that the whole family can learn to love fruits. This is especially attractive to children (Figure 4.6).

After it becomes clear that the patient's appetite is good and his weight stabilized, a slow weight loss diet can be introduced. Rapid weight loss should be discouraged as the evidence appears to indicate that weight regain is almost inevitable (Mann et al., 2007). The only non-surgical approaches that seem to work so far are mild calorie restrictions in combination with regular exercise. The dietitian aimed for about ½ lb weight loss/week from diet restriction alone. Given that a 3500 kcal deficit in a week equates to a 1 lb weight loss, and that this can be achieved with a 500 kcal deficit per day, it is therefore logical that a 250 kcal per day restriction would result in about about a ½ lb of weight loss per week. Hence, the diet prescription for slow weight loss would amount to a 3109 kcal per day diet.

The exercise prescription should not involve rigorous high-intensity workouts, but should be of long duration but mild in intensity. The patient does not have an extensive history of exercise.

5 Walking 3 mi/hr at moderate pace for 2 hours/day for a total of 3 days/week will cause an expenditure of 0.025 kcal/lb/min. This 256 pound man will therefore be able to expend 768 kcals/2 hours of walking. In combination with his dietary restriction of 250 kcals/day, this patient will be able to afford 1.16 lbs of weight loss/week. Below, the calculations are outlined.

A caloric restriction of 250 kcals/day equates to 1750 kcals/week (250 kcal x 7 days). Energy expenditure from walking = 768 kcals/2 hours of waking. If patient walks 3 times per week the total energy expenditure from walking = 2304 kcals/week (3 days x 768 Kcals). The total energy deficit arising from both caloric restriction and exercise equates to 4054 kcal (1750 kcals + 2304 kcals). Since a 3500 kcals deficit equals 1 lb of weight loss, then a 4054 kcal deficit/week will equal a loss of 1.16 lbs/week (4054/3500 kcals).

As this patient loses weight, the risk indicators of heart disease such as waist circumference, hyperglycemia, hyperlipidemia, and BP should greatly diminish. In addition, regular exercise should allow HDLs to rise.

CHAPTER 4 PRACTICE QUESTIONS

1 A 45-year-old female patient presents with a BP= 141/93mmHg and LDL: 165mg/dl, a waist circumference=38 inches, TG= 184 mg/dl, and an HDL= 43 mg/dl. What would you conclude about this patient?

2 A 55-year-old male patient presents with BP= 138/88 mmHg; TG= 167 mg/dl; HDL= 32 MG/DL; waist circumference: 56 inches, BMI=42. Provide the four main diagnoses that reflect this patient's condition.

3 A 67-year-old male presents with a weight=295 lbs, a height = 5 feet and 11 inches and a sedentary activity level; BP= 156/92. Biochemistry indicates LDL= 178 mg/dl; HDL= 31 mg/dl; TG= 487 mg/dl; waist circumference 58 inches; BIA analysis reveals 49% body fat. Assess this patient and prescribe a diet that best fits his condition

REFERENCES

[1] AHA. (2015). *The American Heart Association diet and lifestyle recommendations*. Retrieved from http://www.heart.org/HEARTORG/HealthyLiving/HealthyEating/Nutrition/The-American-Heart-Associations-Diet-and-Lifestyle-Recommendations_UCM_305855_Article.jsp#.V30b0UorKUk

[2] AHA. (2014). *About metabolic syndrome*. Retrieved from https://www.heart.org/HEARTORG/Conditions/More/MetabolicSyndrome/Metabolic-Syndrome_UCM_002080_Sub-HomePage.jsp

[3] AHA. (2014b). *Prevention and treatment of high blood pressure*. Retrieved from: http://www.heart.org/HEARTORG/Conditions/HighBloodPressure/PreventionTreatmentofHighBloodPressure/Prevention-Treatment-of-High-Blood-Pressure_UCM_002054_Article.jsp#.V30dQ0orKUk

[4] AHA. (2006). Diet and Lifestyle Recommendations Revision 2006. A scientific statement: From the American Heart Association Nutrition Committee. *Circulation* 114, 82-96. Retrieved from http://www.heart.org/idc/groups/heart-public/@wcm/@adv/documents/downloadable/ucm_312853.pdf

[5] Balanescu, S. et al. (2010). Systemic inflammation and early atheroma formation. Are they related? *Maedica (Buchar)* 5(4), 292–301.

[6] Bissonnette, D.J. (2014). *It's all about nutrition: Saving the health of Americans*. Lanham, MD: University Press of America, 232.

[7] CDC (2015). Physical Activity Facts. Retrieved from the Centers for Disease Control & Prevention website July 6, 2016: http://www.cdc.gov/healthyschools/physicalactivity/facts.htm

[8] CDC (2014). Prevalence of Overweight and Obesity Among Children and Adolescents: United States, 1963–1965 Through 2011–2012. retrieved from the Centers for Disease Control & Prevention on July 6, 2016: http://www.cdc.gov/nchs/data/hestat/obesity_child_11_12/obesity_child_11_12.pdf

[9] CDC (2014b). Fruit and Vegetable Consumption of U.S. Youth, 2009–2010. retrieved from the Centers for Disease Control & Prevention on July 6, 2016: http://www.cdc.gov/nchs/data/databriefs/db156.htm

[10] CDC (2011). Fruit and Vegetable Consumption Among High School Students—United States, 2010. Retrieved from the Centers for Disease Control and Prevention website July 6, 2016: http://www.cdc.gov/mmwr/preview/mmwrhtml/mm6046a3.htm

[11] Danaei, G., Finucane, M.M., Lu, Y., et al. (2014) Cardiovascular disease, chronic kidneydisease, and diabetes mortality burden of cardiometabolic risk factors from 1980 to 2010: a comparative risk assessment. *Lancet Diabetes Endocrinol*;2: 634–47

[12] Grundy, S. Nutrition in the management of disorders of serum lipids and lipoproteins. In *Modern nutrition in health and disease* 10th edition. New York: Lippincott, Williams, & Wilkins, 1076-1094.

[13] Harvard Health Publication. (March 2010). *HDL: The good but complex cholesterol*. Retrieved from http://www.health.harvard.edu/newsletters/Harvard_Heart_Letter/2010/March/hdl-the-good-but-complex-cholesterol

14 Hegele, R.E. (2009). Overview of lipoprotein metabolism. *Nature Reviews Genetics* 10, 109-121

15 Lozano, R., Naghavi, M., Foreman, K., et al. (2012). Global and regional mortality from 235 causes of death for 20 age groups in 1990 and 2010: A systematic analysis for the Global Burden of Disease Study 2010. *Lancet*; 380: 2095–128

16 Malloy, M.J., & Kane, J.P. (2007). Disorders of lipoproteins metabolism in: D.G. Gardner and D. Shoback, eds *Greenspan's basic and clinical endocrinology*. New York: McGraw-Hill/Lang, 770-795.

17 Mann, T. et al. (2007). Medicare's search for effective obesity treatments: Diets are not the answer. *Am Psychol.* 62(3), 220-33.

18 Mayo Clinic. *Nutrition & healthy living—DASH Diet: Healthy eating to lower your BP.* Retrieved from http://www.mayoclinic.org/healthy-living/nutrition-and-healthy-eating/in-depth/dash-diet/art-20048456?pg=1

19 National Academy of Sciences (NAS), Institute of Medicine, Food and Nutrition Board. (2005). Die*tary reference intakes for energy, carbohydrate, fiber, fat, fatty acids, cholesterol, protein, and amino acids (macronutrients).* *Chapter 12: Physical Activity page: 880* Available at: http://www.nap.edu/catalog/10490/dietary-reference-intakes-for-energy-carbohydrate-fiber-fat-fatty-acids-cholesterol-protein-and-amino-acids-macronutrients

20 National Academy of Sciences (NAS), Institute of Medicine, Food and Nutrition Board. (2005b). *Dietary reference intakes for energy, carbohydrate, fiber, fat, fatty acids, cholesterol, protein, and amino acids (macronutrients). Chapter 11: Macronutrients and healthful diets.* Available at http://www.nap.edu/catalog/10490/dietary-reference-intakes-for-energy-carbohydrate-fiber-fat-fatty-acids-cholesterol-protein-and-amino-acids-macronutrients

21 National Cholesterol Education Program (NCEP). (2001). Expert panel on detection 3rd report on the evaluation and treatment of high blood cholesterol in adults. *JAMA* 16 (285), 2486-97.

22 National Heart, Lung and Blood Institute (NHLBI). (2014). *What is the DASH Eating Plan?* Retrieved from https://www.nhlbi.nih.gov/health/health-topics/topics/dash/

23 National Heart, Lung and Blood Institute (NHLBI). (2014b). *What is atherosclerosis?* Retrieved from https://www.nhlbi.nih.gov/health/health-topics/topics/atherosclerosis/

24 National Heart, Lung and Blood Institute (NHLBI) (2005). *High blood cholesterol: What you need to know.* Retrieved from http://www.nhlbi.nih.gov/health/resources/heart/heart-cholesterol-hbc-what-html

25 National Heart, Lung and Blood Institute (NHLBI). (2001). *ATP-III At-a-Glance: Quick desk reference.* Retrieved from http://www.nhlbi.nih.gov/health-pro/guidelines/current/cholesterol-guidelines/quick-desk-reference-html

26 Roger, V.L., et al. (2012). AHA Statistical update: Heart disease and stroke statistics 2012. *Circulation* 125, e2-e220. Retrieved from http://circ.ahajournals.org/content/125/1/e2.full

27. Sachdeva, A., Cannon, C.P., et al., (2009). Lipid levels in patients hospitalized with coronary artery disease: An analysis of 136,905 hospitalizations in *Get With The Guidelines Am Heart J*;157:111-7.e2

28 Shils, M.E. et al. (2006). Part VIII Appendix Table A-9-b-1-a ATP-III Classification of LDL, Total and HDL Cholesterol. In *Modern nutrition in health and disease* 10th edition. New York: Lippincott, Williams, & Wilkins, 1896.

29 Shils, M.E. et al. (2006). Part VIII Appendix Table A-9-b-6-a Nutrient Composition of the TLC Diet In: *Modern nutrition in health and disease 10th edition.* New York: Lippincott, Williams, & Wilkins, 1898.

30 Stone, N.J. et al. (2014). ACC/AHA guideline on the treatment of blood cholesterol to reduce atherosclerotic cardiovascular risk in adults. *Journal of the American College of Cardiology* doi:10.1016/j.jacc.2013.11.002 Retrieved from https://circ.ahajournals.org/content/early/2013/11/11/01.cir.0000437738.63853.7a.full.pdf

[31] U.S DHHS (Department of Health & Human Services) (2008). *The 2008 physical activity guidelines for americans, chapter 4: Active adults.* Retrieved from http://www.health.gov/paguidelines/guidelines/chapter4.aspx

[32] Whitlock, G., Lewington, S., Sherliker, P., et al. (2009). Body-mass index and cause-specific mortality in 900 000 adults: Collaborative analyses of 57 prospective studies. *Lancet*; 373: 1083–96.

[33] Wing, R.R. et al. (2011). Benefits of modest weight loss in improving cardiovascular risk factors in overweight and obese individuals with type 2 diabetes. *Diabetes Care*; 34(7): 1481–1486.

CHAPTER 4 ANSWERS

1 hypertensive, hyperlipidemic, metabolic syndrome

2 pre-hypertensive, borderline high TGs, metabolic syndrome, extreme obesity class-3

Patient has a BMI = 41 and is therefore extremely obese class-III. Patient has also an unhealthy percent body fat that exceeds 23%. Patient has metabolic syndrome as TGs are greater than 150 mg/dl, BP >or equal to 130/85, HDL <40 for men, and the waist circumference is > or equal to 40 inches. Also the LDLs are considered HIGH and will require cholesterol lowering medication in addition to dietary control.

Patient should be prescribed a DASH DIET and a weight loss diet that will bring her percent body fat down from 49% to less than 23%. Perhaps 18% would be an eventual goal. Now it should be possible to establish the goal weight (see chapter 3). The goal weight = 183 lbs (295 lbs × (100−49%)= 150 lbs lean mass. Goal weight= 150 lbs lean mass/0.82 (assuming 18% fat)= 183.5 lbs) and will require a 111.5 lbs weight loss. This can be prescribed over several years. For instance a 55.75 lbs weight loss per year over 2 years. Clinicians should then determine the caloric deficit per day (55.75 lbs × 3500 kcal/lbs divided by (365 days) which amounts to 535 kcal deficit per day over 2 years.

5

The Problem of Diabetes Mellitus

© donskarpo/Shutterstock.com

5.1 THE PREVALENCE OF DIABETES

Health care in the United States is changing dramatically as the number of young obese and type-2 diabetic patients is exploding. The consequences are terrifying as the medical system is now under siege by patients who are more complicated and more time-consuming to manage. There has been an exponential growth of the diabetic population in the United States in recent decades, going from 5.6 million cases in 1980 to 17.4 million cases in 2007, and more recently jumping to an astounding 29.1 million American adults or 9.3% of the population in 2012 according to the National Diabetes Statistics 2014 report (ADA, 2014). This represents a 420% increase over a 32 year period. Others (Menke et al. 2015) have more recently estimated the prevalence of diabetes to be as high as 12–14% among US adults. But most surprisingly, there are an additional 37–38% of the adult population who are classified as pre-diabetic. In total, then, there are between 49–52% of the US adult population who are either suffering from diabetes or are at risk of developing diabetes (Menke et al., 2015). Epidemiologists have identified the top 10 states forming the diabetes belt with an adult diabetes prevalence that varies between 10–12%; the highest prevalence is exclusively found in the southern states, except for Ohio.

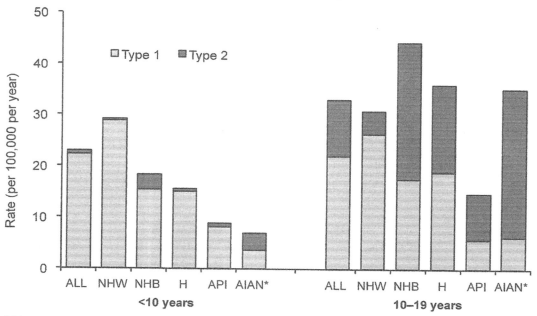

Rate of new cases of type 1 and type 2 diabetes among people younger than 20 years, by age and race/ethnicity, 2008–2009

NHW=non-Hispanic whites; NHB=non-Hispanic blacks; H=Hispanics;
API=Asians/Pacific Islanders; AIAN=American Indians/Alaska Natives

Figure 5.1 *Prevalence of Types 1 and 2 Diabetes among U.S. youth.
(Source: CDC, National Diabetes Statistics Report, 2014)*

Notably, Alabama and West Virginia are the two states with the highest prevalence of adult diabetes in the nation.

While it is understood that 90 to 95% of all diabetes mellitus cases are type-2, it is important to note that the prevalence of type-2 diabetes is still rare in children less than 10 years of age (0.4 per 100,000 cases). The most numerous cases in the youth, nevertheless, have been observed in the 10–19 year olds (8.5 cases per 100,000) (Figure 5.1).

Type-2 diabetes, a disease that was historically documented in adults over the age of 40 is now, in fact, growing in prominence among children and adolescents. A study by Pinhas-Hamiel and co-workers (1996) reported that the incidence of newly diagnosed type-2 diabetes in children jumped from 2 to 4% in 1982 to 16% by 1994, which when stratified represented 33% of the 10–19 year-olds. In the United States the prevalence of type-2

diabetes becomes more accentuated if cases are stratified by ethnicity. Indeed, increases of between 8% and 45% have been observed among recently diagnosed diabetic children and adolescence, depending on their ethnic heritage (American Diabetes Association, 2000). The American Indian children ages 10–14 are particularly vulnerable; the prevalence of type-2 diabetes among Pima Indians for instance, rose 200% between the decades 1967–1976 and 1987–1996, and 150% in the ages 15–19. Also, the Asian Pacific Islanders, Hispanics, and the Non-Hispanic blacks ages 10–19, residing in the United States between 2002–2005, are also specifically at risk, as close to 50% or more of the newly diagnosed diabetics in these groups tend to suffer from type-2 diabetes (Figure 5.1) (CDC, 2011).

In the UK the story is most notable because researchers found that the risk of type 2 diabetes is 13.5 times greater among Asian than white children (Ehtisham et al., 2000; Drake et al., 2002). They also found that girls are 1.7 times more likely than boys to have type-2 diabetes. Worldwide, the prevalence of diabetes has more than tripled since 1985. Dr. Zachary Bloomgarden (2004), an endocrinologist affiliated with Mount Sinai School of Medicine in New York, writes in the April 2004 issue of *Diabetes Care*: "*The topic has become a clinical and health economic priority, with important implications for an increasing health care burden throughout the world.*"

Looking ahead, the Centers for Disease Control and Prevention predict that by the year 2034 there will likely be an estimated 44.1 million diabetics, representing over a 24-year period, a 69.61% prevalence increase, which is projected to be accompanied by a shocking 197.34% increase in direct medical expenses. There is no doubt that the financial burden on the system will be difficult to bear and could ultimately cripple the American Health Care system (Pinhas-Hamiel, 1996; Zeitler, P. et al., 2001). The alarming medical costs only make sense if one considers the treatment costs for many chronic diseases that are attached to diabetes. Indeed, a much bleaker picture gets drawn over the American landscape. Consider that the *2011 National Diabetes Fact Sheet*, published by The Centers for Disease Control and Prevention, reveals that the total costs associated with diagnosed diabetes in 2007 amounted to $174 billion, consisting of $116 billion in direct medical costs and $58 billion in indirect costs involving disabilities, work loss, and premature mortality. Between 2007 and 2012, the total management cost of diabetes in the U.S. jumped 41%, reaching $245 billion (Menke et al., 2015).. These kinds of medical problems become costly but also time-consuming to manage since the life course of diabetes is plagued with crippling secondary conditions and diseases.

The increased prevalence of diabetes in the United States and worldwide is so alarming that it has health care providers struggling with this epidemic as so many of the young appear to be suffering from chronic illnesses at younger ages thereby increasing their risk of developing long-term health problems by middle age (Wilde, 2004).

Type-2 diabetes has risen concurrently in prevalence with obesity, which has been steadily increasing since the mid-1970s. Close to 70% of American adults are either overweight or obese, and approximately 34% of adults are obese (Ogden, et al., 2006). Internationally, the problem is also becoming quite concerning as Scotland reported 25-26% obesity among adults in 2008, and Greece exhibited 26-28% obesity in 2001-2003 (International Obesity Task force).

The consequences of a nation becoming significantly overweight and obese are numerous and profound. This growth is unrelenting, sweeping adults and children into inescapable lives of chronic and debilitating diseases, and unspeakable suffering. Can a nation support this level of illness? What can we do to halt its progress? One thing is certain, and that is we must intervene in haste less we end up ruining the health of our youth and the very fabric of our society.

5.2 TYPE-1 DIABETES

A broader look at diabetes may be necessary at this stage in order to fully appreciate the complexity of this devastating disease. Historically, the most prevalent form of diabetes among children and young adults has always been type-1 or juvenile-onset diabetes, however, type-1 diabetes only represents 5% of the people who have diabetes according to the American Diabetes Association. It is rather type-2 diabetes that is gaining prominence, representing between 90 to 95% of all diabetic cases (Anderson, 2006).

Type-1 diabetes occurs when the beta cells of the pancreas can no longer produce sufficient insulin, a hormone that is secreted in the blood, and which allows serum glucose to enter the cells where it is converted to energy (Figure 5.2). Without insulin, the sugar remains high in the blood after a person consumes complex starches or simple sugars. In type-1 and type-2 diabetics, blood sugars remain elevated for extended periods of time after carbohydrate intakes, a phenomenon known as **hyperglycemia**.

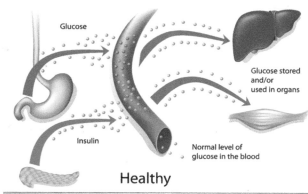

Healthy

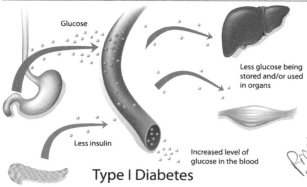

Type I Diabetes

© *Kendall Hunt Publishing Company*

Figure 5.2 *Cause of type-1 diabetes.*

[handwritten: Detenction]

The diagnosis of either type-1 or type-2 diabetes is based on the detection of hyperglycemia using accepted blood glucose concentration standards in various settings:

[handwritten: Hyperglycemia (condition)]

1 When random blood glucose concentrations are≥ 200 mg/dl.

2 When fasting blood glucose levels are ≥126 mg/dl after an eight-hour fast.

3 When blood glucose concentrations following an oral glucose tolerance test (OGTT) of a 75 g glucose challenge are≥200 mg/dl two hours after the challenge.

4 When the hemoglobin A1C is ≥6.5% (ADA, 2011; Anderson, 2006).

There are usually six classic symptoms found concurrently with hyperglycemia in patients with diabetes mellitus.

[handwritten: Symptoms of hyperglycemia]

1 Polyuria: frequent urination.

2 Weight loss: because glucose is not converted to calories.

3 Polydipsia: increased and excessive thirst.

4 Ketoacidosis: acidosis produced by excessive ketone body production.

5 Ketonuria: ketone bodies in the blood reach dangerously elevated levels and spill over into the urine.

6 Glycosuria: glucose concentrations in the blood surpass the renal threshold of 200 mg/dl and begin to spill into the urine.

Of equal importance, at the clinical level, is the detection of a sub-clinical form of diabetes mellitus called pre-diabetes or Impaired Glucose Tolerance using blood screening among patients who are at risk. *[handwritten: Prediabetes]*

Screening for pre-diabetes allows health practitioners to begin early prevention strategies such as weight loss and controlling carbohydrate intake. The criteria for establishing pre-diabetes are featured here and were established in 1979 by the World Health Organization and the National Diabetes Data Group (Ramlo-Halsted, & Edelman, 2000; ADA, 2011): *[handwritten: Prediabetes criteria]*

1 A fasting blood glucose of 100-125 mg/dl

2 Post-prandial plasma glucose of ≥140 mg/dl to 199 mg/dl 2 hrs after drinking a 75 g glucose solution

3 Hemoglobin A_1C: 5.7–6.4%

The importance of detecting and controlling elevated blood glucose is paramount in getting the upper hand on the long-term devastating effects on the vascular systems, the eyes, and the kidneys. The problem with chronically elevated blood glucose levels is the eventual cell and tissue damage that takes place through **glycosylation**. This process is characterized by glucose non-enzymatically attaching to proteins and producing advanced glycation end products (AGEs). When these compounds accumulate, they can damage the integrity of cells and blood vessels thereby leading to macro and microvascular complications in addition to diabetic neuropathies. These problems invariably lead to poor

[handwritten: Glycosylation]

circulation, which slows the healing of injuries such as foot wounds for instance. The neuropathies translate into poor sensitivity thus preventing the recognition of pain as a key signal that injury has occurred. This usually means an important delay in treating these injuries, which lead to infections and ultimately to foot injuries becoming gangrenous, and thus requiring amputation. It is estimated that about 25% of diabetics have a life time risk of developing foot ulcerations, which frequently become infected, requiring hospitalization in 31% of diabetic cases (CDC, 2014b; Wu et., 2007).

It becomes clear that the financial implications that are tied to the secondary effects of type-2 diabetes such as heart disease, retinopathies, neuropathies, nephropathies, and amputations are likely to be financially cumbersome to a health care system that is already overburdened by a populace plagued by chronic disease.

Indeed the 2011 CDC report indicates that of those individuals with diabetes, about 60% to 70% have mild to severe forms of nervous system damage and that 60% of non-traumatic lower-limb amputations occur in people with diabetes. In addition, diabetes accounted for 44% of new cases of kidney disease in 2008 (CDC, 2014).

Though hyperglycemia is the primary disordered outcome of both types of diabetes, each type remains nevertheless distinct in terms of the etiology of these elevated levels of blood glucose. The main physiological impairment in type-1 diabetes is the necrosis or destruction of the pancreatic beta cells that can no longer produce insulin. The only medical treatment available to counter this problem is the subcutaneous injections of insulin along with a well-controlled diet. The reason behind the death of these cells is not clear, but scientists believe that it may be caused by an autoimmune disorder, environmental toxins, or an infection of some sort. The question is: what makes certain individuals more susceptible than others to such viral attacks?

There appears to be some inherited risk factors that can heighten the chance of a person developing type-1 diabetes, but overall, the genetic influence remains relatively weak. In fact, even if both parents have type-1 diabetes the child has between a 1 in 4 and a 1 in 10 chance of also developing the disease (ADA, 2013). By contrast, in type-2 diabetes the primary defect is **insulin resistance**, which also leads to hyperglycemia because of a loss of balance between

insulin sensitivity and secretion (Bloomgarden et al., 2004). The important difference with type-1 is that in type-2 diabetes, even though insulin can still be produced by the pancreas, it is not very effective in allowing glucose to move into the cells because there are insufficient insulin-receptors imbedded within the muscles. In that sense, the body becomes insensitive or resistant to insulin. In type-2 diabetes there can even be hypersecretion of insulin resulting in hyperinsulinemia in response to high sugar intakes, as seen with frequent soda intake and insulin resistance. Over time, a high demand for insulin can exhaust the beta cells thus leading to the possibility of insufficient insulin production. This type of diabetes, in contrast to type-1, is more heavily associated with genetics in that it is more intricately tied to family lineage and history. In fact, if both parents have type-2 diabetes the child has a 1 in 2 chance of also developing diabetes—a genetic association that is much stronger than in type-1 diabetes. This blood glucose disorder has been historically referred to as adult onset diabetes because it was most often diagnosed in adults over the age of 45.

5.3 TYPE-2 DIABETES

The cause of type-2 diabetes is currently unknown, but body fat appears to be an important determinant in causing insulin resistance. Indeed, between 80 to 90% of people with type-2 diabetes are obese, and it appears that it is specifically the visceral fat accumulation or the android-type of obesity that can promote atherogenesis or the buildup of atheromas in the vascular lining, thus leading to atherosclerosis.

The impact of excessive weight in the form of fat is even more worrisome among American Indian children among whom, 40% of the less-than-10-year-old children are classified as overweight or obese (Styne, 2010). In addition, Styne (2001) describes a glucose metabolism that is 40% slower in obese children compared to normal weight children. This is the pre-clinical manifestation of insulin resistance, also called pre-diabetic, which occurs when the tissues of the body begin to lose their sensitivity to the action of insulin, thus preventing the blood glucose from entering the cells and producing energy (Figure 5.3). This culminates in a rise in the blood levels of glucose, which is referred to as hyperglycemia, and it is this kind of diabetes that is called type-2 diabetes.

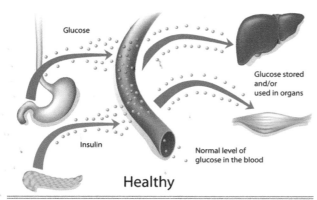

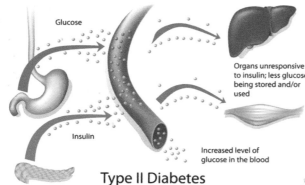

© *Kendall Hunt Publishing Company*

Figure 5.3 *Cause of type-2 diabetes.*

Professor Matsuzawa, abdominal fat

The mechanism was previously reported by Professor Yuji Matsuzawa from Osaka University in Japan. His team showed that accumulated abdominal fat causes impaired glucose metabolism, lipid disorders, and hypertension (Matsuzawa et al., 2008). They report, in their review, that the visceral adipocytes may link directly to the liver via the portal circulation. This fat mass is readily prone to lipolysis, causing abundant free fatty acids (FFA) to flood the portal circulation leading to the liver and thus producing abundant release of VLDLs from the liver into the blood circulation. This lipoprotein circulates to muscles, vascular endothelium, and adipocytes where it deposits its fatty cargo and eventually becomes the more atherogenic lipoprotein called LDL or low density lipoprotein (Kuriyama, 1998). This is likely the mechanism that enhances atherogenesis in obese patients with visceral fat accumulation. However, Dr. Matsuzawa completes the story further, by demonstrating that visceral adipose tissue tends to abundantly secrete bioactive compounds called adipocytokines, which have been tied to thrombogenic vascular disease. Importantly,

VLDC fatty cargo
LDL

they identified an adipocytokine produced mostly by peripheral adipocytes called adiponectin that has been found to be protective against heart disease and diabetes. This is because it appears to induce the production of anti-inflammatory cytokines and thus protect the body against disease. Interestingly, adiponectin is abundantly found in the circulation, when visceral fat reserves are low and suboptimal when there is an accumulation of visceral fat in obesity (Matsuwaza et al., 2004). They proposed that visceral fat accumulation may prevent the release of adiponectin from subcutaneous adipocytes because of the inhibitory effect that comes from abundant secretion of tumor necrosis factor alpha, a nefarious cytokine secreted from visceral adipocytes (Matsuzawa, et al., 2008).

5.4 CAUSES OF TYPE-2 DIABETES

Dr. Lucy Candib, a professor of family medicine and community health at the University of Massachusetts' Medical School, explains the multiple factors that come into play in the etiology of type-2 diabetes. The factors that are the most influential in promoting diabetes to such important degrees that it is likely to afflict entire populations and nations are outlined here:

Lucy's promoting type-2 diabetes.

1 Fetal and maternal explanations
2 The thrifty genotype
3 The nutritional transition
4 The health impact of urbanization and immigration
5 Social attributions and cultural perceptions of increased weight
6 The impact of globalization (Candib, 2007).

The prominent use of high fructose corn syrups in sodas is now being considered as an important source of the obesity and diabetes crisis. In the 1900s fructose coming essentially from fruits represented only 15 g/day or 4% of total calories. Before World War II, fructose consumption had jumped to 24 g/day and then to 37 g/day by 1977. However, with the introduction of high fructose corn syrup into sodas by 1994, fructose consumption sharply rose to 55 g/day. Currently, when stratified by age, it is estimated that

Consumption of high fructose corn syrup.

adolescents consume 73 g/day. The consumption of fructose has in fact increased five-fold since the early 1900s and doubled since the 1980s. If one considers high fruit juice intake in addition to sodas, the total fructose consumption per capita can be adjusted upwards to 194 g/day or a total of 156 lbs per year (Lustig, 2010).

The initial interest in fructose was fuelled by the understanding that intakes of fructose do not increase blood glucose levels. So it seemed like the ideal sweetener for diabetics. However, elevated fructose consumption can drive denovo hepatic lipogenesis or in other words new synthesis of fat from fructose. In a sense the overabundance of fructose consumed through sodas can metabolically overwhelm the mitochondrial TCA cycle, resulting in the abundant deposits of fat in the liver thus producing steatosis and inflammation. In fact, when carbohydrate intakes exceed the energy expenditure of the body, hepatic fat synthesis increases 10-fold (Aarsland, et al., 1996). Most importantly, both fructose and ethanol metabolically produce reactive oxygen species (ROS), which increases the risk of hepatocellular damage. In response to this overabundance of sugar being consumed in the United States, the American Heart Association recommends cutting sugar consumption by more than 50%. Health practitioners and dietitians needs to revise current sugar intake standards as it is clear that things are getting out of hand. Indeed, high fructose corn syrup does not act like other sweeteners. There is now evidence emerging that chronic intakes of fructose may actually prevent dopamine clearance from the brain, thereby stimulating continued caloric intake despite regenerated energy stores (Anderzhanova, et al., 2007).

5.5 THE TREATMENT OF TYPE-2 DIABETES

The increasing numbers of overweight and obese patients are mostly immigrants, low income and people of color who consult doctors more frequently for weight problems, but who also have undiagnosed hypertension, diabetes, and metabolic syndrome with significant dyslipidemia (Candib, 2007). These patients become medical train wrecks, tying up much of the medical practitioners' time with complicated issues such as high blood pressure and heart

disease in addition to all of the medication management problems associated with these diseases.

We are dealing with an insulin-resistant diabetic epidemic that is resulting from obesity and lack of exercise (Bloomgarden, 2004). Logically then, it comes as no surprise that one of the most important goals in the treatment of type-2 diabetes is to lose weight and significantly decrease abdominal fat, as it will greatly assist in diminishing the risks of heart disease and insulin resistance. In fact, increased physical activity will heighten insulin sensitivity thus decreasing fasting blood glucose in children (Schmitz et al., 2002).

An effective treatment to reduce the size of visceral fat is frequent exercise. This is based on the notion that caloric expenditure through aerobic exercise requires fat as the main fuel to support activities such as brisk walking, swimming, running, and hiking. The goal is to engage in exercise routines that occupy significant time commitments such as three hours, and to expend significant calories. A study by Schoeller and colleagues (1997), published in the *American Journal of Clinical Nutrition* (Schoeller et al., 1997) established, using doubly-labeled water, that sizable daily caloric expenditures needed to be attained that equated to 11–12 kcal/kg/day in order to better manage body weight. The National Weight Control Registry estimates that members who have successfully lost weight and kept if off regularly engage, on average, in exercises that expend 2682 kcal/week (ADA, 2009). Also, the Federal Physical Activity Guidelines for Americans 2008 recommend that, in order to achieve significant health benefits, people should engage in 300 minutes per week of exercise of moderate intensity. This represents a five hour weekly commitment to disciplined exercise in order to burn sufficient calories and lose significant weight.

Schoeller's recommendations represent a demanding expenditure that many would have trouble meeting on a daily basis. For instance, a man weighing between 155-210 lbs would need to expend between 1050 to 1144 kcal/day in order to successfully lose weight; this is the equivalent of 5400 to 8000 kcal/week, depending on body weight. This demanding recommendation is nevertheless relatively consistent with the guidelines provided by the **Federal Physical Activity Guidelines for Americans 2008,** which advocates for moderately intense exercise occupying 300 minutes per week. In this setting, a man weighing 189 lbs who runs at a speed of 6 miles/hour—this equates to burning 0.072 kcal/lb/min—for one hour five times per week would in fact expend 4082 kcal/week. Likewise, for individuals who are older and/or compromised by physical disabilities, who cannot engage in rigorous forms of activities, walking becomes a gentler alternative. Hence regular walking at a speed of 3 miles/hour (0.0249 kcal/lb/min), a man weighing 189 lbs would have to walk 3 hours/day or 9 miles per day in order to expend 5929 kcal/week, a total caloric expenditure that becomes meaningful. This is also consistent with the Dietary Guidelines for American.

A more recent recommendation to increase physical activity may not be strictly tied to losing body fat, but also to augmenting lean body mass or muscle mass. An observational study by UCLA medical researcher, Preethi Stikanthan (Srikanthan, and Karlamangla, 2011), concluded that higher muscle mass was associated with a lower risk of diabetes. This is an important study that detracts from the single-minded focus of weight reduction, through dietary caloric restrictions alone, and emphasizes the notion of improved fitness as well. The therapeutic strategy of caloric restriction has not historically been shown to be effective in causing obesity prevalence to decline (Fagot-Campagna, 2001; Mann et al., 2007) and consequently does not appear to be effective in diminishing the prevalence of diabetes.

A more realistic goal in managing overweight and obese children is to aim for weight maintenance or even delaying weight gain (Bloomgarden, 2004) while focusing at guiding the children and parents towards healthier food choices over the long term, in addition to increasing physical activity.

The main conclusions drawn from the 90% weight loss success stories, filed with the National Weight Control Registry, are that individuals with weight problems need to embrace low fat and high carbohydrates diets; they need to regularly eat breakfast, become physically active, and frequently monitor their weight. To be part of the Registry, the more than 3000 subjects had to have lost and maintained 30 lbs of weight for more than one year. Their commitment to weekly exercise is anything but small. On average, they report expending 2682 kcal/week

which involved daily walking schedules of 4 miles/day, 7 days per week. This level of exercise tends to be too taxing for most adults who have professional and family responsibilities (AND, 2009). Bloomgarden (2004) points out several limiting factors in diet management that prevent more positive and measurable outcomes such as weight loss. First, he describes a clear decrease in fitness level among obese and overweight children, thus making physical activity more difficult and continued weight gain more likely. Second, the mean 0.6 kg weight gain that tends to occur prior to and during holidays, that affects both children and adults, is described as a phenomenon that is not offset by the mean 0.1 kg in weight loss that follows after the holidays. Third, physicians tend to consider obese patients as noncompliant to medical directives, leading them to not address weight problems during patient visits (Hiddink et al., 1999).

5.5.1 Public Health Strategies

However, let there be no mistake, obesity is the most significant driver of the diabetes epidemic in the United States and around the world, and there needs to be a long focus on resolving the obesity epidemic according to Dr. Lucy Candib, a researcher in the Department of Family Medicine and Community Health at the University of Massachusetts. Her work suggests that neither enhanced clinical management of diabetes nor improved screening strategies for pre-diabetics will impact death rates from diabetic complication or the enormity of this epidemic (Candib 2007). Dr. Candib advances that for successful outcomes in battling the obesity and diabetic epidemics, *"clinicians need to be involved at a broader level,"* implying that physicians should be engaged in community collaborations that establish relationships, for instance, between health clinics and local fitness centers, thereby fostering safer and easier patient access to exercise programs. It is a strategy that helps front line health care providers assess the sociological and economic factors that define the realities that limit patients' abilities to comply with medical directives. In doing so, physicians are adopting more of a syndemic orientation that sees human affliction intertwined with living conditions and public strength. This approach essentially advocates for a strong public health initiative in combatting obesity and diabetes. As such, physicians need to communicate with community groups and foster ties between their patients and meaningful organizations such as churches, neighborhood associations, and radio stations. In this setting, the clinicians become the instruments for change and education at the community level, teaching, as it were, along with the dietitian, about healthy nutrition, spearheading efforts to rid junk food from local vending machines, schools, community centers, and replace them with healthy choices. They can, along with the dietitian, organize community gardens, farmer markets, and activity programs for children (Candib, 2007).

Nevertheless, **public health** strategies for combatting the rise of type-2 diabetes are plagued with difficulties because multifactorial causes associated with the disease make it difficult to manage. Indeed, weight loss and increased physical activity are difficult outcomes to reach given the complexity of causes tied to overeating and sedentary lifestyles. **The Bienestar School-based Diabetes Prevention Program**, aimed at implementing a total of 93 educational sessions at 27 elementary schools in Texas, is one such effort that intended to implement changes in health behavior among a network of social support personnel that affected 1,420 Hispanic kids. These sessions involved the nutrition education of friends and classmates in the home, classroom, and school cafeteria. Attempts were made to educate cafeteria staff and parents in order to decrease saturated fat levels in food in addition to increasing fruits and vegetables in the diet of the children. The study consisted of separating the students into control and intervention groups. Researchers found, after one year, that the intervention group experienced greater physical activity, and an increase in caloric intake, that was consistent with increased exercise, in addition to a higher BMI. The study also showed a significant decrease in fasting blood glucose in the intervention group but virtually no clinically significant change in body fat (Travino et al., 2003). Other studies, attempting to change school foodservices and introduce healthy lifestyles to the students, failed to show significant changes in the body weight and blood sugar levels, despite some declines in soft drink consumption. However, exercise-based intervention studies such as the **Trim and Fit** program implemented in Singapore between 1992 and 2000, reported that the prevalence of obesity in primary and secondary schools fell from 16 to 14% (Toh & Cutter, 2002). A Japanese exercise intervention study caused the prevalence of overweight in junior high school students to decline 3% in boys and 8% in girls (Kida et al., 2001). These were important studies that magnify the difficulties with changing eating habits, especially in children. They have acquired taste preferences that are conditioned by the high fructose content of the North American diet and that result from habituation and dependence on certain foods. (Lustig, 2010).

5.5.2 Prenatal Nutrition

In the United States, it is the blacks, Hispanics, Native Americans, and the poor or immigrants that represent the groups most vulnerable to the epidemics of obesity and type-2 diabetes. In fact, obesity and diabetes are regarded as markers of inequalities in health in the United States and in other developed nations. These are the very groups that struggle to change dietary habits and exercise more regularly, and who do not consistently take prescribed medications, thus leading to worsening medical problems. From the clinical view point, the difficulties in getting these groups to slim down have been assigned to behavioral decisions or individual characteristics, but recently, there is mounting evidence that compliance with medical directives could be more difficult than initially thought because of a constellation of factors. In a review paper, Dr. Lucy Candib (2007) writes: *"Nevertheless, the epidemic increase in obesity and diabetes around the world suggests that factors far beyond individual behaviors must be at work to explain this recent global process."*

Indeed, one of the most meaningful findings in recent years is the key observation that low birth weight babies, resulting from adverse intrauterine environments, can be predisposed to obesity and metabolic syndrome later in life (Yajnik, 2004). The explanation for this paradox resides with the **thrifty gene phenotype** hypothesis, formulated by the geneticist Dr. James Neel in 1962 from his interest in diabetes mellitus. It was a novel concept that introduced the idea that the phenotype of a fetus could be altered in utero in order to accommodate impoverished conditions during pregnancy such as undernutrition. This phenomena is sometimes coupled with the "Fetal-Maternal Explanations," (Candib, 2007), that highlight the intricate symbiosis that exists between the mother and her unborn child. It has been hypothesized that this relationship is strengthened through specific epigenetic changes (Thrifty Genotype hypothesis) that program the babies of undernourished mothers to survive famine-like conditions by efficiently synthesizing fat stores once they are born. Epidemiological evidence collected from Dutch and Finnish women, who were starved between 1934 and 1945 (Baker et al., 2005; Roseboom et al., 2000, 2001), supports such a notion. Indeed, researchers documented the high prevalence of low birth babies born of these undernourished mothers, and the subsequent rapid weight gain afterwards between 2 and 11 years of age, with higher incidences of coronary artery disease and insulin resistance reported in adulthood (Candib, 2007). Hence, it has been proposed that infants born underweight may likely have a thrifty gene that would permit a rapid and abundant synthesis of fat, once food becomes available, in order to compensate for the low body weight and a possible environment of food scarcity. This gene, however, tends to backfire in a world of abundant and unrestricted calories as we currently see in the North American context. In this environment, the body becomes an efficient synthesizer of fat and eventually produces excessive amounts of body fat thus resulting in obesity, type-2 diabetes, and metabolic syndrome in adulthood (Caballero, 2005). It is common, then, to see premature or underweight babies developing insulin resistance in late adolescence when weight begins to get packed on—the result of rapid fat synthesis directed from the thrifty genotype. In early adulthood, further weight gain becomes apparent as activity levels drop with more academic and professional responsibilities concurrently with unabated food and alcohol intake, and a worsening of dietary practices. In this context, insulin resistance worsens and transitions into type-2 diabetes by early adulthood. In other family environments, low birth weights translate into early fat deposition and obesity in childhood, as poor nutrition and lack of physical activity dominate households. Presently, there are more numerous cases of insulin resistance being reported by clinicians among children older than age 10, a worrisome scenario, as this invariably can lead to an adult population prone to obesity and diabetes (Candib, 2007). However, the notion of a Fetal-Maternal relationship that conditions the intrauterine environment to produce sick children is not limited to suboptimal nutrition environments. In fact, the late 20th and early 21st centuries produced environments of great food abundance that

can also affect the unborn babies negatively. In that sense, the Fetal-Maternal relationship becomes the vector for activating both the Thrifty Phenotype in instances of undernourished mothers and the "hefty fetal phenotype" when obese mothers continue to overeat during pregnancy (Dyck et al, 2001). In this latter context, babies are born overweight, and already preconditioned to develop insulin resistance early in life (Candib, 2007).

A viable solution that needs to be seriously considered is the implementation of programs that influence prenatal nutrition practices at a public health level by using both healthy concepts of nutrition and socioeconomic status of the families. Strategic efforts also need to be placed on promoting breast feeding programs, as it is currently understood that lower rates of obesity are found among breastfed children. According to the CDC 2010 report, 43% of U.S. mothers breastfeed through to 6 months, while only 22.4% are still breastfeeding at 12 months (CDC, 2010), indicating that still significant effort needs to be invested in popularizing this practice.

Internationally, the story appears to be different, since it is not necessarily the poor who are becoming obese, but rather those individuals who have access to cheap food and inexpensive vegetable oils. It is in fact mostly the immigrants, the low income, and minority communities that are disproportionately struggling with obesity and diabetes. The primary reason that developing and emerging nations like Mexico are afflicted with diabetes and obesity is related to global trade policies that lead to the production of cheap cash crops such as corn and soy from which are derived cheap vegetable oils and sugar. These cash crops tend to be produced by large corporate farms, a practice which has invariably led to the closure of the smaller farms as they can no longer compete (Candib, 2007).

Moreover, the industrialization and mechanization of nations influenced by the mass media complex creates urbanization and immigration. Indeed, these become economic driving forces that attract workers from all around the world seeking opportunity and prosperity. However, this trend also creates large urban centers that become **obesogenic environments** that foster poverty, decreased physical activity, and an explosion of fast food restaurants that essentially prey on the poor. These urban environments

More Food than the babie needs.

Industrialzation and mechanization

foster abundant and easy access to high calorie foods within a social environment that offers limited access to nutritious foods but easy embrace of sedentary forms of entertainment. In this context, parents, more concerned about the safety issues in playgrounds, prefer to see their kids playing X-box in the safety of the home, rather than playing in the unsafe parks and neighborhoods. This has a significant impact on the overall energy expenditure of the kids on a daily basis (Candib, 2007).

In addition to obesogenic environments fostering a heavier population, more recent advances in environmental toxicology, have introduced the concept of "obesogens," contaminating our environments and bodies, and possibly facilitating an increased lipogenesis (Janesick, and Blumberg, 2011). Obesogens are dietary, pharmaceutical and industrial compounds that have insidiously made their way into our environments and contaminated our biological system (Holtcamp, 2012). Wendy Holtcamp, a freelance science writer reviewed the literature, looking for whether there was convincing evidence that obesogens represented that much sought after environmental trigger. She writes: " Chemical pesticides in food and water, particularly atrazine and DDE (dichlorodiphenyldichloroethylene—a DDT breakdown product), have been linked to increased BMI in children and insulin resistance in rodents." This newer model of weight gain needs to be followed closely.

The time is short and so we must act in haste to reverse these epidemics. It does appear that government support for community health interventions is needed, if we are, as a society, going to get the upper hand (Green, et al., 2012). In the end, the prevention rather than the treatment of disease appears to be a more affordable and beneficial alternative. But how can we begin the process? The notion that the genetics load the gun, but that the environment pulls the trigger describes fairly accurately how poor dietary and exercise habits can set up genetically-predisposed individuals to developing obesity and type-2 diabetes. By exposing our children to a toxic food environment early on, we trap them into developing a sort of habituation to food, based on heightened taste sensations that create food preferences based on addiction and which clearly competes with the much milder tastes found in fruits and vegetables (Lustig, 2010). Is there any wonder that most of our young in the United States fail to meet

minimum requirements for fruits and vegetables? For nutritionists and epidemiologists, this translates into something of a nightmare since these food habits are, in fact, almost impossible to reverse in the young. Programs focused on prenatal nutrition and teaching mothers how to purchase food and feed their children are possibly the strategies that may carry the greatest impact.

5.6 TYPE-2 DIABETES CASE STUDY-5.1: A 32-YEAR-OLD WOMAN WITH HYPERGLYCEMIA

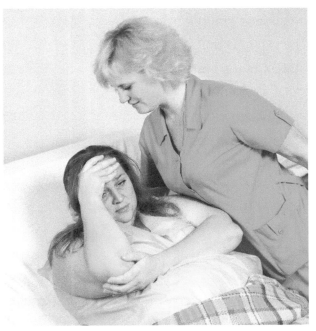

© TijanaM/shutterstock.com

Figure 5.4 *Angela K is a 32-year-old secretary diagnosed with hyperglycemia.*

5.6.1 Presentation

This female patient is a 32-year-old secretary who presents with a recent increase in fatigue, hirsutism, frequent urination (polyuria), extreme thirst (polydipsia), and numbness in her feet and hands. Her weight is 333 lbs; her height: 5 feet 5 inches. She complains of sleep apnea, and of pain in her joints and lower back.

Table 5.1

Patient Chart Information

Angela K... CHART INFORMATION		
Female Age: 32		
Current Weight: 333 lbs		
Usual Weight: 357 lbs		
Height: 5 feet 5 inches		
Patient lost 24 lbs trying to diet in the last year. She has a long history of chronic dieting; she has lost and regained weight frequently		

Diabetes (handwritten)

TESTS	ACTUAL	GOAL
*Glucose (mg/dl)	304	≤100
Insulin (μIU/ml)	9.1	<5.0
LDL Cholesterol (mg/dl)	230	<100
HDL Cholesterol (mg/dl)	27	≥50
BP mmHg	189/98	<120/80
Triglycerides (mg/dl)	475	<150
Total Cholesterol (mg/dl)	380	<200

*Source: NCEP 2001 report JAMA 16 (285), 2486- 97; American Diabetes Association (2011) Standards of Medical Care in Diabetes—2012 Diabetes Care. Suppl. 1, S11-63. * Fasting plasma glucose*

5.6.2 Medical Assessment

Patient's BP is very high and will require antihypertensive medication. Patient complains of extreme fatigue concurrently with polyuria, polydipsia, hyperglycemia, and hypertriglyceridemia, all of which suggest diabetes mellitus. Type-2 diabetes has been diagnosed based on the extreme form of obesity she appears to suffer from, the hyperinsulinemia, and the very noticeable hirsutism on her face and back. Her lipid panel, body weight, and BP indicate Metabolic Syndrome.

5.6.3 Body Composition Assessment

The patient's BMI suggests extreme obesity also called morbid obesity or super-obesity.

$$BMI = Weight\ (Kg)/[Height\ (meters)]^2$$

$$BMI = 151.19Kg/\ (1.65\ meters)^2 = 55.5$$

Waist circumference measurement = 65 inches

Percent body fat measured by bioelectrical impedance assessment (BIA) = 57% fat.

5.6.4 Lifestyle and Diet Assessment

This female patient has a long history of obesity that began around 10 years of age. Both parents are classified as class-2 obesity. She has one brother who is obese and one sister who does not have a weight problem. The patient leads a sedentary life with no real physical activity, except the habitual movements of standing and sitting typically associated with office work. Her total energy expenditure

(TEE) is calculated using the Gerrior equation, (equation-1 below):

1- TEE For women:

$$TEE = [387 - (7.31 \times Age_{\text{-years}})] + [PA \times ((10.9 \times wt._{\text{-kg}}) + (660.7 \times ht._{\text{meters}}))]$$

$$TEE = [387 - (7.31 \times 32) + [1 \times (10.9 \times 151.18Kg) + (660.7 \times 1.65 meters)]$$

$$TEE = [150.08] + [2738 \text{ kcal}] = 2888 \text{ kcals}$$

$$TEE = 2888 kcal/day$$

Her usual food intake (Table 5.2) reveals an excessive amount of calories (**5241 kcals**), which represents a 81.5% calorie excess. Because of the excessive soft drink consumption, she consumes a little over 1 lb of sugar/day. Her fat intake (181g) (Table 5.2), can be looked at from two perspectives: first, as a percentage of her actual caloric intake of 5241 kcal/day. From the outset, it appears that she is only consuming 31.08% of her actual caloric intake as fat, which is within the accepted macronutrient fat range of 20–35%. However, when it is expressed as a percent of her daily caloric need (DRI), which is the correct approach, it jumps to 56.4% of her body's requirement for calories. This is indeed a substantive fat load for her body size and caloric expenditure, and does support her abnormal blood lipid profile. Indeed, LDL and total cholesterol are reported as high. Moreover, her blood glucose, insulin, and triglycerides are consistent with the high sugar intake recorded in her usual food intake. Hyperinsulinemia and hyperglycemia are typically found in cases of type-2 diabetes since it is more of a problem of insulin resistance, rather than insulin insufficiency.

5.6.5 Recommendations

This patient will require first, a weight stabilizing diet that will prevent further weight gain. The purpose of this diet is to get the patient acquainted to healthy eating without the added stress of caloric deprivation. The focus here is to negotiate the elimination of a few critical foods that are greatly affecting her diabetes and lipid profile. The restriction should include soft drinks, donuts, and cakes. Rather than strictly focus on eliminating food, it is psychologically helpful to speak about introducing healthy foods as well. In this instance, vegetables and fruits will need to be slowly introduced. The dietitian needs to recognize that there is quite a high likelihood of these new foods being rejected by the patient. Patience and creativity is called for in this case. Using recipes that are healthy and tasty is essential to the success of this approach. Remember that the dietitian's role is to reeducate the patient and re-sensitize the taste buds to a new standard, which is a task that will take time.

Caloric Recommendation The patient's new caloric intake should be consistent with her sedentary need of 2888 kcal/day. Because the patient has metabolic syndrome, the diet will need to be broken up in accordance with the DASH diet and TLC guidelines:

1 Fat: 27% of calories/day
2 Protein: 18% of calories/day
3 Carbohydrates: 55% of calories/day
4 Saturated fat <6% of calories/day
5 Monounsaturated fats (MUFAs): up to 20% of calories/day
6 Polyunsaturated fats (PUFAs): up to 10% of calories
7 Sodium: <1500 mg/day

The patient should follow this diet for a period of four to eight weeks. During this time, body weight should not increase significantly; there may be a noticeable loss of weight in the first two to three weeks, the consequence of no longer eating junk foods and not being able to fully comply with the new dietary directives—the tendency is to eat less than what is prescribed.

The second step is to establish a new caloric prescription that will favor slow weight loss (0.5–1.0 lbs/week). The calculations pertinent to this new objective are below:

Since 1 lb weight loss arises from a 3500 kcal deficit, then a ½ lb loss would equal a 1750 kcal deficit (3500 kcal/2). Since the goal is to achieve this rate of weight loss over one week, then the daily caloric deficit would equal 250 kcal/day (1750 kcal/7 days). Similarly, a 1 lb weight loss would require a 500 kcal/day deficit (3500 kcal/7 days). The diet prescription for weight loss could vary between **2388–2638 kcal/day**.

The third step should involve setting a healthy goal weight while taking into account the percentage of body fat. This is important because the patient should ideally not lose any lean body mass while following the diet. The body composition assessment, conducted by BIA calculated a 57% body fat or fat mass (FM). Using the two compartment model (Total Body Weight = FFM (Fat Free Mass) + FM (Fat Mass)) it is possible to determine the FFM otherwise known as the lean body mass. It is the latter that should not decrease in size during dieting. The calculations are outlined here:

$$TBW\ (Total\ Body\ Weight) = FFM + FM$$

$$FFM = TBW - FM$$

Since the percent body fat= 57% then the FM is equal to: 0.57 x 333 lbs= 189.81lbs.

This means then that the FFM would equal:

$$FFM = 333\ lbs - 189.81\ lbs = 143.19\ lbs.$$

Remember that this mass must remain constant throughout the weight loss process. The objective at this stage is to aim for a percentage of body fat that is considered healthy (See the obesity chapter for acceptable percent body fat ranges for women). It is best for this patient to aim for the upper healthy range for percentage of body fat; that would be 35% body fat. The equation to determine a healthy body weight goal for this patient is written out below:

$$Goal\ Weight\ (GWT) \times (\%\ FFM) = 143\ lbs$$

$$GWT \times (100\text{-}35\%) = 143\ lbs$$

The premise of this equation is that even once the patient reaches that new body weight, the amount of FFM will not be different than in the original obese body weight, and thus will still be 143 lbs, but will represent 65% of the new GWT. So then, the new goal weight is calculated as follows:

$$GWT = 143\ lbs/65\%$$

$$Weight\ goal = 143\ lbs/0.65$$

$$GWT = 220lbs$$

The plan is to allow the patient to lose a total of 113 lbs over an undetermined amount of time. If the diet prescription is for ½ lb of weight loss/week, then it will take 226 weeks to lose this weight or 4.35 years. Aiming for a 1 lb weight loss/week would require 113 weeks or 2.17 years. Although these calculations are mathematically correct, the reality is that weight loss does not normally take place following this kind of linear model. The general rule is that while a 500 kcal/day deficit should afford 26 lbs over a six month period, only 20 lbs of weight loss actually occurs. Similarly, while a 1000 kcal/day deficit should permit 2 lbs of weight loss/week and 52 lbs of lost weight after six months, the reality is that only 25 lbs is normally recorded (Williamson et al., 1992). The same kind of proportional adjustment can also be made for one year of weight loss.

Practically applied, this adjusted non-linear weight loss model approximates a very different weight loss timeline. A patient weighing 193 lbs who needs to reach a goal weight of 150 lbs, needs to lose 43 lbs within a year. The 3500 kcal linear model would estimate that a 500 kcal/day deficit should take 301 days (0.82 years) to reach her goal (3500 kcals x 43 lbs divided by 500 kcals/day). By contrast, the non-linear model forecasts reaching the GWT in 392 days (1.08 years). Similarly, a 1000 kcal/day deficit should afford a 2 lbs loss/week and attaining the GWT in 150 days, using the linear model (3500 kcals x 43 lbs divided by 1000 kcals). The non-linear model estimates reaching the GWT in 314 days (43 lbs x 6 months (182.5 days) / 25 lbs).

Table 5.2
Usual Food Intake Record

FOODS CONSUMED	QUANTITY CONSUMED	PLACE
PATIENT NAME: ANGELA K	**USUAL FOOD INTAKE**	
BREAKFAST: TIME		
Never consumes breakfast		
AM SNACKS TIME: 10:00 AM		
Pepsi Cola(Reg.)®	30fl-oz (900 ml bottle)	Office/car
Little Debbie Coco cream mini cakes®	8 individual mini cakes	At work
LUNCH TIME:		
Pepsi Cola (Reg.)®	20fl-oz (600 ml can)	Cafeteria
Fish & Chips Medium – Jack in the Box®	2 Medium servings	Restaurant
PM SNACK TIME:		
Pepsi Cola (Reg.)®	20fl-oz (600 ml can)	Dunkin Donuts
Dunkin Donut Muffin-Banana chocolate chips®	1 complete muffin	
DINNER TIME:		
Domino's meat lover pizza®	8 medium slices	Order out
Pepsi Cola (Reg)®	20fl-oz (600ml)	
EVENING SNACK TIME:		
Pepsi Cola (Reg)®	20fl-oz (600 ml)	Home

NUTRIENT BREAKDOWN OF USUAL FOOD INTAKE	
Kcals recommended: 2888 kcal/day (2599–3177 kcals/day)	Kcals eaten: **5241 kcals**
Carbohydrates recommended: 433 g/day (60% DRI kcals) (325–469 g)	Carbohydrates eaten: **823 g**
Protein recommended: 108 g/day (15% DRI kcals) (72 g–253 g)	Protein eaten: **80 g**
Fat recommended: 80 g (25% DRI kcals) (64–112 g)	Fat eaten: **181 g**
Total Maximal Sugar: <144 g (20% DRI kcals)	Total Sugar eaten: **504 g**
Total Maximal Sodium: <2400 mg/day	Sodium eaten: **5911 mg**

Calories measured using the www.myfitnesspal.com website

CHAPTER 5 PRACTICE QUESTIONS

1 A 57-year-old female patient presents with a weight of 243 lbs; a height or 5 feet 4 inches, and a sedentary lifestyle; her FPG: 138 mg/dl; her A1C: 6.2%; her body fat: 42%. Assess whether this patient is non-diabetic, pre-diabetic, or diabetic based on her blood biochemistry; determine the patient's TEE using the Mifflin St. Jeor equation and mean sedentary activity; next establish her goal body weight if the objective is to bring her body fat down to 23%. You will teach her healthy eating principles and book an appointment to see her in 1 month.

2 The same 57-year-old patient presents to clinic three months later with A1C: 6.4%, FPG: 135 mg/dl; LDL: 168 mg/dl; HDL: 48 mg/dl; TG: 189 mg/dl; BP: 158/92; current body weight: 249 lbs. Assess her condition, and prescribe a diet that would best assist her for the next month.

REFERENCES

1. Aarsland, A. et al. (1996). *J. Clin. Invest* 98, 2008-2017.

2. ADA (American Diabetes Association). (2014). *Statistics about diabetes.* Retrieved from the ADA website on March 15, 2016: http://www.diabetes.org/diabetes-basics/statistics/?referrer=https://www.google.com/

3. ADA (American Diabetes Association). (2011). Position Paper: Standards of medical care in diabetes. *Diabetes Care* 34 (suppl. 1), S11–61.

4. ADA (American Diabetes Association). (2013). *Genetics of diabetes.* Retrieved from the ADA website march 15, 2016: http://www.diabetes.org/diabetes-basics/genetics-of-diabetes.html?referrer=https://www.google.com/

5. ADA (American Diabetes Association). (2000). *Diabetes Care.* 23, 381–9.

6. Academy of Nutrition and Dietetics (AND). (2009). Position Paper on Weight Loss Diets. *J. Amer. Diet. Assoc.* 109(2), 330–346.

7. Anderson. J.W. (2006). Diabetes mellitus: Medical nutrition therapy. In: *Modern nutrition in health and disease* 10th edition, (Shils, M.E. et al eds) Baltimore MD: Lippincott, Williams, & Wilkins, 1043–1066.

8. Anderzhanova, E. et al. (2007). *Am. J Physiol. Regul. Integr. Comp Physiol* 293, R603-R611.

9. Barker DJ, Osmond C, Forsen TJ, Kajantie E, Eriksson JG. (2005). Trajectories of growth among children who have coronary events as adults. N Engl J Med;353(17):1802–1809.

10. Bloomgarden, Z. et al. (2004). *Diabetes Care* 27(4), 998–1010.

11. Caballero, B. (2005). *N.Engl.Med.* 352 (15), 1514–1516.

12. Candib, L.M. (2007). Obesity and Diabetes in Vulnerable Populations: Reflection on Proximal and Distal Causes. *Annals of Family Medicine* 5(6), 547–556.

13. CDC. (2014). *National diabetes statistics report, 2014.* Retrieved from the Centers for Disease Control and Prevention website March 18, 2016: http://www.cdc.gov/diabetes/pubs/statsreport14/national-diabetes-report-web.pdf

14. CDC (2014b). Number (in Thousands) of Hospital Discharges with a Lower Extremity Condition (LEC) as First-Listed or Secondary Diagnosis and Diabetes as Any Listed Diagnosis, United States, 1988–2007. Retrieved from the Centers for Disease Control and Prevention website July 6, 2016: http://www.cdc.gov/diabetes/statistics/hosplea/diabetes_complications/fig5.htm

15. Center for Disease Control and Prevention (CDC, 2011). The 2011 National Diabetes Fact Sheet.

16. CDC (2010). Breastfeeding Report Card—United States, 2010. Retrieved from the Centers for Disease Control and Prevention website July 7, 2016: https://www.cdc.gov/breastfeeding/pdf/breastfeedingreportcard2010.pdf

17 Dyck RF, Klomp H, Tan L. (2001). From "thrifty genotype" to "hefty fetal phenotype": the relationship between high birthweight and diabetes in Saskatchewan Registered Indians. Canadian Journal of Public Health. Revue Canadienne de Sante Publique;92(5):340-344.

18 Drake, A.J., Smith, A., Betts, P.R., Crowne, E.C., & Shield, J.P. (2002): *Arch Dis Child* 86, 207–208.

19 Ehtisham, S., Barrett, T.G., Shaw, N.J. (2000). Type 2 diabetes mellitus in UK children--an emerging problem. *Diabet Med* 17, 867–871.

20 Fagot-Campagna, A. (2001). Type 2 diabetes in children. *BMJ* 322, 377-8.

21 Green, L.W. et al., (2012). Primary prevention of type 2 diabetes: integrative public health and primary care opportunities, challenges and strategies. Family Practice 29 (suppl 1): i13-i23. doi: 10.1093/fampra/cmr126

22 Hiddink, G.J. et al. (1999). Cross-sectional and longitudinal analyses of nutrition guidance by primary care physicians *Eur. J Clin Nutr* 53, S35-S43.

23 Holtcamp, W. (2012). Obesogens: An environmental link to obesity. Environmental Health Perspectives; 120 (2): A63-68. Retrieved July 7, 2016 from: http://www.ncbi.nlm.nih.gov/pmc/articles/PMC3279464/pdf/ehp.120-a62.pdf

24 Janesick A, Blumberg B. (2011). Endocrine disrupting chemicals and the developmental programming of adipogenesis and obesity. Birth Defects Res Part C Embryo Today Rev 93(1):34–50; retrieved July 7, 2016 from: http:// dx.doi.org/10.1002/bdrc.20197

25 Kida, K., Ito, T., Yang, S.W., Tahphaichitr, V. (2001) Effects of Western diet on risk factors of chronic diseases in Asia. Bendich, A., Deckelbaum, R.J., eds. *Preventive Nutrition: The Comprehensive Guide for Health Professionals* 435–446.2nd ed., Humana Press Inc Totowa, NJ.

26 Kuriyama, H. (1998). Enhanced expression of hepatic acyl-coenzyme A synthetase and microsomal triglyceride transfer protein messenger RNAs in the obese and hypertriglyceridemic rat with visceral fat accumulation. Hepatology; 27(2): 557–562

27 Lustig, R.H. (2010). Fructose: metabolic, hedonic, and societal parallels with ethanol. *JADA* 110(9):1307–21.

28 Matsuzawa, Y. (2008). The role of fat topology in the risk of disease *International journal of obesity* 32 Suppl 7, S83–S92.

29 Matsuzawa, Y. et al., (2004). Adiponectine and metabolic syndrome. Arterioscler Thromb Vasc Biol; 24(1):29–33.

30 Menke, A., Casagrande, S.,, Geiss L., Cowie, C. C. (2015). Prevalence of and trends in diabetes among adults in the United States, 1988–2012. *JAMA*. 8;314(10):1021–9.

31 Newbold RR, et al. (2009). Environmental estrogens and obesity. Mol Cell Endocrinol 304 (1-2):84–89; retrieved July 7, 2016 from: http://dx.doi.org/10.1016/j.mce.2009.02.024.

32 NIH/NHLBI/NAASO. (2000). *The practical guide identification, evaluation, and treatment of overweight and obese adults.* Retrieved from http://www.nhlbi.nih.gov/guidelines/obesity/prctgd_c.pdf

33 Ogden, C.L. et al. (2006). *JAMA* 295, 1549–1555.

34 Pinhas-Hamiel, O. et al. (1996). Increased incidence of non-insulin dependent diabetes mellitus among adolescents. *J. Pediatrics* 128, 608–615.

34 Romalo-Halsted, B. & Elelman, S.V. (2000). *Clinical Diabetes* 18(2).

35 Roseboom TJ, van der Meulen JH, Osmond C, Barker DJ, Ravelli AC, Bleker OP. (2000). Plasma lipid profi les in adults after prenatal exposure to the Dutch famine. Am J Clin Nutr;72(5):1101–1106.

36 Roseboom TJ, van der Meulen JH, Ravelli AC, Osmond C, Barker DJ, Bleker OP. (2001). Effects of prenatal exposure to the Dutch famine on adult disease in later life: an overview. Mol Cell Endocrinol;185(1-2):93–98.

37 Rosenbloom, A.L., Joe, J.R., Young, R.S., & Winter, W.E. (1999). *Diabetes Care* 22, 345–354.

38 Schmitz, K.H. et al. (2002). *Int. J. Obes Relat Metab Disord* 26, 1310–1316.

39 Schoeller, D.A. et al. (1997). *Am J Clin Nutr* 66, 551–556.

40 Srikanthan, P., and Karlamangla, A.S. (2011). Relative Muscle Mass Is Inversely Associated with Insulin Resistance and Prediabetes. Findings from The Third National Health and Nutrition Examination Survey. The Journal of Clinical Endocrinology and Metabolism; 96 (9): DOI: http://dx.doi.org/10.1210/jc.2011-0435 Retrieved July 7, 2016 from: http://press.endocrine.org/doi/full/10.1210/jc.2011-0435#sthash.t1fMBVt6.dpuf

41 Styne, D.M. (2010). *JPHMP* 16(5), 381-387.

42 Styne, D. M. (2001). Childhood and adolescent obesity: Prevalence and significance. *Pediatric clinics of North America* 48(4), 823-854.

43 Toh, C.M. & Cutter, J. (2002). *BMJ* 324, 427.

44 Travino, R.P. et al. (2003). *Diabetes* 52 (suppl. 1), A404.

45 Wilde, S. et al. (2004). *Diabetes Care* 27, 1047–1053.

46 Williamson, D.F., Serdula, M.K., Anada, R.F., Levy, A., & Byers, T. (1992). Weight loss attempts in adults: Goals, duration, and rate of weight loss. *Am J Pub Health* 82, 1251–1257.

47 Wu, SC. et al. (2007). Foot ulcers in the diabetic patient, prevention and treatment. Vasc Health Risk Manag; 3(1): 65–76.

48 Yajnik, C.S. (2004). *J. Nutr* 134(1), 205–210.

49 Zeitler, P. et al., (2001). *Lancet* 36 (9575), 1823–1831.

CHAPTER 5 ANSWERS

1 Pre-diabetic; TEE= REE x AF= 1673.22 kcals x 1.53= 2560 kcals; goal weight: 183 lbs.

2 Patient is still pre-diabetic, but she can be reclassified as having metabolic syndrome. Since she was last seen, patient has gained an additional 6 lbs over the last one month. Recommend patient be placed on a 2560 kcal diet to prevent any further weight gain (weight loss will be prescribed in one month to ensure normalization of eating habits and weight stability) and prescribe DASH diet cut-offs for saturated fat (≤6%: ≤17g), total fat (≤27%: ≤77.8g), protein (18%: 115g), dietary cholesterol (<150mg), carbohydrates (55%: 352g), and sodium (1500 mg/day).

CHAPTER 6

The Problem of GI Diseases

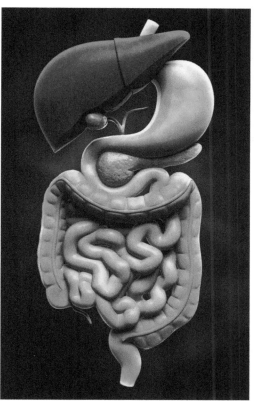

© dream designs/Shutterstock.com

6.1 THE PREVALENCE OF GASTROINTESTINAL (GI) DISEASES

The United States is greatly afflicted by gastrointestinal (GI) diseases of various types, affecting 60 to 70 million people, and causing as many as 245,921 deaths in 2009. These diseases are of such a serious nature that they were responsible for the hospitalization of an estimated 21.7 million Americans in 2010. GI diseases encompass a wide variety of disorders such as abdominal wall hernias, constipation, diverticular disease, gallstones, gastroesophageal reflux disease (GERD), GI infections, liver disease, pancreatitis, peptic ulcer disease, hemorrhoids, viral hepatitis, and inflammatory bowel diseases (DHHS, 2013). Of the GI disorders, GERD affects 70 million people, constipation about 63 million, diverticular disease 2.2 million, and irritable bowel syndrome (IBS) approximately 15.3 million individuals. These disorders are significantly associated with diet and lifestyle, and can be prevented by eating diets high in fiber and low in fat and by implementing good stress management strategies such as regular exercise (DHHS, 2013b, 2013d; Portalatin & Winstead, 2012).

6.2 THE PROBLEM OF CONSTIPATION

Chronic constipation affects 20% of the general US population, costing $821 million/year in over the counter laxatives and physician consultations (Portalatin & Winstead, 2012), but it is particularly in those over 65 years of age that the prevalence rises to 30-40%. Interestingly, women are three times more likely to suffer from constipation than men (Dennison et al., 2005). Criteria for diagnosing functional constipation follow the ROME system of objective diagnosis. The top three standards frequently used by physicians are first, less than three defecations/week; second, straining for >¼ of defecations because of the hardness of the stool; and third, a sensation of incomplete evacuation for >¼ of defecations (Dennison et al., 2005). The symptoms of abdominal pain—usually in the lower left quadrant—and bloating result from the buildup of stool and gas in the descending colon and in the rectum (Figure 6.1), causing an expansion of the colonic wall.

While short-term constipation can be easily treated with laxatives, chronic constipation by contrast represents a greater challenge as it can lead to long-term abdominal discomfort. In rare cases, it can trigger fecal impaction and ultimately bowel perforation, thus requiring hospitalization. In the United States in 2009, there were 4 million ambulatory care visits tied to constipation, 1.1 million hospitalizations in 2010, and 5 million laxative prescriptions in 2004 (DHHS, 2013). These represent a needless cost burden on our healthcare system that would normally be preventable through lifestyle changes at the population level. Chronic constipation is usually the consequence of insufficient dietary fiber (<25 g/day) and fluid intakes. It also arises from extensive immobility or lack of exercise, the aftereffect of an inactive lifestyle, typified by individuals glued to their desks at work or fastened to their sofas at home, either looking at TV, playing video games or surfing the internet. Also medications such as analgesics, antacids, antihistamines, antidepressants, antihypertensive drugs, and iron supplements can cause constipation. A study conducted in the UK found for instance, that up to 40% of hospitalized women over the age of 65—frequently prescribed multiple medications—suffer from fecal impaction

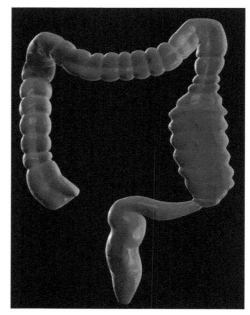

© *Sebastian Kaulitzski/shutterstock.com*

Figure 6.1 *Constipation in the descending colon and rectum.*

(Dennison et al., 2005). This is the result of stool that is so tightly compacted in the large intestine, that it offers a very small likelihood of natural evacuation, but also increases the risk of perforation. A tear or puncture of the colon leads to stool seeping into the peritoneum, causing peritonitis and ultimately sepsis if prompt intervention is not forthcoming. Interestingly, chronic constipation in hospitalized elderly has also been tied to mental confusion, although the actual mechanism is not clearly understood. Individuals who suffer from anxiety and depression have a tendency to exaggerate the severity of their constipation thus consulting physicians more frequently for remedies (Dennison et al., 2005). This impacts the health care system by way of mobilizing expensive resources, for indeed, doctors, PAs and nurse practitioners frequently encounter patients suffering from abdominal pain caused by chronic constipation. Such a diagnosis requires a bit of an expensive workup before other causes can be ruled out, and translates into a sizable expense.

The standard recommendation for people suffering from chronic constipation is to increase dietary fiber to between 25 and 38 g/day (AND, 2008). This can be easily achieved by regularly consuming a high fiber cereal in the morning with dried fruit. For instance, ½ cup of Kellogg's Bran buds has 13g of fiber. Mixed with 1 cup of Total Raisin Bran cereal, containing 5g of fiber, the total fiber intake for breakfast approximates 18g of fiber or 72% of a minimal fiber recommendation (Bissonnette, 2013). If, in addition, the patient opts for whole wheat bread instead of white, complemented with a minimum of five servings of fruit and vegetables, the patient will likely meet fiber requirements by the end of the day. Combined with good fluid intake and regular exercise, high fiber intake will resolve chronic constipation within a week to a month for most individuals; this makes sense given that Americans, on average, only consume 15g of fiber/day (AND, 2008).

6.3 THE REFLUX DISEASES: G.E.R. & G.E.R.D.

Gastroesophageal Reflux Disease (GERD), a condition that caused as many as 8.9 million ambulatory care visits in 2009, is difficult to estimate in terms of prevalence in American society. However, based on pharmaceutical sales, about 1 in 10 Americans purchase antacids at least once/month to relieve the discomfort of GERD, representing in 2010 about $1.2 billion in sales. When the sales of the top four antacids are broken down—Protonix with $690 million in sales; Prilosec OTC racking up $288.5 million; Zantac 150 posting $72.7 million; and Pepcid Complete with $53.9 million in sales—it is relatively easy to grasp the full scale of the problem of overeating in the United States (Hunsinger Benbow, 2011). Indeed, the use of antacids is intimately tied to either overeating, or eating abundant fatty foods or both. It is an indictment of the cultural eating habits of a nation, and represents an urgent cry to intervene in haste before overeating compromises the population. This is no exaggeration as the medical expenses in 2004 tied to GI diseases were estimated at $141.8 billion, with $97.8 billion in direct medical costs and $44 billion in indirect costs related to disabilities and mortality (DHHS, 2013). Another way to look at the importance of GERD in the United States is to consider where antacid sales figure from the perspective of overall pharmaceutical sales. Among the top patented drugs in 2011, an antacid—Pfizer's Protonix—took fifth place in sales. Interestingly, the top position belonged to

Lipitor—a cholesterol-lowering drug—which is another Pfizer product; the second position went to an antipsychotic drug—Ili Lily's Zyprexa (Alazraki, M., 2011). This may not be a coincidence, as obesity is intimately tied to hypercholesterolemia and to overeating, and not surprisingly, obesity is also associated with depression and anxiety. There is a connection here that is worth paying attention to for healthcare providers. More numerous numbers of patients are now coming to outpatient clinics with a broad assortment of diseases and conditions that are secondary to obesity and morbid obesity. It is no longer uncommon for a frontline healthcare provider to encounter a 375 lbs, 5 feet 5 inch female who presents with hypercholesterolemia treated with Lipitor, who takes Zantac for acid reflux, in addition to a selective serotonin reuptake inhibitor (SSRI) to manage depression.

The problem of gastroesophageal reflux (GER) results from a regurgitation of acid from the stomach into the esophagus. Individuals experience what is medically described as acid indigestion or heartburn. It is a widespread digestive problem that can be treated with antacids. (DHHS, 2013b).

This problem of GER can be alleviated through strategic lifestyle and dietary changes. The first is a dietary change that involves consuming less fatty foods in the diet. This can generally be achieved by eliminating junk or fried foods and many unhealthy snack foods as well. The second meaningful change would be to avoid overeating, a common problem in obesity. The third strategy consists of controlling the ingestion of coffee, alcoholic beverages, and spicy foods. There are also lifestyle changes that would be beneficial such as losing weight if the patient is either overweight or obese, not smoking, and not eating two to three hours before retiring for the night (DHHS, 2013b).

GERD is a more chronic condition of heartburn caused by a relaxed lower esophageal sphincter (Figure 6.2) taking longer to shut or not forming a complete seal after the passage of food into the stomach. The consequence is stomach acid—consisting of hydrochloric acid (HCL)—chronically refluxing through the sphincter opening and back into the esophagus, therefore causing a burning sensation in the chest area.

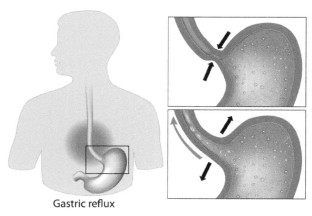

Gastric reflux

© *Alila Medical Media/ shutterstock.com*

Figure 6.2 *Gastroesophageal Reflux Disease (GERD.)*

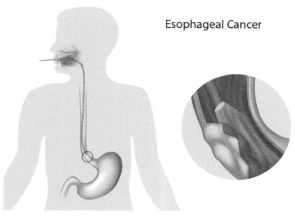

Esophageal Cancer

© *Alila Medical Media/ shutterstock.com*

Figure 6.3 *Esophageal cancer arising from chronic esophagitis.*

Patients suffering from GERD do not consistently experience heartburn. Other symptoms tied to this condition include dry cough, sore throat, nausea, pain in the chest or upper abdomen, bad breath, and difficulty swallowing. These symptoms could be the consequence of a secondary condition called Schatzki's ring. This is a membranous ring structure that partially obstructs the lumen of the esophagus, thus leading to dysphagia or a difficulty swallowing (Smith, 2013). GERD is a condition often associated with obesity, pregnancy, the use of certain medications such as antihistamines, sedatives, antidepressants, analgesics (pain killers), and smoking. If left untreated, GERD can lead to chronic esophagitis that can evolve into an erosive esophagitis. This

signifies an injury to the esophageal lining caused by chronic gastric acid irritation, sometimes leading to bleeding and ulceration. The damage that can ensue, over many years of gastric acid reflux, may culminate in precancerous changes in the esophageal lining. One form of esophageal anomaly is called Barrett's esophagus, characterized by the lining of the esophagus adopting cells similar to those of the intestine. Sometimes it has been known to lead to a rare but deadly form of esophageal cancer (Figure 6.3) (DHHS 2013 B).

The treatment strategies for GERD are to lose body weight, avoid smoking, consuming small but frequent meals as opposed to fewer large meals, and keeping the head in the upright position for at least three hours after a meal. Finally, raising the head of the bed an additional six to eight inches could help control symptoms. Otherwise, antacids such as Alka-Seltzer or Maalox are regularly prescribed. Alternatives to antacids are Tagamet and Zantac, which are proton pump inhibitors (PPIs). Metoclopramide is a class of prokinetic drug that can also be used, but it has many unwelcomed side effects such as nausea, diarrhea, tiredness, depression, anxiety, and problems with physical movement. Antibiotics, such as erythromycin, work just as well as prokinetics, but with fewer side effects (DHHS, 2013).

6.4 PEPTIC ULCER DISEASE

Ulcerations or sores along the inner lining of the esophagus (Figure 6.4), stomach or duodenum affect about 6 million people every year in the United States, and are referred to as peptic ulcers (Feinstein et al., 2010). They create a great deal of abdominal discomfort, often experienced as a dull burning pain, that is accentuated especially when the stomach is empty. Patients with ulcers also experience nausea, bloating, vomiting, and weight loss (DHHS, 2010).

Originally, it had been thought that spicy foods, stress, and excessive alcohol consumption caused ulcers. Consequently the long-term management of ulcers consisted of prescribing bland and tasteless diets with very little spices or alcohol allowed. Over time, the diet prescription evolved to "diet as tolerated," because the practice of over restricting

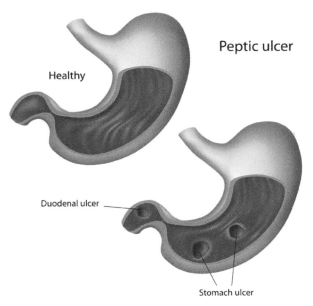

© Alila Medical Media//shutterstock.com

Figure 6.4 *Peptic ulcer disease of the stomach of the duodenum.*

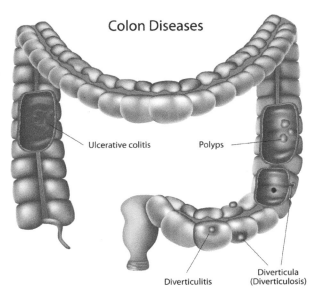

© Alila Medical Media//shutterstock.com

Figure 6.5 *Diverticular disease of the colon.*

foods sometimes compromised the nutritional status of patients. The consumption of milk was encouraged as it relieved symptoms of discomfort fairly rapidly, but it is now known that milk elicits acid secretion and therefore may actually even worsen the ulcers or prevent them from healing. However, back in the 1980s, a bacterium called *Helicobacter pylori (H. pylori)* was identified by Australian scientists Barry Marshall and Robin Warren, and found to be responsible for the majority of gastric and duodenal ulcers (Yamaoka, & DeBakey, 2008). The therapeutic goals are to kill the bacterium using the antibiotic amoxicillin, reduce acid production using proton-pump inhibitors (PPIs) or histamine receptor blockers (H2 blockers), and protect the lining of the stomach and duodenum through the use of bismuth subsalicylates like Pepto-Bismol. However, in recent years antibiotic-resistant bacteria have become more prominent throughout the world, making it more difficult to kill *H. pylori*. Therefore doctors now verify the efficacy of antibiotic therapy by using breath and stool tests, and often implement several rounds of therapy in order to successfully kill the bacterium (DHHS, 2010). Nevertheless, resistance to amoxicillin specifically is still relatively rare.

6.5 DIVERTICULAR DISEASE

Diverticulosis, a condition characterized by the formation of out pouches, most often found along the transverse and descending colon, and created through an increased intra-luminal pressure on the colonic wall (Figure 6.5), arises from chronic constipation in most cases (DHHS, 2007).

This intraluminal pressure, resulting from the hard and voluminous stool compacted inside the colon, pushes along the colonic wall and creates out pouches called **diverticula** over 10 to 20 years. When pieces of fecal material get caught in the out pouches they become infected, thereby creating an inflammatory condition called **diverticulitis**, which is characterized by an inflammation of and around the infected area, abdominal pain, nausea, and fever. Sometimes there can be numerous diverticula that begin to bleed and become infected. These advanced forms of diverticulitis will often require surgery, such as a partial colectomy or surgical resection of the infected segments of the colon. The disease normally begins to appear in people over the age of 40, but the prevalence increases significantly every 10 years afterwards; between the ages of 60 and 80; about 50% of people suffer from diverticular disease, but almost every individual over the age of 80 has diverticulosis (DHHS, 2007). In 2009 there were 2.7 million ambulatory care visits linked to diverticular disease in the United States, which only represents those individuals acutely affected by diverticulosis (DHHS, 2013). The physician will use a **barium enema** in order to observe through X-ray the extent to which the out pouches or diverticula are spread throughout the colonic wall. A **colonoscopy** can be used by a gastroenterologist to visually observe the colonic wall using a miniature camera attached to a tube that moves along the colon after it enters through the anus.

The causes, from an epidemiological perspective, are tied to the low fiber westernized diet. Fiber's role in maintaining a healthy GI tract tends to be greatly underestimated. Food processing has been responsible for the most significant loss of fiber in the United States diet. This has mostly taken place in the processing of wheat used for bread making and breakfast cereals. Also the shift from a fruit and vegetable-based diet to more animal-based and calorically-dense food choices, has had inevitable consequences on he health of the American population (DHHS, 2007).

6.5.1 Recommend a High Fiber Diet

The low fiber content of the U.S. diet translates into harder stools and longer transit times through the GI tract. The soluble fibers, found mostly in fruits and vegetables, are colloidal in structure and richly found in the pectin of fruits for instance. This means that the colloids attract and trap water within the structure. This feature is responsible for softening the stool and thus making it less hard; the payoff is less intraluminal pressure against the intestinal wall. The insoluble fibers, by contrast, are mostly located in cereals and tend to not capture and bind water. Instead, the insoluble fibers draw water into the GI tract without binding it. Hence, its role is less for softening the stool, but more for flushing the stool down the GI tract. In other words, insoluble fibers provide a shorter transit time or a faster flow of stool down the colon and into the rectum (Gropper & Smith, 2013; Lupton & Trumbo, 2006).

The notion of disease prevention applies to this condition very well, because once the disease sets in, there is no escaping it afterwards. The out pouches become permanent features of the colon, and potentially susceptible to infections. The prevention strategy, most suitable to averting this condition all together, is to begin early on to consume a diet that is rich in fruits such as apples, pears, peaches, nectarines, prunes, dates, figs, raisins, and dried apricots. It is also pertinent to include vegetables of all sorts, such as broccoli, squash, carrots, turnips, cauliflower, spinach, and cabbage. Most forgotten in the North American diet are legumes, like navy, lima, kidney and romano beans, soybeans, and lentils. These need to find their way back into the diet as sources of vegetable protein and soluble fiber. This should ideally decrease the reliance on animal protein from beef and pork. The added benefit from frequently ingesting soluble fibers is that it decreases the risk of cardiovascular disease (Lupton & Trumbo, 2006). In addition, soluble fibers tend to be fermented by gut bacteria that line the GI tract. Fermentation produces short and medium chain fatty acids that play an important role in managing an ideal pH that favors the colonization of a friendly microflora, considered instrumental in minimizing GI diseases and some cancers (Gropper & Smith, 2013). It has been proposed that fermentation lowers the pH enough to decrease the conversion of primary bile acids to the more carcinogenic secondary bile acids (Gropper & Smith, 2013). The insoluble fibers, found in whole wheat bread, brown rice, bran flake and bran bud cereals are important in minimizing chronic problems of constipation by increasing fecal bulk and weight. Soluble and insoluble fibers consumed regularly can work together preventing diverticular disease in many people.

6.6 HEMORRHOIDS, ANAL FISSURES AND FISTULAS

About 75% of the U.S. population will develop hemorrhoids at some point during their lives. Hemorrhoids affect mostly adults between the ages of 45 to 65, and are diagnosed when there is inflammation of the veins surrounding the lower rectum or the anus (DHHS, 2013). Hemorrhoids can bleed, thereby leaving bright red blood in the toilet bowl or on toilet paper after defecating. Hemorrhoids can be internal,

Anal Disorders

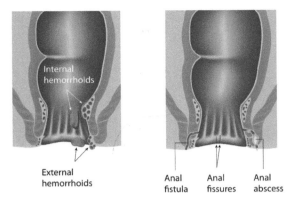

© *Alila Medical Media/shutterstock.com*

Figure 6.6 *Hemorrhoids, anal fistulas and fissures resulting from constipation.*

and thus located in the lower end of the rectum, and can prolapse or fall through the anus (Figure 6.6). Prolapsed hemorrhoids tend to be painful, uncomfortable and associated with itching, but will tend to recede on their own. However, sometimes prolapsed hemorrhoids protrude permanently and may require treatment or surgery. Non-prolapsed hemorrhoids tend to not be painful or uncomfortable. Hemorrhoids are also classified as external, and thus are situated under the skin in proximity of the anus. Hemorrhoids occur from chronic straining resulting from constipation and from the increased pressure on the abdominal wall during pregnancy, and from pushing during delivery. Pregnancy-derived hemorrhoids tend to disappear after parturition (DHHS, 2013c).

Anal fissures are really only slight linear cracks or tears of the mucosa lining the anus. These fissures are often observed in young infants more than in children, and will generally heal on their own if the anal area is kept clean; otherwise anal abscesses can arise. A perianal abscess is an infected area surrounding the anus that fills up with white blood cells and debris in a process of a pus pocket formation. This can occur from blocked anal glands, sexually transmitted infections, or from an infected anal fissure (NLM, 2012). Anal fissures are prevalent as well in young adults—both men and women are equally susceptible—and are less prevalent in older adults. Fissures can occur in adults who tend to strain when defecating large hard stools or who experience frequent bouts of diarrhea, but in about

90% of cases these fissures spontaneously heal over time with constipation management (Jonas & Scholefield, 2001). The solution is the ingestion of a diet containing somewhere between 25 to 38g of fiber per day (AND, 2008). This can be achieved by ingesting a high fiber bran-based cereal such as raisin bran, bran flakes, bran buds, or regular cereals with added natural bran. Adding dried fruits like raisins, apricots, figs, and dates will provide soluble fibers and some natural laxative agents that assist with stool softening and shortening the transit time of the stool. If dietary changes are not implemented, then fissures can evolve to abscesses (Figure 6.6), which most often pierce through into the anal canal and spontaneously heal; however, occasionally the abscesses can undergo a submucosal spread that produces a transphincteric route or track that pierces through the buttocks, and that is medically termed a **fistula** (Figure 6.6). In these circumstances, the area surrounding the fistula exit site becomes tender and sore, and will tend to have purulent drainage and thus must be surgically treated with a fistulotomy (Mappes & Farthmann, 2001).

6.7 INFLAMMATORY BOWEL DISEASE (IBD)

The onset of inflammatory bowel disease is more frequently seen in 15 to 30 year olds of Caucasian and Ashkenazic Jewish origin with about 10% of cases occurring under the age of 18. This condition, because it is chronic, involves a lifetime of medical care, and currently carries a price tag of $1.7 billion a year in healthcare costs; it is, in fact, the most prevalent form of gastrointestinal disease in the United States (DHHS, 2013). IBD generally refers to Crohn's disease and ulcerative colitis, and is primarily an immune response characterized by chronic inflammation of the gastrointestinal (GI) tract (CDC, 2014). Recent studies have been able to show that the incidence of IBD is more frequent in developed countries, particularly in urban centers. It has been advanced that the westernized lifestyle may be a significant contributor to the disease. It has also been hypothesized but nor proven that the western diet, oral contraceptives, perianal and childhood infections, in addition to atypical myocardial infections may be playing a role in the onset of the disease (CDC, 2014).

6.7.1 Crohn's Disease

This is a type of inflammatory bowel disease, characterized by abdominal pain, chronic or nocturnal diarrhea, weight loss, fever, and rectal bleeding, commonly affects roughly 700,000 people/year in the U.S., mostly between the ages of 13 to 30, and costs approximately $2 billion/year in medical expenses (CCFA, 2016; Hanauer et al., 2001). It characteristically causes deep transmural fissures through all the layers of the intestinal wall, potentially affecting both the small and large intestine (Figure 6.7).

6.7.1.1 Diagnosing Crohn's Disease

The symptoms of abdominal pain and diarrhea are, however, common with other types of inflammatory bowel disease such as ulcerative colitis and irritable bowel syndrome (IBS); this makes it difficult to diagnose unless confirmed by sigmoidoscopy, colonoscopy, a Computerized Tomography (CT) scan or an upper or lower GI series using barium (DHHS, 2011). However, Crohn's disease (CD) will mostly affect the ileum (Ileitis) in 35% of cases, the ileum and the beginning of the colon in 45% of individuals (Ileocolitis), and only the colon in 20% of patients (granulomatous colitis) (CDC, 2014; Merck, 2012; CCFA, 2016). Consequently Crohn's disease, if not well managed, causes a great deal of malabsorption and weight loss; many nutrients such as vitamins D and B12 in particular, and iron in children, are of concern as they cannot be completely absorbed in the inflamed areas, thereby causing anemia and growth retardation (Merck, 2012). Moreover, there are significant protein losses resulting from the fissure damage of the intestinal wall and villi. Low dietary intake of calories and protein, secondary to the anorexia that accompanies the disease, further contributes in a significant way to the weight loss (DHHS, 2011). Typically, then, patients will tend to present with pallor, cachexia, perianal fissures, abdominal masses or tenderness, fistulaes, or abscesses (Lichtenstein et al, 2009).

The Vienna Classification of Crohn's and its recent Montreal modification identify three clinical presentations of Crohn's that provide a broad perspective to the disease: First, it presents primarily as an inflammation that persists over several years; second, it evolves into a stenotic or narrowing of the GI tract leading to obstruction; and third, it becomes

Inflammatory Bowel Disease

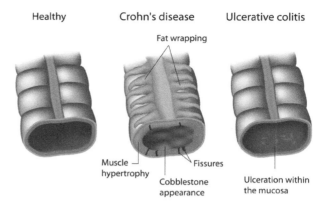

© Alila Medical Media/shutterstock.com

Figure 6.7 *Crohn's disease & ulcerative colitis.*

penetrating in the way it affects the mucosa, submucosa, and muscularis layers of the intestinal tract. It is also fistulizing in that fistulas become more prevalent in about 30% of patients (Figure 6.7), which exacerbates the discomfort and heightens the fear of eating (CDC, 2014) (Figure 6.7). Moreover, Crohn's disease, because of the sequelae ensuing from the chronic inflammation and malabsorption, can elicit secondary medical complications such as anemia, cholelithiasis, nephrolithiasis, or metabolic bone disease (Hanauer, et al., 2001). When CD remains limited to the colon, it will normally present with rectal bleeding, and hence will tend to be difficult to distinguish from ulcerative colitis unless a biopsy is conducted for histological features (Lichtenstein, et al., 2009). In both instances, when the colon is affected, red blood becomes apparent in the stool. However, in an upper GI bleed (stomach, duodenum, jejunum and ileum, even including the right ascending colon), typically seen in CD, a **melena**-type blood appears in the stool (Merck, 2016e). This is when the stool takes on a black tarry consistency, and is therefore very different from the rather bright red blood, typically seen in ulcerative colitis, emanating from the transverse and descending colon. A diagnosis of CD can be further supported by using diagnostic tools of the blood that confirm the presence of inflammation such serum acute-phase reactants. The most noteworthy blood biochemical markers are an elevated erythrocyte sedimentation rate, orosomucoid, and C-reactive protein (Lichtenstein, et al., 2009).

As a means of monitoring patients with Crohn's, it is advisable to conduct lab tests for anemia, hypoalbuminemia, and electrolyte imbalances. Every one to two years, patients need to have their serum hydroxy-25 (OH-25) vitamin D and B12 status checked. Other vitamins such a niacin and folic acid in addition to the minerals zinc, selenium, and copper can be monitored. No matter the patients' ages, bone density measurements using DEXA (Duel Energy X-Ray Absorptiometry) should be conducted periodically (Merck, 2012). Those individuals prone to Crohn's disease are people of Jewish heritage and smokers, and those less likely to contract this disease are African Americans (DHHS, 2011). The causes of this condition are still being studied, but presently it is believed to be the result of an interaction between inherited genes, a compromised autoimmune system, and some elements in the environment (DHHS, 2011). One credible hypothesis suggests that the immune system attacks friendly bacteria and foods located in the GI tract, causing white blood cells to migrate to specific sites along the lumen of the intestine. This sets into motion an inflammatory response which, over time, results in inflammation, followed by ulcerations and sores that chronically injure the intestinal wall (DHHS, 2011). Crohn's patients are at risk of cancer. Symptoms experienced by patients tend to be frequent watery stools, abdominal cramps, fever, and rectal bleeding (CDC, 2014). Historically, it had been theorized that feelings of guilt, stress, and anxiety were associated with the onset of the disease; this has since been shown to be false (Sajadinejad, et al., 2012). However, emotional conditions such as Alexithymia (difficulty verbally expressing feelings), anxiety and depression are frequently documented conditions in Crohn's disease patients (Sajadinejad, et al., 2012), and have most certainly been tied to the worsening of the problem particularly in concert with chronic stress, which has been shown to heighten abdominal pain and cause frequent diarrhea (CCFA, 2014).

6.7.1.2 Treatments of Crohn's Disease

This condition can be managed by a combination of medications, surgery, and nutritional supplementation to ensure the patient is adequately fed. This kind of disease can often times go into remission for many years before reappearing; there is really no cure for this condition, (Hanauer et al., 2001), but rather long-term management strategies that involve the use of anti-inflammatory medications like Sulfasalazine—the most popular in use—and as an alternative, patients are put on Asacol, Dipentum, or Pentasa—all mesalamine-based medications classified as 5-aminosalicylic acid (5-ASA) agents—which are reported to have side effects such as nausea, diarrhea, vomiting, and headaches (DHHS, 2011). Patients who remain unresponsive to standard medications and who persist with vomiting, high fever, and cachexia are often suffering from an obstruction or abscesses, and therefore should be hospitalized (Lichtenstein et al,. 2009). This fulminant form of CD requires surgery, and only 5–7 days post-operatively is nutritional support through elemental feeding or parenteral hyperalimentation advised (Lichtenstein et al,. 2009).

In order to manage inflammatory flare ups of the disease, especially in the early onset, when inflammation is prominent and symptoms are difficult to manage, steroids such as prednisone and budesonide are frequently prescribed in large doses. About 67% of patients suffering from Crohn's will require surgery to deal with intestinal blockages, perforations, bleeding, or abscesses. Intestinal resections are at times performed because of extensive and irreparable damage to the intestine or colon (DHHS, 2011).

During periods of inflammation, doctors will prescribe intravenous nutrition in the form of total parenteral nutrition otherwise known as TPN. Bypassing the GI tract for a brief period is a strategy aimed at providing bowel rest so that lesions, inflammation, or abscesses can heal, often with a combination of antibiotics and prednisone (DHHS, 2011). Although it is very clear that foods do not cause Crohn's disease, hot spicy foods, bulky fiber-containing grains such as wheat, rye and barley, fatty foods, unabsorbable sugars like sorbitol and mannitol, alcohol, and milk products are known to cause diarrhea and cramps in some patients; these foods tend to be on a cautionary list. Otherwise, patients are encouraged to eat a liberal diet as tolerated (CCFA, 2013).

6.7.2 Ulcerative Colitis

This is also an inflammatory bowel disease that is more prevalent than Crohn's disease, with peak incidences occurring in the age range of 14 and 24, and later in life between 50 and 70 (Merck, 2016b). It usually begins in the rectum and slowly progresses to involve part of the colon, but rarely the entire large intestine. Unlike Crohn's disease, ulcerative colitis (UC) is strictly limited to the large bowel or colon and does not affect all the layers of the intestine (**Figure 6.7**), but rather the inflammation remains in the mucosa and the submucosa with a complete absence of abscesses or fistulas; the longterm risk for cancer remains nevertheless high depending on the length of the colon affected and the duration of the disease. For instance, patients affected for 20 years with this condition, have between a 7–10% chance of developing colon cancer; after 35 years, the risk jumps to 30% (Merck, 2016). In severe cases of the disease, there are mucosal ulcers formed with purulent exudates. Consequently, patients experience abdominal cramps followed by frequent bowel movements, often in the form of diarrhea containing blood and mucus. For most, UC is experienced as a chronic inflammatory disease, but in 10% of cases an initial flare up can become fulminant, leading to hemorrhage, perforation, or sepsis and toxemia, with only 10% of patients recovering with treatment (Merck, 2016). Because only the mucosa is affected, gross rectal bleeding is frequently observed (Merck, 2016b), but malabsorption is less of a problem compared to Crohn's disease. The implication is that there are fewer nutrients at risk of becoming deficient. Nevertheless, iron deficiency anemia is likely and should be monitored closely in these patients because of the blood loss in the stool. Hence, it is appropriate for physicians to measure hemoglobin levels to ensure proper iron status. Also, a loss of appetite with weight loss is commonly observed in patients with ulcerative colitis, and can lead to poor growth in children (Merck, 2016; CDC, 2014). Symptomatically, adult patients with UC present with recent weight loss, frequent watery and bloody stools, a general malaise, anorexia, and Fe-deficiency anemia (Merck, 2016). It is therefore a good practice to monitor patients for anemia, hypoalbuminemia, and electrolyte abnormalities (sodium ($Na+$); potassium ($K+$); calcium ($Ca2+$); bicarbonate ($HCO3-$);

magnesium ($Mg2+$), chloride ($Cl-$), and hydrogen phosphate ($HPO42-$)). Additionally, liver function needs to be assessed using key hepatic enzymes such as alanine aminotransferase (ALT), formerly called SGPT, or Aspartate aminotransferase (AST), formerly called SGOT (NLM, 2014), in order to rule out hepatic disease as an underlying cause for the abdominal pain.

About half of the individuals with ulcerative colitis experience only mild symptoms with long periods that can last months and years that are asymptomatic between flare ups. Therefore, far fewer patients with UC—only 25%—require surgical interventions (Merck, 2016; CDC, 2014). Hence, the most frequent treatment protocol revolves around the use of -aminosalicylic acid, corticosteroids, immuno-modulators, biologics, and antibiotics. The dietary management of this condition (Merck, 2016), is limited to restricting raw fruit and vegetables from the daily menu as they are known to exacerbate the inflamed colonic mucosa. Restricting milk has been shown to help some patients, but not all. It is important to reintroduce milk, if limiting its consumption does not produce any clear benefits (Merck, 2016).

6.8 IRRITABLE BOWEL SYNDROME (IBS)

This is not an inflammatory bowel disease, but a functional GI disorder with symptoms of abdominal pain and diarrhea that resemble what would be observed in IBD (DHHS, 2013d). The onset of the disease usually takes place in the early 20s and tends not to occur after 45 years of age (FDA, 2014). Historically this disorder was given different medical terms such as colitis, mucous colitis, spastic colon, nervous colon, and spastic bowel. The expression, irritable bowel syndrome, was finally adopted to enforce the notion that the condition had both a mental and physical dimension. Although the GI tract has no physical damage to it when viewed by colonoscopy, the symptoms of abdominal discomfort, distension, constipation, and diarrhea are still real, and therefore affect the patient's quality of life (DHHS, 2013d). IBS is diagnosed in individuals who experience abdominal pain or discomfort at least three times a month for at least three months in the absence of diseases or injuries that could explain the pain. While there is no physical sign that is diagnosable, the functional disorder impacts normal motility or movement of the GI tract that moves the chyme down the small intestine towards the colon and onwards to the rectum. Instances of slow motility translate into constipation, whereas fast motility produces diarrhea. Spasms that contract the GI muscles can generate mild to acute cramps that are very uncomfortable. The reasons for the erratic and unpredictable irregularities in motility are not very well understood. The research is unanimous however, in identifying a strong mental health component that appears based in anxiety, depression, panic disorder, and post-traumatic stress disorder. Some have also found an inexplicable link between bacterial gastroenteritis and IBS, however, the mechanism remains elusive (DHHS, 2013d). Certain foods like carbohydrates, spicy or fatty foods, coffee, and alcohol do appear to trigger symptoms. The mechanism may be tied to suboptimal bile secretion for fat emulsification that leads to poor fat digestion and intestinal discomfort. Additionally, it has been proposed that large amounts of fructose, mannitol, and sorbitol may be poorly absorbed, thereby leading to cramps and osmotic diarrhea (DHHS, 2013d; Merck, 2013).

6.8.1 Therapeutic Strategies for IBS

The treatments for IBS are based on making important dietary modifications. The general rule is to follow a liberal but healthy diet as tolerated. If discomfort is experienced it is best to follow these four basic steps: First, eat small frequent meals at a slow pace or small portions at mealtime; second, consume foods low in fat; third, include foods high in complex carbohydrates such as pastas, rice, and whole grain breads and cereals; fourth, consume many varieties of fruits and vegetables, but avoid those that are gas-producing like cabbage and legumes such as lentils, navy beans, and kidney beans as these may cause some abdominal distress. The goal behind steps three and four is to heighten the total fiber intake, which appears to alleviate most of the symptoms of IBS. One tablespoon of raw bran can be added to some foods at meals in order to boost fiber. Fiber supplements have also been recommended with some success, but it is important to keep total daily fiber intake below 40 g to avoid gas and abdominal distention; individual tolerance must be considered. The frequent consumption of probiotics has had significant benefits in patients with IBS. Probiotic foods like yogurt with *Bifidobacteria* help recolonize the microflora of the GI tract. The idea here is that the gut of IBS patients may not have a healthy microflora possibly because of previously poor dietary habits involving a lot of junk and processed foods that caused more nefarious bacteria to dominate the lumen of the GI tract (DHHS, 2013d). The possibility of lactase deficiency can be addressed by restricting milk. Antispasmodic drugs such as hyoscine, cimetropium, and pinaverium have been used with some success, in addition to antidepressant medications (DHHS, 2013d). A more natural approach using aromatic oils such as peppermint are popularly used and effective in relaxing the GI muscles and minimizing cramps (Merck, 2013). Regular exercise has also been documented as an effective approach to manage both stress and the symptoms of IBS (Asare et al., 2012)

6.9 SHORT BOWEL SYNDROME

Also called malabsorption syndrome, this problem arises from the surgical resection of more than two thirds of the small intestine—overall less than 2 meters of bowel (6.6 feet) remaining—usually because of damaged gut from Crohn's disease, cancer, or congenital anomalies (Merck, 2012b; Nightingale & Woodward, 2006).

Resection of the distal small intestine that includes more than 100 cm of the ileum almost always leads to diarrhea and malabsorption, which are the typical symptoms of short bowel syndrome. By contrast, when the jejunum is partially resected with >100 cm of remaining jejunum, there is a moderate but temporary malabsorption of many nutrients that takes place. However, the ileum will tend to adapt and compensate for this loss by increasing the size and absorptive capabilities of its villi (Merck, 2012b). The removal of a significant section of the ileum—more than 100 cm—is critical as it will tend to compromise absorption of bile and vitamin B12. This has serious consequences because normally most of the bile is reabsorbed in the ileum via the enterohepatic pathway (Figure 6.8), which brings bile acids back to the liver for the regeneration of new bile, and the conversion of **cholic acid**—main compound of bile—to cholesterol. In short bowel syndrome, large amounts of bile therefore move into the colon and causes a secretory diarrhea to occur. The ileum is also critical for water absorption; researchers have found that it can absorb about 70% of the ingested fluid load. Hence, a resection of the ileum would therefore signify a significant loss of fluid and electrolytes (Jeejeebhoy, 2006). If <100 cm of the jejunum is left after resection and the ileum is completely resected, then the GI tract loses its ability to absorb fat and many micronutrients, which normally occurs in the jejunum. In addition, vitamin B12 absorption, which exclusively takes place in the ileum, with the help of **intrinsic factor** (IF), is compromised, justifying the need for intramuscular injections of vitamin B12 (Merch, 2012b; Jeejeebhoy, 2006). Patients left with only the duodenum, <65 cm of small bowel and no colon, or who have <100 cm of jejunum remaining, require a lifetime of exclusive total parenteral nutrition (TPN), otherwise known as intravenous feeding (Merck 2012b; Jeejeebhoy, 2006). Surgeons tend to want to preserve at least 100 cm of jejunum, as it is the minimal length needed to ensure an adequate absorption of protein and fat. Carbohydrates, by contrast, especially simple carbohydrates, contribute such a significant osmotic load to the GI tract, that it exacerbates short bowel syndrome. The dietary goal, when there is no colon, is to recommend a high calorie diet consisting of 30–40% fat—steatorrhea must not be observed—20–30% protein and 40–50% carbohydrates consumed as small but frequent meals, with liquids taken between meals. Higher carbohydrates (50–60% and lower fat (20–30%) can be prescribed when fat malabsorption is observed (steatorrhea) or when there is still a colon (IFFDID, 2015; Fessler, 2007; Jeejeebhoy, 2006). Often supplements of potassium, magnesium (Mg), calcium, fat-soluble vitamins and zinc (Zn) are prescribed (Jeejeebhoy, 2006) to compensate for the significant malabsorption. Hypomagnesemia frequently occurs because unabsorbed fatty acids form chelating compounds with Mg, leading to poor Mg absorption. The consequence is serious since Mg is necessary to activate parathormone (PTH). In short bowel syndrome, the likelihood that less PTH is

activated translates into greater renal secretion of Mg, and in less 25 (OH) vitamin D3 being activated to calcitriol also known as 1, 25 Hydroxy vitamin D3. This invariably carries over into less calcium and Mg absorption and greater net bone loss (Nightingale & Woodward, 2006).

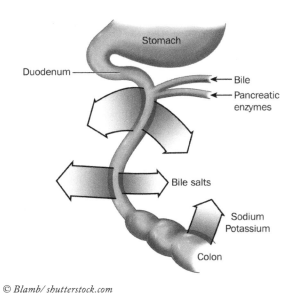

© Blamb/ shutterstock.com

Figure 6.8 *The enterohepatic circulation.*

The carbohydrates should be mostly in the form of complex starches such as potatoes, rice, pastas of all types, couscous, and cereals like oats, rye, and bulgur. It important to minimize the intake of simple sugars like table sugar (sucrose), drinks with high fructose corn syrup, corn syrup, and maple syrups, as they will precipitate diarrhea in many circumstances (Fessler, 2007). There are three standard medications commonly used in managing short bowel syndrome. The first is an anti-diarrheal medication, Loperamide, taken about one hour before a meal. It acts via the enterohepatic (EH) circulation by reducing GI motility. A higher than usual dose may be needed as the EH circulation is compromised in short bowel, resulting in a short transit time through the intestine. The second strategy is to prescribe cholestyramine at meal time as it will bind the bile salt pool in the gut, thereby diminishing the availability of bile salt that serves as vector for secretory diarrhea (Nightingale & Woodward, 2006). The third involves taking proton (H2) pump inhibitors to mitigate the larger than usual gastric acid secretions and ensuing diarrhea (Merck, 2012b). The acid, in this instance, leaks into the proximal end of the duodenum and deactivates the pancreatic enzymes, lipase and amylase, therefore causing poor digestion of sugars and fats (Nightingale & Woodward, 2006).

Preserving the integrity of the colon is essential in preventing the excessive loss of fluids—water is reabsorbed back into the body through the colonic wall—and electrolytes such as sodium (Na+), potassium (K^+), calcium ($Ca^{2}+$), magnesium (Mg^{2+}), chloride (Cl^-), hydrogen phosphate (HPO_4^{2-}), and hydrogen carbonate (HCO_3^-). Should the terminal ileum and ileocecal valve be resected in surgery, the risk of bacterial overgrowth then becomes elevated. Colonic bacteria, in this instance, can move into the intestine and populate the anastomotic area linking the intestine and the colon (Merck, 2016d).

6.10 BOWEL DISEASE CASE STUDY 6.1: A 45–YEAR-OLD MALE WITH ABDOMINAL PAIN

Background: A 45-year-old male presents to urgent care with a complaint of (c/o) a gradual worsening of abdominal (ABD) pain in the lower left quadrant (LLQ) that has lasted for the last three days. His pain is described as aching, at times sharp. Associated symptoms include low grade fever of 100.2 F°, fatigue, nausea without vomiting and malaise. Past medical history (PMH) is significant for chronic constipation but no history of inflammatory bowel disease or irritable bowel syndrome. Otherwise the patient is in good health, with no daily medications taken.

Table 6.1
Patient Chart Information

ROBERT B. CHART INFORMATION		
Male Age: 45		
Current Weight: 220 lbs has poor dietary habits.		
Usual Weight: 230 lbs		
Height: 5 feet 11 in.		
Patient lost 10 lbs in last three months from ABD pain impacting appetite. He has a long Hx of chronic constipation; he has frequently dieted for weight loss. Regular BP: 110/79		

TESTS	ACTUAL	GOAL
*Glucose (mg/dl)	98	≤100
Albumin (g/dl)	4.7	3.9–5.0
Sodium (Na) (mEq/L)	138	136–144
Hemoglobin (g/dl)	10.8	14–18
Alkaline Phosphatase (IU/L)	48	44–147
ALT (Alanine Aminotransferase) IU/L	12	8–37
AST (Aspartate aminotransferase) IU/L	15	10–34

Source: NCEP 2001 report JAMA 16 (285), 2486– 97; American Diabetes Association (2011) Standards of Medical Care in Diabetes—2012 Diabetes Care. Suppl. 1, S11-63. * Fasting plasma glucose.

MedlinePlus: comprehensive metabolic panel: http://www.nlm.nih.gov/medlineplus/ency/article/003468.htm

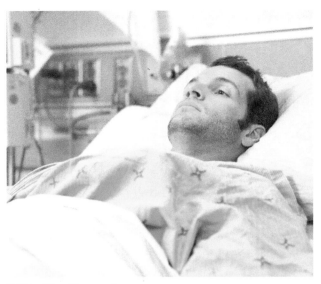

© *Tyler Olson/shutterstock.com*

Figure 6.9 *Robert B. is a 45-year-old construction worker with abdominal pain.*

Pertinent negatives: No diarrhea, rectal bleeding, melena, chest pain, shortness of breath (SOB), or anorexia.

Exam: Adult male, appearing mildly ill, but in no distress. Exam is normal except for moderate tenderness with palpation of LLQ, no guarding or rebound tenderness.

Summary of Biochemistry

Complete blood count (CBC): normal except White Blood Count (WBC) elevated 13.1 cells/L

Comprehensive metabolic Panel (CMP): normal

Erythrocyte Sedimentation Rate (ESR): normal

C-Reactive Protein (CRP): normal

Urine Analysis (UA): normal

Liver enzymes (ALT & AST): normal

Imaging Assessment

Flat and Upper Right Abdominal X-Ray (UR ABD XR): unremarkable gas pattern.

CT Abdominal with contrast: left-sided colonic diverticulitis.

Treatment: stool softeners, cipro 500 mg BID 14 days, Flagyl 500 mg TID 14 days. Constipation prevention strategy of high fiber diet recommended. Referral to dietitian was made. Dietitian will teach patient a 35 g/day high fiber diet beginning with a high fiber cereal (at least 5 g of fiber/serving). Total of 8 serving of whole wheat bread and/or whole grain cereals will be prescribed/day. A minimum of 5 fruits and vegetables will be recommended for this patient /day.

Using **Table 6.2** a minimum of 34 g can easily be achieved with ½ cup of Fiber-One® cereal, 3 slices of multi-grain whole wheat bread, ½ cup of carrots, ½ cup of broccoli, ¼ cup of raisins, and one medium apple/day.

6.11 INFLAMMATORY BOWEL DISEASE CASE STUDY 6.2: A 23-YEAR-OLD FEMALE WITH INFLAMMATORY BOWEL DISEASE (IBD)

Background: A 23-year-old female presents to family practice with a two-week history of a gradually worsening right-sided abdominal (ABD) pain and diarrhea. At the onset of illness, loose stools occurred 3-4 times per day but have gradually progressed to frequent liquid stools 8–9 per day and sometimes bloody. Pain location right upper and lower ABD. Pain described as aching and at times burning, initially mild but gradually worsening to severe. Patient states she is now so ill she cannot work; she is weak and has noticed her clothes are loose due to weight loss. Her boyfriend says she looks pale and miserable. Pain becomes worse two hours after a meal and is milder with the avoidance of food.

Table 6.2

Fiber Content of Grains and Fruits

PRODUCT	G /SERVING	# SERVING	TOTAL G
Fiber One	28g/cup	½ cup	14g
All bran buds	26g/cup		
Apple	4.4g/1 Med	1 med	4.4g
Apricots dried	5.0g/ ½ cup		
Pear	6g/ 1 med		
Raisins	3.5g/½ cup	¼ cup	1.75g
Banana	3g/1 med		
Cabbage	1.8g/cup shredded		
Carrots	3.6g/1 cup	1/2 cup	1.8g
Navy beans	51g/1c raw		
Broccoli	2.6g/1/2 cup	1/2 cup	2.6g
Multi-grain bread WW	3g/1 slice	3 slices	9g
TOTAL			34G

Source: USDA, National Nutrient Database for Standard Reference Release 27. Retrieved from http://ndb.nal.usda.gov/ndb/nutrients/index

© Alexander Raths/shutterstock.com

Figure 6.10 *Sally C. is a 23-year-old female college student with abdominal pain.*

Associated symptoms: nearly complete loss of appetite, fever is up to 102 F° and does not decrease entirely with ibuprofen. Patient also c/o debilitating fatigue, malaise, pallor and bloody stools.

Pertinent negatives: Melena, body aches, chills

Past Medical History (PMH): Patient has been in excellent health until this illness, no chronic health problems, no daily medications.

Social history: college senior, works part time at a grocery store.

Family History (FH): Mother has rheumatoid arthritis, otherwise negative.

Exam: Young adult female who appears her stated age, ill and tired but in no distress. Thin body habitus but no cachexia. Skin: pale, slightly diaphoretic but no cyanosis, turgor normal. Heart: tachycardic

120, rate regular, no murmur. Lungs: clear to auscultation, no cough or dyspnea. ENT: mucous membranes moist, no urinary tract infection (UTI).

Abdomen: Soft, non-distended, but pain with palpation over right upper and lower abdomen. No palpable masses or enlarged organs. Rectal: hemoccult positive

Biochemistry:

CBC: normal except low hemoglobin 8.2 g/dl

CMP: normal except low potassium 3.3 mEq/L

Urine Analysis: moderate proteinuria

Erythrocyte Sedimentation Rate (ESR): elevated 12.1—reveals general inflammation

C-Reactive Protein (CRP): elevated 7.1 mg/L—confirms inflammation as it is more accurate than ESR

Imaging Assessment:

Flat and UR ABD XR: normal

CT of abdomen with contrast: transmural colonic inflammation at ileocecal valve consistent with active Crohn's disease

Course of Action: Patient is hospitalized and transfused with 2 units PRBC's, IV rehydration. NPO is prescribed for bowel rest. Colonoscopy findings were significant for inflammation and constriction at the ileocecal valve. Colitis is consistent with Crohn's disease. Biopsy results also consistent with inflammation associated with Crohn's.

Treatment: Patient stabilized initially with prednisone then changed to immune modulator therapy to affect remission. Patient will need lifetime monitoring of this condition with up to twice yearly colonoscopy and monitoring of serum inflammatory markers: C-Reactive protein. While the inflammation of the colon subsides, patient will be placed on Peripheral Parenteral Nutrition (PPN) which is intended to be a short-term feeding through the peripheral veins, whereas total parenteral nutrition (TPN) is more of an option for long-term feeding using a central catheter. Once the inflammation subsides, the patient can be prescribed clear fluids for 1–2 days while maintaining the PPN, after which she can transition to full fluids and then to a soft diet. Concomitantly, the the caloric delivery from PPN can be gradually decreased. After about 3–4 days on a transitional diet, the patient can be given a regular diet and the PPN discontinued. Initially a lactose-free diet with an avoidance of alcohol, hot spices, and bulky grains will be prescribed, but patient should transition on their own to a more liberal diet as tolerated. The Crohn's and Colitis Foundation of America (CCFA, 2013) recommends small frequent meals eaten in a relaxed atmosphere and the avoidance of any trigger foods known to the patient. Foods rich in soluble fiber, typically seen in seeds, nuts, beans, leafy greens, and fruit should be minimally consumed as this kind of fiber is known to irritate the inflammed ares of the G.I tract (CCFA, 2013).

CHAPTER 6 PRACTICE QUESTIONS

1 Identify the GI disease for which there is no pathophysiology but yet the symptoms of abdominal pain are real.

2 Identify the GI condition that has deep fissures of the intestinal wall that affect the mucosa and the muscularis layers.

3 Identify the known cause of most peptic ulcers.

4 Identify the nutrients that are most closely monitored in Crohn's disease.

5 Identify the GI disease likely to be diagnosed with inflammation of mucosa, some blood in stool, no melena, and Fe-deficiency anemia.

REFERENCES

1 Alazraki, M. (2011). The 10 biggest-selling drugs that are about to lose their patents. *Daily Finance*. Retrieved from http://www.dailyfinance.com/2011/02/27/top-selling-drugs-are-about-to-lose-patent-protection-ready/

2 Academy of Nutrition and Dietetics (AND). (2008). Position of the ADA: Health implications of dietary fiber. *J Am Diet Assoc* 108, 1716–1731.

3 Asare, F. et al. (2012). Meditation over medication for irritable bowel syndrome? On exercise and alternative treatments for irritable bowel syndrome. *Curr Gastroenterol Rep* 14(4), 283–9. Retrieved from http://www.ncbi.nlm.nih.gov/pubmed/22661301

4 Bissonnette, D. (2013). *It's all about nutrition: Saving the health of Americans*. Lanham, MD: University Press of America, 232.

5 CDC. (2014). *Inflammatory Bowel Disease (IBD)*. Retrieved from: http://www.cdc.gov/ibd/

6 Crohn's & Colitis Foundation of America (CCFA, 2013). Diet and Nutrition and Inflammatory Bowel Disease. Retrieved July 7, 2016 from: http://www.ccfa.org/assets/pdfs/diet-nutrition-2013-1.pdf

7 Crohn's & Colitis Foundation of America (CCFA). *(2016).* What is Crohn's Disease. Retrieved July 7, 2016 from: http://www.ccfa.org/what-are-crohns-and-colitis/what-is-crohns-disease/

8 Dennison, C. et al. (2005). The health-related quality of life and economic burden of constipation. *Pharmacoeconomics* 23 (5), 461–476.

9 FDA. (2014). Irritable bowel syndrome treatments aren't one size fits all. *FDA's Consumer Update*. Retrieved from http://www.fda.gov/ForConsumers/ConsumerUpdates/ucm392396.htm

10 Feinstein LB, Holman RC, Yorita Christensen KL, Steiner CA, Swerdlow DL. (2010). Trends in hospitalizations for peptic ulcer disease, United States, 1998–2005. Emerg Infect Dis; 16(9). Retrieved from the Centers for Disease Control and Prevention website July 7, 2016: http://wwwnc.cdc.gov/eid/article/16/9/09-1126_article

11 Fessler, TA. (2007). A Dietary Challenge: Maximizing Bowel Adaptation in Short Bowel Syndrome. Today's Dietitian; 9 (1):40

12 Gropper, S.S. and Smith J.L. (2013). Advanced Nutrition and Human Metabolism, 6th edition. Belmont, CA: Wadsworth, 586 pp

13 Hanauer, S.B. et al., (2001). management of Crohn's Disease in Adults. *The American Journal of Gastroenterology*; 96 (3): 635– 643 retrieved July 9 2016 from: http://usatoday30.usatoday.com/money/industries/health/2011-03-01-antacid-shortage_N.htm

14 International Foundation for Functional Gastrointestinal Disorders (IFFDID) (2015.) Nutritional Strategies for the Management of Short Bowel Syndrome.

15 Jeejeebhoy, KN. (2006). Chapter 75: Short Bowel Syndrome. In: *Modern Nutrition in Health & Disease* (Maurice E. Shils, Moshe Shike et al., eds) 10th edition. Baltimore MD: Lippincott, Williams & Wilkins, pages :1201–1208

16 Lichtenstein, G.R. et al., (2009). Management of Crohn's Disease. Am. J. Gastroenterology doi: 10.1038/ajg.2008.168

17 Lupton, J.R., Trumbo PR. (2006). Dietary fiber. In: Shils, M.E., Shike, M., Ross, A.C., Caballero, B., Cousins, R.J., eds. *Modern Nutrition in Health and Disease*. 10th ed. Philadelphia: Lippincott Williams & Wilkins, 83–91

18 Mappes, H. J. & Farthmann, E. H. (2001). Anal abscess and fistula. In Ibid. Retrieved from http://www.ncbi.nlm.nih.gov/books/NBK6943/

19 Merck Manual for Healthcare Professionals. (2012). *Inflammatory bowel disease: Crohn's Disease*. Retrieved from http://www.merckmanuals.com/professional/gastrointestinal_disorders/inflammatory_bowel_disease_ibd/crohn_disease.html?/

20 Merck Manual for Healthcare Professionals. (2016). *Inflammatory bowel disease: Ulcerative Colitis*. Retrieved from http://www.merckmanuals.com/professional/gastrointestinal_disorders/inflammatory_bowel_disease_ibd/ulcerative_colitis.html

21 Merck Manual for Health Professionals (2016b). Overview of Inflammatory Bowel disease. Retrieved from: http://www.merckmanuals.com/professional/gastrointestinal-disorders/inflammatory-bowel-disease-ibd/overview-of-inflammatory-bowel-disease#v894291

22 Merck Manual for Healthcare Professionals (2016c). Overview of Malabsorption. Retrieved from: http://www.merckmanuals.com/professional/gastrointestinal-disorders/malabsorption-syndromes/overview-of-malabsorption

23 Merck Manual for Healthcare Professionals. (2012b). *Gastrointestinal disorders: Short bowel syndrome*. Retrieved from http://www.merckmanuals.com/professional/gastrointestinal_disorders/malabsorption_syndromes/short_bowel_syndrome.html

24 Merck Manual for Professionals (2016d). Bacterial Overgrowth Syndrome. Retrieved from: http://www.merckmanuals.com/professional/gastrointestinal-disorders/malabsorption-syndromes/bacterial-overgrowth-syndrome

25 Merck Manual for Healthcare Professionals (2016e). Overview of GI bleeding. Retrieved from: http://www.merckmanuals.com/professional/gastrointestinal-disorders/gi-bleeding/overview-of-gi-bleeding

26 Merck Manual for Healthcare Professionals. (2013). *Inflammatory bowel disease: Irritable bowel syndrome*. Retrieved from http://www.merckmanuals.com/professional/gastrointestinal_disorders/irritable_bowel_syndrome_ibs/irritable_bowel_syndrome_ibs.html?qt=IBS&alt=sh#v896655

27 National Library of Medicine (NLM). (2012) NIH. *Abscesses*. Retrieved from http://www.nlm.nih.gov/medlineplus/ency/article/001519.htm

28 National Library of Medicine (NLM). (2014) NIH. Liver Function Tests. Retrieved from: https://www.nlm.nih.gov/medlineplus/ency/article/003436.htm

29 Nightingale, J. & Woodard, J.M. (2006). Guidelines for the management of patients with a short bowel. *Gut*. 55 (5), iv1-iv12. Retrieved from http://www.ncbi.nlm.nih.gov/pmc/articles/PMC2806687/

30 Portalatin, M., and Winstead, N. (2012). Medical Management of Constipation. Clin Colon Rectal Surg; 25(1): 12–19. retrived July 7, 2016 from: http://www.ncbi.nlm.nih.gov/pmc/articles/PMC3348737/

31 Sajadinejad, M. S., Asgari, K., Molavi, H. Kalantari, M. and Adibi, P. (2012). Psychological Issues in Inflammatory Bowel Disease: An Overview. Gastroenterology Research and Practice; 2012 retrieved July 7, 2016 from: http://www.hindawi.com/journals/grp/2012/106502/

32 Smith, M.S. (2010). *Diagnosis and management of esophageal rings and webs gastro-enterol hepatol* (N Y). 6(11), 701–704. Retrieved from http://www.ncbi.nlm.nih.gov/pmc/articles/PMC3033540/

33 Stevenson, W.F. The esophagus and stomach. In Disorders of the alimentary tract (2006). In *Modern nutrition in health and disease*, 10th edition. (Shils, M.E. et al., eds). New York: Lippincott, Williams & Wilkins, 1179–188.

34 U.S. Department of Health & Human Services (DHHS). (2013). National Digestive Diseases Information Clearinghouse (NDDIC). *Digestive Disease Statistics for the United States NIH Publication No. 13–3873*, Retrieved from http://digestive.niddk.nih.gov/statistics/statistics.aspx

35 U.S. Department of Health & Human Services (DHHS). (2013b). *National Digestive Diseases Information Clearinghouse (NDDIC). Gastroesophageal Reflux (GER) and Gastroesophageal Reflux Disease (GERD) in Adults. NIH Publication No. 13–0882*. Retrieved from http://digestive.niddk.nih.gov/DDISEASES/pubs/gerd/

36 U.S. Department of Health & Human Services (DHHS). (2013c). *National Digestive Diseases Information Clearinghouse (NDDIC). Hemorrhoids, NIH Publication No 11–3021*. Retrieved from http://digestive.niddk.nih.gov/ddiseases/pubs/hemorrhoids/index.aspx#what

37 U.S. Department of Health & Human Services (DHHS). (2013d). *National Digestive Diseases Information Clearinghouse (NDDIC). Irritable Bowel Syndrome (IBS) NIH Publication No. 13–693*. Retrieved from http://digestive.niddk.nih.gov/ddiseases/pubs/ibs/index.aspx#what

38 U.S. Department of Health & Human Services (DHHS). (2011). *National Digestive Diseases Information Clearinghouse (NDDIC). Crohn's Disease. NIH Publication No. 12–3410*. Retrieved from http://digestive.niddk.nih.gov/ddiseases/pubs/crohns/

39 U.S. Department of Health & Human Services (DHHS). (2011b). *National Digestive Diseases Information Clearinghouse (NDDIC). H Pylori and Peptic Ulcers. NIH Publication No. 12–1597*. Retrieved from http://digestive.niddk.nih.gov/ddiseases/pubs/colitis/index.aspx#what

40 U.S. Department of Health & Human Services (DHHS). (2010). *National Digestive Diseases Information Clearinghouse (NDDIC). H Pylori and Peptic Ulcers. NIH Publication No. 10–4225*. Retrieved from http://digestive.niddk.nih.gov/ddiseases/pubs/hpylori/#1

41 U.S. Department of Health & Human Services (DHHS). (2007). *National Digestive Diseases Information Clearinghouse (NDDIC). What I Need to Know about Diverticular Disease NIH Publication No. 07–5535*. Retrieved from http://digestive.niddk.nih.gov/ddiseases/pubs/diverticular/#cause

42 Yoshio Yamaoka Michael E. DeBakey (eds) (2008). *Helicobacter pylori: Molecular genetics and cellular biology*. Veterans Affairs Medical Center, Caister Academic Press, 262pp.

CHAPTER 6 ANSWERS

1 Irritable bowel syndrome

2 Crohn's disease

3 Helicobacter Pylori

4 vitamin D, iron, B12, niacin and folic acid, in addition to the minerals zinc, selenium, and copper

5 ulcerative colitis

The Problem of Cancer

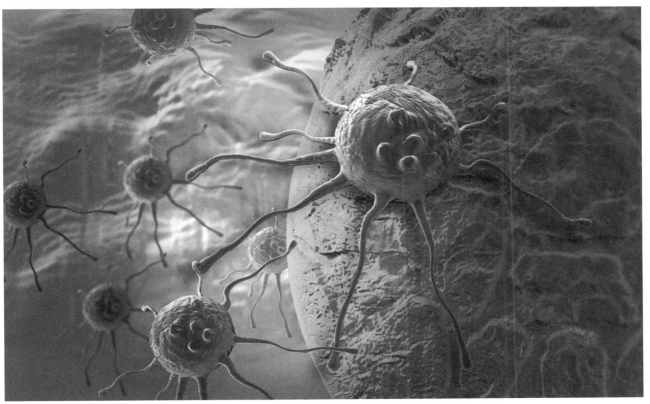

7.1 PREVALENCE OF CANCER

The prevalence of cancer is widespread throughout the United States with total cancer deaths increasing between 1971 and 2004 for lung, colorectal, prostate, and pancreatic cancers (Sporn, 2006). Cancer carries financial and human costs that are troubling. Even though death rates from overall cancers have been recently declining in the United States (NCI, 2014), the lifetime risk of contracting cancer at some point, for a U.S. male, is still 1 in 2 or 42.05%, and it is 1 in 3 or 37.58% for a female (ACS, 2016). According to the NIH, cancer takes the second position after heart disease for the greatest number of deaths in the United States, and the future does not look any better, as forecasters in 2010 ranked cancer as the leading cause of death by 2015. The economic burden to this country is alarming because of the direct long-term treatment costs that tax the healthcare system. In 2010 alone, cancer cost an estimated $263.8 billion in both direct and the indirect costs associated with mortality, losses to the labor force, and sick time (ACS, 2010). The human cost is dreadfully high as well, as it affects the physical, emotional, and spiritual dimensions of the person; it changes people's lives and the lives of their families in a significant manner (CDC, 2013). A total of 1.45 million people reportedly had a cancer diagnosis in 2010, and there were roughly 575,000 people who died from the disease that same year (CDC, 2013).

163

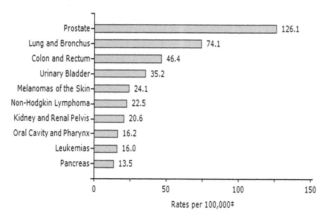

Top 10 Cancer Sites: 2010, Male, United States—All Races

Source: CDC 2014: http://apps.nccd.cdc.gov/uscs/toptencancers.aspx

Figure 7.1 *Prevalence of male cancers in the United States in 2010 in all races.*

After cardiovascular disease, cancer is the most significant cause of death in the United States and in most westernized nations (Willett & Giovannucci, 2006). The highest risk of cancer in men is prostate cancer (CDC, 2014) (Figure 7.1) whereas in women it is breast cancer (CDC, 2013b). The second most prevalent form of cancer, in both men and women, is bronchial and lung cancer, and in third position, is the prevalence of colorectal cancer in both genders (CDC, 2014; 2013b). It is reassuring that the three most prevalent forms of cancer, currently in the United States, are directly associated with lifestyle. Indeed, if Americans would quit smoking, start to exercise regularly, and consume a diet rich in fruits and vegetables, cancer rates would begin to dramatically decline over the following 10 to 20 years. Worldwide, the prevalence of cancer is on the rise. The CDC estimates that between 2010 and 2020, new cases of cancer in men are expected to rise 24%, whereas a 21% jump is forecasted in women, culminating in over one million new cases in the United States per year. This will represent $156 billion/year in medical costs (NCI, 2016; CDC, 2016). The incidence of new cancers is shocking and motivates a fear-driven population to find a remedy or a prevention strategy that works.

This is especially true since it is now recognized that 39.6% of U.S. men and women will get cancer in their lifetime (NCI, 2016). Internationally the W.H.O. predicts that new yearly cancer incidences are expected to rise to 15 million by 2020,

and 22 million by 2030. These are values that have significantly jumped from the 12 million new cases reported in 2012 (NCI, 2016; WHO, 2003).

7.2 PREVENTION OF CANCER

It is clear that many cancers are preventable by modifying dietary practices and lifestyles. Overall, epidemiologists have linked 45% of cancer deaths in men and 59% in women to diet and lifestyle (Anand, 2008). For instance, making a firm decision not to smoke would greatly decrease the risk of lung, bronchial, and bladder cancers. Incidence rates of melanomas of the skin would also fall with the use of sunscreen and limited exposure to tanning beds. Likewise, colon and rectal cancers would decline concomitantly with the ingestion of more fruits and vegetables in addition to maintaining a healthy weight (CDC, 2014; ACS, 2012). High physical activity levels were also tied to lower incidence of cancer at the population level (Willett & Giovannucci, 2006).

Screening is another tactic used in public health to detect a disease early before it becomes too invasive and compromises the health of the individual. The CDC has many cancer prevention programs that are used to screen and tract the population for cancer. There is the **National Breast and Cervical Cancer Early Detection Program** (NBCCEDP), the **National Comprehensive Cancer Control Program** (NCCCP), the **National Program of Cancer Registries** (NPCR), and the **Colorectal Cancer Control Program** (CRCCP). They have all successfully coordinated either the screening or monitoring of tens of millions of Americans every year (CDC, 2013).

The most powerful incentive, however, is to study preventative ways to avoid developing cancer in the first place. Epidemiological research has also focused on the prevention strategies built in our lifestyles and eating habits that can contain and possibly eliminate the scourge.

As far back as the early 1940s, studies on rats showed that **caloric restrictions** could hinder mammary tumor development. Much later on, in the mid-1980s, researchers demonstrated that a 30%

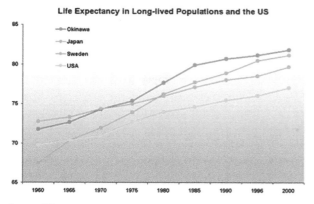

Source: WHO 1996 and Japan Ministry of Health and Welfare. (2004). U.S. Department of Health & Human Services/CDC 2005

Figure 7.2

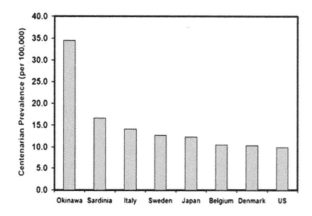

Source: Wilcox, DC et al. AGE 2006. 28(4), 313–332.

Figure 7.3 *Prevalence of centenarians in Okinawa versus United States in 2002.*

energy restriction in rats diminished mammary rat tumors by as much as 90% (Willett & Giovannucci, 2006). The results were fascinating and had significant implications on human epidemiological cancer research. This was especially true for an overweight and obese population plagued with numerous secondary diseases. The growing onslaught of obese and overweight patients—the obese most typically carry a morass of costly and debilitating medical problems—began to clog the efficient delivery of medical services in the United States as far back as the 1990s, and were becoming very expensive to manage. Indeed, by 2008, the total direct cost to manage overweight and obese U.S. adults rose to $147 billion per year (Finkelstein et al., 2009). It is

not just that we are getting bigger, but also sicker; medically, an obese individual is at high risk of cancers of the breast, endometrium, prostate, pancreas, colon and rectum (NCI, 2012; NCI, 2010). In addition to these devastating conditions, obese persons will tend to have chronic problems with their gallbladders; they will suffer from osteoarthritis, sleep apnea, asthma, and possibly depression, in addition to hypertension, atherosclerosis, and type-2 diabetes (CDC, 2014b; NIH, 2012). All these conditions come with a hefty price tag because they are serious and complicated chronic diseases that require constant management by medical practitioners.

At a societal level, the goal of a public health preventative program is to increase longevity and quality of life. There is no point in living longer if it means extending lives plagued with chronic disease and suffering; the idea is to live long and healthy.

The Okinawa study, which began in 1976, is a clear example of how temperate living in an isolated Japanese sub-culture, resistant to modernization, appears to translate into health and longevity. Here is a society with a mean life expectancy of 81.2 years—much longer than the United States's 76.8 years (Figure 7.2)—and an astounding 2.5 to 5 times greater number of centenarians in the population (Figure 7.3) than found in most industrialized countries (Suzuki, 2001; Willcox et al., 2006).

These are decisive statistics that greatly suggest there is an interaction between genetics and the environment. Research in the field of heritability concludes that between 10–50% of longevity is inherited with most agreeing that 25–33% of our lifespan is likely determined by genes. This translates into 67–75% of our longevity possibly being greatly influenced by factors in our environment (Wilcox, 2006b; Christensen et al., 2006). So then what is it in the Okinawan environment that increases longevity?

The Okinawans tend to consume only 80% of their caloric needs, or in other words, they follow a style of eating known as "*hara hachi bu.*" In this form of eating, the person is encouraged to consume low glycemic foods such as legumes and vegetables. In concrete terms, this means Okinawans rise from the table without being fully satisfied at that moment. Does this mean they remain in a state of hunger?

Not likely, since that slight hungry feeling dissipates a little later as the food settles in the stomach.

The Okinawa diet, so it appears, slows the aging process and prevents disease. In fact, the prevalence of breast and prostate cancers is 80% lower than in Western societies; also, the rates of colon and ovarian cancers are less than 50% of the rates reported in industrialized nations. One of the accepted aging theories is that free radical production can overwhelm the concentrations of antioxidants in the body and therefore overcome cellular integrity and cause cell damage and even death (apoptosis). It is this cell damage that plays into the aging process and the etiology of disease. Consistent with this theory, a population that consumes abundant antioxidants in its diet can keep the free radicals in check, slow down the aging process, and prevent coronary artery disease and some cancers (Suzuki et al., 2001). In Okinawa, the centenarians tend to consume almost 10 times (10 x) the amount of isoflavones—an antioxidant—found in the diet of Japanese Canadians.

The isoflavones—genistein and daidzein—are protective against hormone-based cancers such as breast, prostate, and endometriosis, and are found in soy-based foods such as soybeans, tofu, and tempeh. Researchers have also measured elevated lignans in foods like flaxseed and grain products. Combined together, the diet content of antioxidants is elevated enough that, compared to Westerners, Okinawans have an 80% risk reduction in cardiovascular disease (Willcox, 2006: 2006b).

Okinawa residents manage to maintain a consistent Body Mass Index (BMI) that varies between 18 and 22. This rather lean physical consistency is achieved through a combination of kcalorie-controlled intakes and regular physical exercise. From a very young age, the martial arts like karate are taught to their children. Judo, in particular, is Japan's national sport and one of the most effective self defence systems around. The warm ups alone are intense and can cause even the most adept aerobics instructor to run for the vomit bag before the end of the 20-minute warm up; the vigorous judo training then lasts an additional hour and ten minutes.

Agility, resistance and flexibility are the main physical attributes that are developed by the martial arts, which are often practiced for 20–30 years, and in some cases up to 70 years of age; it is not uncommon to see a 70-year-old Okinawan still practicing judo or karate regularly. Over time, joints tend to be more flexible, physical resistance, and endurance significantly greater in the Okinawan compared to a typical Westerner. It would not be surprising to see a 70-year-old Okinawan demonstrate greater flexibility and agility than a typical middle aged Westerner. The schedule followed by Japanese youth is a 90-minute judo practice three to five times per week. In this setting, a Japanese teenager, weighing 150 lbs, would expend 0.075 kcal/lb/minute for a total of 844 kcal per practice, or 2531 kcal per week if practiced three times (3x) per week.

Maintaining energy balance appears to be the strategy that works. Other epidemiological studies appear to reaffirm the position that visceral body fat accumulation in humans, invariably lead to the development of several cancers (Nightingale & Giovannucci, 2006).

The important point that comes out of the Okinawa studies is that a diet high in antioxidants does appear to protect the body against cancer and aging. Suzuki and colleagues (2001) report that with high antioxidant intakes from the diet, there are lower levels of plasma lipid peroxides (LPO) compared to controls. Numerous animal studies also confirmed that exogenous antioxidants given to rats help decrease free radical levels and damage to cells and tissue (NCI, 2014b). The relevant question right now is whether antioxidant supplements can prevent cancer. There are nine randomized clinical trials that have tested the efficacy of antioxidant supplements in cancer prevention (NCI, 2014b), and they mostly show no decrease in cancer incidence rates, or increased risk of cancer with supplementation. Two of the studies had to be stopped early. One study—**Alpha-Tocopherol/Beta-Carotene Cancer Prevention Study**—reported in 1994 that those subjects receiving beta-carotene supplements were developing lung cancer at rates greater than controls. The other study—**Carotene and Retinol Efficacy Trial**—was a U.S.-based investigation that found in 1996 that smokers on beta-carotene were developing lung cancer at a faster rate than non-smokers, and that the cause of death from all studied sources was also more elevated. More surprising and troubling was that cancer risk persisted up to six years after ending the intake of supplements. Interestingly, another study during the late nineties as well—**Physicians' Health Study I (PHS I)**—found that a 50 mg beta-carotene supplement, taken over the long term, had no effect on either mortality or cancer incidence rates in smokers and non-smokers. In 2001, a U.S. trial—The **Selenium and Vitamin E Cancer Prevention Trial**—was stopped in 2008 because it showed that daily vitamin E supplements taken alone over a 5.5 year period had no effect in reducing the incidence of prostate or other forms of cancers in men 50 years of age and older. However, a 2011 follow up reported that subjects who took only vitamin E supplements had a 17% greater risk of developing prostate cancer than those on a placebo (Klein et al., 2011). Finally the Physicians' Health Study II (PHS II) showed that daily supplementation of two popular antioxidants (400 IU vitamin E every other day, 500 mg vitamin C) over a median 7.6 years had no impact on a wide variety of cancers notably, prostate, melanomas, leukemia, and colorectal (NCI, 2014b). The effect of supplementation on cancer prevention is certainly not convincing at this time, and should cause some degree of alarm.

The idea of preventing cancer appears now to centrically revolve around the issue of good and wholesome nutrition. It is not enough to take a supplement, while continuing to eat poorly, and expect to be protected from the long-term devastation of chronic diseases like cancer. The Dietary Guidelines for Americans 2015 recommend the daily consumption of varied vegetables, notably dark green vegetables of the cruciferous type (Brassica genus). These include vegetables such as broccoli, Brussels sprouts, cabbage, cauliflower, turnips, rutabaga, collard greens, radishes, and kale, which are rich in biologically active compounds called phytochemicals. For instance, they contain indols, isothiocyanates, and thiocyanates that have been shown in vitro and in rat studies to be protective against cancer (NCI, 2012). However, human prospective studies have not convincingly shown that abundant and regular intake of cruciferous vegetables imparts strong protection against varied types of cancers (NCI, 2012). Clearly more research is needed to elucidate this vegetable controversy. The challenge is to begin these long-term prospective studies early enough—that is before the promotional phase of cancer is advanced—in order to truly measure the protective effect of these vegetables against cancer

(Giovannucci et al., 2003). The more persuasive findings, regarding dietary components that increase the risk of cancer, are from those studies measuring the impact of meat consumption on cancer incidence.

Rat studies and in vitro tests have shown that heterocyclic amines (HCA) and polycistic aromatic hydrocarbons (PACs) formed from the high temperature treatment of beef, pork, chicken, and fish have mutagenic effects on DNA with the potential of leading to development of cancer cells. High doses of PACs and HCAs, fed to monkeys and rats, caused mutagenic changes in their cells, and eventually cancer. Using large epidemiological human studies, it became evident that there was a significant association between the consumption of well-done, fried or barbecued meats, and colorectal, pancreatic, and prostate cancers in humans (NCI, 2010). However, the link between HCAs and PACs, and cancer has not been decisively established in humans. And while several prospective studies have shown a 13–17% increase in the risk of cancer for every 100 g (~3oz-wt) of red meat consumed, it was the incremental risks tied to processed meat that was alarming. Prospective studies and a meta-analysis demonstrated a 49% jump in cancer risks for every 25 g (~1oz-wt) of processed meat consumed (Willett & Giovannucci, 2006). Another set of 21 studies found a 30% to 40% risk of developing prostate cancer with increased red meat consumption. Most notable was a study by Pan et al. (2012) that looked at data from two very large prospective studies—Health Professionals Follow-up Study (HPFS) and Nurses' Health Study (NHS)—that followed over many years 51,529 men and 121,700 women, respectively. Researchers are uncertain whether the cancers are caused by the fats from the meats or something else in the meat. One thing remains, and that is that frequent red meat consumption should not be encouraged, especially processed meats according to American Cancer Society Guidelines on Nutrition and Physical Activity (Willett & Giovannucci, 2006; ACS, 2012).

7.3 PATHOPHYSIOLOGY OF CANCER

Cancer, rather than being a static state, is now seen more as a dynamic process or an evolving cellular process, and thus is referred to as carcinogenesis.

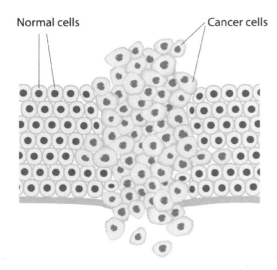

Normal cells   Cancer cells

© *Alila Medical Media/shutterstock.com*

Figure 7.4 *Cancer cell proliferation.*

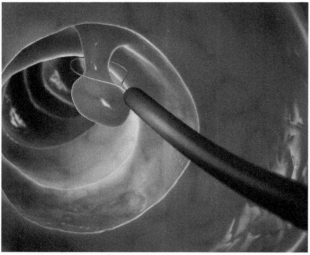

© *Sebastian Kolitzski/shutterstock.com*

Figure 7.5 *Polyp being removed from colon.*

This is consistent with the medical community's understanding that there is a 20 year or greater latency period that spans the point of cancer initiation, in which DNA mutation occurs, to the promotional phase in which cancer becomes invasive and metastatic (Sporn, 2006).

The size, structure, function, and growth rate of malignant cancer cells are very different than what is observed in normal cells. The problem begins when a cell's ability to differentiate becomes altered because

of DNA mutations, taking place in the nucleus of the cell, that alter the normal functions, cell division, growth, and appearance of the cell (NCI, 2014). The consequence is an important change in the way the tissue works, ultimately leading to pain, cachexia, lowered immunity, anemia, leukopenia, and thrombocytopenia (NCHPAD, 2014). The mutated cells begin to divide, producing numerous anomalous cells that grow at irregular rates that are sometimes fast other times slow (Figure 7.4) (ACS, 2014).

They can **metastasize**, or in other words **proliferate**, in distant organs and tissues via the complex and far reaching lymphatic and cardiovascular circulatory systems (NCI, 2014). Most malignant cells form tumors (Figure 7.5), however leukemia does not form tumors, but rather leukemic cancer cells invade blood and bone marrow cells. Representing 3.3% of all cancer cases, leukemia, despite being responsible for only 4.1% of all cancer deaths, nevertheless afflicted 318,389 people in 2012 (NCI, 2014c). In 2011, the National Cancer Institute estimated that there would be by 2015 approximately 54,270 new cases of leukemia diagnosed in the United States, and about 24,450 deaths due to leukemia (NCI, 2014c). These predictions tend to be very close to actual prevalence values, since the prediction model follows longstanding prevalence graphs that have been closely monitored since 1992.

The rapid development of cancer in the West coincides remarkably well with the growth of obesity in adults and the earlier onset of menarche in young girls, which has been attributed to rapid growth rates prior to puberty.

Whereas in China the onset of menstruations begins around 17 years of age, in the United States the age of menarche starts at 12 or 13 years of age. What is of interest is that this early onset of the menstrual cycle is associated with future risk of breast and other types of cancers (Nightingale & Giovannucci, 2006). Moreover, cancer risk increases with body weight in adults and young people. The mechanism is likely tied to metabolic and hormonal changes such as increased circulating sex hormones, insulin, and insulin-like growth factor (IGF). These are now recognized as powerful vectors for cell differentiation, proliferation, and apoptosis. Human studies have shown that high serum IGF-1 and insulin are strongly linked to colon cancers in the more prosperous populations (Giovannucci, 2001). These findings suggest then that weight loss should be associated with a decline in cancer risk. This however, has not been investigated very thoroughly in the human population. Nevertheless, one prospective study (Parker & Folsom, 2003) had found that women, who had purposely lost at least 20 lbs, experienced a significant reduction in breast cancer risk.

7.4 COLON CANCER AND THE U.S. DIET

Colon cancer is the third most prevalent form of cancer, in both men and women in the United States, and is responsible for as many as 51,000 deaths/year (ACS, 2010); but most interesting, 90% of colorectal cancers are diagnosed after 50 years of age, and the risk of a genetic predisposition is only weighted at 5% (NCI, 2014E). This means that most colorectal cancers are the result of either endogenous or exogenous factors that damage genes, and therefore are considered preventable (ACS, 2010). A colonoscopy is the preferred method of screening for colonic polyps, which could be benign or malignant. From a preventative perspective, it is best to consider polyps as potentially cancerous. Polyps found in the colon are generally raised (Figure 7.5) or flat, and should be surgically removed in order to decrease the risk of the polyp becoming cancerous. Research conducted at the Memorial Sloan-Kettering Cancer Center, reported a 53% decline in death rates when all polyps were systematically removed from subjects during standard colonoscopies (ACS, 2012b).

It was this study that helped establish the extent to which early detection of polyps with colonoscopies could help reduce the risk of colon cancer. Findings from long-term epidemiological prospective studies, over the last 10 years, reveal that individuals at risk of developing polyps regularly consume fatty foods; they tend to have a diet high in red and processed meat; they consume few fruits and vegetables, exercise very little, smoke, and drink alcohol excessively, and tend to be either overweight or obese (DHHS, 2008; ACS, 2010). Moreover, high fruit and vegetable intake tends to decrease risks of oral, esophageal, stomach, and colorectal cancers. Indeed, those who tend to eat more abundant fruits and vegetables will also be more likely not to consume as many fatty foods. The research findings are not always consistent since not all vegetables are equal. Those studies that have found vegetables to be anticarcinogenic, almost unfailingly point towards carotene-rich vegetables that contain a vast array of carotenoids such as lutein, zeaxanthin, criptoxanthin, lycopene, ß-carotene, and α-carotene. Visually this means the lunch and dinner plate must be loaded up with yellow/red and yellow/orange vegetable combinations—a dramatic shift from the dreary monotonous brown and beige plates often seen throughout popular restaurant chains. In fact, the ß-carotene rich fruits and vegetables appear to inhibit cancer-induction events. But be warned that ß-carotene supplements have been shown, in the beta-Carotene and Retinol Efficacy Trial, published in the high impact *New England Journal of Medicine* (Omenn, et al., 1996), to increase lung cancer risks among smokers. It becomes clear that the full protective effect of phytochemicals can be better felt using minimally processed vegetables and fruits, not supplements. The prevalence of colon cancer has declined considerably since screening for patients >50 years of age became a more common practice by physicians in 1998. Consequently, the prevalence declined from 63.3 to 45.5/100,000 people over age 50, but did increase since 1994 in those men and women younger than 50 (ACS, 2010).

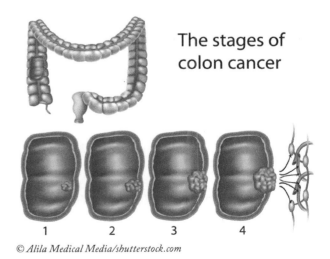

The stages of colon cancer

1   2   3   4

© *Alila Medical Media/shutterstock.com*

Figure 7.6 *Colon Cancer*

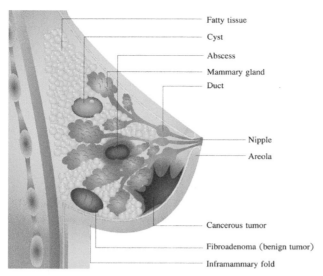

© GRei/shutterstock.com

Figure 7.7 *Breast cancer and other breast anomalies*

Experts believe that it is the routine colonoscopies, conducted in men and women over 50 years of age, that have led to lowering the incidence rates in the >50 years age group through early detection and treatments. The main reason is that the early phases of colon cancer are virtually asymptomatic or without noticeable symptoms (DHHS, 2008). By the time the polyp has evolved to a cancerous stage-4 (Figure 7.6) and caused more frequent and noticeable lower abdominal cramping in addition to bloody stools, the cancer has more likely begun to spread systemically throughout the body. In that sense the cancer is said to have metastasize or spread to other tissues.

7.5 BREAST CANCER AND THE U.S. DIET

The National Cancer Institute predicted that there would likely be an estimated 231,840 new cases of invasive breast cancer in the United States in 2015. Using a predicted 17.4% death rate, the NCI forecast of approximately 40,340 deaths was not far from actual reported values (NCI, 2014d). Ductal breast carcinoma represents about 70% of invasive breast cancers (Figure 7.7) and is the leading cause of cancer deaths in women (NCI, 2014d; CTCA, 2014). There are a few non-modifiable factors that heighten the risk of breast cancers in women, starting with an early age at menarche or late onset of menopause, and a family history of breast cancer. The breast cancer susceptibility genes (BRCA1 and BRCA2) are very rare, representing between 5–10% of all breast cancer cases (ACS, 2010). It is however encouraging to note that between 1999 and 2006 the incidence of breast cancer has been declining at a rate of 2% per year, and experts believe this decrease is likely the result of two events: first, a 2002 publication that came out of the Women's Health Initiative (WHI), which reported the findings of a 15 year NIH study program that followed 161,808 post-menopausal women. Researchers in that study had successfully linked hormonal menopausal therapy (HMT), consisting of a combined use of estrogen and progestin, to higher risks of breast cancer (ACS, 2010); second, there has also been a decline in the use of mammography as an early screening tool for cancer which may have simply delayed early breast cancer detection and falsely brought down incidence rates. The findings from the WHI study persuaded professional medical bodies to change therapeutic approaches for managing menopausal women.

It is hopeful that breast cancer incidences can be reduced in the population by modifying medical therapies. But even more encouraging is the fact that there are lifestyle and diet changes that can be embraced by women in order to greatly decrease their risk of developing breast cancer in future years. The main risk factors for breast cancer that can be modified include: first, significant weight gain after the age of 18; second, becoming overweight or obese; third, adopting a physically inactive lifestyle; fourth, the intake of one or more alcoholic drinks per day; fifth, recent use of oral contraceptives; sixth, never having children; or seventh, delaying having the first child until after the age of 30 (ACS, 2010). In order to further decrease risks, women are encouraged to breastfeed, engage in moderate to vigorous exercise, and maintain a healthy body weight (ACS, 2010). The good news is that five-year survival rates have significantly improved since the 1960s, going from a mere 63% to an impressive 90% today. If the cancer is localized in the breast and has not spread, the survival rate jumps to 98%. By contrast, patients with breast cancer that metastasize to the lymph nodes, have a five-year 84% survival rate, however, metastatic cancer that invades other organs brings survival rates down to 23% (ACS, 2010).

7.6 ASSESSMENT OF CANCER PATIENTS

A little over 50% of all newly diagnosed cancers in women are lung, breast, and colorectal, whereas in men, 55% are lung, prostate, and colorectal. These four types of cancers are responsible for more than 50% of the half million cancer deaths reported every year in the United States. Moreover, the direct cost to manage cancer is estimated at $40 billion a year, and the forecast is for health care costs to continue to rise as the absolute number of cancer patients is expected to increase (Shattener & Shike, 2006). There is a clear incentive to improve cancer management strategies, because rates have not declined in a manner consistent with the 1970s National Cancer Institute goals of halving cancer mortality rates by the year 2000 (Sporn, 2006).

One of those possible strategies is to improve the nutritional status of cancer patients undergoing treatments. There are several factors that need to be considered in a nutritional assessment: first, the primary goal is to accurately provide a prognosis or in other words, a reasonable forecast of the patient's ability to fare well physically during the treatment process. A poor nutritional status translates into a poor prognosis for patients undergoing chemotherapy, and therefore a poor outcome. Malnutrition is so prominent in cancer that among the 1.3 million patients newly diagnosed with invasive cancer in 2003, 80% were malnourished and experienced significant weight loss (Shattener & Shike, 2006). In fact, between 54% to over 80% of patients suffering from prostate, lung, pancreatic, colon, and gastric cancers, experienced moderate to severe weight loss about six months prior to the official cancer diagnosis. It is generally accepted that an involuntary weight loss greater than 10% of usual body weight, over a six-month period, is concerning, and needs to be addressed (Shattener & Shike, 2006).

The reasons for the weight loss are multifactorial, but the most significant contributor is a decline in caloric intake, generally attributed to an early sense of satiety in 71% of patients, anorexia in 56% of cases, and a change in taste perception 60% of the time (Komurcu et al., 2002).

The second most influential cause of weight loss are metabolic alterations that affect the way the body metabolizes carbohydrates, proteins, and lipids (Shattener & Shike, 2006).

7.7 METABOLIC CHANGES DURING CANCER

There is indeed a distinct metabolic pattern in cancer patients that contrasts with the metabolism seen in patients suffering from simple starvation (Gullett et al., 2011). Otto Warburg, a doctor of medicine and chemistry, was the first to observe, as early as the 1930s, that cancer cells have an altered metabolism. This phenomenon was later called the **Warburg Effect** in his honor and depicted a faster aerobic glycolysis inside the tumor cells, which utilized much higher than normal glucose and generated abnormally elevated lactate (Wu & Zhao, 2013). **Warburg** published his findings in 1956 and forever changed the fundamental understanding of cancer (Warburg, 1956). Consequently, the medical field interpreted this heightened glycolysis as part of the process needed to nourish uncontrollable cell proliferation and ultimately, tumor growth. Interestingly, the acidic environment, created from the overproduction of lactate, appears to be specifically harmful to normal cells but of no consequence to cancer cells (Wu & Zhao, 2013).

Another phenomena observed in cancer is hyperglycemia. Carbohydrate metabolism, during cancer-induced weight loss, favors a heightened glucose

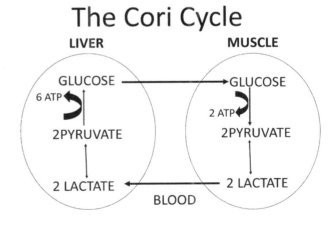

Figure 7.8 *The Cori cycle.*

turnover, as depicted by an increased endogenous production of glucose, thus leading to hyperglycemia; this is likely the consequence of glucose intolerance, insulin resistance and possibly a decline in pancreatic release of insulin. In simple starvation, by contrast, weight loss is intimately associated with a decline in glucose turnover. What does this mean? In starvation, the lack of food intake leads to a decline in food and sugar ingestion, and therefore sugar absorption. Likewise, insulin secretion from the beta cells of the pancreas also decreases, which normally leads to an increased secretion of hormone-sensitive lipase, and to an ensuing increase in lipolysis or breakdown of fat via oxidative metabolism. In cancer patients, this process is altered, thereby leading to a rate of glucose oxidation that increases proportionally with the tumor size, and that never really completely relents, even when exogenous glucose is infused through the veins of these patients. Still, endogenous glucose production persists maximally first, through the continued breakdown of hepatic glycogen reserves—maximal output lasts 12–24 hours after the start of fasting—followed by a persistent gluconeogenesis that catabolizes protein in order to form glucose. Researchers have also noted a persistent Cori cycle (Figure 7.8) that is metabolically

inefficient as it costs the body a net 4 ATPs to revert anaerobically-produced muscle lactate via glycolysis back to glucose using a gluconeogenic pathway in the liver, only for the muscle to reuse the glucose again. In cancer, the body can relentlessly breakdown muscle lactate, via the Cori cycle, thus representing as high as 50% of the glucose turnover in cancer patients (Holroyde et al., 1975) and causing a 0.9 kg loss of fat mass per month (Tisdale, 1997). The body then proceeds to more completely revert to the degradation of skeletal muscle protein and to the inhibition of muscle protein synthesis, both causing, over time, a visible wasting of the skeletal muscle mass that so characteristically leads to the state of **cachexia** or significant wasting, which is often seen in advanced cancer (Tisdale, 1997). More specifically, the 2006 Cachexia Consensus Conference, has officially defined cachexia as "a complex metabolic syndrome associated with underlying illness and characterized by loss of muscle with or without loss of fat mass" (Evans et al., 2008).

Also, concomitantly, liver protein synthesis increases during this time, perhaps to produce C-reactive proteins and other stress-related proteins. Interestingly, the relentless muscle protein breakdown, observed

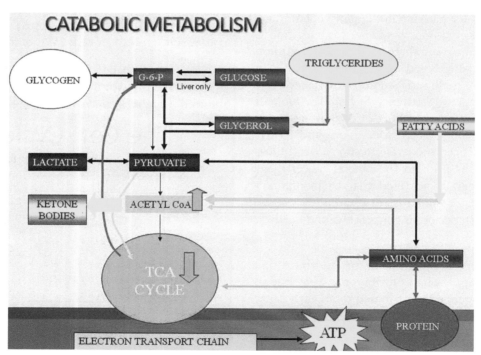

Image courtesy of David Bissonnette

Figure 7.9 *Catabolic Pathways during fasting..*

during carcinogenesis, is not naturally diminished over time, as in simple starvation, nor is it completely prevented with nutritional support, whether it be given parenterally (veins) or enterally (gut). In other words, hyper-alimentation is not capable of completely preventing continued muscle breakdown in cancer-generated anorexia. In addition, fat reserves are also depleted in cancer patients, in part because of a lipid-mobilizing factor (LMF) generated from the tumor, which causes a persistent lipolysis, and in part by insulin resistance, and a heightened catecholamine secretion due to metabolic stress (Shattener & Shike, 2006). In ordinary starvation, by contrast, the body's reliance on glycogen quickly changes to gluconeogenesis within about 12 to 14 hours, then by about two days, 90% of the body's glucose needs is derived from protein, and about 10% from glycerol in order to maintain neurological function (Figure 7.9). Afterwards, dependency on protein rapidly shifts again, so that by the 10th day of starvation the nervous system's reliance on ketone bodies, rather than glucose, is at its peak (Rolfe et al., 2009). In this manner, long-term dieting leads to a high reliance on fat and thus spares protein. However, because fat is effectively oxidized in the flame of carbohydrate metabolism, the production of ketone bodies becomes more prominent during fasting because of the absence of dietary carbohydrates. This is nicely depicted in Figure 7.9 with the TCA cycle's downward arrow, which occurs with a less active glycolysis. The abundant fat being broken down for energy (lipolysis), rather than being oxidized through the TCA cycle, is diverted towards the synthesis of ketone bodies. The upside is that the brain can use ketones instead of glucose. Fortunately, gluconeogenesis, by this time, has dropped by 67% in light of this adaptation. Carcinogenesis, contrariwise, persistently taxes both muscle protein and adipocytes, causing a significant depletion of both body reserves; in this way, the body appears cachectic, or severely emaciated.

7.7.1 Nutritional Assessment of Cancer Patients:

A proper determination of the patient's nutritional status should be established by the dietitian. This information is vital to the medical team who must assess the patient's prognosis or likelihood of recovery or surviving the chemotherapy. The understanding here is that the dietitian has two possible roles: first, should the physician want to pursue an aggressive treatment protocol, the dietitian should determine a feeding regimen to ensure the patient's nutritional status is sufficient to enable him to tolerate and recover from the chemotherapy and/or radiation therapy (CTCA, 2015); or second, determine the kind of nutritional support that will be needed to help maintain an acceptable quality of life for patients receiving hospice care (Fuhrman, 2008).

Patients aggressively treated for their cancer need to receive strong nutritional support. The baseline nutritional status before medical treatments is important to establish, as it will help the medical team determine pre-treatment nutritional support in order to increase the likelihood of the patient tolerating and successfully getting through the chemo and radiation relatively unscathed. The nutrition support prevents complications that may arise from surgery, chemotherapy, or radiation therapy and increases survival rate (NCI, 2014g). The Prognostic Nutritional Index (PNI) and the Patient-Generated Subjective Global Assessment (PG-SGA) are prognostic nutritional indicators, currently in use, that assist medical teams in establishing reliable and accurate patient prognosis (NCI, 2014g).

The Prognostic Nutritional Index (PNI) equation is depicted here and represented as a percent (Buzby and Mullen, 1984):

$$PNI = 158 - [16.6(alb) + 0.78(TSF) + 0.2(Trn) + 5.8(DH)]$$

Used as a method of predicting the occurrence of complications in patients that are undergoing non-emergency surgery, this method relies on: serum albumin (Alb) expressed in g/dl [normal: 3.4–5.4 g/dl]; delayed hypersensitivity (DH) [normal: 2], with assessment ranges represented here: (no reaction = 0, < 5mm induration =1, and > 5mm induration = 2) (Dempsey et al., 1983); triceps skinfold (TSF) measured in mm [normal for men: 5–28mm; women: 11–38 mm] (Stoudt et al., 1970); and serum transferrin (Tns), measured a mg/dl [normal: 200–360 mg/dl]. The major limitation is that the index has difficulty differentiating between the effects of malnutrition and those of disease; patients with iron deficiency anemia, for instance, would tend to have

PATIENT-GENERATED SUBJECTIVE GLOBAL ASSESSMENT

NAME:_____; AGE:_____; DATE:___/___/_____

Complete this form by questioning the patient or selecting the most likely option

WEIGHT HISTORY

Current Weight_____ Kg Percent usual weight: _____

Usual Weight _____ Kg

Weight 3 Months Ago: _____ Kg % weight loss:_____

Weight 6 months Ago:: _____ Kg % weight loss:_____

Goal Weight to Achieve:_____ Kg

DIET ASSESSMENT

My FOOD INTAKE compared to 1 month ago:

□ I am eating more

□ I am eating the same

□ I am eating less

The type of FOOD I am eating:

□ Normal diet

□ Very little solid food

□ Only liquids

□ Only nutritional supplements

□ Very little food of any kind

ACTIVITY ASSESSMENT

Daily activity level over the last month:

□ Normal

□ Less than usual

□ Don't feel like doing anything

□ I spend half of the day in bed or sitting down

ABILITY TO EAT/TOLERATE FOOD

I have problems eating:

□ YES

□ NO

If the answer is "YES" indicate below the problem (s) you are having

□ I have no appetite

□ I have nausea

□ I am vomiting

□ I have constipation

□ I have gas /bloating

□ I have diarrhea

□ Smells bother me

□ Foods are tasteless

□ Foods have funny taste

□ I feel full quickly

□ I have problems swallowing

□ I have problems with my teeth

□ I have pain. Where is the pain located? _____

_____

□ I have depression

□ I have money problems

□ I am worried

□ I am anxious

□ I am nervous

Source: adapted from Gomez–Candela et al., 2012.)

Figure 7.10A *A patient-generated Subjective Global Assessment (PG-SGA) form-1 for the nutritional assessment of cancer patients.*

PATIENT-GENERATED SUBJECTIVE GLOBAL ASSESSMENT

THIS PART OF THE FORM WILL BE FILLED OUT BY YOUR DOCTOR

DISEASE ASSESSMENT

CURRENT DISEASES: _____

_____

ONCOLOGICAL TREATMENTS:_____

_____

OTHER TREATMENTS:_____

_____

SERUM ALBUMIN before oncological treatments:

_____g/dl

PRE-ALBUMIN after oncological treatments:

_____mg/dl

PHYSICAL EXAM

Body fat deficit: ☐ YES ☐ NO

If YES rate: ___mild to moderate ___severe

Body muscle deficit: ☐ YES ☐ NO

If YES rate: ___mild to moderate ___severe

Body edema/ascites: ☐ YES ☐ NO

If YES rate: ___mild to moderate ___severe

Pressure sores: ☐ YES ☐ NO

Fever: ☐ YES ☐ NO

% weight loss over 3 months:_____%

% weight loss over 6 months:_____%

Current weight as a % usual weight:_____%

ASSESSMENT CRITERIA & GUIDELINES

A. **WELL NOURISHED**: A well nourished patient will have <5% body weight loss. In addition, the patient will not experience any loss of muscle or fat tissue. There will be no observable gastrointestinal problems or symptoms, nor will there be any documented decline in physical activity levels

B. **MODERATELY MALNOURISHED**: A mild to moderately malnourished patient will experience a 5%-10% weight loss over the previous 3-6 months. The patient will have had a mild loss of fat and muscle tissue, and will report having digestive problems and /or difficulties consuming adequate amounts of food.

C. **SEVERELY MALNOURISHED**: A severely malnourished patient will experience > 10% weight loss over the previous 6 months. There will also be a severe loss of fat and muscle tissue, a significant loss of physical function (activity level will be low), many gastrointestinal problems, and edema in extremities and possible ascites.

A serum albumin <3.0g/dl is a poor prognostic indicator and is tied to poor tolerance of treatment and poor survival independent of nutritional status (Lien et al, 2004)

(Source: Rolfes et al 2008; Gibson, 1990; Gomez-Candela, et al. 2012)

Source: adapted from Gomez-Candela et al., 2012; Rolfe et al., 2008; Gibson, 1990

Figure 7.10B *A patient-generated Subjective Global Assessment (PG-SGA) form-2 for the nutritional assessment of cancer patients.*

high circulating transferrin which would render the PNI calculation invalid. This is because transferrin, in a state of protein malnutrition and disease is expected to decline in the blood because of the catabolic state. Therefore this technique can only be effectively applied to patients that are not suffering from trauma, Fe-deficiency anemia, sepsis, and disease states that increase metabolism significantly. The criteria, utilized to interpret the PNI percentages, are represented below (Gibson, 1990).

PNI > 50: High risk

PNI = 40–49%: Intermediate risk

PNI ≤ 40%: Low risk

So then a male patient with albumin: 3.2 g/dl, transferrin: 230 mg/dl; DH: 2mm; TSF: 10mm would have a PNI= 158 - 16.6(5.1 /dl) - 0.78(10mm) - 0.20(230 mg/dl) - 5.8(2mm) = 7.94 or ~ 8% which places him at low risk. However, if instead, a male patient has a serum albumin: 2.4 g/dl; transferrin: 150 mg/dl, TSF: 4mm and a DH=0mm, then his PNI= 158 - 16.6(2.4 /dl) - 0.78(4mm) - 0.20(158 mg/dl) - 5.8(0mm) = 83.44 ~83%. This puts the patient at high risk of complications and morbidity.

Patient-Generated Subjective Global Assessment (PG-SGA), on the other hand, was developed for assessing the nutritional status of cancer patients specifically (Laky, et al., 2008; Bauer et al., 2002). This method does not utilize a numeric system for quantifying risk, such as in the PNI determination, but purely a subjective approach as indicated in Figures 7.10A and 7.10B. The most sensitive indicator of poor nutritional status and increased risk of not tolerating cancer treatments is a significant weight loss of 5–10%

or >10% of the usual body weight, within a three month or six month period, respectively (NCI, 2014J).

7.8 NUTRITION THERAPY

7.8.1 Method of Nutrition Delivery

The overall goal of any nutritional intervention is to optimize the patient's quality of life whether active treatment or palliation is being pursued. Specific goals have to do with preventing or reversing nutrient deficiencies, impeding the loss of lean body mass, preserving strength and energy levels so as to better tolerate the cancer treatments, minimizing infections and preventing complications arising from malnutrition (ACI, 2014h).Even in cases of advanced cancer, when weight gain is no longer the primary objective, nutrition support can be of some assistance; it can aid in increasing the patient's sense of wellbeing, in addition to minimizing the risk of infections, side effects, and asthenia, which is an abnormal sense of physical weakness, in which patients will experience a pronounced lack of energy (ACI, 2014h). Nutritional support in the form of oral supplemental nutrition or oral nourishment is recommended as the method of choice as it preserves gut function by maintaining GI integrity of the villi. A high protein and calorie meal plan is provided to patients who have unintentionally lost >10% body weight within six months (NCI, 2014j). It is also recommended for patients with advanced cancer who suffer from malnutrition—a prevalent problem in 85% of advanced cancer patients. Moreover, 80% of patients experience both weight loss and anorexia, which have been linked to 20% of cancer deaths (McCreery and Costello, 2013). The loss of

Table 7.1
Protein Requirements in Critical Illness Based on BMI

PATIENT BMI	PROTEIN NEED
BMI <30kg/m²	1.2–2.0g protein/kg
BMI 30-40kg/m².	2g/kg ideal weight
BMI >40kg/m²	2.5g/kg ideal weight

McClave et al. (2009)

appetite in cancer is common, and if left unchecked, can lead cachexia, an advanced physical wasting in which an aggressive erosion of fat and protein reserves leaves the patient extremely emaciated; it is enough of a problem that cachexia has been responsible for between 20–40% of cancer deaths (NCI, 2014j). In one study, patients with advanced cancers could only manage to eat between 22–23.6 kcal/kg body-weight, which was far below the 34 kcal/kg needed for at least weight maintenance (Hutton, et al., 2006).

Patients suffering from cancer will at times experience a heightened resting energy expenditure (REE) and protein turnover (ONDPG, 2006), but also a decline and maintenance in REE (NIC, 2014j). The American Society of Parenteral and Enteral Nutrition (ASPEN) recommends the technique of indirect calorimetry as the preferred method for determining energy needs; predictive equations like Harris Benedict or the quick estimate of 25–30 kcal/Kg body weight are certainly acceptable alternatives (McClave et al., 2009). Protein requirements have a tendency to also be higher (Table 7.1) because of the aggressive and relentless breakdown of protein seen in cancer patients.

This kind of caloric and protein prescription in combination with appetite stimulants can help stabilize patients and diminish any risk of infection or complication. High calorie and protein nutritional support is prescribed to patients who have been unable to eat or drink adequately for more than five days, probably because of alteration in taste, xerostomia, mucositis, nausea, and/or diarrhea following cancer therapy (ACI, 2014h). Refeeding patients who have not eaten for more than five days must be done cautiously to avoid **refeeding syndrome**; no more than 20 kcals/kg/24 hrs is recommended, but a more cautionary protocol with a usual start rate of ≤10 kcals/Kg/24 hrs is strongly advocated with a slow progressive increase towards meeting patient energy requirement over four to seven days (NICE, 2006). Refeeding syndrome can occur when infusion rates of enteral nutrition, and even TPN, are too elevated, causing rapid and fatal cellular shifts in fluid and electrolytes such as potassium, magnesium, and phosphorus (Mehanna, et al., 2008). The dietitian is usually in charge of determining the degree of malnutrition using various assessment techniques, and, based on the findings, a type of nutritional support is usually recommended.

Total parenteral nutrition (TPN) is considered as a viable strategy for providing much needed nutrition through the veins, in instances when the gastrointestinal tract is compromised either from injury, obstruction, resection, or inflammation, often resulting in malabsorption or short bowel syndrome (ACI, 2014h). There is, however, insufficient data to support the consistent use of TPN for patients receiving anti-cancer therapy at this time; more studies are required to further investigate if there are notable benefits. Otherwise, enterally administered nutritional support through the gut, in the form of a nasogastric tube, gastrostomy, or jejunostomy is popularly given precedence in order to minimize atrophy of the GI villi, and infections that would otherwise possibly occur through TPN (Shattener & Shike, 2006).

Enteral Nutrition Tube Feedings: A polyurethane or silicone tube is place up the nose and down the back of the throat (nasopharynx) until it reaches the gastric pouch—this is a nasogastric feeding or NG feed—in order to facilitate the delivery of a liquid nutritional supplement, often over the short term (<2 weeks). The tube, which is 30–43 inches long, can also be positioned in the duodenum (nasoduodenal feeding), or the jejunum (nasojejunal feeding) depending on the risk of aspiration. Patients, prone to aspiration, will be particularly vulnerable to aspirating stomach contents into the trachea (NCI, 2014h). The preferred alternative would be the duodenum or jejunum, which are locations along the GI tract less likely to cause aspiration. In instances, when the vulnerability to aspiration is very high, TPN will be prescribed. If the long term plan (>2 weeks) involves enteral nutrition, then it is customary to implement **percutaneous endoscopic gastrostomy tubes** (PEGs) or **percutaneous endoscopic jejunostomy tubes** (PEJs). A patient with a PEG (Figure 7.11) can conceal the tube better than with an NG tube feeding (NCI, 2014).

These methods are particularly suitable for patients who are unable to tolerate tubes in their mouths,

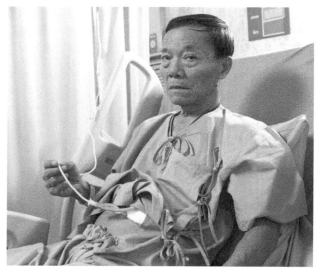

© Stockphoto Mania/ shutterstock.com

Figure 7.11 *Percutaneous endoscopic gastrostomy (PEGs) tubes.*

© CandyBox Images/shutterstock.com

Figure 7.12 *Jennifer F. is a 46-year-old wife and mother of four who presents with 12% weight loss, anorexia, occasional nausea.*

noses, and throats because of mucositis, esophagitis, or some kind of fungal lesions in the mouth or throat (NCI, 2014h). The PEG tubes tend to be wider and placed through the abdominal wall in order to allow liquid nutrition to flow directly into the stomach (gastrostomy) or jejunum (jejunostomy) as in the case of a PEJ.

The school is still out as to whether aggressive nutritional support is warranted for cachectic patients with malignant tumors as the increased calories may promote tumor growth. Quality of life most certainly improves with nutrition but not necessarily longevity (Gullett, et al., 2011). There is also the problem of refeeding syndrome.

7.9 PATIENT WITH CANCER EXPERIENCES WEIGHT LOSS—CASE STUDY 7.1

Background: 46-year-old female presents with six-month history of gradually worsening fatigue, appetite loss, and weight loss. In the last two weeks she has developed some shortness of breath (SOB) with exertion and family members think she looks

pale. Over the course of the last six months she has lost some weight and has noticed her clothes fitting loosely but she has not weighed herself.

Pertinent negatives: no diarrhea, melena, or chest pain.

Exam: Adult female, in no distress, appears mild to moderately ill and tired, and somewhat older than her stated age. Skin is pale but turgor is normal, and there is no rash. Heart and chest exam is normal. Abdominal (ABD) exam is also normal. Rectal exam is normal except for hemo-occult positive stool indicative of a possible malignant tumor, which will need to be confirmed by colonoscopy.

Lab Results Interpreted: low hemoglobin is observed most likely because of bleeding from the colon; this will be confirmed with a colonoscopy. The elevated liver enzymes (ALT, AST, alkaline phosphatase) reveal the possibility of metastases in the liver. This should prompt the physician to further explore this likelihood by referring the patient to surgery for a liver biopsy.

Serum albumin is low, indicating an overall advanced disease state, and a poor prognosis. Elevated glucose is typically seen in an advanced catabolic state. It is

Table 7.2

Body Composition and Blood Biochemistry Case 7.1

Usual Weight:	214 lbs	S-Hemoglobin (Hb):	8g/dl [Normal: 12–16 g/dl]
Current Weight:	189 lbs	S-ALT:	74 u/l [Normal: 8–37 iu/l]
Height:	5 feet 9 inches	S-AST:	57 u/l [Normal: 10–34 iu/l]
Tricep skinfold:	5 mm [Normal: 8–15 mm]	S-Alkaline phosphatase (AP):	203 iu/l [Normal: 44–147 iu/l]
Delayed cutaneous hypersensitivity test (DH):	1	S-tranferrin:	137 mg/dl [Normal: 188–341 mg/dl]
Serum Albumin:	2.3 g/dl [Normal: 3.5–5.5 g/dl]	BUN:	42 mg/dl [Normal: 6–20 mg/dl]

specifically a failure of the balance between glucose production and clearance that is really taking place

(Schlichtig & Ayres, 1988). Catabolism means a metabolic breaking down of tissue which occurs concomitantly with significant wasting as evidenced by the 25 lbs weight loss in three months; it is also tied to a higher mortality rate (Pakhetra et al., 2011). This represents an 11.7% weight loss, which is clinically significant. Indeed, as the extent of weight loss approaches 30% so also is death regarded as imminent (Gullett, et al., 2011).

The PNI can be measured in this patient to establish the prognosis. The value obtained equals 82.72%, indicating a very poor prognosis or high risk of complications.

Again the general assessment guidelines recognize that involuntary weight loss is clinically significant when more than an 8% weight loss occurs over three months, and when there is a greater than 10% weight loss over six months. Increased circulating catecholamine, cortisol and glucagon, in concert with cytokines such as tumor necrosis factor-a (TNF-a), cause blood glucose to soar and insulin resistance to become more prevalent in this kind of acute catabolic state (Pakhetra et al., 2011). The

increased secretion of glucagon from the α-cells of the pancreas favors a heightened glycogenolysis. This is the biochemical step that breaks down the glycogen reserves of the liver into glucose, which is then abundantly released as glucose into the blood. The low insulin also promotes lipolysis which can lead, in catabolic states, to lipotoxicity and an aggravation of the inflammatory state.

The high levels of BUN reveal an unusually elevated urea synthesis occurring in the liver from the breakdown of large amounts of amino acids, which lead to ammonia and then to urea. The urea moves into the blood as BUN and enters the kidney where it is expelled in the urine. This overabundance of amino acids can come from large amounts of protein—likely via intravenous feedings like TPN—or from extensive muscle erosion or break down, the consequence of metabolic stress—the largest proteolysis is seen in burn patients. The implications of catabolizing protein and creating a negative nitrogen balance (see chapter 8 for definition) environment are that wound healing can be impaired and susceptibility to infections heightened (Pakhetra et al., 2011). Not even nutritional support can completely reverse the negative balance.

The creatinine is only slightly elevated in this patient, indicating no real kidney dysfunction. So then the BUN is not elevated because of decreased renal function, but rather from increased proteolysis (breakdown of protein in the body).

Nutritional Assessment of Patient:

The first part of a nutritional assessment involves determining the actual dietary intake of the patient. Here there are three goals the dietitian will attempt to achieve: first, assess the amount of calories, protein, carbohydrates, and fat consumed; second, determine how long the patient has been eating this way; and third, establish if dietary patterns have changed significantly from her usual intake (Table 7.3).

The next step is to establish the patient's resting energy requirements using the Harris Benedict equation for hospitalized patients and then, using the appropriate activity and metabolic stress factors, determine total energy needs. The equation, found in **Table 7.3** below will assist in determining the patient's resting energy expenditure (REE):

$$♀REE = [665 + 9.56\ W\ (kg) + 1.85\ H\ (cm)] - 4.6\ A$$

$$REE = [665 + 9.56\ (85.81Kg) + 1.85\ (175.26)] - (4.6 \times 46)$$

$$REE = [665 + 820.34 + 324.23] - (211.6)$$

$$REE = 1812.23 - 216.2$$

$$REE = 1597.97\ kcal \sim 1598\ kcal$$

The patient is bedridden while in hospital, and is therefore assigned a 1.2 activity factor (Table 7.4)

$$REE \times AF = 1596\ kcal \times 1.2 = 1915\ kcal$$

Work done by Vernon Young out of Cambridge, MA, showed that cancer patients, taken as a whole, require upwards of 10% all the way to 120% of normal energy requirements with various types of cancers (Young, 1977). Assigning a stress factor (SF) is not an exact science. The stress factor is indeed difficult to predict, as energy needs will depend on the stage of the cancer, the size of the tumor and the location of the cancer (NCI, 2014i). Applying an approximate stress factor of 1.25 based on the published work of Kohr and Mohd (2011) would appear reasonable and conservative for this patient's possible GI malignant tumor. The patient's total energy expenditure (TEE) would then be the resting energy expenditure (REE) multiplied by an activity factor (AF) of 1.2 since she is bedridden and then multiplied again by a stress factor (SF) of 1.25:

$$TEE = REE \times AF \times SF$$

$$TEE = 1596\ kcal \times 1.2 \times 1.25$$

$$TEE = 1596 \times 1.5 = 2394\ kcal/day$$

This is the patient's total daily energy requirements. Based on her recent usual intake reported on the **usual food intake form** (Table 7.3) in which she reports a daily intake of 1186 kcalories, it is not surprising to find that she has been experiencing weight loss.

Her protein intake is 54g, which is deficient when expressed per kilogram body weight:

54g / 85.8Kg = 0.63g/kg body weight. This does not meet the minimal physiological requirement of 0.8 g/kg body weight, nor does it meet the 10–35% of DRI calories recommended by the Good Health Eating Guide (Table 7.3). It is important to note that, in the hospital setting, the g/kg protein intake that is <0.8 g/kg indicates suboptimal protein even though, based on calories, the patient may be taking in 11% of DRI calories, for instance. The body weight is always considered the superior standard to follow. Moreover, there is evidence that additional protein may be needed because of the persistent catabolic state that is often seen in cancer patients. Long (1984) recommends 1.5–2.0g/kg for moderately stressed patients. Also fat intake represents only 16.7% of her actual caloric intake and only 8.27% of her DRI calories, which is far below the

Table 7.3

Usual Food Intake Record

PATIENT NAME: Jennifer F.	USUAL FOOD INTAKE	
FOODS CONSUMED	QUANTITY CONSUMED	PLACE
BREAKFAST: TIME 7:00 AM		
Porridge (homemade)	1 cup	Kitchen
AM SNACKS TIME: 10:00 AM		
Applesauce (Mott's Natural) ®	1 cup	Dining room
LUNCH TIME: 12:30 PM		
Egg sandwich on white bread (Homemade)	1s/w	Hospital Cafeteria
Milk skim	1 cup	
PM SNACK TIME: 2:15 PM		
Pudding (vanilla) Jell-O ® pudding cup	1 cup	Home
DINNER TIME: 7:00 PM		
Strawberry Milkshake (McDonald's) ®	Medium	Restaurant
EVENING SNACK TIME:		
None		
NUTRIENT BREAKDOWN OF USUAL FOOD INTAKE		
Kcals recommended: 2394 kcal/day (1796–2992 Kcals/day)	Kcals eaten: **1186 kcals**	
Carbohydrates recommended: 359 g/day (60% DRI Kcals) (269–389g)	Carbohydrates eaten: **193 g**	
Protein recommended: 90 g/day (15% DRI Kcals) (60–209 g)	Protein eaten: **54 g**	
Fat recommended: 66 g (25% DRI Kcals) (53–93g)	Fat eaten: **22 g**	
Total Maximal Sugar: <100 g (20% DRI Kcals)	Total Sugar eaten: **60 g**	
Total Maximal Sodium: <2400 mg/day	Sodium eaten: **1189 mg**	

Calories measured using the www.myfitnesspal.com website

Table 7.4
Total Energy Expenditure in Health and Disease

EQUATIONS	DESCRIPTIONS
♂REE= [66.47 + 13.75 W(kg) + 5 H (cm)]– 6.76 A ♀REE = [665 + 9.56W(kg) + 1.85 H (cm)] – 4.6 A	Harris-Benedict equation for hospitalized patients with disease.
♂REE= [10W(kg) + 6.25 H (cm)] – (5A -5) ♀REE =[10W(kg) + 6.25 H (cm)] – (5A +161)	Mifflin St. Jeor equation for non-hospitalized patients without disease. Mifflin, M.D. (1990). *Am.J.Clin.Nutr.* 51, 241-7.
♂REE = 879 + 10.2 WT (kg) ♀REE (non-athletes) = 795 + 7.18 WT (kg) ♀REE (athletes) = 50.4 + 21.1 WT (kg)	Owen equation for the estimation of caloric requirements in healthy lean and obese men, healthy women. Owen, O.E. et al. (1986). *Am.J.Clin.Nutr.* 44, 1-19; Owen, O.E. (1988). *Mayo Clin Proc* 63: 503-510.
♂REE = 1 kcal/kg/Bwt/hr · 24 hrs (subtract 0.1 kcal/hr sleep) + activity increment + spec dynamic action: 10% ♀REE = 0.95 kcal/kg/Bwt/hr · 24 hrs (subtract 0.1 kcal/hrs sleep) + activity factor + specific dynamic action of food: 10%	Rule of thumb method for estimating energy needs.

ACTIVITY FACTORS FOR HOSPITALS	INJURY FACTORS
Confined to bed: 1.2 Out of bed: 1.3 *Source: Long, CL., 1984*	**1** Surgery – Minor: 1.0–1.1 　　　　　– Major: 1.1–1.2 **2** Infections –Mild: 1.0–1.2 　　　　　– Moderate: 1.2–1.4 　　　　　– Severe: 1.4–1.8
ACTIVITY FACTORS FOR GERRIOR EQUATION	**3** Skeletal Trauma: 1.2–1.35 　　　　+ Head injury + steroids: 1.6
Sedentary: 1.0 . . . . . . normal range: (1.0–1.39) Low activity: 1.13 . . . . normal range: (1.4–1.59) Active: 1.27 . . . . normal range: (1.6–1.89) Very active: 1.54 . . . . . normal range: (1.9–2.49) *Source: Gerrior et al., 2006; Food & Nutrition Board, 2005.*	**4** Blunt trauma: 1.15–1.35 **5** Burns. 20% BSA: 1.0–1.5 　　　　20–40% BSA: 1.5–1.85 　　　　>40% BSA: 1.85–1.95 **6** Cancer: severely aggressive: 1.5–1.7 　　　　Tumor & leukemia: 1.20–1.36

(Continued)

ACTIVITY FACTORS FOR MIFFLIN EQUATION	
Sedentary: 1.27	range:1.0–1.39
Sedentary/low activity: 1.53	range:1.4–1.59
Active: 1.76	range:1.6–1.89
Very active/heavy activity: 2.25	range:1.9–2.5

Source Long, C.L, 1984; Young, Y., 1977; Khor, S.M. and Mohd, B.B. (2011); FAO, 2001; Food & Nutrition Board, 2005.

20%–35% recommended by Healthy Eating Guidelines for Americans. Carbohydrate intake equals 193g or 32.25% of DRI calories, a value that is much below the 45–65% of DRI calories recommended by Healthy Macronutrient Range Guidelines.

Treatment Recommendations of Patient:

The persistent nausea and red blood found in her stool, in concert with the colonic tumor found by colonoscopy, suggests a cancer. Slightly elevated liver enzymes raise suspicions of possible metastases, which must be confirmed by an oncologist. Even if the patient's BMI of 27.9 (85.81 Kg / (1.753 meters)^2) is classified as overweight, the recent weight loss of 11.7% over a three month period reveals a high likelihood of malnutrition. Patient will be given 1676 kcalories per day through TPN because of a likely obstruction in the colon from the tumor. The patient is purposely prescribed 70% of her energy needs in order to decrease the possibility of overfeeding the patient. Gradually, calories can be increased to 2394 kcal/day based on patient's stability and biochemical markers. Underfeeding critically-ill patients with the intent of meeting 60–70% of the patients' energy needs, has been shown to decrease serum blood glucose, insulin insensitivity, the length of hospitalization and mortality (Arabi, 2011). In this instance, intravenous nutrition makes good sense, as her GI tract will be compromised until after the surgical removal of the tumor. This amount of calories is intended to prevent weight gain, minimize weight loss, and decrease the risk of complications. The elevated PNI in concert with the very low serum albumin (<2.6 g/dl) are indicative of a high risk of complications and possibly death, and therefore supports the need for a conservative nutritional support strategy (underfeeding) (Sung et al., 2004; Buzby et al., 1980).

CHAPTER 7 PRACTICE QUESTIONS
[Answers not provided—class discussion encouraged]

1 Define and explain the nutritional support problem called **refeeding syndrome**.

2 Define and explain the metabolic alteration in cancer called the Warburg Effect.

3 Explain the role of the Cori cycle in cancer metabolism.

4 Explain the differences between the metabolic processes taking place during normal starvation versus during cancer.

5 Explain what has been learned from the Okinawa study regarding the possible causes of cancer.

6 What has been learned from the Okinawa study about healthy lifestyles and longevity?

7 How effective have nutritional supplements been in cancer prevention?

8 What is currently known about the relationship between meat and the risk of cancer?

9 What is the wisest council that could be given to a patient regarding the relationship between meat and the risk of cancer?

10 What are the top five lifestyle and nutrition recommendations that can be given to the population in order to decrease the risk of cancer?

11 Differentiate the usefulness of the Prognostic Nutritional Indicator (PNI) versus the Patient-Generated Subjective Global Assessment (PG-SGA).

12 Discuss the conditions that would favor TPN versus enteral nutrition in cancer patients.

13 Argue why underfeeding patients that are critically ill is likely to decrease the length of hospital stay, in addition to morbidity and mortality rates.

REFERENCES

1 American Cancer Society. (2016). *What is cancer?* *Retrieved* from http://www.cancer.org/cancer/cancerbasics/what-is-cancer

2 American Cancer Society. (2016). *Lifetime risk of developing or dying from cancer.* Retrieved from http://www.cancer.org/cancer/cancerbasics/lifetime-probability-of-developing-or-dying-from-cancer

3 American Cancer Society. (2012). *Guidelines on nutrition & physical activity for the cancer prevention.* Retrieved from http://www.cancer.org/healthy/eathealthygetactive/acsguidelinesonnutritionphysicalactivityforcancerprevention/acs-guidelines-on-nutrition-and-physical-activity-for-cancer-prevention-summary

4 American Cancer Society. (ACS, 2012b). *Colon/rectum cancer, prevention/early detection. Removing polyps prevents colon and rectal cancer deaths.* Retrieved from http://www.cancer.org/cancer/news/news/removing-polyps-prevents-colon-and-rectal-cancer-deaths

5 American Cancer Society. (ACS, 2010). *Cancer Facts & Figures 2010.* Retrieved from http://www.cancer.org/acs/groups/content/@epidemiologysurveilance/documents/document/acspc-026238.pdf

6 Anand, P. et al. (2008). Cancer is a preventable disease that requires major lifestyle changes. *Pharmaceutical Research* 25(9).

7 Arabi Y.M., Tamim H.M., Dhar G.S., et al. (2011) Permissive underfeeding and intensive insulin therapy in critically ill patients: a randomized controlled trial. Am J Clin Nutr; 93:569–577

8 Bauer, J., Capra, S., & Ferguson, M. (2002). Use of the scored patient-generated subjective global assessment (pg-sga) as a nutrition assessment tool in patients with cancer. *Eur J Clin Nutr* 56 (8), 779–85.

9 Bissonnette, D. (2014). *It's all about nutrition: Saving the health of Americans.* Lanham, MD: University Press of America, 232.

10 Buzby, G.P. & Mullen, J.L. (1984). Analysis of nutritional assessment indices-prognostic equations and cluster analysis. In *Nutritional Assessment* (Richard A Wright and Steven Heymsfield eds). Boston: Blackwell Scientific Publications, 141–155.

11 Buzby, G.P., Mullen, J.L., Matthews, D.C., Hobbs, C.L. & Rosato, E.F. (1980). Prognostic nutritional index in gastrointestinal surgery. Am J Surg; 139: 160–167.

12 Cancer Treatment Centers of America (CTCA). (2015). *How we treat cancer: Nutrition therapy.* Retrieved from CTCA website, March 30, 2016: http://www.cancercenter.com/treatments/nutrition-therapy/

13 Cancer Treatment Centers of America (CTCA). (2014). *Breast cancer types.* Retrieved from http://www.cancercenter.com/breast-cancer/types/tab/invasive-breast-cancer/?source=GGLPS01&channel=paid%20search&c=paid%20search:Google:Non%20Brand:{campaignName}:invasive+breast+cancer:Exact&OVMTC=Exact&site=&creative=36290882721&OVKEY=invasive%20breast%20cancer&url_id=190113679&adpos=1s2&device=c&gclid=COnhpseZqb4CFaY-MgodbXUAXQ

[14] CDC. (2016). *Cancer prevention and control. Expected new cancer cases and deaths in 2020.* Retrieved from http://www.cdc.gov/cancer/dcpc/research/articles/cancer_2020.htm

[15] CDC. (2014). *National program of Cancer Registries. About United States Cancer Statistics reported from 1999-2010.* Retrieved from http://www.cdc.gov/cancer/npcr/about_uscs.htm

[16] CDC (2014b). Depression and Obesity in the U.S. Adult Household Population, 2005–2010. Retrieved from: http://www.cdc.gov/nchs/products/databriefs/db167.htm

[17] CDC. Chronic Disease Prevention and Health Promotion. (2013). *Cancer: Addressing the cancer burden at a glance.* Retrieved from http://apps.nccd.cdc.gov/uscs/toptencancers.aspx

[18] CDC. Cancer Prevention and Control. (2013b). *Cancer among women.* Retrieved from http://www.cdc.gov/cancer/dcpc/data/women.htm

[19] Dempsey, D.T., Buzby, G.P., & Mullen, J.L. (1983). Nutritional assessment in the seriously ill patient. *J Am Coll Nutr.* 2, 15–22.

[20] Evans W.J., Morley J.E., Argiles J., et al. (2008). Cachexia: a new definition. Clin Nutr;27:793–9.

[21] FAO. (2001), Energy requirements of adults. In *Human energy requirements, food and nutrition technical report series# 1* Report of a Joint FAO/WHO/UNU.

[22] Finkelstein E.A., Trogdon J.G., Cohen J.W., Dietz W. (2009). Annual medical spending attributable to obesity: payer- and service-specific estimates. Health Aff (Millwood);28(5):w822–w831

[23] Food and Nutrition Board. (2005). *Dietary reference intakes for energy, carbohydrate, fiber, fat, fatty acids, cholesterol, protein and amino acids (macronutrients).* Washington. D.C.: National Academy Press.

[24] Fuhrman, P. (2008). Nutrition support at the end of life: A critical decision. *Today's Dietitian*; 10 (9): 68.

[25] Gibson, R.S. (1990). *Principles of nutritional assessment.* New York: Oxford University Press, 691.

[26] Giovannucci, E. et al. (2003). A prospective study of cruciferous vegetables on prostate cancer. *Cancer Epidemiol. Biomarkers Prev.* (12), 403–9.

[27] Giovannucci, E. (2001). Insulin, insulin-like growth factors and colon cancer: A review of the evidence. *J. Nutr.* 131, 3109S–20S.

[28] Gomez-Candela, C. et al. (2012) Nutrition intervention in onco-hematological patient. *Nutr. Hosp.* 27(3), 669–680.

[29] Gullett, N.P. (2011). Nutritional Interventions for Cancer-induced Cachexia. Curr Probl Cancer; 35(2): 58–90.

[30] Holroyde, C.P., Gabuzda, T.G., Putnam, R.C., Paul, P., & Reichard, G.A. (1975). Altered glucose metabolism in metastatic carcinoma. *Cancer Res* ;35:3710-4.

[31] Hutton, J.L., Martin, L., Field, C.J., Wismer, W.V., Bruera, E.D., Watanabe, S.M., & Baracos, V.E. (2006). Dietary patterns in patients with advanced cancer: Implications for anorexia-cachexia therapy. *Am J Clin Nutr* 84 (5), 1163–1170.

[32] Khor, S.M. & Mohd, B.B. (2011). Assessing the resting energy expenditure of cancer patients in the Penang General Hospital. *Mal J. Nutr* 17(1), 43–53.

[33] Klein, E.A. et al. (2011). Vitamin E and the Risk of Prostate Cancer The Selenium and Vitamin E Cancer Prevention Trial (SELECT). JAMA; 306(14):1549-1556. doi:10.1001/jama.2011.1437.

[34] Komurcu, S., Nelson, K.A., Walsh, D., et al. (2002). Gastrointestinal symptoms among inpatients with advanced cancer. *Am J Hosp Palliat Care* 19, 351–355.

35 Laky, B. et al. (2008). Comparison of different nutritional assessments and body composition measurements in detecting malnutrition among gynecologic cancer patients. *Am J Clin Nutr* 87, 1678–85.

36 Lien, Y.C et al. (2004). Preoperative serum albumin level is a prognostic indicator for adenocarcinoma of the gastric cardia. *J. Gastrointest Surg* 8(8), 1041–8.

37 Long, C.L. (1984). The energy and protein requirements of the critically ill patient. In *Nutritional Assessment*, (R.A. Wright and S. Heymsfield, eds). Boston: Blackwell Scientific Publication, 157–181.

38 McClave, S.A., Martindale, R.G., Vanek, V.W., McCarthy, M., Roberts, P., Taylor, B., Ochoa, J.B., Napolitano, L., & Cresci, G., (2009). The ASPEN Board of Directors, and the American College of Critical Care Medicine. Clinical guidelines for the provision and assessment of nutrition support therapy in the adult critically ill patients: Society of Critical Care Medicine (SCCM) and American Society for Parenteral and Enteral Nutrition (ASPEN). *JPEN* 33(3), 277–316.

39 McCreery, E. & Costello, J. (2013). Providing nutritional support for patients with cancer cachexia. *Int J Palliat Nurs* 19(1), 32-7.

40 Mehanna, H.M. et al. (2008). Refeeding syndrome: What is it? And how to prevent and treat it. *BMJ* 336(7659), 1495–1498.

41 Merck Manual for Health Professionals. (2013). *Modalities of cancer therapy.* Retrieved from http://www.merckmanuals.com/professional/hematology_and_oncology/principles_of_cancer_therapy/modalities_of_cancer_therapy.html?qt=CANCER&alt=sh

42 National Cancer Institute (NCI). (2016) *Cancer Statistics.* Retrieved from http://www.cancer.gov/about-cancer/what-is-cancer/statistics

43 National Cancer Institute (NCI). (2014). *What is cancer?* Retrieved from http://www.cancer.gov/cancertopics/cancerlibrary/what-is-cancer

44 National Cancer Institute (NCI). (2014b). *Antioxidants and cancer prevention.* Retrieved from http://www.cancer.gov/cancertopics/factsheet/prevention/antioxidants#r8

45 National Cancer Institute (NCI). (2014c). *Leukemia.* Retrieved from http://www.cancernet.nci.nih.gov/cancertopics/types/leukemia

46 National Cancer Institute (NCI). (2014d). *Breast cancer.* Retrieved from http://www.cancernet.nci.nih.gov/cancertopics/types/breast

47 National Cancer Institute (NCI). (2014e). *Colorectal cancer prevention.* Retrieved from-http://www.cancernet.nci.nih.gov/cancertopics/pdq/prevention/colorectal/HealthProfessional

48 National Cancer Institute (NCI). (2014f). *Nutrition in cancer care. Nutrition implications of cancer therapies.* Retrieved from http://www.cancer.gov/cancertopics/pdq/supportivecare/nutrition/HealthProfessional/page3

49 National Cancer Institute (NCI). (2014g). *Nutrition in cancer care.* Nutrition screening and assessment. Retrieved from http://www.cancer.gov/cancertopics/pdq/supportivecare/nutrition/HealthProfessional/Page4#Section_50

50 National Cancer Institute (NCI). (2014h). *Nutrition in cancer care—Nutrition therapy.* Retrieved from http://www.cancer.gov/cancertopics/pdq/supportivecare/nutrition/HealthProfessional/page4#Section_50

51 National Cancer Institute (NCI). (2014i). *Nutrition in cancer—Tumor induced effects on nutritional status.* Retrieved from http://www.cancer.gov/cancertopics/pdq/supportivecare/nutrition/HealthProfessional/page2

52 National Cancer Institute (NCI). (2014j). *Nutrition in cancer care: Overview.* Retrieved from http://www.cancer.gov/cancertopics/pdq/supportivecare/nutrition/HealthProfessional/page1

53 National Cancer Institute (NCI). (2012). Obesity and Cancer Risk. Retrieved from: http://www.cancer.gov/about-cancer/causes-prevention/risk/obesity/obesity-fact-sheet

54 National Cancer Institute (NCI). (2010). *Chemicals in meat cooked at high temperature and cancer risk.* Retrieved from http://www.cancer.gov/cancertopics/factsheet/Risk/cooked-meats

55 National Center on Health, Physical Activity, and Disability (NCHPAD). (2014). Retrieved from-http://www.nchpad.org/163/1257/Cancer~and~Exercise

56 National Cancer Institute (NCI). (2012). *Cruciferous vegetables and cancer prevention.* Retrieved from http://www.cancer.gov/cancertopics/factsheet/diet/cruciferous-vegetables

57 National Institutes of Health (NIH). National Heart, Lung and Blood Institute. (2012). What are the Risks of overweight and Obesity?. Retrieved from: https://www.nhlbi.nih.gov/health/health-topics/topics/obe/risks

58 National Institute for Health and Clinical Excellence (NICE). (2006). Nutrition support in adults: Oral nutrition support, enteral tube feeding and parenteral nutrition. *The Royal College of Surgeons of England, London,* 1–247.

59 Omenn, G.S. et al. (1996). Effects of a combination of beta-carotene and vitamin A on lung cancer and cardiovascular disease. *N. Engl. J. Med.* 334(18), 1150–155.

60 Oncology Nutrition Dietetic Practice Group (ONDPG, 2006). *The Clinical Guide to Oncology Nutrition.* Second Edition ed. American Dietetic Association.

61 Pakhetra, R. et al. (2011). Management of hyperglycemia in critical illness: Review of target and strategies. *MJAFI* 67, 53-57.

62 Parker, E.D. & Folsom, A.R. (2003). Intentional weight loss and incidence of obesity-related cancers: The Iowa Women's Health Study. *Int J. Obes. Related Metab. Disorder* 27, 1447–52.

63 Rolfes, S.R., Pinna, K., & Whitney, Ellie. (2009). *Understanding normal and clinical nutrition* 8th Edition. Belmont, CA: Wadsworth, Cengage Learning, 925.

64 Schattner, M. & Shike, M. (2006). Nutritional support of the patient with cancer. In *Modern nutrition in health and disease* 10th edition (Shils, M.E., Shike, M. et al. eds). New York: Lippincott, Williams & Wilkins, 1290–1313.

65 Schlichtig, R. & Ayres, S.M. (1988). *Nutritional support of the critically ill.* Chicago: Yearbook Medical Publishers Inc., 223.

66 Sporn, M.B. (2006). Chemoprevention of cancer. In *Modern nutrition in health and disease* 10th edition (Shils, ME., Shike, M. et al. eds). New York: Lippincott, Williams & Wilkins, 1280-89.

67 Stoudt, H.W., Damon, A., & McFarland, R.A. (1970). Skinfolds, body girth, biacromial diameter and selected anthropometric indices of adults US 1960-1962. *Vital and health statistics from the National Health Survey.* Washington DC: US Dept. of Health Education & Welfare, 63.

68 Sung, J. et al. (2004). Admission serum albumin is predicitve of outcome in critically ill trauma patients. Am Surg;70(12):1099-102. Retrieved from: http://www.ncbi.nlm.nih.gov/pubmed/15663053

69 Suzuki, M. et al. (2001). Oxidative stress and longevity in Okinawa and investigation of blood lipid peroxidation and tocopherol in Okinawa centenarians. *Asia Pac J Clin. Nutr.* 10(2), 165-71. Retrieved from http://www.ncbi.nlm.nih.gov/pmc/articles/PMC3068305/

70 Tisdale, M.J. (1997). Biology of Cachexia. *JNCI J Natl Cancer Inst* 89 (23): 1763–1773.

71 U.S. Cancer Statistics Working Group (USCS). (2013). *United States Cancer Statistics: 1999–2010 Incidence and Mortality Web-based Report.* Atlanta: U.S. Department of Health and Human Services, Centers for Disease Control and Prevention and National Cancer Institute. Available at www.cdc.gov/uscs

[72] U.S. Department of Health & Human Services (DHHS). (2008). National Digestive Diseases Information Clearinghouse (NDDIC). *What I need to know about colonic polyps.* NIH Publication No. 09–4977. Retrieved from http://digestive.niddk.nih.gov/ddiseases/pubs/colonpolyps_ez/

[73] Warburg, O. (1956). On the origin of cancer cells. *Science* 123, 309–314.

[74] WHO. (2003). *Global cancer rates could increase by 50% to 15 million by 2020.* Retrieved from http://www.who.int/mediacentre/news/releases/2003/pr27/en/

[75] Willcox, B.J. et al. (2006). Siblings of Okinawan centenarians exhibit lifelong mortality advantages. *J Gerontol A Biol Sci Med Sci* 61, 345–54.

[76] Willcox, C., Willcox, B.J., Hsueh, W-C., & Suzuki, M. (2006b). Genetic determinants of exceptional human longevity: Insights from the Okinawa Centenarian Study. *AGE* 28(4), 313–332.

[77] Willett, W. & Giovannucci, E. (2006) Epidemiology of diet and cancer risk. In *Modern nutrition in health and disease* 10th edition (Shils, M.E., Shike, M. et al. eds). New York: Lippincott, Williams & Wilkins, 1267–79.

[78] Wu, W. & Zhao, S. (2013). Metabolic changes in cancer: Beyond the Warburg Effect. *Acta Biochim Biophys Sin* 45, 18–26.

[79] Young, V.R. (1977). Energy metabolism requirements in the cancer patient. *Cancer Research* 37, 2336–2347

CHAPTER

8

The Problem of Malnutrition

© Nielsklim/Shutterstock.com

1) Chronic disease
2) Psyc. disorders
3) Elderly

8.1. UNDERNUTRITION IN NORTH AMERICAN SOCIETY

8.1.1 Hospital Malnutrition

While nutritional deficiencies in Western industrial societies in general, and in the U.S. population specifically, have not been prevalent or widespread, they have been a problem in hospitalized patients since the mid-1970s (Bistrian et al., 1976; Weinsier et al., 1979). The concern about malnutrition, within the clinical setting, stemmed from observations in the 1930s, by Hiram Studley, who reported a 10-fold hike in mortality rates among patients with peptic ulcers who had lost in excess of 20% of their usual weight (Compher & Mehta, 2016). There are likely two main explanations behind the rise in hospital malnutrition: first, the patients were malnourished

1970s

prior to hospitalization, and second, the nutritional status of patients deteriorated while in hospital (Fessler, 2008). There are likely three main driving forces responsible for patients being malnourished prior to admission: The first may well be attributable to the degree to which chronic diseases or malignancies have been affecting the patients prior to being hospitalized; second, psychological disorders leading to self-neglect, and or substance abuse can significantly compromise a person's nutritional status, especially if accessing medical services is delayed because of socioeconomic conditions such as poverty or lower education (Fessler, 2008); and third, the elderly are at high risk of being in financial difficulties, and becoming functionally compromised, resulting in less mobility and capacity to purchase nutritious foods. Moreover, ambulatory elderly patients are also less likely to be closely monitored and treated for significant weight loss by physicians (Manson & Shea, 1991).

reasons why malnutritioned

There are several circumstances that can cause or further worsen a poor nutritional status after admission to hospital: 1) Patients who are unable to properly swallow food because of oral or esophageal cancer or strictures; 2) those affected by degenerative neurological disorders that eventually lead to dysphagia; 3) trauma and ventilator-dependent patients whose nutritional requirements are often heightened by their condition; 4) often patients loose significant weight while waiting for appropriate nutritional support to be implemented (Fessler, 2008). Finally, patients suffering from gastrointestinal (GI) disorders such as inflammatory bowel diseases are prone to malabsorption, weight loss and various degrees of malnutrition, depending on the severity of the conditions and the extent of the delays prior to implementing adequate nutritional support protocols (Fessler, 2008; ASPEN, 2007). These circumstances have unfortunately led to a significant rise in the prevalence of hospital malnutrition in Westernized countries (Fessler, 2008).

8.1.1.1 Prevalence of Hospital Malnutrition

Malnutrition is defined as nutritional imbalances of energy and nutrients that become observable in either over-nutrition or undernutrition (Morley, 2014). In many developed and developing nations over-nutrition is on the rise and has led to an increased prevalence of obesity in many countries worldwide in which excessive calories, and nutrients such as cholesterol, saturated fat, sodium, salt, and sugar are ingested, but key nutrients are under-consumed (Via, 2012). Undernutrition, in contrast, is typically seen in underdeveloped and developing nations, in addition to Western hospitals and long term care facilities and residences (Barker et al., 2011). Here in the United States, suboptimal protein intake is almost never seen except as protein-energy malnutrition (PEM) in hospitalized patients suffering from cancer, AIDS, gastrointestinal diseases, alcoholism, and drug abuse (Lee and Nieman, 1996).

The prevalence of hospital malnutrition was documented as far back as the 1970s by Bruce Bistrian and colleagues (1976), who reported a 44% prevalence of malnutrition among general medicine patients (Bistrian et al., 1976). It is shocking that malnourished patients are still prevalent in our hospitals despite decades of improved nutritional support protocols and nutritional supplements widely available in the market. Currently, the prevalence of hospital malnutrition in the United States is estimated at between 20–50% with the majority of clinical studies showing a tighter cluster varying between 30–36% (Barker et al., 2011). Worldwide, the prevalence of hospital malnutrition between 1976 and 2008 varied greatly, with some estimates as low as 13% and others as elevated as 69% depending on the countries and the criteria used to measure malnutrition (Fessler, 2008). The medical implications of such an elevated prevalence of malnutrition are worrisome, as they translate invariably into more frequent infections, slower wound healing, greater loss of muscle mass and mortality, and hospital stays that are on average three to six days longer. Others have reported 43% longer hospital stays when patients were malnourished (Barker et al., 2011).

8.1.1.2 Basic Concepts of Starvation

There is no doubt that starvation represents a state of crisis for the body as it forces it into a sort of metabolic emergency that involves the rapid breakdown of endogenous tissues in order to provide vital fuel for oxidative phosphorylation and energy production. There is, in fact, a shift from a reliance on exogenous sources of food for energy to an internal breakdown of fat and protein stores to keep the body alive. Total starvation and semi-starvation both restrict sufficient calories to cause weight loss. The rate of weight loss is, however, not linear in that the body does not experience weight loss at rates that are proportional to the degree of restriction, the length of the caloric restriction, or the drop in resting energy expenditure. Early experimental work by Benedict and colleagues in 1912 investigated this paradox. They held a man in an enclosed area for 31 days, feeding him only distilled water. He lost 16.7% of his original body weight within the first three weeks, yet experienced a 30% drop in bodily heat production, clearly demonstrating that the body metabolism had dropped more sharply than the body weight. Hence, it was not only the lower body weight that accounted for the decline in basal metabolic rate, but some other unknown factor (Kinney, 2006). The question was picked up again, during WWII, by Ancel Keys and his colleagues at the University of Minnesota. Wanting to emulate the semi-starvation

Definition of

undernutrition prevalence

hospital malnutrition. Bruce Bistrian.

Benedict keeping man only water

diets imposed by the Nazis in concentration camps, they fed young healthy men 1600 kcal/day over a six month period. They found that while the men lost 24% of their body weights, they lost on average 39% of basal metabolic rate (BMR). Interestingly, at the end of the six months the BMR ceased decreasing and stabilized (Kinney, 2006).

Metabolically, the body has an ability to adapt to fasting or reduced food intake. This is likely related to how our primitive genes saved our ancestors from death during the many prolonged famines throughout history. After several famines the body becomes more efficient at preserving valuable fuel reserves in the body, and does this by making significant metabolic readjustments. About 12–24 hours after beginning a fast, the drop in insulin concentrations signals the alpha cells of the pancreas and the adrenal gland to respectively secrete glucagon and catecholamines like epinephrine. These endocrine compounds in combination with the increased glucagon-to-insulin ratio enhance the breakdown of liver glycogen stores for the release of glucose into the blood by a biochemical process called **glycogenolysis**. It takes between 48–72 hrs of fasting for the complete depletion of liver glycogen to take place (Hoffer, 2006). This release of glucose is necessary to keep the blood sugars homeostatic, as the nervous system, renal medulla, erythrocytes, and leukocytes rely on glucose for normal activity. Slowly, as liver glycogen concentrations become depleted, gluconeogenesis will account for a greater percent of the glucose released. Gluconeogenesis will contribute 64% of the glucose released into circulation by the 22 hour of fasting; that percentage jumps to 80% by the 40th hour; indeed, all of the hepatic glucose produced will originate from gluconeogenesis once hepatic glycogen reserves are fully depleted. Interestingly, serum glucose concentrations only modestly decline because there is a concomitant reduction in glucose absorption as well (Hoffer, 2006). Following 3.5 days, the brain's reliance on glucose drops 25% as it shifts to an adaptive uptake of ketone bodies for fuel. It is common to expect to smell acetone—a prominent ketone—in the breath of patients who have fasted for three to four days (Hoffer, 2006). Leading up to that time, the overall hepatic glucose output declines 40–50% by the 24th to 48th hour (Rothman et al., 1991) as the synthesis of ketone bodies begins to gradually increase as a fuel utilized by the brain

and muscles. In fact, between days 4 and 7 of a fast, the body relies on 30-40% of its energy needs from the oxidation of ketone bodies in the mitochondria (Hoffer, 2006). Gradually, however, over the following week, the muscles entirely shift from ketones to fatty acids a source of calories. This means that by week two of a fast, the breakdown of fat—a process called known as lipolysis—begins to gain in importance, resulting in the increased release of free fatty acids (FFA) into the blood, which remain relatively stable over the remainder of the fast. The release of FFA is further aided by the fall in insulin early on. The glycerol fractions of the triglycerides that are being broken down along with glucogenic amino acids, catabolized from protein, are used for glucose production through **gluconeogenesis**.

Translated into quantifiable terms, the state of starvation will cause a 75 kg man to breakdown 160 g of fat and 180 g of glucose per 24 hour period in the early stages of the fast. The glucose is primarily coming from hepatic glycogenolysis early on, whereas after about day 1 gluconeogenesis begins to supply glucose to the blood from lactate, glycerol, pyruvate, and from about 75 g of catabolized protein coming mostly from skeletal muscle. This loss of protein translates into increased content of urinary nitrogen (Schlichtig & Ayres, 1988). Based on the fact that 1 g of nitrogen is found in 6.25 g of protein, it can be assumed that these 75 g of protein would result in 12 g of urinary nitrogen. Overall, the quantity of skeletal muscle protein catabolized during pure starvation is approximately the same during metabolic stress (Schlichtig & Ayres, 1988); the difference is that nutritional support is effective in suppressing protein catabolism in pure starvation, whereas it is not in situations of metabolic stress (Gibson, 1990). In the late phase of starvation—about 5–6 weeks of fasting—the need for glucose is downsized from 180 g to a mere 80 g/d, thus conserving muscle mass. This shift takes place because of a greater reliance on fat from adipose tissue. Consistent with this shift, there is a decrease in urinary nitrogen loss from 8 g/d to 3 g/d within about two weeks (Schlichtig & Ayres 1988). The drop in the amount of lost nitrogen, resulting from a decline in protein erosion, is also attributed to a downward shift in metabolic rate. This is a kind of adaptation process that allows people on semi-starvation and starvation diets to survive a long time before dying. This downward

(margin notes: glycogen used; week 2 Fast Ketone ↓ Fatty acid)

(handwritten note at bottom: Skeletal muscle protein during starvation catabolizes the same as Metabolic Stress.)

adjustment in metabolic rate with fasting translates into a 15% decline in resting energy expenditure (REE) by two weeks, and another 25–35% by the third and fourth week of fasting (Hoffer, 2006). Death can be precipitated by a 40% loss of body weight in non-stressed starvation. In a situation of stressed starvation, a 25% loss of body weight or a 70–94% loss of adipose tissue is considered to be associated with a high risk of mortality (Schlichtig & Ayres, 1988; Bistrian, 1984).

8.1.1.3 Assessment of Hospital Undernutrition

The degree to which hospitalized patients are undernourished before entering or while under hospital care, especially in acute and chronic care settings, necessitates nutritional risk screening as the best strategy to decreasing the problem (Charney & Marian, 2008). Ideally, a nutritional screening should take place within the first 24 hours of admission of all patients according to the Joint Commission for the Accreditation of Health Care Organizations Guidelines (Kudsk et al., 2003). Those patients found to be at risk are then referred to a clinical dietitian for a more complete nutritional assessment (Barker et al., 2011). The notion of risk is best framed within three paradigms normally encountered within the hospital setting, and that were recognized as a valid assessment framework by the Academy of Nutrition and Dietetics and the American Society for Parenteral and Enteral Nutrition (ASPEN) in 2012. The first is recognized as a starvation-related malnutrition in the absence of inflammation; the second is malnutrition emanating from chronic disease and a persistent mild to moderate inflammation; the third is malnutrition derived from acute disease or injury with which is associated severe inflammation. Dietitians are encouraged to assess patients, using this frame-work of malnutrition, for improved patient outcomes (Compher & Mehta, 2016).

There are several steps the dietitian or clinician must follow to complete a meaningful nutritional assessment. First, in a nutritional risk assessment the health professional is interested in monitoring the patient's weight, height, non-desired weight changes, food allergies, dietary practices, recent changes in appetite, whether they had recently experienced vomiting or nausea, bowel habits that may intimate constipation or diarrhea, the presence of chronic disease, and a compromised ability to chew or swallow. In instances when laboratory turnaround time is fairly rapid, then serum albumin or hematocrit can used in screening patients at risk (Charney & Marian, 2008).

A patient would be classified nutritionally at risk if he meets at least one of the following criteria:

a Weight loss or gain that is >10% of the usual body weight within 6 months.

b A weight loss or gain >5% of the usual body weight within 1 month.

c A body weight that is either at 80% or less or 120% or more of the patient's healthy weight.

d Recently affected by disease, surgery, or trauma.

e Affected by some kind of chronic disease or a change in metabolic requirements.

f Has not ingested adequate amounts of food or nutrition supplements for > 7 days.

g Has experienced difficulty swallowing or absorbing food for > 7 days.
(Source: Charney & Marian, 2008).

There is also a rapid nutritional screening tool, popularly used by nurses in American hospitals in order to quickly and efficiently identify patients who are at risk of malnutrition. The **Rapid Nutrition Screen for Hospitalized Patients** is made up of a three question scoring questionnaire that can be completed promptly; a numeric value can be generated that will position the patient on a nutritional risk scale (Charney & Marian, 2008).

a Have you lost weigh recently without trying: No (0) / Unsure (2)

b If yes, how much weight (Kg) have you lost?
   1 1–5 kg (1 point)
   2 6–10 kg (2 points)
   3 11–15 kg (3 points)
   4 >15 kg (4 points)
   5 Unsure (2 points)

c Have you eaten poorly because of poor appetite
   1 Yes (1 point)
   2 No (0 point)

A score that is ≥2 implies the patient is at risk of malnutrition, and a nutritional assessment is advised (Charney & Marian, 2008).

The **Malnutrition Universal Screening Tool (MUST)** is also popularly used by medical professionals because it uses familiar weight parameters and is part of one of the recommended approaches advocated by the European Society of Enteral and Parenteral Nutrition (Kondrup, et al., 2003). Using this screening technique, the dietitian, nurse or physician who measures a BMI >20 can conclude that the patient is at no risk, and assign a score of 0; a score of 1 is indicated for a medium problem if the patient's BMI is 18.5–20; and a score of 2 is given when the BMI <18.5, indicating a more serious risk (Kondrup et al., 2003). In a second step, any unintentional weight loss can be assessed by assigning different numerical values to variable degrees of weight loss. For instance, a score of 0 is assigned to weight loss < 5% over 3–6 months; a score of 1 is given for a loss of between 5–10%, and a score of 3 is allocated to a weight loss >10% over 3–6 months (Kondrup et al., 2003). In the third step, the provider needs to give a score of 2 if the patient has been, is or will be at risk of going without food for more than 5 days because of illness. Depending on the cumulative score, the patient would be categorized as low, medium or high nutritional risk (Charney & Marian, 2008). So then, a score of zero would indicate low nutritional risk and to proceed with routine clinical care. A score of 1 would suggest medium nutritional risk and a need to observe the patient's diet and fluid intake closely. Finally, a score of 2 or greater implies high risk of undernutrition, and a need to treat the patient by referring them to a dietitian for dietary information or nutritional support (Kondrup et al., 2003). The criteria used in these assessment tools illustrate the fundamental reliance on body weight, appetite and disease state in screening patients for nutritional risk.

The Nutritional Risk Screening (NRS-2002) consists of an initial screening and assesses four major points: a) Is the BMI <20.5? b) Has patient lost weight in last 3 months? c) Has there been a reduction in dietary intake over the last 7 days? d) Is the patient receiving intensive therapy because of serious illness? Answering **Yes** to any of the above questions would prompt a second more involved final screening (Table 8.1) that measures both the extent of wasting and the severity of disease (Kondrup et al.,

2003). Follow the score assessment indicated in the table below to interpret the numerical score.

Once the screening is complete, then a dietitian can engage in a more thorough nutritional assessment of the patient. This step will rely on medical, nutritional, and medication histories; physical examination, anthropometric measurements, and laboratory data to complete a more comprehensive understanding of the patients nutritional status (Charney & Marian, 2008). The assessment will also likely be able to assign a prognostic risk based on the nutritional status (Buzby & Mullen, 1984). A prognosis is an estimation of a patient's risk of morbidity or mortality. A poor nutritional status is likely to increase the risk of post-surgical complications. This is because the prognostic determination is based on four important measures: first, serum albumin levels which, when low (<2.6 g /dL), indicate a high risk of mortality; second, triceps skinfold, which measure the degree of subcutaneous fat; it is a measure of emaciation which, when low, correlates poorly with good health; third, serum transferrin is a measure of both iron status and protein status. When low, it can be an indirect measure of poor protein status; however, elevated transferrin is expected in anemia; fourth, delayed cutaneous hypersensitivity. It is a skin reactivity test to three antigens. The idea here is when nutritional status is compromised so will the immune system (Buzby & Mullen, 1984). Students can review more details of the Prognostic Nutritional Index in chapter 7 section 6.

8.1.1.4 Treatments of Hospital Undernutrition

a) *Energy Determination*—Following a complete assessment of the patient's nutritional status, it is possible for the clinician to prescribe an appropriate strategy to enhance or rebuild the nutritional status if it is suboptimal. The first thing to consider is the type of nutritional support needed by the patient. In hospital settings, patients are in a disease state and may have undergone some kind of trauma such as multiple bone fractures as seen in an automotive accident. The patient may have experienced burns to a broad surface area of the body. All these are traumas and are responsible for increasing both the energy and protein needs of the patient. DeSouza and Green (1998) report that, on average, burn patients require 40–45 kcal/kg body weight/day.

Table 8.1

Nutritional Risk Screening 2002

Score	Weight Loss & Diet Intake	Score	Disease State
0	No reported weight loss/meets enrgy needs	0	Disease state not reported
1	>5% Wight loss in 3 months/ingests 50–75% of normal food intake in last week	1	Hip fractures/Chronic disease with acute complications: cirrhosis, COPD, diabetes, oncology, hemodialysis
2	>5% Weight loss in 2 months or BMI: 18.5–20.5/ingests 25–60% of normal food intake in last week	2	Abdominal surgery/Stroke/Severe pneumonia
3	>5% Weight loss in 1 month or BMI: <18.5/ingests 0–25% of normal food intake in last week	3	Head injury/Bone marrow Transplant/ICU patient/APACIIE >10

Age if >70 years: add 1 to total score above /

Age-adjusted total score:_____

Total Score Assessment: Score ≥3: the patient is nutritionally at-risk and a nutritional care plan is initiated. A Score <3: weekly rescreening of the patient and a preventive nutritional care plan is considered.

Source: Adapted from the Nutritional Risk Screening (NRS 2002) published in Kondrup et al., 2003)

The burn patient's energy needs work out to be about 1.47 times the resting energy expenditure (REE) calculated using the Harris-Benedict formula. According to Long (1984) this upward caloric adjustment is typically seen in patients with about 20% of their body surface area (BSA) burned. And so with a greater burned BSA, that is 40 to 100%, then the energy needs jump 1.85–2.05 times the value of the REE or the basal metabolic rate (BMR) (Long, 1984).

There are traumas of lesser intensities that carry decreased injury factors. Energy estimations using the Harris-Benedict formula and a set of injury factors were previously described by Long (1984) and represented in Table 8.2.

b) *Protein Requirements*—Traumatic injuries and sepsis (systemic infection) produce a hypermetabolic state in which energy and protein requirements are heightened in the body (Frankenfield, 2006). Protein requirements will vary depending on whether the injury is classified as mild, moderate, or severe, because of the impact of trauma/injury on body proteolysis and lipolysis. Indeed, the greater the trauma or the infection the greater the protein catabolism and fat breakdown (DeSouza & Greene, 1998).

Historically, research from the 1980s espoused the notion that significant protein ingestion was necessary during trauma in order to offset the greater negative nitrogen balance observed in the post-traumatic period. The therapeutic recommendations for protein are outlined below:

a Elective surgeries: 1.1 g/kg/day

b Fractures and infections: 1.5–2.0 g/kg/day

c Multiple fractures, injuries, infections, and burns greater than 40% BSA: 2.0–4.0 g/kg/day (Long, 1984)

Table 8.2
Energy Requirements of Hospitalized Patients Calculated Using the Harris-Benedict Equation

Women's BMR Formula	
$[(665.10 + 9.56 \times W_{kg})+(1.85 \times H_{cm})]-(6 \times A_{years})$	
Men's BMR Formula	
$[(66.47 + 13.75 \times W_{kg}) + (5.0xH_{cm})]-(6.76xA_{years})$	
Total Energy Expenditure	
BMR x AF(Activity Factor) x IF (Injury Factor)	

Activity Factor	Injury Factor
1.2 (confined to bed)	Surgery: 1.0–1.2
1.3 (out of bed)	Infection: 1.0–1.8
	Skeletal Trauma: 1.2–1.35
	Multiple Traumas + Steroids: 1.6
	Blunt Trauma: 1.15–1.35

Source: Adapted from Long, CL. (1984).

Despite the higher protein prescription, no amount of protein appears able to completely halt the rate of protein catabolism that occurs during injury; large ingestion of protein can mitigate somewhat the protein erosion, but not stop it entirely (Weissman, 1999). Overfeeding protein does however leave the body with a high nitrogen burden that needs to be excreted. This paradox has created some controversy and a lack of agreement with respect to protein needs during critical illness. Graham Hill's group out of Auckland New Zealand studied this problem more closely by implementing nutritional support protocols with varied protein levels on 18 trauma and 8 sepsis patients. Researchers found that, by increasing protein intake from 1.1 to 1.5 g/kg fat free mass (FFM), protein losses declined by 50%. However, they reported that further increases up to 1.9 g/kg FFM did not continue to abate nitrogen losses from the body. The group concluded that the current practice of prescribing protein to between 1.2–2.0 g/kg bodyweight, is likely excessive, especially if post-traumatic body weights—which tend to be overhydrated—are used in the calculation (Ishibashi et al., 1998). Assuming exaggeratedly high weight estimations because of edema and ascites, then the most efficient prescription of 1.5 g/kg FFM should be adjusted to 1.0 g/kg body weight/day after correcting for a water and fat mass (FM) totaling 33%. The team recommended a prescription of 1.2g/kg body weight/day to critically ill patients using pre illness body weights (Ishibashi et al., 1998). In the instance when body weights prior to illness are unknown, then the conservative 1.0 g/kg body weight/day prescription is advised. This lower protein recommendation has, however, been disputed by others who argue that protein intakes >2.0 g/kg body weight/day can indeed heighten the rate of protein synthesis. Frankenfield (2006) contends that very elevated protein prescriptions are necessary in order to achieve nitrogen balance in critically ill patients; some of the data is convincingly linked with greater survival (Frankenfield, 2006). A review by Hoffer and Bistrian (2012) could not find, however, strong enough studies that favored clinical recommendations for elevated protein intakes above 2.0 g/kg body weight in critically ill patients. Consistent with these findings, the Canadian Clinical Practice Guidelines (CCPG), considered the most thorough data base on best practices in critical care management, also concluded that the data available in 2013 prevented the committee from making formal recommendations for high or escalating protein doses in critical illness (CCPG, 2013). Nevertheless, although the most common practice in the United States is to prescribe on average 1.5 g/kg body weight/day of protein in critical care medicine (Wolfe, 1996; Hoffer & Bistrian, 2012), the few good studies that have been published do nevertheless suggest some benefits like better survival rates with protein intakes between 2.0–2.5 g/kg/day (Hoffer & Bistrian, 2012).

8.1.2 Prevalence of Malnutrition in the U.S Population

It would appear on the surface that nobody is really undernourished in the United States or Canada, but paradoxically, the malnutrition of obesity affects increasing numbers of the U.S. population (Via, 2012).

8.1.2.1 Obesity as a Form of Malnutrition

It is controversial that an obese person could suffer from malnutrition, but it is recognized as the modern face of malnutrition, especially in the pediatric population (Compher & Mehta, 2016). The classic image of an emaciated child or adult comes to mind when trying to conceptualize what a malnourished person looks like. As previously discussed, most or our malnourished are in our hospitals, however, the commercialization of our food supply has led to an abundant processing of food in order to sell and distribute large volumes of stable and safe food to the population. The problem is that much of what we eat has undergone an extrusion process that uses thermal heat and therefore destabilizes vitamins A, E, D, and C especially (Riaz et al., 2009).

8.1.2.2 Vitamin D Deficiency and its History

Historically, vitamin D deficiency was prominent in the United States, Canada, Western Europe, and Asia in the early years of the 20th century. The fortification of the U.S. milk supply with vitamin D by the 1930s caused the prevalence of rickets to begin

to decrease (Holick, 2006). Rickets is a devastating bone malformation that caused the long bones of the legs of children to bow outwards under the increasing weight of the growing child (Figure 8.1), or to cause knock knees because of a poorly formed calcified bone matrix (Gibson, 1990). It also caused a curvature of the spine and disturbed gait. Weakened muscles and beaded ribcages are also common symptoms (Holick, 2006). It was considered eradicated by the late 1960s. This was a public health success because in the early 1900s about 90% of children living in the North Eastern United States and in large Northern European cities suffered from rickets (Holick, 2006).

Rickets, although documented by Francis Glisson among the city dwelling children of 17th century Europe, did not begin to be understood until 1822, when Sniadecki observed that the disease was prominent inside of Warsaw and absent outside the Polish capital. This raised suspicions about the need for sunlight in order to cure the disease, a recommendation that Sniadecki began to promote (Holick, 2006). However, the medical establishment

© *Getty Images*

Figure 8.1 *Children with rickets in the 1940s presented here with bowed legs.*

continued to pay little attention to the environment as the cause of rickets. Meanwhile, French physician, Bretonneau was able to quickly heal a 15-month-old child with rickets in 1827 by administering cod liver oil, a practice thought to be more folkloric than true medical science (Holnick, 2006). Nevertheless, cod liver oil, and the use of fish oils in general, in combination with exposure to sunlight became medical recommendations which Bretonneau's student, Trousseau, began to advocate.

Still, this belief that the environmental conditions played no real role in the onset of the disease was further promoted in light of an 1889 epidemiological study, conducted by the British Medical Society, in which a lack of sunlight did not appear as a risk factor. A cure for rickets continued to evade the larger sphere of scientists and medical researchers, despite another epidemiological survey in 1890 by Palm that pointed again at the importance of sunlight for prevention. His team found that children of middle class families, living in industrialized cities of Britain, had the greater prevalence of rickets, whereas those in Chinese, Japanese and Indian cities showed no signs of the disease. So it would seem the evidence was not convincing enough to alter medical practice (Holick, 2006). The world would have to wait until 1920, some 30 years later, for Huldschinsky to demonstrate the curative effect of mercury vapor arc lamps on the rachitic bones of children. He argued that the lamps produced a melanization effect on skin that was identical to the effect of sunlight. This was the indisputable evidence needed to confirm that sunlight could be considered an appropriate therapy for rickets (Holick & Adams, 1998).

Meanwhile, the curative features of fish oil, continued to interest a researcher by the name of Edward Mellanby who, in 1918, created a dog model of rickets, which he produced using a strict oatmeal diet, and cured with butter fat. He did however observe that cod liver oil cured the disease more effectively (Wolf, 2004). He concluded that either vitamin A, which had been discovered a few years earlier, or some other factor was the curing agent. McCollum, the discoverer of vitamin A, which his team isolated from butter fat in 1914, wondered whether the curative factor in butter and cod liver oil was vitamin A. After treating the cod liver oil, in order to oxidize the vitamin A, and then feeding it to rachitic

rats in 1922, his team found that although the rats developed xerophthalmia—blindness due to vitamin A deficiency—it still held its rachitic curative properties, thus concluding that another factor, other than vitamin A, was healing the animals of rickets (Wolf, 2004). The next major finding occurred in post-WWI Vienna, where Hariette Chick and her team successfully cured rickets in children by feeding them either whole milk or cod liver oil (Wolf, 2004).

At this historical juncture, the race to uncover the cure for rickets was taking place in two fronts: The first was the role of sunlight and the second was the food factor apparently present in cod liver oil, butter, and whole milk. It was the work of Huldschinsky on the influence of sunlight that was gaining some attention. It was perhaps the bold clinical trial of both doctors, Hess and Unger, who brought irrefutable evidence, in 1922, that sunlight was able to cure rickets. They placed seven kids with rickets on the rooftop of a New York City hospital, where they remained exposed to sunlight daily for various lengths of time; the epiphyses of the bones began to calcify (Holick, 2006). These two avenues of investigation made it particularly difficult to fully understand the cause of rickets, for indeed, both diet and sunlight were curing rickets, but no researcher was able to find the common factor that linked both treatments. It was in 1924 that this dichotomy began to be unraveled with key observations made by three distinct laboratories (Wolf, 2004). First, Hess' lab showed that the irradiation of linseed oil with U.V. light activated some kind of antirachitic factor. A second lab cured rats of rickets by irradiating, not only rachitic rats with U.V. light, but after removing the rats, the air inside the empty jar as well. A third lab further explored the impact U.V. light had on the rats. What was going on that had a curative effect? The team killed standard non-irradiated rats, extracted their livers and irradiated them with U.V. light. Researchers minced up the irradiated livers to create an additive to the standard rat meal. They found that non-irradiated rats with rickets that were fed the irradiated livers also were cured of rachitic symptoms.

What was going on that irradiating liver gave it an increased antirachitic potency? It was this question that eventually led to uncovering, in 1937, the cholesterol-derived precursor to vitamin D,

7-dehydrocholesterol, which is formed under the skin of humans and some animals when exposed to U.V. light or sunlight (Wolf, 2004; Carpenter, 2003). About 80% of vitamin D (calcitriol) is synthesized subcutaneously from U.V. sunlight directly interacting with 7-dehydrocholesterol—the precursor to naturally occurring vitamin D_3. The diet provides a vitamin equivalent called vitamin D_2. Both D_3 and D_2 are metabolized in the liver to 25-hydroxyvitamin D (25-OH-D3), and then transformed in the kidney to the biologically active form of 1, 25-dihydroxyvitamin D (1,25-(OH)2-D3), also called **calcitriol** (WHO, 2006). Because vitamin D plays a central role in regulating calcium and phosphorus homeostasis in the body, it should not be a surprise that a deficiency of this vitamin could cause rickets in infants (Figure 8.1), and osteomalacia in adults, which leads to osteoporosis and frequent bone fractures (WHO, 2006). Rickets characteristically presents with a poor calcification of femoral, tibia, and rib matrix, thus resulting in soft bone that bends to the growing weight of the child (Figure 8.2). The typical risk factors for rickets have been well accepted and include living in a temperate environment above latitudes 40°N and below 40°S, poor sun exposure, dark skin pigmentation, exclusive breast feeding, and mothers with a deficient vitamin D status (WHO, 2006). Infants particularly vulnerable to rickets and adults susceptible to osteomalacia are those with complete skin covering, typically seen in the Middle East.

In recent times, vitamin D insufficiency has been reported to be alarmingly high among U.S obese and type-2 diabetics, with prevalence rates of 80–90%. This finding prompted some epidemiologists to recommend vitamin D supplementation to improve glucose metabolism and insulin sensitivity in type-2 diabetics (Via, 2012). The problem however, is more widespread than originally thought. Up until 2003, the FDA had given the okay for only milk, and a few cereals and bread to be fortified with vitamin D (Holick, 2006); without exposure to sunlight the U.S. population had access to very few foods rich in vitamin D. This was especially true within geographic areas where dietary shifts of young people toward greater soft drink consumption meant that there was less milk consumed by children and young adults. Women of color have been identified as

particularly at risk. Indeed, NHANES-III reported that 43% of African women between the ages of 15 and 49 had suboptimal vitamin D levels in their blood. In Boston, at the end of the winter of 2001, nutrition researchers documented that 32% of Caucasians between the ages of 18 and 29 were vitamin D deficient (Holick, 2006). Those individuals over the age of 50 are also prone to insufficient vitamin D. It is currently estimated that 50% of Americans and Europeans over 50 years of age are likely at risk of a poor vitamin D status. Stratifying by ethnicity really brings out the disparity. Among free living elderly, residing in the Boston area in 2001, 84% of African American elderly, 42% of Hispanics, and 30% of whites were found to be vitamin D deficient (Holick, 2006). These findings raised concerns, among public health officials, that something was not right. In 2003, the FDA approved vitamin D fortification of orange juice and other juice products in order to counter the dietary shift away from milk (Holick, 2006). Is this enough of a measure, or is soft drink consumption more widespread and insidious than originally believed?

8.1.2.3 Vitamin E Deficiency and its History

Isolated from wheat germ in 1936, vitamin E's main role, documented in monkeys, pigs and dogs, appeared to be the prevention of necrotizing myopathy in these and many other animals. However, after 80 years of research, vitamin E remains, in humans, the vitamin without a disease (Traber, M.G., 2006). In the 1950s and 60s, researchers could only find that erythrocytes, taken from men that were induced with vitamin E deficiency, were more susceptible to hemolysis. No other symptoms were evident, until 1960s when cholestatic liver disease and abnormal lipid profiles became evident in children with malabsorption syndrome. It was clearer, by the 1980s, that peripheral neuropathy defined the main symptom of vitamin E deficiency. There were also much longer and potentially more devastating implications around chronically suboptimal vitamin E intakes. By the turn of the new millennium, vitamin E's involvement in antioxidant activity became a game changer. The vitamin interrupted the free radical chain reactions that threatened biologic membranes. Seen as a peroxyl radical scavenger, vitamin E, also known as α-tocopherol, protected the polyunsaturated fatty acids (PUFAs) that made up the phospholipid layer of the cellular membranes. In this manner, the vitamin prevents the oxidation of the fatty acids that make up the cellular membrane (Traber, 2006). Absorbed within the chylomicron during digestion, it circulates to the liver via the chylomicron remnant where it is taken up by hepatic cells and then recirculated to the tissue again as VLDLs, LDLs and HDLs (Traber, 2006). Only but rarely is vitamin E deficiency, resulting from suboptimal dietary intakes, ever reported in humans. The individuals most susceptible to outright vitamin E deficiency are those with fat malabsorption syndromes. Whenever there is an inability to properly secrete adequate amount of bile into the intestine to form micelles, which is part of the normal emulsification process of fat, then malabsorption occurs. This is referred to as a hepatobiliary disorder. Cystic fibrosis, in children, usually involves poor pancreatic secretions of the lipase enzyme, therefore leading to steatorrhea, which occurs when a significant amount of fat remains in the stool. There is a tendency here for the child to develop vitamin E deficiency even when supplements of pancreatic enzymes are administered orally (Traber, 2006). Intramuscular injections of vitamin E are a preferred treatment option as these patients with malabsorption are unable to absorb the actual vitamin. The other instance of vitamin E deficiency has been documented in patients receiving total parenteral nutrition. Here the lipid component of the intravenous feeding is generally made up of soybean emulsions that contain γ-tocopherol and not the preferred α-tocopherol. In these patients there is evidence of higher than normal levels of lipid peroxidation. This means the fat oxidation is occurring too easily because it does not have enough of vitamin E's antioxidant protection (Traber, 2006).

8.1.2.4 Vitamin C Deficiency in the United States and its History

Although scurvy—having long plagued sea explorations to the new world, as far back as the 15th century—has been considered eradicated since the late 19th to early 20th centuries, there have been concerns that people in the United States may be at risk of vitamin C (Figure 8.3) deficiency or depletion because of a growing trend in poor dietary practices (Hampl et al., 2004).

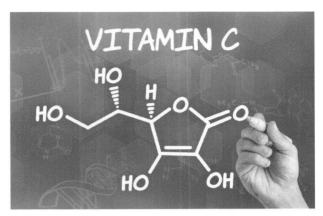

© Zebor/shutterstock.com

Figure 8.3 *Ascorbic acid molecule (Vitamin C).*

The W.H.O, using 1988–1994 data from the National Health and Nutrition Examination Survey (NHANES) in the United States that showed about 9% of women and 13% of men had a mild form of ascorbic acid deficiency, concluded that there was a likely mild vitamin C deficiency prevalent worldwide (WHO, 2006). Although the symptoms of scurvy, which include follicular hyperkeratosis, hemorrhagic manifestations, swollen joints, swollen bleeding gums and peripheral edema, with a risk of death, have been well documented, the milder form of deficiency, which could be referred to as subclinical vitamin C deficiency, does not have such clearly defined symptoms. There are some suspicions that poor bone mineralization—because of poor or slower collagen synthesis—lassitude, fatigue, anorexia, muscular weakness and increased susceptibility to infections could very well be the most common subclinical symptoms. Understanding ascorbic acid's involvement in enhancing non-heme iron absorption could very well help explain the fatigue and lassitude typically observed in people who ingest inadequate vitamin C (WHO, 2006).

Because vitamin C (ascorbic acid) is a water soluble vitamin, and is thus not stored in the body for long periods of time, it is important to regularly consume adequate amounts—the RDA is 75 mg/day for women and 90 mg for men (Levine et al., 2006)—through the regular consumption of a broad assortment of fruits and vegetables. Smokers in particular have higher needs—about 110-125 mg/day—because smoking causes increased oxidative stress in the body (Hampl et al., 2004). Jeffrey Hampl a nutrition researcher from Arizona State University, Mesa, and his colleagues, in reviewing the literature, described previous studies done in the late 1970s that found that 25% of nonsmoking men, and up to 50% of adult male smokers had depleted vitamin C reserves (Hampl et al., 2004). Internationally, this groups notes that when fruit and vegetable intakes are low in a population, the prevalence of vitamin C deficiency tends to be elevated. They write that even though many Americans do meet the American Cancer Institute's 5-A-DAY recommendation for fruit and vegetable intake—a feat only possible by including French fries—it turns out that the quality and variety of the produce consumed is not actually elevated in ascorbic acid. The truth of the matter is that Americans have a rather narrow intake of fruits and vegetables, with about 30% of all produce consumed in the United States being primarily iceberg lettuce, raw tomatoes, French fries, bananas, and orange juice, in descending order of importance (Hampl et al., 2004).

The problem is that vitamin C is the least stable of the vitamins and thus prone to be destroyed by heat, air, alkali and metals. Consequently, cooking and long storage time can cause a significant drop in vitamin C content. For instance, once orange juice is exposed to air, the rate of vitamin C degradation approaches 2% per day (Hampl et al., 2004).

The growing prevalence of obesity has raised some concern about the caloric and nutrient densities of the food consumed by the obese. It has been established that between 35–45% of obese individuals tagged for gastric bypass surgery in the United States are likely deficient to some degree in vitamin C. Diabetics are also more predisposed towards suboptimal vitamin C compared to healthy controls (Via, 2012). Although fruit and vegetable consumption continues to be encouraged by health professionals, Vitamin C supplementation has been proposed, in recent years, for vulnerable groups like poor eaters and smokers (Hampl et al., 2004).

Ascorbic acid deficiency causes scurvy, which is characterized by weakness and lassitude, swollen, receding bleeding gums, perifollicular hyperkeratosis, petechial hemorrhage, as well as bleeding into the skin, subcutaneous tissues, muscles and joints. In its severe form, scurvy can cause the loss of teeth,

bone damage, internal hemorrhage and infection (Levine et al., 2006). Historically, there is evidence from Egyptian hieroglyphs that scurvy existed at least as far back as 3000 BC. The great Greek physician, Hippocrates described the condition in 500 BC. But it is really in reading the history books recounting sea explorations to the new world in the 16th and 17th centuries, that most became aware of the condition for the first time. Long term travel at sea, lasting more than one month, was responsible for causing many sailors to succumb to the scourge of the sea because of the poor vitamin C content of their diet, which arose from the inability of the ship's cargo bays to hold fruits and vegetables, rich in vitamin C, for extended periods (Carpenter, 1986). It was also a prominent condition that developed in northern European cities during the 19th century because of the city dwellers' limited access to fresh fruits and vegetables (Carpenter, 1986). It was not until 1753 that James Lind wrote the first treatise on scurvy in which he proposed that acidic fruits could heal scurvy, and yet, despite his findings, scurvy continued to devastate maritime travel. The main reason was that his discovery went against popular beliefs of the time that scurvy was caused by things like cold climate, dampness, foggy weather and lack of fresh air (Levine et al., 2006). Despite Lind's treatise, it took until 1795, before the British Royal Navy, under advisement by Scottish physician Sir Gilbert Blane, ordered that all British sailors at sea for more than two weeks take one ounce of citrus juice—eventually adapting lime juice as a stable—on a daily basis. This practice resulted in British sailors being nicknamed "limeys." Interestingly, there were still cases of scurvy that persisted among sailors and the merchant navies until the Merchant Shipping Act of 1854 which made it mandatory for all ships to carry citrus fruits (Levine, et al., 2006).

Surprisingly, soldiers during the American Civil War and WWI were widely affected by scurvy. Albert Szent-Gyorgyi, a Hungarian biochemist, managed to isolate the antiscorbutic principle in 1928, a feat that completely rid the national landscape of scurvy, and that afforded him the Nobel Prize in 1937 (Levine et al., 2006). It was specifically Dr. J.H. Crandon who, while still a surgical resident at Harvard's School of Medicine, placed himself on a diet containing no vitamin C for 26 weeks, in order to clinically prove the medical efficacy of the synthetic vitamin C supplement (Crandon, et al., 1940). During that time, he ensured that all other nutrients and micronutrients were supplemented. The terrible hemorrhaging from his legs, physical exhaustion and poor wound healing were quickly reversed with vitamin C supplements (Carpenter, 2003).

Frank scurvy, eradicated from industrialized countries since the early 20th century, has not been considered a threat except in cases of hospital malnutrition often seen in cancer cachexia, malabsorption, alcoholism, and drug addiction; subclinical forms of vitamin C deficiency have, however, been seen in recent years in individuals with inadequate and idiosyncratic diets (Levine et al., 2006). Unfortunately, non-specific symptoms make detection more difficult; in fact clinicians have mistaken early signs of scurvy in children for rickets as both are known to impair bone growth (Levine et al., 2006). Strategies to help maintain a good ascorbic acid status consist of helping the population consume greater varieties of fruits and vegetables on a daily basis. Both the U.S. Department of Agriculture (USDA) and the National Cancer Institute encourage the consumption of a minimum of 5 servings of a wide variety of fruits and vegetables daily. Despite such a minimal target, NHANES data from between 1988 and 1991 revealed that 37% of men and 24% of women in the United States took in less than 2.5 servings/day, with French fries representing a large proportion of their intake. Moreover, between 10–25% of the Americans met or fell below the DRI for vitamin C (Levine et al., 2006). Excellent fruit sources of vitamin C are fortified grape juice (120 mg), strawberries (95 mg), papaya (85 mg), kiwi (75 mg), oranges (70 mg) and cantaloupe (60 mg), whereas the best vegetable sources of vitamin C are fresh broccoli (60 mg), kale (55 mg), raw green or red peppers (60 mg) and Brussels sprouts (50 mg). Cabbages of various types and preparations contain between 10–25 mg per serving (Levine, et al., 2006). Vitamin C supplementation is a less preferred alternative by dietitians, even though it is popularly ingested in megadoses. The popularity of vitamin C supplementation really began with Linus Pauling's 1970 bestselling diet book: *Vitamin C and the Common Cold.* In it, he recommended daily mega-doses of 3,000 milligrams of vitamin C to stop the common cold. Three time Nobel Prize laureate, his book began to sell amazingly well with two reprints: one in 1971 and the other in 1973 (Offitt, 2013). It did not take too long before the scientific community discredited him, after his claims were tested by acclaimed research centers and shown to be unfounded. It soon became evident that Pauling, now in his seventies, had actually not done any scientific research on vitamin C (Offitt, 2013).

8.1.2.5 Thiamin (Vitamin B1) Deficiency in the U.S and its History

Thiamin (**Figure 8.4**) is richly abundant in wheat germ, brown rice, eggs, liver, legumes, pork and green vegetables (Kennedy, 2016). In diets that rely on the refinement or processing of wheat, rice and other cereals, in addition to including excessive alcohol and frequent raw fish, the risk of thiamin deficiency greatly increases. Raw fish is of particular interest in the context of frequent sushi consumption, as it contains the enzyme, thiaminase, which catalyzes the breakdown of thiamin (WHO, 2006). Thiamin deficiency, also known as beriberi, although documented in Chinese texts as early as 2700 BC, and then again in 1611 by the first Governor General of the Dutch East Indies, and by European physician, Bontius in 1642, has only sporadically occurred. Thiamin deficiency did not become a public health problem until wheat and cereals like rice were being highly processed in the 19th century. Numerous cases began to emerge in two separate geographic areas: First, in Japan around 1880, and a second cluster, around that same time, was reported in the Dutch West Indies among native army recruits in the vicinity of Djarkarta (Carpenter, 2003b).

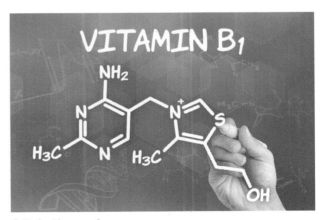

© *Zerbor/shutterstock.com*

Figure 8.4 *Thiamin (Vitamin B1) molecule.*

Many sailors in the Japanese navy were developing a disease known as "kakké" which characteristically presented as a polyneuritis with symptoms of weakness in the lower limbs, heart failure, shortness of breath and edema (Carpenter, 2003b). The degeneration of the peripheral nerves (polyneuritis) was a condition which led essentially to a paralysis of the hands and feet. An English-trained naval surgeon by the name of Kanehiro Takaki was commanded to resolve the problem. After investigating European and Japanese naval practices, he concluded that the only really noticeable difference was that the Japanese naval diet was significantly lower in protein. He ordered the menu on a ship headed to New Zealand to be readjusted to include more meat, condensed milk, bread and vegetables. A year earlier, this same voyage resulted in 25 dead sailors and numerous others sick with beriberi. This second voyage resulted in no death an in only a few cases of beriberi that were limited to sailors who refused to eat the newly-adapted diet (Carpenter, 2003b). Takaki concluded that a protein deficiency was the primary cause of the disease. Consequently, his dietary recommendations, which were implemented throughout the Japanese fleet, eventually led to the resolution of the problem. Still in Japan another problem was mounting among its newborn babies and their mothers. A disease called "taon" appeared to poison the mothers' breast milk and thus endangered the newborn Japanese infants with alarming symptoms of vomiting, edema, low urination rates, and unusually high death rates.

At the same time, back in Indonesia, a different approach was being proposed. The Dutch government sent a medical team, headed by bacteriologist, professor Pekelharing, for an eight-month investigation (Carpenter, 2003b). He concluded that the disease had to originate from some unknown bacteria, and proposed that his assistant, Dr. Christian Eijkman, a young army physician, continue the investigation. Eijkman was relieved of military duties and assigned to an army hospital that had many beriberi cases, just outside of Djakarta, Indonesia, where he became research director. Eijkman's first approach was to thoroughly investigate the contagion of the disease using an affordable animal model that would allow him to study large numbers. This was particularly important given the inter-animal variability in symptoms that had been typically observed until that time. His choice of chicken was a rather

lucky one as he was able to duplicate the polyneuritis symptoms in chickens by injecting them with blood of infected human patients. This was a logical step as he assumed the disease to be infectious. The problem was that his control chickens, also kept in the same compound were also developing similar symptoms. Suspecting that the infection had jumped from the infected group to the controls, he repeated the experiment, this time keeping the control chickens in a separate facility; this time the symptoms did not develop in either of the controls or infected animals, causing Eijkman to doubt the validity of using chickens as an experimental animal. He later discovered, by chance, that a cook, several months previously, was supplementing the chickens' diet with leftover polished rice from the hospital compound, but that a recent cook, who had begun his work a few weeks earlier, no longer requested leftover rice to supplement the chicken feed. Eijkman then began to test the leftover rice and was able to duplicate the disorder repeatedly. He suspected that cooked rice, stored overnight, caused the proliferation of bacteria-producing toxins that generated the polyneuritis. However, he later found that feeding raw polished rice also caused beriberi. This left him in a bit of a quandary, as his experiments were not consistently proving microbial infestation as the cause of the degenerative polyneuritis. This became even more evident when he discovered that feeding brown unprocessed rice healed the condition in the birds. Another set of experiments that tested tapioca versus meat, demonstrated that tapioca caused the disease and that meat cured it; this finding raised suspicions that starches in general were likely the problem not just rice. He hypothesized that starch was possibly fermenting in the intestine and producing a bacterial toxin that was behind the polyneuritis. Adding the rice bran back to the starches also healed the birds, confirming that the bran contained an antidote to the starch toxin. Having lost his wife and contracted malaria while in Indonesia, he had to promptly conclude his research. Eijkman's work however, never really evolved to include human experimentation, which was a great weakness that prevented him from uncovering the truth. Upon submission of his final report, the scientific community was critical of his work, questioning whether the disease he produced in the chickens was even beriberi (Carpenter, 2003b).

It is at this point that a recent acquaintance, Dr. Adolphe Vorderman with whom he had discussed his work before departing, was going to attempt to build on Eijkman's unfinished research. Working as a medical prison inspector in Java, he realized that there was already a human experiment in progress within the vast 101 prisons on the island of Java. He observed that the disease beriberi was rampant among prisoners who consumed white rice and relatively rare in the prisons serving brown rice, thus confirming Eijkman's work. However, the Dutch government did eventually send Eijkman's replacement, a bacteriologist named Gerrit Grijns, who managed to disprove that starch was the culprit. Rather, he demonstrated, in a 1901 published paper, that a nutrient located in the outer bran layer of the rice in addition to some legumes was necessary to cure and prevent the disease (Butterworth, 2006; Carpenter, 2003b). This finding was not well accepted in other parts of Asia where beriberi was prevalent. It took excellent work, by the Malaysian Institute for Medical Research, to decidedly produce convincing evidence that the white rice was deficient in some kind of factor. They showed that an alcoholic extract of the rice bran, when added to white rice, prevented beriberi, and that brown rice from which alcohol extract had been taken actually caused the disease (Carpenter, 2003b).

Following the Spanish-American war of 1898, the United States had a sizable proportion of native troops, stationed in the Philippines, who had contracted beriberi. The Philippine government called a meeting, which experts from the United States, Japan, and many other countries attended, in order to find a solution. Agreement had been reached that it was indeed the populations that had white polished rice as a stable that were at greater risk of developing beriberi. The solution for the Americans was to recommend banning the rice all together or taxing it so heavily that the poor, who were most vulnerable, would abandon it from their daily menu. Around that time, American Medical Corp physicians found that the symptoms of "taon," documented several years earlier in Japan, looked suspiciously similar to those adult with beriberi, and thus began to investigate. Using alcohol extracts from the bran of brown rice which they added to the breast milk, the babies quickly recovered. The Asian populations adopted

the white rice so readily because brown rice would become rancid too quickly when stored in tropical conditions. By 1911, the Polish chemist, Casimir Funk, who had been working at the Lister institute in London, was the first to isolate the thiamin crystal (Carpenter, 2003b).

In the United States, the adulteration of the food supply had become a significant problem by the 19th century so that with the advent of sophisticated food processing technology, a safer and more hygienic food supply began to appear but at a cost. Indeed, with processing, many food ingredients were devoid of nutrients. Three things were occurring that hinted that this pure American food was scandalously compromised nutritionally. First, by the 1930s and 40s, as the United States continued to manufacture and market cheap processed foods, food chemists were identifying sizable amounts of food products that were nutritionally deficient. At the same time, cases of malnutrition were popping up everywhere in the early 1930s, as the United States' reliance on bleached white bread continued to grow (Bobrow-Strain, 2012). Second, the FDA in the United States and Health and Welfare Canada, proposed a number of bills intended on regulating the food industry, which had, prior to WWII, been increasingly producing refined foods that had lost much of their nutrients. The goal of one of the bills was intended to force the food industry to "enrich" the foods they were manufacturing. The bill was, however, defeated in the United States, where the enrichment of flour and cereals became voluntary after WWII. Eventually, by 1964, Canada passed legislation, requiring the food industry to enrich its foods with thiamin, riboflavin, niacin and iron. Even today, the U.S. government still does not enforce enrichment, although much of the flour in the United States is enriched.

Today, the obesity crisis in the United States is setting off alarm bells, as the evidence seems to be pointing to a population with extremely poor eating habits that is being fed a food supply made up of cheaper calories, but a food quality that is more nutrient impoverished (Bissonnette, 2013). It is however among the obese population that a prevalence of thiamin deficiency of 15–25% has been reported, with prevalence rates as high as 79% observed among type-2 diabetics (Via, 2012). It is also found among hospitalized patients, who are ill with anorexia nervosa, alcoholism, HIV-AIDS, gastrointestinal, liver diseases, and persistent vomiting (Butterworth, 2006).

The RDA for adults is 1.1 mg/day and there is no known toxicity concern. Normally it is fairly easy to meet the RDA for this vitamin since it is abundantly found in the U.S. flour supply, breads, breakfast cereals, and grains such as polished rice, whole brown rice, peas, legumes of various types (soybeans, lentils, navy beans, kidney beans, etc.), beef, and lamb. So long as the diet is varied, and there are no absorption problems, then there should be little concern for the risk of being deficient in this nutrient. However, the heavy use alcohol has raised some concerns, as there is a tendency to eat poorly, experience diminished absorption, and a reduced hepatic storage of the vitamin because of frequent cases of steatosis and fibrosis that are reported (Butterworth, 2006). One of the diseases derived from abusive intakes of alcohol is called Wernicke-Korsakoff syndrome (WHO, 2006), which consists of two separate disorders: Wernicke Encephalopathy (W.E.) and Korsakoff Psychosis. W.E. is a disease that affects the activities of all three of the enzymatic reactions—transketolase in the monophosphate shunt pathway, pyruvate dehydrogenase in glycolysis and alpha-ketoglutarate dehydrogenase in the tricarboxylic acid (TCA) cycle—that have needed the co-factor, **thiamin diphosphate** (TDP), which was previously called thiamin pyrophosphate (Butterworth, 2006). This cofactor has been found to be suboptimal in the brain of deceased alcoholics with W.E. Erythrocyte thiamin transketolase activity (ETKA) and thiamin pyrophosphate effect (TPPE) are therefore two enzymes involved in carbohydrate metabolism that are sensitive indicators of tissue concentrations of thiamin, and thus should be used together in confirming thiamin deficiency (Gibson, 1990; WHO, 2006). Medical students are classically taught to look for a triad of symptoms consisting of ophthalmoplegia, ataxia, and confusion, which do not frequently occur in W.E. Rather, the condition is often missed because although it does involve ocular palsies, nystagmus, ataxia of gait, and a decline in mental processing, it will more likely present as apathy and a psychomotor fatigue or slowness (Butterworth, 2006). Korsakoff Psychosis is a confabulatory syndrome that involves amnesia, loss of spontaneous initiatives, and abnormal conceptual functions

(Butterworth, 2006). Beriberi can present as a wet cardiomyopathy which can lead to heart failure, or as a dry peripheral neuropathy.

8.1.2.6 Niacin and Riboflavin Deficiencies in the U.S and their History

a) *Niacin (Vitamin B3)*—Abundantly found in meats, fish, whole grains, legumes, mushroom and nuts, this vitamin, when deficient, has been associated with depression, memory loss, paranoia, vertigo, and psychotic symptoms (Kennedy, 2016). Structurally, niacin (Figure 8.5) is known as nicotinic acid and nicotinamide. It is specifically nicotinamide that is an important component of the nucleotides, nicotinamide adenine dinucleotide (NAD) and nicotinamide adenine dinucleotide phosphate (NADP). They are heavily involved in oxidation reduction reactions within the TCA cycle, which is the common pathway for the oxidation of carbohydrates, proteins and fats (Bourgeois et al., 2006).

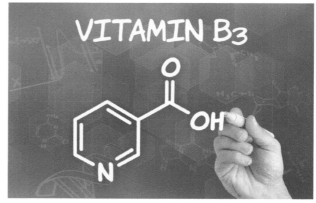

© Zebor/shutterstock.com

Figure 8.5 *Niacin molecule (Vitamin B3).*

Beginning in 1905, the niacin deficiency disease, pellagra, became more prominent in the American south, and by 1909 pellagra had widened its grip, spreading to several southern states (Carpenter, 2003). Symptomatically, those afflicted with pellagra presented with dermatitis, muscle weakness and twitching, burning sensation in the extremities, alopecia, and disturbed gait (Kennedy, 2016). The problem became widespread and so persistent that a physician by the name of Goldberger had been put in charge of the U.S. Public Health Service's pellagra program by 1914. The medical community was convinced that the cause was some kind of pathogenic fungi that had gotten into the food supply, or the consequence of excreta from flies that invaded outdoor food storage facilities. These ideas arose from a long standing pellagra problem in Italy, where moldy corn was suspected to be the cause.

When Goldberger became head of the investigation, he quickly ruled out the suspected infectious nature of the disease on the basis that none of the healthcare practitioners were getting ill from treating the sick patients. Suspecting an inadequate diet was at the source of the disease, he persuaded Mississippi authorities to allow him to recruit 12 prisoners from their prison system, who he intended to make sick with the disease. The motivation to participate was that if the prisoners survived six months they would be set free. He fed them a diet poor in protein and elevated in maize, which was the staple of the southern poor. By the sixth month, the volunteers had developed dermatitis in several regions of the body—a typical symptom seen in pellagra—but escaped from the hospital before Goldberger could confirm with other colleagues that he had produced pellagra in the prisoners. He studied whole families afflicted with the disease and found, after comparing to healthy families, that the difference was that the control families that did not have pellagra had a dairy cow, from which they extracted daily rations of milk.

The inclusion of both milk and rice in the diet, for instance, ensured a proper ingestion of tryptophan, which invariably converted to niacin in amounts considered sufficient to ensure a recovery or a prevention of pellagra, and this, despite both foods being poor sources of niacin (Bourgeois et al., 2006).

Golberger's group eventually developed a dog model of pellagra that exhibited black tongue after feeding them cornmeal, no milk, milk powder, or meat. Most surprising, the animals were healed very rapidly upon feeding them yeast. It took until 1937 before researchers conducted assays on fractions of yeast that allowed them to identify nicotinic acid as a key co-factor in the yeast reaction. Even though researchers were confident at that point that niacin deficiency was at the source of the pellagra, recent reports out of India created some confusion. Polished rice, which was heavily consumed in India, where pellagra was far from being a public health problem, actually contained much less niacin than in the maize consumed in the American south. Why then were they not afflicted with pellagra? The other problem, which deepened the mystery, was that pellagra was not prominent in Mexico where the Indian maize was heavily used (Carpenter, 2003c). In attempting to unravel this paradox, researchers discovered that the amino acid tryptophan, which is an essential amino acid, found in protein of high biological value (meat, poultry, fish and dairy), could chemically be transformed into niacin. Though the conversion rate of tryptophan to niacin is low (60 g tryptophan creates 1 g niacin), it was sufficient to prevent pellagra from occurring. There is however a catch, as this reaction requires vitamin B6 (pyridoxine), B2 (riboflavin), iron and copper to complete the biotransformation. So then, a diet deficient in any one of those additional nutrients could increase the risk of pellagra in the population (Bourgeois, et al., 2006). Also, the native people in Mexico knew to soak their maize in lime or some other kind of alkaline, which helped release the niacin from the maize for absorption. There were two main problems with the southern United States. Most of the maize was purchased as highly processed corn flour, which was used for cornbread—most of the niacin removed—and the overall diet was poor in protein (Carpenter, 1981). Those two things created a medical catastrophe; the poor began developing gastrointestinal malabsorption and **diarrhea**, **dermatitis**, followed later by **dementia** and finally **death**; these are commonly referred to as the 4 D symptoms (Bourgeois et al., 2006). Moreover, pellagra is a deficiency disease that should not be thought of in a linear fashion, in that, unlike other nutrient deficiency diseases, this one does not strictly take place when there is poor intake of niacin (WHO, 2006).

This is not surprising given niacin is involved as a key biochemical co-factor in so many biochemical reactions within the TCA cycle, and the electron transport chain, notably as nicotinamide adenine dinucleotide (NAD), and all of the metabolite derivatives such as NADH, NADP and NADPH (Bourgeois, et al., 2006).

The RDA for niacin in adults varies between 14–16 mg/day or niacin equivalents (NE)/day. Nowadays the good and excellent sources of niacin are well known; nuts, fish, and meat, along with enriched breads and cereals (Figure 8.7) regularly consumed as part of a well-balanced diet, prevent deficiency.

Additionally, milk and eggs, even though their niacin content is low, are still considered good sources of niacin because of the elevated tryptophan content in the high quality proteins of these foods (Bourgeois et al., 2006). Niacin has only but recently been used therapeutically in the management of hyperlipidemias, even though its hypocholesterolemic effect had been known since the 1960s (Goldsmith, 1965). Underutilized because of its secondary flushing effect, it has nevertheless been shown at doses of 2 g/day to effectively reduce many cardiovascular risk factors, notably an 18.4% reduction in LDL-C and a 31.2% decrease in the LDL:HDL ratio (Maccubbin et al., 2008). Its use as an alternative to statins has been increasing in both the US and Canada (Jackevicius, et al., 2013) despite the fact that there are no good quality randomized studies to confirm its efficacy (HPS2-THRIVE group, 2014). Recently, a double blind multi-center trial has demonstrated that niacin had no real cardiovascular therapeutic benefit, but appeared instead to heighten the risk of worsening known cases of diabetes, as well as increasing the incidences of infections and hemorrhages (HPS2-THRIVE group, 2014). It has been advanced that by inhibiting lipolytic reactions in adipose tissue—this decreases the release of triglycerides—and the synthesis of triglycerides in the liver, the nicotinic acid prevents the formation of VLDLs and LDLs. There are as well in vitro findings that suggest that the vitamin may promote heightened synthesis of HDL, the cholesterol scavenger (Bourgeois et al., 2006).

b) *Riboflavin (Vitamin B2)*—Riboflavin (Figure 8.6) is a key nutrient found in milk, some meats, whole grains, and processed grains, legumes, leafy greens, mushrooms, oily fish, and liver (Kennedy, 2016). This vitamin is, in fact, richly abundant in milk, making it truly unique among the B-complex of vitamins (Powers, 2003). So much so, that riboflavin deficiency tends to become endemic in populations that consume suboptimal amounts of milk and meat (Powers, 2003). It is also a precursor to two important nucleotides, flavin mono-nucleotide (FMN) and flavin adenine dinucleotide (FAD) that function as coenzymes in beta oxidation, the tricarboxilic acid (TCA) cycle and in the electron transport chain located in the wall of the mitochondria (Newsholme & Leech, 1983).

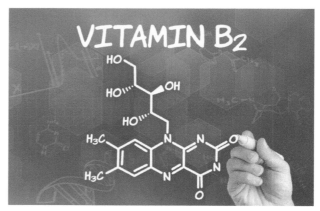

© *Zebor/shutterstock.com*

Figure 8.6 *Riboflavin (Vitamin B2) molecule.*

It would not, therefore, be difficult to infer that a deficiency could biochemically compromise fatty acid oxidation. FAD-dependent erythrocyte glutathione reductase is regarded as the most accurate measure of riboflavin status, which is expressed as the activation coefficient, EGRAC (WHO, 2006, Powers, 2003; Gibson, 1990).

A riboflavin deficiency is a serious concern, as it interferes with iron absorption and utilization, thus leading to iron deficiency anemia (Powers, 2003). The role of riboflavin in the hemopoietic system has been known since the 1950s. By the 1960s, studies on primates identified riboflavin's role in both the bone marrow production of red blood cells, and in their distribution throughout the body. More animal work throughout the 1970s and 80s demonstrated that the reduced form of the flavins assists in the release of iron from the ferritin protein, which is reflective of iron reserves. Consistent with this finding, vitamin B-2 deficient diets fed to rats resulted in less mobilization of iron from key tissues. Studies in the mid to late 1980s, also implicated riboflavin status with improved iron absorption, inferring its importance in gastrointestinal development (Powers, 2003). The milder symptoms of fatigue, weakness, mouth pain, burning eyes, and itching are truly non-specific, but can influence the quality of life of individuals. The more advanced deficiency symptoms, characterized by dermatitis with cheilosis and angular stomatitis, brain dysfunction, and microcytic anemia are more specific and recognizable (WHO, 2006).

Deficiencies of this vitamin are mostly found in regions like Guatemala and the United Kingdom, where milk consumption has significantly declined; a reported 47% decrease in whole milk intake, for instance, has taken place in the United Kingdom since 1990, among 4 and 8 year olds, concomitantly with a drop in vitamin B-2 status (Powers, 2003). There is some evidence of riboflavin deficiency causing neurological abnormalities in humans, which were reversed with supplementation (Leshner, 1981), but more research is needed to confirm the mechanism. Interestingly, animal studies have shown peripheral nerve demyelination resulting from B-2 deficiency, a finding that has not yet been confirmed in humans. More recently, the role of riboflavin in thyroxine activity has been identified, therefore raising some serious concerns about a potential role of B-2 deficiency in the pathophysiology of mental illness (Bell et al., 1992).

Deficiency tended to also occur to varying degrees at the same time as niacin deficiency (Carpenter, 2003). The yeast experiments had also uncovered that riboflavin, like niacin, was part of a rather complex enzymatic system. Indeed, they found that riboflavin was part of flavin adenine dinucleotide (FAD), which acted as a co-factor in numerous enzymatically controlled reactions in glycolysis, the TCA cycle, and electron transport chain. The characteristic symptoms of glossitis, angular stomatitis, and cheilosis tended to be documented as well in pellagra patients because the poor quality diet that typically produces pellagra can and does tend to also generate riboflavin deficiency (Carpenter, 2003).

Riboflavin is richly found in milk as well as in eggs, lean meat, broccoli, and enriched breads and cereals (McCormick, 2006). With an RDA of 1.1 mg/day for women and 1.3 mg/day for men, only very poor dietary selections or disease can compromise an individual's riboflavin status.

Hence, those individuals susceptible to a deficiency of this vitamin tend to be patients with anorexia (poor appetite) who eat too little food overall. Vulnerable as well are athletes who restrict energy intake as an unhealthy method of weight loss. Here too, the ingestion of riboflavin tends to be suboptimal (McCormick, 2006). Additionally, pregnant and lactating women, infants, along with school children and the elderly, become the groups most vulnerable to a deficiency. The NHANES survey reported a prevalence of riboflavin deficiency, among the elderly, varying between 10-27% (Powers, 2003; Guthrie & Guthrie, 1976; Fonelli & Woteki, 1989). To ensure a good riboflavin status today, with so much of our food fortified, would simply require consuming a breakfast cereal in the morning complemented with a cup of milk (Powers, 2003).

©Hurst Photo/shutterstock.com

Figure 8.7 *Good and excellent sources of riboflavin and niacin.*

8.1.2.7 Pyridoxine, Pantothenic Acid and Biotin Deficiencies in the United States and their Histories

a) *Pyridoxine (Vitamin B₆)*—Abundantly found in meat, fish, legumes, bananas, nuts, and potatoes (Kennedy, 2016), vitamin B_6 (Figure 8.8) is naturally found in three distinct forms: pyridoxine (PN), pyridoxal (PL), and pyridoxamine (PM). Since its discovery in the 1930s, the understanding of pyridoxine's role in human health and metabolism continued to grow. This vitamin in the phosphorylated form of pyridoxal phosphate (PLP) serves as a coenzyme in protein and amino acid metabolism (WHO, 2006).

Low serum pyridoxal-5'-phosphate (PLP) below the cut-off of 20 nmol/L has been used as the most reliable indicator of poor vitamin B_6 status (Mackey et al., 2006). Because this vitamin is widely found in the food supply, a deficiency of is difficult to find. Nevertheless, lower plasma concentrations have been frequently documented in patients with celiac disease, Crohn's disease and ulcerative colitis (Mackey, et al., 2006). These malabsorption syndromes affect not only vitamin B_6 absorption, but a multitude of other nutrients. Hence, a deficiency usually takes place concomitantly with other suboptimal nutrients. For instance, the activation, through phosphorylation of B_6, is done with the help of zinc. Conversely, niacin, folate and carnitine require pyridoxine for their biosynthesis. Severe cases of B_6 deficiency typically show symptoms of dermatitis, glossitis, and cheilosis because of its ties to other nutrients such as riboflavin. In fact, both B-6 and B-2 deficiencies show similar clinical signs (Powers, 2003). This is not surprising, since the metabolism of pyridoxine depends on FAD. Consequently, treating a riboflavin deficiency in humans with supplements almost invariably leads to an improved activity of erythrocyte pyridoxamine phosphate oxidase (Powers, 2003).

But the link to anemia is related to the critical role played by pyridoxal phosphate (PLP) in hemoglobin synthesis. In the absence of PLP a microcytic hypochromic anemia ensues (Mackey et al., 2006).

Elevated blood **homocysteine** is generally thought to occur in folate deficiency, but should not be unexpected in vitamin B_6 deficiency as its role in folate metabolism is well documented (See chapter 9). What is unclear is whether B_6 plays any significant role in carnitine metabolism in humans (Mackey et al., 2006). The fact that B_6 is a critical step in neurotransmitter synthesis explains the impact of a deficiency on the incidence of convulsions (Mackey, et al., 2006).

Although the symptoms of a pyridoxine deficiency are not well documented nor as overtly clear as in the cases of scurvy, beriberi and pellagra, there are convincing indicators that suboptimal intakes of this vitamin can lead to some long term diseases. There is epidemiological data, in 10 to 30 year olds, that documents a significant association between low B_6 status and increased risk of breast and other cancers. However, there is hardly any kind of clinical trial confirming causality (Mackey et al., 2006). It is specifically PLP's role in neurotransmitter synthesis—serotonin and α-amino-butyric acid are

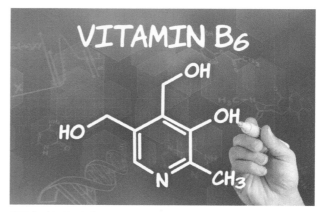

© Zebor/shutterstock.com

Figure 8.8 *Pyridoxine molecule (Vitamin B6).*

sensitive to B_6 in rats—that has inspired some to advance a role in cognitive development, but the evidence is not strong in humans (Agnew-Blais et al., 2015), except in the elderly (Riggs et al., 1996; Gottfries, 1998). It seems that getting old may make us particularly vulnerable to low plasma concentrations of PLP. The reason why levels would drop with aging is not clear, but some have advanced that the lower intake of food, typically seen with advanced age, a decline in renal function and perhaps increases in acute phase reactants and inflammation, may be behind these changes. What is even more convincing is that large doses of pyridoxine supplementation, administered to elderly patients, successfully restored biochemical, functional and immunological indices of PLP in the elderly. The fact that plasma levels tend to be suboptimal in cases of rheumatoid arthritis, dementia and Alzheimer's disease (Agnew-Blais et al., 2015) gives further credence to the consequence of neurological impairment and increased inflammation in B_6 deficiency.

Despite not being able to pinpoint a neurological mechanism, there are non-specific symptoms of peripheral neuropathy and symptoms resembling those of pellagra, along with seborrheic dermatitis, glossitis, and cheilosis in cases of protein-energy malnutrition, and in patients receiving anticonvulsant drug therapy (Merck, 2013). Additionally, in adults, there is evidence of increased depression, confusion, EEG abnormalities, and seizures when plasma B_6 levels are below the cutoff (Merck, 2013). The mechanism tying B_6 deficiency to dementia may well be associated with its involvement in regulating serum homocysteine levels, rather than just in neurotransmitter synthesis (Agnew-Blais et al., 2016). Indeed, cellular and blood concentrations of homocysteine tend to rise in instances of poor vitamin B_{12}, B_6 and/or folate status, which heightens the risk of cardiovascular disease and vascular dementia (Agnew-Blais et al., 2015). In fact, higher concentrations of serum homocysteine have been linked to an increased sensitivity to cerebral infarcts. So then, the role of vitamin B_6 in cognition and depression remains nonetheless documented, especially among the elderly (Moorthy et al., 2012), but there are some equivocal findings reported by other researchers (Agnew-Blais et al., 2015).

The key noteworthy areas of pyridoxine's biochemical involvement are outline below:

a It acts as a co-enzyme in glucose production via glycogenolysis and gluconeogenesis in the liver.

b PLP is a recognized co-factor that aids in enzymatic reactions involving amino acid and lipid metabolism (Mackey et al., 2006).

b) *Pantothenic acid*—A deficiency is unlikely given that this B vitamin is found in almost every food, notably, all meats, whole grains and broccoli (Kennedy, 2016). Consequently, the only early recorded cases of deficiency were in malnourished prisoners of war found in WWII Japanese, Filipino, and Burmese concentration camps. They experienced strong burning sensations on the bottom of their feet in addition to toe numbness, which were reversed with pantothenic acid, and not any other of the B vitamins (Trumbo, 2006). Additionally, diarrhea, dermatitis, encephalopathy, and demyelination have also been reported (Kennedy, et al., 2016). Dr. Lipmann discovered in 1947 that this was a key component of coenzyme A (CoA) in human metabolism. As such, it is directly involved in ß-oxidation of fatty acids and in the breakdown of amino acids as they prepare to be oxidized in the TCA cycle. The CoA plays a critical step in the formation of citrate from oxaloacetate in the TCA cycle. A component of hydroxyl-3-methylglutaryl-CoA, it exercises a vital role in cholesterol synthesis (Trumbo, 2006). It is no wonder that a deficiency of this vitamin produced, in subjects tested during the 1950s and 80s, symptoms of irritability, restlessness, sleep disturbances, numbness, and gastrointestinal problems. An unintentional acute deficiency caused, in Japanese individuals, mental retardation and suffering from dyskinesia, lactic acidosis, hypoglycemia, and hyperammonemia leading to encephalopathy (Trumbo, 2006). More recently, a 1 g calcium pantothenate supplement, taken daily, was found to be effective in the pain management of patients with rheumatoid arthritis (Trumbo, 2006).

c) *Biotin (Vitamin B7)*—Found in eggs, liver, pork, and leafy green vegetables (Kennedy, 2016), the essentiality of this nutrient (Figure 8.9) was first suspected in the 1980s by Velasquez and his co-workers. They surmised that biotin deficiency was occurring in severe cases of pediatric malnutrition, based on the activity of the lymphocyte carboxylase enzyme (Mock, 2006). The certainty, however, of its essentiality was documented only by the mid-1990s. Two events clearly outlined the consequences of a deficiency: the first case arose from a prolonged ingestion of raw egg white, which contains the biotin binding compound identified as avidin. This is a sequestering agent that is naturally found in raw egg, and that binds the biotin, preventing its absorption. The avidin is deactivated with cooking, and no longer poses a threat of deficiency, even when abundant eggs are consumed. The second event that confirmed biotin as an essential nutrient was in cases of exclusive prolonged intravenous nutrition or total parenteral nutrition (TPN) with an infusion mix that contained no biotin. Administered to patients with short gut syndrome, symptoms of periorificial dermatitis, occurring either as a seborrheic (scaly) or red eczematous skin rash is observed in frank deficiencies. Additionally, conjunctivitis, also known as red eye, alopecia, and ataxia were clinically observed (Mock, 2006). There are several other neurological symptoms such as lethargy, depression, and hallucinations that are commonly documented in adults with biotin deficiency. Children, by contrast, present with clear developmental delays, lethargy, and hypertonia (Mock, 2006).

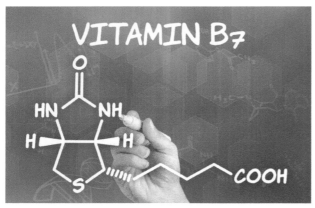

© Zerbor/Shutterstock.com

Figure 8.9 *This is a chemical structure of vitamin-B$_7$ or biotin.*

There are several other conditions for which biotin deficiency has been reported as a cause, but only two appear to be solidly founded on good research findings. The first appears to be a condition known as "brittle nails." The treatment with 2.5 g/day of biotin reversed the condition, successfully generating increased nail thickness. The second type of biotin deficiency is reliably confirmed in cases of alcoholism and in gastrointestinal diseases (Mock, 2006).

Biochemically, this vitamin plays a key role as a co-factor in the ß-oxidation of fatty acids. It is richly bound to the proteins of meats and cereals (Mock, 2006).

8.1.2.8 Vitamin K Deficiency

Dr. Henrik Dam, working out of Copenhagen in 1929, observed subdural and muscular hemorrhages in chicks that had been fed a diet from which cholesterol had been extracted using a solvent. Subsequent blood extractions from these chicks consistently showed a slowed clotting process. Early in the 1930s, McFarlane and his colleagues, while assessing the nutritive value of various protein sources, also noticed a hemorrhagic disease in chicks that were fed purified diets of fish meal (Suttie, 2006). A new fat soluble dietary factor (Figure 8.10) was suspected to be involved in the blood clotting mechanism—at the level of prothrombin synthesis—but it took researchers at the University of California in Berkeley to find, by the mid-1930s, that this factor was present in lipid extracts identified in green plants such as collards, spinach, and salad greens. Unexpectedly, bacteria-treated fish meal also had the same factor, a finding which eventually led to uncovering the existence of vitamin K-producing gut bacteria. This led researcher, Frick and co-workers, in 1967, to demonstrate that prolonged antibiotic treatments, in intravenously-fed starved patients, actually did lead to a decline in gut bacteria production of vitamin K and to significant hypothrombinemia (Suttie, 2006).

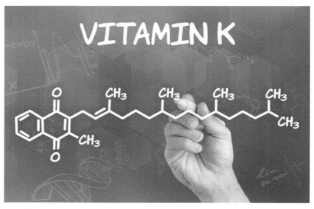

© Zerbor/shutterstock.com

Figure 8.11 *Vitamin K chemical structure.*

Vitamin K's role is also most important in bone metabolism. The most abundant bone-matrix protein, osteocalcin, depends on vitamin K to help catalyze the gamma-carboxylation of calcium in bone, a most critical step in the calcification of bone (Suttie, 2006).

The most prevalent dietary form of this vitamin was identified as **phylloquinone**, and it is absorbed into the chylomicrons of the enterocytes of the small intestine and, from there transported to the lymphatic system. Afterwards, it is found in the circulating VLDLs that deposit their triglycerides in adipose and muscle tissues (Suttie, 2006). Pure dietary deficiencies of this vitamin are extremely rare because it is abundantly found in a variety of vegetable oils (soybean, canola, cottonseed, and olive oils) and in an assortment of green leafy vegetables (collards, spinach, salad greens, broccoli, Brussels sprouts, and cabbage). The concern with vitamin K deficiency is associated more with newborn babies.

212 *Chapter 8*

In fact, one out of every 100,000 live births (CSPS, 2002), not treated with vitamin K, has hemorrhagic disease of the newborn (HDNB) which is characterized by intracranial bleeding (Suttie, 2006). These babies have a vitamin-K deficient clotting mechanism that shows up, in the classical presentation, about two to seven days after birth. This is a risk in newborn infants since all newborns are actually deficient in vitamin K because of very poor placental transfer from the mother. This is why intramuscular injections or an oral dose of the vitamin is administered within the first few minutes of birth (CSPS, 2002). In even more rare circumstances, mothers who are taking anticonvulsants place their babies at risk of HDNB within the 24 hours after birth because these drugs impair the vitamin's action. The third manifestation of this disease is seen about three to eight weeks after the birth of babies who have been exclusively breastfed by mothers with poor dietary K status. Additionally, this hemorrhagic disease is reported in infants, with neonatal hepatitis, or biliary atresia, who cannot absorb fat or the fat-soluble vitamin K (CSPS, 2002). In adults, vitamin K deficiency has rarely been documented from poor dietary intakes, but is reported more often in patients on long-term TPN or with malabsorption syndromes, and gastrointestinal diseases such as celiac disease, ulcerative colitis, and short bowel syndrome to name a few (Suttie, 2006). It would have to take an unfortunate set of circumstances to cause a primary deficiency of vitamin K. A woman who chronically follows a very low fat weight-reducing diet, who does not consume vegetables and who is being treated with wide spectrum antibiotics, would be a high risk candidate. In such a case, she would be ingesting suboptimal amounts of vitamin K since the oils and the green vegetables—touted as the primary sources of K—are absent from the diet. Moreover, there are insufficient amounts of bacteria in the gut to produce acceptable amounts of the vitamin. In theory this could greatly increase the risk of a deficiency.

8.1.2.9 Folate and Cyanocobalamin (B12)

a) *Folate*—British-born hematologist, Lucy Wills arrived in India in 1928, intrigued by the prevalent form of macrocytic anemia that was affecting especially Mohammedan women living in Bombay. Suspicions were high that it was infectious—Pasteur's work on the germ theory of disease by then had gained importance and notoriety. Having ruled out the communicable nature of the condition, Wills suspected that it could be of nutritional origin; she first determined that it was neither vitamin A or C deficiencies that were the causes of the disease. Soon after being dumbfounded by the mystery, she discovered, perhaps serendipitously, that an English food spread called Marmite, made of yeast extract, was instrumental in patient recovery. Back in England in 1937, Wills successfully duplicated the macrocytic red blood cells in a group of rhesus monkeys fed a Bombay peasant's diet (Carpenter, 2003). The monkeys also recovered consuming Marmite and a crude form of liver extract. But interesting, the more refined liver extraction, administered parentally (through the veins) to patients with pernicious anemia, had no effect on the macrocytosis. Realizing, that they might be dealing with an unknown nutrient, researchers labeled this factor vitamin-M. It was not until 1944, when interest in poultry nutrition had gained some popularity, that the story of folate was finally unraveled. Slow growth in chicks had become a problem for industry researchers despite using purified feed that contained all the known vitamins. It was the extract of some bacterial growth factor that normalized the growth in the chicks. It was labeled vitamin B_c until a similar compound was also extracted from spinach and found to be effective in correcting the growth rates. They named it folate, after the word foliage (Carpenter, 2003).

The most common cause of folate deficiency in the United States is poor dietary intake (Carmel, 2006b). Back in the late 1980s to early 1990s the National Health & Nutrition Examination Survey (NHANES, 1988-1994) detected suboptimal intakes of folate among young women of childbearing age, which the researchers attributed to poor fruit and vegetable consumption (Raiten & Fisher, 1995). Ever since the 1980s there has been an important shift in the eating habits of young American women, who began dieting for weight loss, and ingesting ready-to-eat process dinners and less fresh produce. Although folate is broadly found in the food supply, in the methylated inactive form with no more than 50% bioavailability, the richest sources of folate are leafy green vegetables such as asparagus, spinach, Brussels sprouts, and broccoli, it is also very prominent in oranges and orange juice, lima beans, and kidney beans, peanuts, yeast, and liver, with much smaller concentrations in milk, chicken, and beef (Carmel, 2006b). The NHANES findings in addition to the higher than expected prevalence of neural tube defects (NTDs)—the most common form being spina bifida, now occurring at a rate of one out of every 1000 newborns (Carmel, 2006b)—were sufficient for the FDA to implement a folate fortification program. And so, in 1998 the FDA began to require folate fortification of enriched breads, cereals, flours, cornmeal, pastas, and rice with the biologically active folic acid (Honein, 2001). This poor dietary trend of eating fewer vegetables and fruits became concerning enough for the Healthy People 2000 campaign to encourage five or more fruits and vegetables per day. It was a diet marketing plan to ensure good health that completely failed; although the USDA data did show a rise in fruits and vegetables being eaten, a closer look revealed that it was French fries and non-dark leafy greens with little health benefit that were being selected (Johnson, 2000). Moreover, meeting daily folate requirements is that much more difficult because the vitamin is labile and thus susceptible to being lost depending on cooking, storage, and preparation methods (Carmel, 2006b). Consequently, the FDA's folate fortification program, which raised folate concentrations in grains and cereals to very high levels, did manage to decrease the prevalence of NTDs by 20% since its implementation in 1998 (Carmel, 2006b; Honein, 2001). More prevention strategies are essential, as NTDs are disabling and lethal. One aspect to consider is that neurulation begins in the fetus as early as day 21, which is often much before the pregnancy is known by the women; this means that even at the point of conception, if the mother's folate is suboptimal or deficient, the fetus is already at risk of NTDs. A beneficial strategy has been to give young women, of reproductive age, 400 mcg/day of folic acid and 4 mg/day (4000 mcg) to those who are known to be at risk of having babies with NTDs (Carmel, 2006b).

Folate deficiency is clinically manifested in the form of megaloblastic anemia which, for the hematologist reviewing the blood smears, is seen as higher preva-

lence of larger than normal red blood cells (RBC) or erythrocytes. Because of the absence of folate, the DNA cannot be replicated in preparation for mitotic cell division (Figure 8.11). The consequence of this abnormal nuclear maturation, is that the red blood cell cannot divide and therefore grows larger than normal; the RBC is said to be macrocytic.

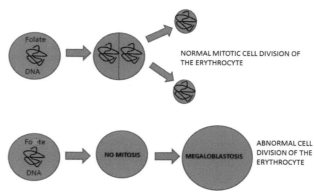

Image courtesy of David Bissonnette

Figure 8.11 *Megaloblastic red blood cells in folate deficiency.*

The macrocytic cell is identified when the mean corpuscular volume (MCV) is larger than the range of 83–97 fl. If the causes of this macrocytosis are folate or cobalamin deficiencies, then the large RBC is labeled a megaloblastic cell (Carmel, 2006b). Folate is unique in that it is intimately related to cobalamin in such a way that without B12, the inactive methyltetrahydrofolate cannot be activated to the biologically active tetrahydrofolate form. Megaloblastic anemia and the biochemical link between folate and B12 are further developed in chapter 9.

b) *Cobalamin (vitamin B12)*—The story of vitamin B12 (Figure 8.12) deficiency begins in 1849 with Dr. Addison's observation of a usual form of anemia associated with restlessness, languor or lassitude, and which often ended in fatality. He erroneously attributed the cause to some dysfunction of the adrenal glands, and so its true cause remained hidden for several decades (Carmel, 2006).

It was, however, the fatalities that came from this disorder that inspired Dr. Biermer to name it **pernicious anemia** (PA) in 1872. Although pernicious

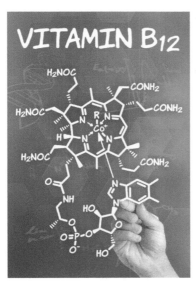

Figure 8.3 *Cyanocobalamin (vitamin B12) molecule.*

anemia remains an official medical diagnosis, it is nevertheless a bit of a misnomer. Indeed, in many instances the megaloblastosis is either a minor trait or completely absent, while the neurological symptoms that typify B12 deficiency worsen. It was the research of Minot and Murphy in 1926 that showed that feeding liver to patients with the neurological problems reversed the course of the disease. The B12 in the liver was, in fact, the effective therapeutic agent (Carmel, 2006). The next breakthrough came in 1929 when Dr. Castle discovered that an extrinsic factor, found in liver and in the gastric juice, greatly facilitated the rehabilitation of the patients. However, in 1956, cyanocobalamin was identified as the extrinsic factor in liver, which was a finding that officially launched B12 injections as the therapeutic approach of choice for PA. Later on, the other extrinsic factor in gastric juices—called **Intrinsic Factor** (IF)—would be identified, setting the stage for a more complete understanding of the rather complex process of B12 absorption.

There are several notable steps in B12 absorption that can help better understand the propensity for deficiencies of this vitamin in some segments of the population. The first step is the secretion of HCL from the parietal cells of the stomach. The acid plays an important role in denaturing the polypeptides making up the ingested animal proteins. This enables the pepsin and pepsinogen to hydrolyze the peptide bonds and release the B12 into the mix of gastric chyme and juices. A series of glycoproteins, secreted from the salivary glands, then bind to the B12 until it is set free again by pancreatic proteases secreted in the duodenum. The parietal cells in the stomach also secrete IF, which binds to the B12 not long after being set free in the duodenum. The IF's main role is to facilitate the absorption of B12 in the ileum, the only site where B12 is absorbed (Carmel, 2006). It is noteworthy to remember that when the ileum is compromised, either through surgical resection or inflammation, that B12 status is most certainly at risk. Also important to note that up until the fortification of B12, in many non-dairy milks and processed breakfast cereals, that B12 could only be acquired by ingesting animal proteins such as milk, cheeses, yogurts, eggs, and all meats (Carmel, 2006). This of course has historically put pure vegans at greater risk of B12 deficiency compared to the rest of the population.

Today, rather than seeing outright cases of pernicious anemia, it is rather the subclinical form that has become more prevalent and which can fortunately be detected using sensitive biochemical assays (Carmel, 2006). (See chapter 9 for biochemical indices of pernicious anemia).

The main cause of B12 deficiency (subclinical or PA) seen in the clinical setting is malabsorption (Carmel, 2006). Detectable using the Schillings test (see chapter 9), it is often observed in middle aged to older adults who have lost the ability to synthesize IF—between 10–15% of elderly white people have low cobalamin (Carmel, 2006). The deficit in IF arises from a condition called atrophic gastritis that is usually limited to the gastric fundus. PA becomes inevitable once the parietal cells are damaged enough to cause **achlorhydria** or a deficient release of HCL and a loss of IF. Once IF is no longer available, it takes several years for the PA to become diagnosable because of the significant B12 that is reabsorbed— roughly 70%—through the enterohepatic circulation. It can take three to five years for PA symptoms to become evident (Carmel, 2006).

On the other hand, older patients suffering from atrophic gastritis, who tested negative for the Schillings test—in other words, the test was normal— and who presented with B12-like symptoms, have been consistently found to have food-cobalamin malabsorption. In this situation, the low acidity and pepsin levels make it difficult for B12 to be released from the meat proteins—primary source of B12 (Carmel, 2006).

Research into the growing prevalence of dementia among the elderly—10% of European adults >65 years of age—has also uncovered evidence linking hyperhomocysteinemia to decreases in cognitive performance (Argawal, 2011). These high levels of serum homocysteine, commonly documented among the elderly (Gottfries et al., 1998), raise the possibility of an involvement of folate, B12 and/or B6 deficiencies in the pathogenesis of cognitive impairment in the elderly (Riggs et al., 1996). Work by Clark et al., (1998) intimate a strong link between low serum folate and B12 and the onset of Alzheimer's disease, however, Argawal (2011), in reviewing the literature, found some studies that have not uncovered links between B12 and cognitive performance.

The next clinical manifestation of B12 deficiency, that has gained some prominence in recent years, are partial gastric resections—often implemented as an obesity treatment. While in some cases there is a documented loss of IF, in about 15–30% of gastric resections there is a **food-cobalamin** malabsorption. This occurs when the upper duodenum becomes parasitically infested because of higher pH, therefore resulting in a bacterial proliferation that is invasive enough to capture B12, making it unavailable for absorption.

Motility disorders of the GI tract that result in stasis, or lack of movement of food stuff, will increase the risk of bacterial overgrowth in the small bowel. Once captured by the microorganisms, cobalamin can no longer be properly absorbed resulting in PA.

The last manifestation of B12 deficiency is observed in patients with any number of disorders of the ileum including surgical resections (partial or total), tropical sprue, or radiation treatments. These conditions will inhibit B12 absorption and require B12 injections to stave off any deficiency symptoms (Carmel, 2006).

Vegetarians, specifically vegans, who do not consume any kind of animal products, are susceptible to B12 deficiency. It takes years, however, for any

symptoms to become visible because of the body's incredible ability to reutilize B12 through the enteropathic circulation. Also, the fortification of soy, rice, and almond milks with vitamin B12, here in the United States, has created a safer food inventory for vegans (USDA, 2011).

Vitamin B12 deficiency is all the more difficult to detect today because of the fortification of the food supply with folic acid and the use of supplements. Whereas the physician historically would often use megaloblastic red blood cells to screen for the possibility of B12 deficiency, now the fortification of the food supply with folic acid (the active form of folate) has greatly reduced the prominence of megaloblastosis—B12 is no longer necessary to activate the folate. In that sense, the fortification of the food supply with folate has masked B12 deficiencies.

8.1.2.10 Key Macromineral and Micromineral Deficiencies and their Histories

This section will discuss only the relevant and significant minerals and microminerals as they pertain to human health and disease. Calcium, phosphorous, magnesium, and potassium will be the main macrominerals that will be discussed; iron is tackled in a separate section dedicated to anemias. In addition, iodide, copper, zinc, and selenium will be discussed as they are most relevant to the formation of healthcare professionals.

a) *Calcium, Phosphorus and Magnesium*—**Calcium** is the second most abundant nutrient mineral in the body with 99% of its concentration found in bone and teeth. The rest of the calcium is distributed between blood and also tissue where it functions more specifically in muscle contractions (Weaver & Heaney, 2006). The body maintains a tight homeostatic control of blood calcium levels. Hence a 10% or greater deviance away from the general mean standard blood value, is indicative of either hypocalcemia or hypercalcemia. These are blood conditions that reflect a disease state, and need to be resolved quickly. Understanding the homeostatic mechanism is important in order to have a better grasp of calcium's involvement in the disease process. There are surface receptors located in the parathyroid, thyroid glands, kidney, intestine, and bone marrow that monitor the concentrations of calcium in the plasma. Whenever the calcium concentrations begin to rise, less parathyroid hormone (PTH) is released and a greater secretion of calcitonin (CT) takes place, which inhibits the calcium release from bone. Conversely, when plasma calcium levels begin to decline, there is a greater release of PTH and less calcitonin, which facilitates bone resorption (Weaver & Heaney, 2006). In response, the renal tubules begin to reabsorb more calcium, and at the same time a greater renal phosphate clearance occurs. In a separate location, the **osteoclast** cells of the bones become activated, thus generating greater bone resorption or breakdown. Concomitantly, the inactive form of vitamin D is activated to 1, 25–dihydroxy vitamin D (1, 25(OH)2 D), also called **calcitriol**, which is instrumental in increasing intestinal absorption of calcium. Conceptually then, PTH and calcitriol work together to increase calcium renal tubular reabsorption, resorption of calcium from the bone, and intestinal calcium absorption. All three processes assist in bringing serum calcium levels back to normal. In contrast, a rising concentration of serum calcium leads to an increase in calcium binding to the receptors on the parathyroid, which in turn inhibits the release of PTH. The direct consequence is less calcium tubular reabsorption in addition to a drop in bone resorption rates and a diminished activation of vitamin D in the kidney. At the cellular level, osteoclast activity is diminished and osteoblasts are activated; the latter will translate into greater calcium bone deposition. All three of these adjustments will lead to a downward realignment of serum calcium levels (Weaver & Heaney, 2006). It is specifically during the growth period that the bone can become vulnerable to the under mineralization of newly formed bone matrix. Chronically low intakes of dietary calcium can ultimately lead to hypocalcemia even with the hypersecretion of PTH aimed at regaining serum calcium balance. The **osteoblast** dysfunction that ensues has been shown to lead to rickets, even without a vitamin D deficiency. Moreover, the hyper-secretion of PTH lowers serum phosphate concentration. It is the low level of phosphate and calcium in the blood that favor a poor mineralized nation of the bone (Weaver & Heaney, 2006). Calcium's relationship with phosphorous is an important one for bone health, especially in light of the excessive phosphorus consumed with process foods that use phosphate-based additives (Whybro et al., 1998), and the significant decline in calcium intake related to a 25% lower milk consumption seen in the transition from childhood to adolescence in the United States (Weaver & Heaney, 2006). An ideal molar Ca: P ratio of 1:1 or a weight Ca: P ratio of 1.3:1 (700mg: 550mg), have been associated with bone health because of the concomitant lower parathyroid hormone (PTH) (Calvo et al., 1988). An elevated ratio, resulting from lower phosphorus has been linked to greater bone mineralization and calcium absorption (Kemi et al., 2010), however a lower ratio <0.65 was associated with greater PTH (Calvo et al., 1988) and bone resorption even with ideal calcium intakes (Kemi et al., 2010). Significant alterations in this ratio has been observed notably in teenagers whose diet has consistently kept calcium intake low by displacing milk and dairy products at the expense of soft drinks and other sugary beverages. The overall ratio reported in the NHANES-1976-1980 survey, for men and women, averaged 0.63. Some teenagers and adults in the United States had Ca: P ratios that fell as low as ≤0.25 (Calvo, 1993). This is concerning since the peak bone health is achieved between the ages of 20 and 30 years, after which the risk of osteoporosis increases if optimal bone density is not achieved leading up to the cut-off age (Calvo, 1993).

Because the dietary requirements for calcium are so elevated—the RDA varies between 1000–1300 mg per day—it is imperative that youth specifically but also adults be judicious in their dietary choices. Dairy products are the richest supplier of calcium in the diet. In fact, 1 cup of milk, 1 cup of yogurt or 1 ½ ounces of cheddar cheese all contain approximately 300 mg of calcium. This means that 3 cups of milk a day contains about 900 mg of calcium or 69% of the highest RDA value. Regularly consuming milk, yogurt and cheese increases the chances of meeting the daily requirement. Indeed, 78% of calcium consumption in the United States comes from dairy products whereas only a mere 17% of calcium is ingested from fruits, vegetables and grains. There is a good reason why Healthy Eating Guidelines prioritize dairy products. It has to do with both the high calcium content and absorbability. This is especially important for the young who have up to the age of 25 to achieve maximal bone density. Although somewhere between 60% and 80% of the bone mass is genetically determined, it is specifically how the calcium is utilized that is genetically predetermined. So then it is not surprising that calcium intake in adolescent girls is the most significant determinant of bone density. The other reason that dairy products are encouraged in the North American diet is that the overall nutritional quality of the diet tends to increase. In fact, whenever milk is regularly consumed, vitamin A intake jumps 35%, folate increases 38%, riboflavin rises 56%, and there is a 22% rise in magnesium intake. Along with an 80% increase in calcium, there is also a 24% jump in potassium compared to non-dairy consumers.

Once the full genetic potential of peak bone density has been achieved there are several things that can be done after the age of 25 to minimize bone loss:

a regular exercise

b continued dairy consumption

There is also growing evidence in the literature in support of calcium's role in reducing the risk of colonic cancer in animal models, but still more research is needed before this protective role is confirmed in humans. So far, two prospective studies have shown that neither calcium nor milk influenced the incidence of colorectal adenomas (Weaver & Heaney, 2006).

The role of **phosphorus** in bone is important as 80% of the body's phosphorus is located in the hydroxyapatite structure of bone. It is also a structural component of the phospholipids such as phosphotidyl choline (lecithin). In the form of adenosine triphosphate (ATP) and creatine phosphate, it becomes essential in energy production and storage within the cell. Phosphate is abundant in animal protein foods, such as meats, fish, poultry, dairy, and processed foods (Knochel, 2006). In recent years the "acid-ash" hypothesis has been proposed as a mechanism for the advanced prevalence of osteoporosis in North American society. The theory posits that because of the high meat and dairy intake, and the unusually elevated amounts of processed foods consumed in the United States, including soft drinks, there is a significant intake in phosphates and reduction in the Ca: P ratio. This excessive intake of phosphates contributes to the body's diet acid load, which in turn accelerates bone decalcification and increased urinary calcium losses (Fenton et al., 2009). Although this hypothesis has been embraced as truth by the Institutes of Medicine, there still remains some debate about the accuracy of the science.

About 60% of **magnesium** in the body is mainly located in bone and the rest in muscle (Rude and Shils, 2006). In the clinical setting, magnesium deficiency usually presents with biochemical, neuromuscular and cardiac abnormalities. The biochemical change that is most common with low magnesium is hypokalemia. Low potassium may be a logical consequence because of the importance of Mg-dependent Na+/K+-ATPase in electrolyte regulation. This is an active energy-dependent cross membrane regulatory system; in the absence of sufficient Mg, there would be insufficient intracellular K released into the extracellular space.

Neuromuscular hyperexcitability is one of the repercussions found in patients with low serum magnesium but normal calcium levels. It would appear that magnesium plays a role in modifying the release of the neurotransmitters into the neuromuscular junction, by competitively preventing calcium from reaching the presynaptic terminal. However, when magnesium levels are low, more calcium reaches the presynaptic terminal thereby resulting in greater release of neurotransmitters into the synaptic cleft, which leads to hyper-responsiveness; this could also translate into a greater propensity to develop leg cramps. Magnesium has also been found in both clinical and epidemiological studies to regulate blood pressure. Indeed, hypomagnesemia correlates with hypertension; the DASH study also supported that finding. In the long term, a low level of serum magnesium can also translate into bone demineralization. The mechanism is actually very similar to calcium in that acutely elevated serum magnesium concentrations can prevent PTH secretions from the parathyroid glands, and that acutely suboptimal plasma levels will elicit abundant PTH release leading to bone resorption (Rude & Shils, 2006).

There has been some concern that the U.S. population may not be receiving sufficient amounts of magnesium in the diet, because the food supply is highly processed. The USDA's Continuing Survey of Food Intakes by Individuals, in addition to the NHANES-III cross-sectional survey, have both found that 75% of the U.S. population regularly consumes below the RDA for Mg. Although this does not confirm an outright deficiency, it raises some concerns that the population may be at risk (Institute of Medicine, 1997). Some have even advanced that it has reached a public health concern. Nobody knows for sure whether there is a nutritional problem here or not. Further studies have been encouraged in this area in light of growing concerns that highly processed foods tend to be low in magnesium.

Potassium (K+) is a significant intracellular cation in human health, as it is critical in the contraction of smooth, skeletal and cardiac muscles. About 95–98% of the body's potassium is found inside the cells, and its intracellular concentration is maintained constant through the action of the Na^+/K^+ pump (Gropper & Smith, 2013). Potassium is widely distributed in the diet, and abundantly found, especially in non-processed foods, including a wide assortment of meats and fish, fruits such as avocado, banana, cantaloupe, honey dew melon, and mango in addition dried fruits like raisins, prunes and apricots. Winter squash, leafy greens, legumes and yams are good vegetable sources of this mineral, and so are dairy products, yet the mean U.S. intake is estimated at the suboptimal level of 3,300 mg/day (Gropper & Smith, 2013). There is no RDA for potassium, but the AI is equal to 4,700 mg/day, thus making relatively difficult to meet this requirement on a daily basis, especially in the U.S. population, where there are suboptimal intakes of fruits and vegetables. In recent years, because of the highly processed food supply to which North Americans have access, there is increasing evidence that potassium intakes are dropping even lower in the diet (He & MacGregor, 2008). From an epidemiological perspective this is concerning since the role of potassium in the prevention of hypertension is well known; in fact the FDA has approved this health claim for potassium rich foods (Gropper & Smith, 2013). A concerted effort must be made to ensure that a judicious selection of foods high in K^+ be regularly made (Gropper & Smith, 2013). Potassium plays a pivotal role, as well, in the prevention of osteoporosis; it accomplishes this by reducing urinary calcium secretion, diminishing likewise the risk of hypercalciuria and kidney stones. Low potassium intakes are especially correlated with increased glucose intolerance; hence dietary potassium may play a role in diminishing the risk of type-2 diabetes that typically occurs in hypertensive patients chronically taking thiazide diuretics. In instances when patients suffer from ischaemic heart disease, heart failure and left ventricular hypertrophy, dietary potassium can take on a critical role in the prevention of lethal ventricular arrhythmias (He & MacGregor, 2008). Metabolically, potassium plays a significant intracellular position of importance in the cross membrane flow of both sodium and potassium via the Na^+/K^+ pump, critical in nutrient absorption, and in ensuring the outward flow of Na^+ and the inward movement of K^+, which is necessary for maintaining the serum concentration of both serum K^+ and Na^+ within narrow ranges. Suboptimal serum levels are referred to as **hypokalemia**, which is typically seen in refeeding syndrome, and can cause cardiac arrhythmias or hyperexcitability, muscular weakness, nervous irritability, hypercalciuria, polyuria, glucose intolerance, and mental disorientation (Gropper & Smith, 2013). This is condition occurs either from an excessive loss from the kidneys through the use of diuretics (Thiazides, loop and osmotic diuretics) or from the GI tract, the consequence of chronic diarrhea, or from the chronic use of laxatives or the ingestion of clay (Merck, 2016b). Contrariwise, excess concentrations of serum potassium is equally serious and is medically identified as **hyperkalemia**. This condition can occur first, from excess potassium intake; second, from ingesting medication that impairs potassium excretion from the kidneys; and third, from either an acute kidney injury, or from chronic renal disease (Merck, 2016). Hyperkalemia is a condition that is usually asymptomatic up until the start of cardiac arrhythmias. However, episodes of weakness and paralysis leading to frank paralysis have been documented (Merck, 2016).

b) *Zinc*—The essentiality of **zinc** in human health was first demonstrated in 1961, when a 21-year-old Iranian farmer was diagnosed with anemia, hypogonadism, and dwarfism. His diet had been limited to unrefined flat breads, potatoes, and milk (King and Cousins, 2006). As part of the glutathione oxidase system, zinc is critical in providing the body with protection against oxidative stress. Richly found in liver and the flesh of beef, fowl, fish and crustaceans, with lesser amounts in eggs and dairy products, deficiencies due to poor dietary intakes would be rare in affluent societies such as the United States that are big meat consumers. Although modest amounts are found in legumes and cereals, their phytate levels are high enough to significantly diminish zinc absorption. It is for this reason that non-meat consuming Middle Eastern countries and those affected by poverty are prone to zinc deficiency. The problem is so widespread that the FAO estimates that close to 50% of the world's population is at risk of being deficient in zinc (King & Cousins, 2006). Here in the United States zinc deficiency is encountered in preterm and low birth weight babies, in instances of chronic diarrhea, and cases of malabsorption disorders such as Crohn's disease, celiac sprue, and short-bowel syndrome. Zinc deficiency especially in children can cause growth retardation, delayed sexual maturation, and hypogonadism; in adults, symptoms of skin lesions adjacent to bodily orifices, poor appetite, impaired taste (hypogeusia), delayed wound healing, and immune deficiencies of various types are observed. In severe enough cases, alopecia and the hypopigmentation of the hair which may take on a reddish hue has been observed (King & Cousins, 2006). The latter resembles the reddish coiling hair seen in kwashiorkor.

c) *Iodine, Copper, and Selenium*—**Iodine** has been briefly covered in a section on mineral deficiencies in developing countries. The focus of this section is **iodine** deficiency in the United States. Historically, in the United States, iodine deficiency was endemic to certain areas that formed the "goiter belt" in the surrounding regions of the Great Lakes. The soil was impoverished in iodine, therefore causing low iodine levels in the vegetables produced in that region. Consequently, the prevalence of goiter—a medical term referring to the thyroid gland protruding from the neck like a pouch—was on the rise in that area of the United States. In the absence of iodine in the diet, thyroid stimulating hormone (TSH), secreted from the pituitary gland, remains elevated, causing the thyroid to become abnormally large. TSH would normally cause an increased uptake of iodine by the thyroid, the first step before it can synthesize thyroxin (T4) and triiodothyroxine (T3), which are the key hormones secreted by the thyroid. They regulate biochemical processes, metabolism, skeletal, and neurological development in the fetus. A severe iodine deficiency can be significantly more compromising when a pregnant mother's intake is suboptimal, as it will invariably lead to hypothyroidism. The low functioning maternal thyroid would be a high risk for cretinism in the newborn. This is a condition involving dwarfism, deaf mutism, and severe mental retardation. While in utero, the fetus experiences irreversible neuro-developmental deficits because of the hypothyroidism that can be responsible for growth retardation after birth (Patrick, 2008). This is because the thyroid hormone plays a critical role in brain development, in as much as it modulates crucial myelination of the central nervous system (Dunn, 2006). In the United States, the most important natural food source of iodine are dairy products, whereas seafood represents a moderate, and meats, modest sources of the nutrient. There was considerable hope placed on the efficacy of iodized salt in containing the prevalence of goiter and cretinism in the United States back in the 1920s, when the salt iodization program was implemented. The problem is that in recent years, the has been a population shift towards preferentially consuming much large amounts of processed foods manufactured, for the most part, using salt that has not been iodized (Dunn, 2006).

Richly found in nuts, seeds, legumes, and dried fruits (Gropper & Smith, 2013), **copper** was utilized as a therapeutic compound back in 400 BC by Hippocrates. Copper belonged in the medical pharmacopeia until the 19th century, at which point its therapeutic efficacy could no longer be upheld in light of scientific scrutiny. However, as early as 1912 copper's involvement in human disease was identified in Wilson's disease, which is an autosomal recessive disorder that typically presents with copper accumulation in the liver, brain, and cornea of the eyes. Several decades later, in 1962, Menke's disease was also linked back to copper. Trapped within the intestinal mucosa, kidney, spleen, and muscle, copper is unable to be transported to organs and tissue, thus leading to mental retardation, and poorly pigmented skin and hair (Turnlund, 2006).

Copper's role in iron deficiency anemia began to be suspected in rats that did not improve despite being administered iron supplements. It took until 1930 before scientists began to suspect a link between copper deficiency and anemia in humans, but the mechanism remained obscure (Turnlund, 2006). By the 1980s, it had been found that the copper-containing glycoprotein, ceruloplasmin, was necessary to catalyze the oxidation of ferrous iron to its reduced ferric state (Fe^{+3}). In this way the iron could be stored in the body and ultimately be used in erythropoiesis or the synthesis of red blood cells. If copper is deficient, then iron cannot be oxidized to its active storage form and be used for the formation of red blood cells; the consequence is a poor production of red blood cells, leading to anemia. It has also been suspected that copper is needed for the normal synthesis of bone marrow, the site of red blood cell production (Turnlund, 2006). Copper is also involved in **copper/zinc superoxide dismutase**. Located in the cytosol of the cell, this enzyme's role is to shield the cell from oxidative damage by scavenging superoxide radicals (Turnlund, 2006). This process protects cellular integrity and, some suspect it can, over the long term, lessen the disease and aging processes. In the North American diet, copper can be richly found in shellfish, nuts, seeds, legumes, and within the bran and germ factions of the grains. There are only moderate amounts of copper in dried fruits, mushrooms, tomatoes, bananas, potatoes, and meats. Frank outright deficiency of this micromineral is relatively rare. However, in the 1980s, a set of Japanese cases of copper deficiency, involving children and young adults who were mentally retarded, had been documented. Patients consumed a long-term enteral diet, deficient in copper. It is important, therefore to make broad food selections that focus on fruits, vegetables, and grains, with less attention on meat consumption (Turnlund, 2006). Zinc supplementation is also a concern, since it is well known that excessive zinc intake can inhibit both copper and iron absorption (Gropper & Smith, 2013).

Selenium's role in human nutrition was documented only 35 years ago, in 1979. Keshan's disease was known to afflict Chinese children and young women with irreversible cardiomyopathy characterized by a diminished heart function. Researchers found that selenium supplements protected the young who were living within the northeastern to southwestern regions in China, where there was selenium-depleted soil (Burk & Levander, 2006). This specific mineral should be remembered for its biochemical function in glutathione peroxidase (GSHPx), which protects cells against oxidant molecules that threaten the integrity of cells. Abundantly found in all bodily cells, GSHPx is the most abundant and widespread antioxidant system of the body.

8.2. UNDERNUTRITION IN DEVELOPING COUNTRIES

Historically, between the 1950s and 1960s, international relief had been primarily preoccupied with a type of protein deficiency identified in children as *kwashiorkor*. However, in the 1960s and 70s, interest shifted towards protein and energy malnutrition (PEM). Worldwide, there are an estimate 200 million pre-school aged children that are afflicted with chronic undernutrition, causing stunted growth, and representing 35.8% of pre-school children in developing countries. Geographically, about 80% are located in Asian countries, 15% in Africa and 5% in Latin America (de Onis et al., 1993).

8.2.1 Protein Energy Malnutrition

Protein intake has been historically central to the WHO's efforts to eradicate malnutrition since the 1950s (WHO, 2007), because of the vital role of protein in ensuring immuno-competence, growth, lactation, the maintenance of body composition, biological structure and function, and ultimately **nitrogen balance** (Woodward, 2009; WHO, 2007). Protein foods of high biological value (BV)—proteins of animal origin like milk, cheese, eggs and meat—which contain all indispensable amino acids, tend to be of limited availability in underdeveloped countries where malnutrition is prevalent, especially during famines, droughts, and during periods of war and civil unrest. Very simply, the role of protein cannot be overestimated at the international level. A Jamaican pediatrician, Dr. Cicely Williams, introduced, in 1935, the medical term, **kwashiorkor** to describe cases of pediatric chronic protein malnutrition observed in the African nation of Ghana. Derived from the African Ga language of coastal Ghana, the term refers to the sickness that the baby contracts after the arrival of the newborn (Williams, 1935). The condition was observed in long-term breast-fed babies after they had been displaced from the breast with the arrival of a newborn baby. The infants most prone to the condition were often between 9 weeks and 5 years of age, and presented with dry and sparse hair, enlarged fatty liver, dermatitis observed as dark patchy skin on the elbows, knees, wrist and ankles, and a reddish dull and muddy skin discoloration (Williams, 1933). Additionally, there was edema (water accumulation in the extremities) present in the feet and hands (Williams, 1933), hypo-albuminemia (Hoffer, 2006), and very little erosion of fat or muscle mass (Woodard, 2009; Badaloo et al., 2006). It has been argued that this inability to breakdown fat and protein reserves may explain the much higher death rates in kwashiorkor children compared to those with marasmus (Badaloo et al., 2006). The predominantly maize-based diet that was consumed by children with kwashiorkor came in the form of "arkasa" or "kenki." The former, when prepared, was served as a light gruel, or it could be fixed as acorn dough, whereas the latter, was corn-soaked and boiled extensively in water, ground up and served with plantain leaves. The Ga also complemented their diet with other root vegetables such as cassava and yams, and so they tended not to lack calories (Williams, 1933). The main difficulty with this diet was that the maize was deficient in tryptophan and lysine—2 essential amino acids—making the maize very poor in protein quality. Since there was no other main sources of dietary protein in the rest of the diet, the children's protein status became compromised and so did their immune systems, which led to increased infections, diarrhea, and higher death rates (Woodward, 1998; Williams, 1933, 1935). A second form of malnutrition, called **marasmus**, occurs when both calories and protein are deficient in the diet (Lee & Nieman, 1996). This condition results in advanced emaciation, and is the consequence of suboptimal calories and protein leading to stunting and both fat and muscle erosion, but with no edema or noticeable change in blood proteins. In this situation, the person experiences emaciation and a significant decline in body weight (Lee & Nieman, 1996).

Both kwashiorkor and marasmus emphasize the importance of protein and calories in survival. Today the expression "protein-energy malnutrition" (PEM) is more commonly used, but in its more severe expression, is referred to "marasmus," "kwashiorkor," or "marasmic kwashiorkor" (Torun, 2006).

To ensure that amino acids from protein are efficiently used for tissue maintenance and growth, it has been determined that calories and micronutrients must be provided from carbohydrates and fats; also, that all essential amino acids be in adequate amounts, and that total protein quantity be sufficient to meet the body's need, estimated at 0.83 g/kg body weight for adults (WHO, 2007; Rand, et al., 2003).

The aim of nutrition relief was to originally provide protein in adequate amounts to quell the negative nitrogen balance that is so prominent in malnutrition. The notion of nitrogen balance stemmed from original work by Rose (1957) in the 1950s that intended to identify the minimal amino acid requirements for humans using nitrogen balance (Mathews, 2006; Carpenter and Harper, 2006). He had identified nitrogen excreted from the urine and feces as byproducts of protein. The use of nitrogen balance for protein determination was later popularized after Johan Kjeldahl invented the **Kjeldahl method** for the nitrogen determination of organic material in 1883, after which it was approved for protein determination in food (Moore et al., 2010). The main assumption was that protein was certainly the most significant nitrogen-based compound in the body—about 95% of all nitrogen is derived from protein—and thus, any losses or gains had to be attributable to protein losses and gains in the body. Nitrogen balance (Figure 8.13) is a physiological state in which nitrogen (N) intake equals the nitrogen excreted from feces, urine, hair, and sloughed off skin (Pike & Brown, 1975). That balance is dependent on an equilibrium between protein catabolism and synthesis. Increased catabolism or breakdown, leads invariably to more nitrogen excreted than consumed. By contrast, more synthesis than catabolism, results in less nitrogen expelled than consumed (Figure 8.13). The actual calculation is shown and is based on the notion that about 16% of protein consists of nitrogen (N) (Hoffer, 2006). If a person consumes 120 g of protein, then it could be inferred that he ingested 19.2 g of nitrogen (0.16 x 120 g). This is also commonly represented as 1/6.25 x 120 g or 120 g /6.25 (Bistrian, 1984). The second main assumption that should be made in nitrogen balance studies is that 85% of total urinary nitrogen is in the form of urea nitrogen (Long, 1984). The corrected estimation of total urinary N can then be represented below:

[Total urinary N (g) = Urinary Urea N(g)/0.85]

This then means that if urinary urea N equals 1.4 g then the total urinary N that should be used in the nitrogen balance study would equal 1.65 g of nitrogen (1.4g/0.85). At this point, it is now possible to calculate the nitrogen balance of an individual using the two previous assumptions. The formula is indicated here:

$$\text{N-balance (g/d)} = \left[\frac{\text{protein intake(g)}}{6.25} \right] - \left[\left(\frac{g\ N_{urea}}{0.85} \right) + g\ N_{stool} + g\ N_{skin} \right]$$

Because nitrogen in the stool is relatively stable, except in chronic diarrhea, an alternative adjustment to the formula has been proposed by Long (1984) that uses 4 g as an estimate for non-urea nitrogen, skin and stool losses.

$$\text{N-balance (g/d)} = [(\text{Protein intake (g)})/6.25] - \frac{[(g\ N_{urea} + 4g)]}{0.85}$$

So then if a man consumes 120 g of protein, and then excretes 12 g of urea nitrogen, his nitrogen balance can be estimated:

$$\text{N-balance} = (120\ g/6.25) - \frac{(12\ g + 4\ g)}{0.85} =$$

$$19.2\ g - 18.12\ g = +1.08\ g$$

This person would then be in positive nitrogen balance, which translated means that he is excreting less N than what he consumed. This +1.08 g of N, if not excreted in urine, is utilized in the biological system after it is absorbed through the gastrointestinal tract. The idea here is that most of that nitrogen is used in the synthesis of protein and other nitrogenous compounds. A negative nitrogen balance, by contrast, implies that the person is excreting more N than he is consuming. This N would be derived from the breaking down of body protein as would be expected in a catabolic state (Pike & Brown,

1975). Attaining N balance (Figure 8.13) means that protein degradation equals protein synthesis (WHO, 2007).

Much of what is understood about our need for protein has to do with the concept of **Biological Value** (BV) of protein, measured using the formula below (WHO, 2007):

BV= Nitrogen utilized/Digestible Nitrogen Intake

First, the digestibility of protein is established by measuring the amount of nitrogen excreted in the feces, which reflects the nitrogen that was not absorbed through the gut (Matthews, 2006). In that sense, high digestibility infers that, of the N ingested in the form of protein, most was absorbed through the gastrointestinal tract. Low digestibility, by contrast, means that of the nitrogen ingested, very little was absorbed. Protein sources that are considered as highly digestible tend to be of animal origin, such beef, eggs, and dairy products, whereas vegetable proteins sources, such as kidney beans, Romano beans, soy beans, and lentils, have a lower digestibility factor. If most of the protein ingested is of vegetable origin, then greater amounts would be needed to meet the body's requirement. In the same way, if most of the protein was of animal origin, then less would be required (Gropper & Smith, 2013). Consistent with that logic, a person consuming a diet with an overall digestibility of 72% would have to consume greater amounts of protein to meet his requirement. Hence, if it had been found that a patient needed to ingest 57 g of protein to reach nitrogen balance, using egg, which has 100% digestibility, then his requirement for protein, while on a 72% digestibility vegetarian diet, would be: 57 g/0.72 = 79 g.

The formula below best reflects how to calculate digestibility (WHO, 2007). The I represents the N intake, the F, is the N found in the feces, whereas the Fo, refers to the N measured while fasting, and thus reflects the endogenous N produced by sloughed off intestinal cells and bacteria.

$$\text{DIGESTIBILITY} = \frac{I - (F - F_o)}{I} \times 100$$

By contrast, the N found in the urine is really, for the most part, the end products of amino acid oxidation showing up as urea and ammonia. Hence, suboptimal intakes of N, resulting from a poor protein diet, leads to an increased breakdown or mobilization of body proteins for oxidation and energy. The outcome would be an unusually large amount of N expelled compared to N consumed or, in other words, negative N-balance (Matthews, 2006).

Second, the utilization of N can now be better understood in light of the significance of urinary N. Indeed, utilized N is used, in a pure sense, in the synthesis of protein, and is therefore not oxidized and excreted in the urine. So then, lower urinary content of N signifies greater utilization.

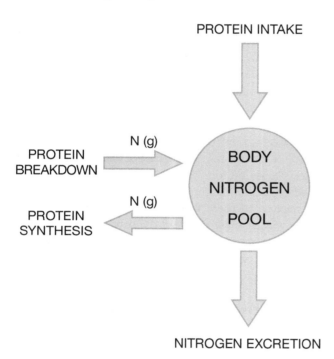

PROTEIN INTAKE

N (g)

PROTEIN BREAKDOWN

BODY NITROGEN POOL

N (g)

PROTEIN SYNTHESIS

NITROGEN EXCRETION

Figure 8.13 *Nitrogen balance achieved when N intake equals N excreted, assuming body breakdown and synthesis are equal (Adapted from Matthews, 2006).*

To better understand the concept of biological value (BV) we can now measure N utilized relative to digested and absorbed N. This can be visualized using the following equation (WHO, 2007):

$$BV = \frac{I - [\,(F-F_o) + (U-U_o)/0.85\,] \times 100}{I - (F-FO)}$$

The **I** refers to N intake, the **F** is the fecal N and the **Fo** the fecal N when fasting, whereas the **U** refers to the urinary N and the **Uo** is the urinary N measured in a fasting state. The numerator of the formula essentially subtracts from N intake, the N found in both urine and feces, thus equaling the amount of N utilized by the body. Now the denominator indirectly derives how much of the N ingested was actually absorbed through the gut. So the completed calculation would express the following: of the N digested and absorbed through the gut, what percent was utilized by the body and not oxidized for energy (Gropper and Smith, 2013).

8.2.2 Economic Development

At the 1974 World Food Conference in Rome, economists took over as the main policy makers as opposed to the nutritionists and pediatricians, who had been, up that time, concerned about PEM. Economists shifted the WHO's attention towards **food security**. The ability to access, pay for, and consume adequate amounts of nutritious foods, on a daily basis, in order to support a healthy and active life, is referred to as food security. It is, however, specifically food insecurity—the inability to access nutritious foods daily—that was responsible for limiting regular access of an estimated 840 million people worldwide to nutritious foods between 1990 and 1992, according to the 6th World Survey administered by the WHO. Moreover, despite the millennium development goal of reducing by half the prevalence of hunger and poverty in the world, which was formulated by the WHO in 2000, the number suffering from food insecurity jumped to 1.023 billion by 2009. But it was mostly pre-school children, women, and girls who were the most vulnerable to malnutrition. In fact, it has been estimated that up to 60% of people suffering from hunger are female (Pinstrup-Andersen & Cheng, 2007). Malnourished women of reproductive age pose a particular risk to their offspring by increasing the chances that they will be born underweight. There are an estimated 20 million babies born every year from undernourished mothers. These underweight infants are at risk of chronic disease later in life (Caballero, 2006).

The World Bank strategically began promoting increased income generation as a solution to poverty and malnutrition. Contrary to popular belief, it was not the lack of food, but rather the poverty itself that became the greatest threat for undernutrition. Since the 1990s the origin of that poverty was more clearly understood to be part of a much broader network of social and political struggles. It was, in fact, the dictatorships, wars, sectarian violence, famines, earthquakes, droughts, poverty, and social conflicts of various types that compromised population access to nutritious foods and water. It is especially the mass migration and individual poverty that is behind the selloff of properties and livestock in order to access the money necessary to purchase food. More recently, greater emphasis on the economic development of countries, aimed at boosting the gross national product (GNP) of underdeveloped nations, has been recognized as having the potential of greatly decreasing world hunger (Quandt, 2006). Indeed, the **economic development approach** suggests that greater family income can translate into improved purchasing power, thus better food and improved nutrition. The paradox and contention here is that an enhanced GNP does not necessarily translate into better food purchases and nutrition. In contrast, adherents of the **world systems theory**, advance that greater GNPs invariably translate into a lowering of living standards and heightened nutrition problems such as obesity (World Bank, 1993). The main difficulty is that while countries may be able to increase their GNP by transitioning from subsistence-based farming to cash cropping, they also appear to cause an important drop in the nutritional status of the population (Quandt, 2006). Traditional farming practices, consisting in multi-plot and multi-crop farming, a practice encouraged by the world systems theory, provide a diverse assortment of agricultural products to the food supply. This accomplishes two goals: first, it manages to smooth out anomalies in nutrient content in the food supply, and second, it protects the farmer from the devastation that could come from crop failure (Feuret & Fleuret, 1980). Transitioning to a cash crop-based agriculture necessitates greater imports of diverse and more expensive foods in order to feed the population. These imports invariably create a dependency on the surplus grains that influx into these countries from the industrialized west. The cash earned

from this kind of singular crop agriculture does not necessarily translate into better nutrition because of two main phenomena: first, the money earned is usually paid in two annual bulk sums that do not always go towards nutritious foods, but often towards competing non-food needs; second, the influx of cash usually drives up food prices, thus making nutritious foods more difficult to obtain, and tends to subject the population to the dangers of significant market price fluctuations (Fleuret and Fleuret, 1980).

Eradicating poverty was the main thrust of the WHO international relief efforts right up until the early 1980s, at which point the International Monetary Fund (IMF) began to make structural adjustments at around the same time that the WHO and UNICEF renamed the Applied Nutrition Program (ANP), the Joint Nutrition Support Programs (JNSPs). This joint effort to reduce severe and moderate malnutrition internationally, led to remarkable results, in Iringa, Tanzania specifically, where the prevalence of severe and moderate malnutrition declined 70% and 32% respectively between 1984 and 1989. Strategically, the focus was placed on improving the nutritional status of children and women. Priorities were set on six main efforts: 1) developing and supporting infrastructure; 2) allowing women and children to more easily access health services; 3) improving the quality of water concomitantly with environmental sanitation; 4) increasing food security for individual households; 5) focusing on developing a competent, affordable and accessible child care system; and 6) creating income-generating projects that can provide financial sustainability to communities (Moneti & Yee, 1989).

8.2.3 Key Vitamin and Mineral Deficiencies in Developing Countries

Not long after, in the 1990s, nutritionists successfully set the stage for the interest to shift towards micronutrient deficiencies in response to goals that were set by 1989 World Summit on Children, and the 1992 International Conference on Nutrition (FAO, 1997). Suddenly, PEM and poverty got pushed to the background, while an urgent need to eradicate three of the most prevalent micronutrient deficiency diseases—vitamin A, iron and iodine—rose to the top of the international agenda (FAO, 1997). These were deficiencies that demanded quick fixes as it was clearly recognized that retinol, iodine and iron deficiencies in combination with vitamin D, folate and zinc were linked to 7.3% of human diseases worldwide, and thus represented a significant threat to human health in developing countries (WHO, 2006).

An estimated two billion people around the world are affected by micronutrient deficiencies, and subject to a greater risk of diseases, disabilities and death (Pisciano, 1999). Internationally, the WHO has identified **vitamin A**, **iodine** and **iron** as the three most prominent nutrient deficiencies in underdeveloped and developing countries. Together, they affect up to 33% of the world's population (WHO, 2006). Ever since 1992, the Health and Nutrition Monitoring System, established from the World Health Resolution WHA45.33, has been set up to assess the degree to which these three nutrient deficiencies are affecting populations, and to what extent control programs have been effective in containing the magnitude of the threat (WHO, 2006).

Vitamins A, folate and D, have also been identified as most prominent and treatable vitamin deficiencies in the population of underdeveloped and developing countries.

8.2.3.1 Vitamin A/Retinol Deficiency

The active form of Vitamin A is represented by a complex of compounds, consisting of retinol, retinal, retinoic acid, and retinyl esters, that are referred to as retinoids (Gropper & Smith, 2013). The RDA for men is 900 mcg/day and for women, it is 700 mcg/day Retinol Activity Equivalence (RAE). These biologically active forms are known a **pre-formed vitamin A** and are strictly found in the animal components of the diet such as milk, cheese, butter, eggs, liver, oily fish like tuna, herring, and sardines. Fish oils, like cod liver oil contain high concentrations of retinol. Consequently, it is not surprising that developing countries, with difficulties accessing fish and meat protein of high biological value, such as in South East Asia and the Middle East, might experience retinol deficiency. With the advent of food fortification, which has become more widespread since the 1990s, retinol can be regularly found in breakfast cereals (Gropper & Smith, 2013). There are also non-animal sources of precursors to vitamin A, called **pro-vitamin A**, found in the vegetable pigments of plants, which are classified as carotenoids. Of the hundreds of carotenoids—there are over 600 varieties—present in our food supply, less than 10% can be considered as precursors to vitamin A or in other words, potentially exhibiting vitamin A activity. Indeed, the carotenoid that is strongly pro-vitamin A, is identified as β-carotene; other carotenoids, considered as having weaker, but nonetheless, significant pro-vitamin A contents, are α-carotene and β-cryptoxanthin. The conversion of β-carotene to retinal, which in turn becomes retinol only occurs to the degree that the body needs retinol. There is no danger of consuming toxic amounts of retinol by ingesting β-carotene. In fact the conversion is roughly 50% depending on retinol stores. Consequently, because of the abundant presence of pro-vitamin A in the diet, dietary intakes are expressed as Retinol Activity Equivalence (RAE) or Retinol Equivalence (RE). This means that in general, 12 mcg of β-carotene or 24 mcg of α-carotene or β-cryptoxanthin will yield 1 mcg of retinol. To understand this equivalence system, it is important to recognize that 1 RAE = 1 mcg of Retinol. Vitamin requirements and content of food can also be expressed in International Units (I.U.), thereby allowing the conversion of RAE to I.U. to occur following this equation: 1 IU retinol = 0.3 mcg RAE. This equation is adapted, if the food source is a carotenoid: 1 IU beta-carotene from food = 0.05 mcg RAE; if ingested as a supplement, then 1 IU beta-carotene from dietary supplements = 0.15 mcg RAE (NIH, 2016; Gropper & Smith, 2013). In practical terms, a person who ingests one carrot containing 4,142 micrograms of beta-carotene, will in actuality be ingesting 345 mcg of RAE or mcg Retinol (NIH, 2016, Gropper & Smith, 2013). By contrast, carotenoids such as lycopene, canthaxanthin, lutein and zeaxanthin, although not considered good sources of pro-vitamin A, nevertheless, are of some physiological importance, and potentially play protective roles against diseases (Gropper & Smith, 2013). Those vegetables and fruits with red, orange, and yellow-colored pigments, such as carrots, cantaloupe, sweet red peppers, sweet potatoes and papaya tend also to be rich in β-carotene and/or β-cryptoxanthin (NIH, 2016; Ross, 2006). Dark green vegetables like broccoli, spinach and peas, in which the chlorophyll masks the colored pigments, are also elevated in carotenoids (Gropper & Smith, 2013). Of significance, is the fact that many carotenoids, but lycopene and β-carotene specifically, have a high antioxidant activity, capable of scavenging singlet oxygen free radicals. The oxidative stress generated from these free radicals can damage the integrity of cells, protein, lipids, and nucleic acids, right down to the biochemical processes of the cytosol of cells. In that sense, oxidative stress that overwhelms the oxidant-antioxidant balance can be responsible for the genesis of disease (Bissonnette et al., 2012; Gropper & Smith, 2013; Lobo et al., 2010). Indeed, the role of carotenoids as antioxidants cannot be underestimated over the long term, as they have the potential to minimize the incidence of chronic diseases (Paiva & Russell, 1999). The WHO estimates, that every year, there are 3 million children that are diagnosed with xeropththalmia, and between 250,000 to 500,000 who progress to blindness (Ross, 2006), resulting from vitamin A deficiency with most of the incidences occurring in young children (Merck, 2014, 2014b; Ross, 2006). In fact, internationally, it is specifically infants, children, pregnant and lactating women who are most vulnerable to vitamin A deficiency (NIH, 2016). Interestingly, the WHO considers vitamin A deficiency as the most preventable cause of blindness in the world (UNICEF, 2003). There are two functions, specific to vitamin A, that are critical to the integrity of the eye. The first, consists of the role off vitamin A in night vision. The earliest preclinical sign of vitamin A deficiency is in fact **night blindness**. This condition can be assessed in the dark, by exposing the eye to a flash of light and then measuring the time it takes to recover the night vision. A delayed recovery could intimate pre-clinical vitamin A deficiency (Gropper & Smith, 2013). Night blindness develops because of vitamin A's involvement in the rejuvenation of the rhodopsin protein, located in the rods of the retina, where it serves as a light receptor. Once light enters through the cornea of the eye, it moves through to the retina, which is made up of rods and cones that act as photo-receptors at night. The rods contain a vitamin A-based protein called rhodopsin, which consists of a protein named, opsin, a vitamin A derived compound, 11-cis-retinal. When light reaches the retina, the rhodopsin reacts by cleaving into opsin and 11 cis-retinal; the brain does not register sight until the cis-retinal is converted to trans-retinal. If the reformation of rhodopsin is slow and inefficient, after the light exposure in the dark, then an early sign of vitamin A deficiency can be concluded, since it could indicate insufficient 11-cis-retinal concentrations (Gropper & Smith, 2013).

In the second function, retinol plays an important role in maintaining the health of the skin's epithelial cells, and of the epithelial cells of the cornea of the eye in particular. The involvement of vitamin A in epithelial cell morphology had been known since the mid 1920s from the work of Wolbach and Howe. They had observed, in deficient rats, that the epithelial cells of many tissues became dry, squamous an keratinized. With continued research, it became clearer that vitamin A's action affected specifically cell differentiation, and that it was retinoic acid's regulatory action on gene transcription that was critical in favoring this cell differentiation (Ross, 2006). Clinically, a vitamin A deficiency can therefore lead to a progressive drying of the eye's conjunctiva and cornea, which is the result of poor cell differentiation leading to the keratinization of the corneal epithelial cells, but also of the drying out of the eye's lacrimal or tear glands. The first symptoms to appear are white foamy and patchy spots in the conjunctiva, formed from sloughed off cells, and known as **Bitôt spots**. The condition progresses towards corneal xerosis, or drying out of the cornea's mucus membrane, and epithelial cells, thus leading to **xerophthalmia** or the condition of temporary blindness. If not treated with retinol, the condition can progress towards a permanent form of blindness, called keratomalacia. This condition, refers to a more advanced keratinization and softening of the of the cornea, often depicted with corneal ulcerations (Merck, 2014).

At the international level, children suffering from measles and diarrheal disease have been identified by the WHO as being at high risk of vitamin A deficiency. Consequently, supplementation has been recognized as an acceptable treatment protocol (COID, 1993). It is noteworthy to point out that when diets are also suboptimal in calories, protein, and zinc, vitamin A deficiency tends to also be prominent. This is because the synthesis of the transport protein, retinol binding protein (RBP), requires proteins, calories, and zinc (COID, 2013). There are several other areas in which vitamin A is suspected to have a significant role, notably in growth and immunity, but the mechanisms have not yet been identified. The role of vitamin A in growth, for instance, has been suspected from research that showed that normal fetal development was linked to good retinoid status. Developmentally, retinoids appear to be responsible, either through cell differentiation and proliferation, as well as by gene expression, in the growth of the skeletal, cardiovascular, and central nervous systems. Of significance, clinically, is the documented involvement of vitamin A in anemia (Ross, 2006; Semba & Bloem, 2002). The anemia of vitamin A deficiency is caused by a complex system that is associated with the growth and differentiation of the cells of the erythrocyte right down to the role of retinoids in potentiating the immune response in disease and thus thwarting the promotion of anemia of chronic disease (Semba & bloem, 2002).

8.2.3.2 Folate Deficiency

At the international level, folate and B12 deficiencies have been identified as a potential public health problem that could possibly affect several millions of individuals (de Benoist, 2008). Folate, which tends to be high in green leafy vegetables—the name folate is derived from foliage—legumes and a variety of fruits, will tend to be deficient in populations that consume suboptimal diets containing unfortified wheat, maize, or rice, and poor in legumes and folate-rich vegetables, and fruits (de Benoist, 2008). Countries such as India and Chile have a high prevalence of folate deficiency because of the heavy reliance on processed white flour. This tends not to be a problem in Mexico, Guatemala, or Thailand where erythrocyte folate levels were found to be elevated (WHO, 2006). This poor form of nutrition can be found in both developing and developed nations alike. Low blood erythrocyte folate concentrations—the most reliable indicator of long term folate status—have been tied to a high risk of low birth weights. Moreover, there is strong evidence, in support of a direct link between suboptimal maternal folate intake or status, measured by blood values, and the risk of **megaloblastic anemia** and neural tube defects (NTD) such as spina bifida in the offspring (de Benoist, 2008). Large scale supplement studies in China in addition to postfortification trials in Canada, Chile and the United States have successfully confirmed this association. By contrast, the evidence in support of orofacial clefts and heart defects and poor folate intake is modest at this time (de Benoist, 2008).

8.2.3.3 Vitamin D Deficiency and Its History

The surge in the international prevalence of rickets appears to be mostly tied to both exclusive breast feeding and to the practice of shielding the skin from the sun. The problem is particularly exacerbated by the immigration of individuals with heightened skin pigmentation coming from non-European countries, and settling in the northern hemisphere, where daylight hours are significantly shortened during winter (Pettifor, 2004; WHO, 2006). In this context, full body garments that shield the sun completely, in combination with prolonged exclusive breastfeeding practices have made infants and young children susceptible to rickets, and the elderly to osteomalacia (WHO, 2006). Also, surprisingly, there are some countries where suboptimal calcium intake has been linked to a surge in rickets, despite having adequate vitamin D status with blood 25(OH) D concentrations that are >10–12 ng/mL (Pettifor, 2004). These tend to be cultures with limited dairy intake, in combination with elevated cereal-based phytate consumption, which tends to bind available calcium (Williams, 1998). The lower calcium intake also defines the important shift from traditional food habits to a more impoverished urban nutrition, high in sweetened beverages, that displace dairy out of the diet (Popkin, 1994). The most reliable method of determining poor vitamin D status is measuring low plasma 25-OH-D3. However, measuring Parathyroid hormone (PTH) levels can be helpful in ruling out hyperparathyroidism which tends to occur with vitamin D deficiency (Gropper & Smith, 2013; Kennel, et al., 2010).

8.2.3.4 Key Micromineral Deficiencies

Internationally, **iodine, iron**, and **zinc** have contributed most significantly to the onset of disease worldwide (WHO, 2006). The devastating impact of iron and iodine deficiencies on the prevalence of anemia and mental retardation worldwide, respectively, has forced the international community to prioritize the elimination of iodine deficiency and the reduction of the prevalence of anemia by one third. Iron status, specifically, is of great interest as it is the most prominent nutrient deficiency in the world, and because it is linked to national productivity and health (Basta et al., 1979).

Since the WHO identified iodine deficiency as the most preventable cause of mental retardation in the world, there has been a strong impetus to eliminate this deficiency. The fortification of salt with iodine—a process called iodization—has been helpful in eradicating the problem in western industrialized countries. However, there are still developing countries that have not yet fortified their food supply with iodine. Moreover, they also rely too heavily on cassava as a main carbohydrate staple even though it is a goitrogen that binds iodine, thus making it unavailable for absorption. Iodization is a priority as many countries have iodine-impoverished soil, the result of the leaching effect of heavy rain, snow fall and past glaciation (WHO, 2006).

Roughly 20% of the world's population is at risk of zinc deficiency, with countries like Bangladesh and India, Africa and the Western Pacific being particularly prone to deficiency (WHO, 2006). Zinc's roles in cell division and protein synthesis mean that it can directly impact the growth and maturation of children, and when deficient in the diet, stunted growth becomes prominent in the children. About 33% of children in developing countries are reported to be stunted. The causes can vary, but suspicions run high that poor dietary zinc intake, compromised absorption because of parasitic infestations, or high prevalence of phytates, are somehow involved. Plant- and cereal-based diets tend to have elevated phytates, which bind both iron and zinc, and diminish their bioavailability (Groper & Smith, 2013). However, recent work on zinc bioavailability in diverse diets has not shown conclusively that phytates bind zinc to the extent of limiting availability (WHO, 2006). While the symptoms of severe zinc deficiency are overt and easy to document such retarded growth, dermatitis, and diarrhea, mild to moderate deficiencies are more difficult to track. Nevertheless, zinc supplementation directly reduced the frequency of pneumonia and diarrhea, in addition to the duration of diarrheal episodes (WHO, 2006). Iron and zinc deficiencies tend to occur concurrently as they are found in similar foods.

8.2.3.5 Other Varied Nutrient Deficiencies in Developing Nations

Although not as prominent as iron, retinol, iodine, and zinc deficiencies, on the global stage, there are still numerous types of vitamin B deficiencies prominently reported internationally among nations that consume little meat, eggs, and dairy products, where cereals and wheat are over processed through extensive millings, and where fruits and vegetables are not abundant and varied (WHO, 2006).

a) *Cyanocobalamin (B12) Deficiency.* The prevalence of B12 deficiency is widespread internationally with 15% of German women of reproductive age, 31% of the elderly in the United Kingdom, and 11–12% of Venezuelan pre-school and school aged children with reported suboptimal serum values.

The highest prevalence was found among 46% of Indian adults and 40% of Kenyan school-aged children, whereas the lowest incidences were reported in the United States (0–3% of the population), Botswana, Japan, and Thailand. A vitamin B12 deficiency is determined by serum levels that drop to <150 pmol/L. In developing countries, it appears that the infestation of *Helicobacter pylori* infection and aging is at the source of the gastric atrophy that compromises the secretion of intrinsic factor (IF) from parietal cells of the stomach. The IF is a transport protein that is necessary for the absorption of B12 in the ileum. The main symptom is pernicious megaloblastic anemia (See chapter 9 for more details about the deficiency). Blood levels are also low among strict vegetarians, but surprisingly also among lacto-ovo-vegetarians. Only those who consume meat have adequate plasma concentrations of B12 (WHO, 2008, 2006).

b) *Thiamin (Vitamin B1) Deficiency.* Although thiamin deficiency—beriberi is the deficiency disease—has been mostly eliminated in industrialized nations, with the enrichment of the wheat and cereal supplies, beriberi is still documented in Asian and African countries such as Ethiopia, Guinea, Nepal, and Thailand. It is in these countries, specifically, where refined and unenriched white rice is a staple of the diet. Beriberi is additionally documented in countries afflicted with civil unrest, or torn apart by war and compromised by famines (WHO, 2006).

c) *Riboflavin (Vitamin B2) Deficiency.* The WHO has conducted several international assessments of riboflavin status, and has reported a surprisingly elevated prevalence in over 90% of pregnant Gambian women, 50% of elderly Guatemalans, and 70% of lactating women. Urinary flavin concentrations, which reflect recent intake more than status, were low in 90% of China's adults (WHO, 2006).

d) *Niacin (Vitamin B3) Deficiency.* Deficiencies of this vitamin are usually seen in populations that rely a lot on cereal-based diets that are low in both niacin and tryptophan. This is the only known vitamin that can be synthesized from protein. Indeed, tryptophan, an essential amino acid, can convert to niacin through the involvement of vitamins B2 and B6, in addition to iron and copper. In a protein-poor diet that is based on overly-processed wheat or cereal, there is a propensity to develop pellagra. This deficiency can seemingly occur when either copper, iron, riboflavin, or pyridoxine are suboptimal or missing, within the context of poor quality protein and unprocessed maize or overly processed non-enriched cereal products (Bourgeois, 2006). Internationally, pellagra can still be found in countries such as India and in some regions of Africa, and China, where the diets of maize, sorghum and polished rice predominate. Pellagra also rears its ugly head in refugee camps such as the one for Mozambicans in Malawi (WHO, 2006). Interestingly, abundant coffee consumption in Latin America may be playing a significant role in why pellagra is absent those countries. The roasting of the coffee bean appears to greatly increase the bioavailability of nicotinic acid.

e) *Pyridoxine (Vitamin B6) Deficiency.* Despite these complex and intricate links with other nutrients, there are indications of suboptimal blood levels in about 40% of Indonesian children in rural and 10% in urban centers. In Egypt, vitamin B6 concentrations, in about 40% of the milk of breastfeeding mothers, were low (WHO, 2006). Epidemiologically, diets that rely extensively on refined grains with very little meats, vegetables, and nuts will be prone to be deficient in B6. Chronic forms of alcoholism will also increase the risk of deficiency (WHO, 2006).

f) *Ascorbic Acid (Vitamin C) Deficiency.* Severe ascorbic acid deficiency has been almost completely eradicated in industrialized nations, but remains a brutal reality for populations that are displaced into refugee camps, because of civil unrest, for periods of three to six months as recently seen in places like Ethiopia, Kenya, Somalia, Sudan, and Nepal. Somalian refugees in the mid-1980s had scurvy outbreaks that affected between 7% and 44% of refugees (WHO, 2006). All it takes is consuming three to four consecutive months of a vitamin C-impoverished diet (<10 mg per day) to cause scorbutic symptoms to appear (Levine et al., 2006).

8.2.4 Societal Causes of Malnutrition

The result of a broad analysis of international malnutrition concluded that there were six key factors that were in play. **Agricultural production** became a critical component in the discussion, for indeed, the shift from subsistence agriculture to cash cropping will tend to impoverish population diets. Also, the question of **food preservation**, as it pertains to processing after harvest, plays a significant role in population nutrition because of excessive wastage. In fact, roughly 25% of grains and 50% of fruits, vegetables, and roots are lost in post-harvest storage in developing countries. There is also the question of over-processing, which leads to poor nutritional food quality and a greater susceptibility to nutrient deficiencies of thiamin (vitamin B1) and niacin (vitamin B3). **Overpopulation** has been argued as central to the discussion in so far as limited child spacing represents a financial burden felt by families that have too many children. **Poverty** of the family has now been recognized as a determinant of nutritional status. When the purchasing power of the family becomes constricted because of economic strife, then access to food is limited with direct consequences on the health of family members. The **geopolitical landscape** will also influence population nutrition as it becomes central to political stability. Dictatorships are infamous for creating strife, poverty, and social upheaval. In the midst of social unrest, lawlessness, and poor government policies, food production can be hampered. Finally, the prominence of certain **pathologies**, especially infections, can seriously devastate the nutritional status of a population (FAO, 1997).

More recently, since the turn of the new Millennium, there has been an important reduction in the prevalence of undernutrition and mortality among children younger than 5 years of age. Yet, despite this improvement, there still remain 170 million undernourished children worldwide of which about three million indirectly die from diseases that are worsened by undernutrition. However, the paradox is that overnutrition also afflicts populations of underdeveloped transitioning countries at the same time. Of particular concern are the one billion overweight adults in addition to the 300 million clinically obese adults around the world who are emerging because of a nutrition transition (Caballero, 2006).

8.2.5 The Nutrition Transition

The concept of a nutrition transition was first proposed in the 1990s by Dr. Barry Popkin, a leading epidemiologist and obesity researcher out of the University of North Carolina, Chapel Hill (Popkin, 1994). The premise was that food consumption over the last 50 years in developing countries such as Egypt, Mexico and South Africa was changing and fueling a rise in chronic diseases internationally. The transition refers to **technological**, **economic** and **demographic** changes taking place in developing countries that increase population access to cheap vegetable oils and animal foods such as meats and dairy products, in addition to soft drinks, all of which have contributed to a spike in obesity rates that began to rival those of the United States (Caballero, 2006).

At the very heart of the international jump in overweight and obesity prevalence, however, is the demographically significant **population shift** of rural agricultural workers moving to cities to find work. This occurred with the disappearance of small subsistence farming, and the emergence of cash crop mega farms. It also describes populations that began to immigrate to westernized countries, looking for opportunities. The improved **technology** they encountered in urban centers and western nations transformed what used to be heavy labor into more mechanized work with fewer calories expended on a daily basis. The other factor coming into play here is greater **urbanization**. The city dweller produces very little food products, but actually becomes a great purchaser or consumer of commodities. He also drives everywhere and walks very little. Moreover, access to cheap and affordable high calorie foods is facilitated by a **globalization** of the food production and marketing (Caballero, 2006). The end result is a 600 kcal/day increase in energy availability per capita in many developing countries, with China exhibiting as much as 1000 kcal/day jump in available energy per person. The biggest culprit appears to be a dramatic increase in caloric sweeteners which takes place with urbanization (Caballero, 2006). Hence, the face of malnutrition is changing in a dramatic way, as it now includes a preponderance of over-nutrition alongside much undernutrition in intermediate-income countries. The repercussions are mostly observed in the form of spikes in many secondary diseases such as type-2 diabetes, cardiovascular disease and hypertension (Caballero, 2006)

CHAPTER 8 PRACTICE QUESTIONS

1 If patient presents with goiter, what nutrient deficiency should you suspect?

2 What vitamin(s) is directly involved in the synthesis of the hemoglobin protein?

3 Identify the vitamin deficiency disease that was affecting both the Japanese navy and native army recruits in Indonesia around the late 19th century.

4 Identify the young Dutch physician who managed to determine that beriberi was caused by the lack of a dietary factor rather than from a bacterial infection.

5 Identify what food predisposed the Indonesian army recruits to develop beriberi?

6 What is the name of the deficiency disease associated with poor thiamin intake and metabolism in alcoholics?

7 Identify the nutrient deficiency disease associated with the 4 D symptoms.

8 Identify the co-enzyme forms in which niacin can be found.

9 Identify the nutrients that actively participate in the conversion of tryptophan to niacin.

10 Describe how large doses of niacin can effectively treat hypercholesterolemia.

11 Identify the vitamin involved in the synthesis of the neurotransmitters, serotonin and aminobutyric acid.

12 Identify the vitamin that causes brittle nails when deficient.

13 Identify the vitamin prominently found in the diet in the form of "phylloqinone."

14 Identify the vitamin critically required for blood clotting to occur.

15 A patient presents with angular stomatitis, cheilosis, and glossitis. What vitamin deficiency do you suspect?

16 If a patient presents with xerophthalmia, follicular hyperkeratosis, and night blindness, what deficiency do you suspect?

17 What other nutrient deficiency would you suspect in a case where there are documented deficiencies in calories, zinc, and protein?

18 Calculate the nitrogen balance of an individual, consuming 130 g protein, who has a net urea nitrogen output of 12 g, a net fecal nitrogen output of 4 g, and an estimated skin loss of 1.5 g of nitrogen.

19 Calculate the biological value (BV) of a food that contains 156 g protein, and after consumption, results in a net 14 g of urea output, and 2 g net fecal output.

20 A patient presents with a serum hemoglobin = 7.6 g/dl, serum ferritin = 18 mg/L, an erythrocyte protoporphyrin (EP) = 2.23 mg/L, and suboptimal serum ceruloplasmin. What should the clinician suspect?

21 If the digestibility of a specific plant protein is 70%, how much protein would need to be consumed if, nitrogen balance was achieved with 16 g of nitrogen coming from egg white, which has a 100% digestibility?

22 When parathyroid hormone (PTH) is secreted in response to a lowering of blood calcium, identify which bone cell becomes activated in order to normalize the blood calcium.

23 When PTH activates vitamin 25-OH-D3 to calcitriol, what action does this vitamin have on bone?

24 When PTH activates vitamin 25-OH-D3 to calcitriol, what action does this vitamin have on the gastrointestinal tract?

25 When PTH activates vitamin 25-OH-D3 to calcitriol in the kidneys, what action does the PTH have on the kidney tubules?

REFERENCES

1 Agnew-Blais, J.C. et al., (2015). Folate, vitamin B-6, and B-12 intake and mild cognitive impairment and probable dementia in the Women's Health Initiative Memory Study. *J. Academy of Nutrition and Dietetics*; 115 (2) 231–241.

2 Argawall, R. (2011). B12 deficiency & cognitive impairment in elderly population. *Indian J Med Res*;134(4): 410–412.

3 ASPEN. (2007). *The American Society of Parenteral and Enteral Nutrition ASPEN Nutrition Support Core Curriculum: A Case-Based Approach — The Adult Patient.* Silver Spring, Md: American Society of Parenteral and Enteral Nutrition.

4 Badaloo, A.V., Forrester, T., Reid, M., & Jahoor, F. (2006). Lipid kinetic differences between children with kwashiorkor and those with marasmus. *Am J Clin Nutr*; 8 (6): 1283–1288.

5 Basta, S.S., Soekirman, D.Sc., Karyadi, D., & Scrimshaw, M.S. (1979). Iron deficiency anemia and the productivity of adult males in Indonesia . *Am. J.Clin. Nutr.* 32: 916–925.

6 Barker, L.A., Gout, B.S., and Crowe, T.C. (2011). Hospital malnutrition: Prevalence, identification and impact on patients and the healthcare system. *Int J Environ Res Public Health.* 8(2): 514–527. Retrieved from: http://www.ncbi.nlm.nih.gov/pmc/articles/PMC3084475/

7 Bell IR, Morrow FD, Read M, Berkes S, Perrone G. (1992). Low thyroxine levels in female psychiatric patients with riboflavin deficiency: implications for folate-dependent methylation. Acta Psychiatr Scand;85:360–3.

8 Bissonnette, D.J. (2013). *It's all about nutrition: Saving the health of Americans.* Lanham, MD: University Press of America.

9 Bissonnette, D.J. et al., (2012). The Effect of Intra-Muscular Injections of Alpha-tocopherol on the Activity of Phospho- Fructokinase in the Slow- and Fast-Twitch Skeletal Muscles of Metabolic Stress-Induced and Malnourished Rats. International Journal on Bioinformatics & Biotechnology; 2 (1):12–24

10 Bistrian, B. (1984) Nutritional assessment of the hospitalised patient: A practical approach. In *Nutritional Assessment*, R. and Heymsfield, S. eds) Blackwell Scientific Publications, Boston.

11 Bistrian, B.R., Blackburn, G.L., Vitale, J., Cochrane, D., & Naylor, J. (1976). Prevalence of malnutrition in general medical patients. *JAMA.*235: 1567–1570.

12 Bobrow-Strain, A. (2012). *White bread: A social history of the store-bought loaf.* Boston: Beacon Press.

13 Bourgeois, C., Cervantes-Laurean, D. & Moss. (2006) J. Niacin. In *Modern Nutrition in Health and Disease* 10th edition, (Shils, M.E. et al. eds). Baltimore MD: Lippincott, Williams & Wilkins.

14 Burk, R.F. & Levander, O.A. (2006) Selenium. In *Modern nutrition in health and disease* 10th edition, (Shils, M.E. et al., eds). Baltimore MD: Lippincott, Williams & Wilkins.

15 Buzby, P. & Mullen, J.L. (1984). Analysis of nutritional assessment indices—prognostic equations and cluster analysis. In *Nutritional Assessment*, R. and Heymsfield, S. eds) Blackwell Scientific Publications, Boston.

[16] Butterworth, R.F. (2006) Thiamin. In *Modern nutrition in health and disease* 10th edition, (Shils, M.E. et al. eds). Baltimore MD: Lippincott, Williams & Wilkins.

[17] Caballero, B. (2006). The Nutrition Transition: Global Trends in Diet and Disease. In *Modern nutrition in health and disease* 10th edition, (Shils, M.E. et al. eds). Baltimore MD: Lippincott, Williams & Wilkins.

[18] Calvo, M.S. (1993): Dietary phosphorus, calcium metabolism and bone. *J. Nutr.* 123, 1627±1633.

[19] Calvo, M.S., Kumar, R., & Heath, H. (1988): Elevated secretion and action of serum parathyroid hormone in young adults consuming high phosphorus, low calcium diets assembled from common foods. *J. Clin. Endocrinol. Metab.* 66, 823±829.

[20] Canadian Clinical Practice Guidelines (CCPG) (2013). *Composition of enteral nutrition: High protein vs low protein.* Retrieved from: http://www.criticalcarenutrition.com/docs/cpgs2012/4.2c.pdf

[21] Canadian Pediatric Surveillance Program (CPSP). 2002. Vitamin K Injection: Best prevention for newborns. *Paediatr. Child Health* 7(8).

[22] Carmel, R. (2006). Cobalamin (vitamin B12). In *Modern nutrition in health and disease* 10th edition, (Shils, M.E. et al. eds). Baltimore MD: Lippincott, Williams & Wilkins.

[23] Carmel, R. (2006b). Folic Acid. In *Modern nutrition in health and disease* 10th edition, (Shils, M.E. et al. eds). Baltimore MD: Lippincott, Williams & Wilkins.

[24] Carpenter, K.J., and Harper, A.E. (2006) Evolution of Knowledge of Essential Nutrients. In *Modern nutrition in health and disease* 10th edition, (Shils, M.E. et al. eds). Baltimore MD: Lippincott, Williams & Wilkins.

[25] Carpenter, K.J. (1981). Pellagra Stroudsburg, PA: Hutchinson Ross Publishing.

[26] Carpenter, K.J. (1986). *The history of scurvy and vitamin C.* Cambridge: Cambridge University Press.

[27] Carpenter, K.J. (2003) A short history of nutritional science: Part-3 (1912–1944). *J. Nutrition.* 133.

[28] Carpenter, K.J. (2003b). A short history of nutritional science: Part-2 (1885–1912). *J. Nutr.* 133: 975–984,

[29] Carpenter, K.J. (2003c). A short history of nutritional science: Part-4 (1945–1985). *J. Nutr.* 133.

[30] Charney, P. and Marian, M. (2008) Nutritional Screening and Nutritional Assessment. In *ADA Pocket guide to nutrition assessment.* Pamela Charney, and Ainsley M. Malone, (eds) 2nd edition. Chicago: American Dietetic Association.

[31] Clarke, R., Smith, A.D., Jobst, K.A., Refsum, H., Sutton, L., Ueland, P.M. (1998). Folic acid, vitamin B_{12} ad serum homocysteine levels in confirmed Alzheimer's disease. *Arch Neurol*; 55.

[32] Committee on Infectious Diseases (COID). (1993). Vitamin A treatment of measles. *Pediatrics.* 91.

[33] Compher, C., & Mehta, N.M. (2016) Diagnosing malnutrition: Where are we and where do we need to go? *J. Academy of Nutrition and Dietetics*; 116 (5).

[34] Crandon, J.H., Lund, C.C., &Dill, D.B. (1940). Experimental human scurvy. *New England J. Med.* 223(10).

[35] De Benoist. B. (2008) Conclusions of a WHO technical consultation on Folate and B12 deficiencies. *Food and Nutrition Bulletin*, vol. 29, no. 2 (supplement).

[36] de Carvalho Pereira, D. et al. (2013). Association between obesity and calcium: phosphorous ratio in the habitual diets of adults in a city of northeastern Brazil: An epidemiological study. *Nutrition Journal*, 12:90.

[37] de Onis, M. et al. (1993). The worldwide magnitude of protein-energy malnutrition: An overview from the who global database on child growth. *Bulletin of the World Health Organization*—WHO.71(5).

38 De-Souza, D.A. & Greene, L.J. (1998) Pharmacological nutrition after burn injury. *J. Nutr.* 128.

39 Dunn, J.T. (2006). Iodine. *In Modern nutrition in health and disease* 10th edition, (Shils, M.E. et al. eds). Baltimore MD: Lippincott, Williams & Wilkins.

40 Fanelli M.T., Woteki C.E. (1989). Nutrition intakes and health status of older Americans. Data from the NHANES II. Ann New York Acad Sci;561:94–103.

41 FAO. (1997). Human nutrition in the developing world. *FAO Food and Nutrition Series #29.* Retrieved from http://www.fao.org/docrep/w0073e/w0073e00.htm

42 Fenton, T.R. et al. (2009). Phosphate decreases urine calcium and increases calcium balance: A meta-analysis of the osteoporosis acid-ash diet hypothesis. *J. Nutr.* 8(41).

43 Fessler, T.A. (2008). Malnutrition: A Serious concern for hospitalized patients. *Today's Dietitian*; 10(7).

44 Fleuret, P. & Fleuret, A. (1980). Nutrition, consumption, and agricultural change. *Human Organization.* 39 (3).

45 Frankenfield, D. (2006). Energy expenditure and protein requirements after traumatic injury. *Nutr. Clin. Pract.* 21(5).

46 Gibson, R.S. (1990). *Principles of nutritional assessment.* New York: Oxford University Press.

47 Goldsmith, G.A. (1965). Niacin: Antipellagra factor, Hypocholesterolemic agent. JAMA 194 (2): 147–153

48 Gottfries, C.G., Lehman, W., & Regland, B. (1998) Early diagnosis of cognitive impairment in the elderly with the focus on Alzheimer's disease. *J Neural Transm*;105.

49 Gropper, S.S. & Smith, J.L. (2013). *Advanced nutrition and human metabolism.* 6th edition. Belmont, Ca: Wadsworth Cengage Learning.

50 Guthrie H.A., Guthrie G.M.(1976). Factor analysis of nutritional status data from Ten State Nutrition Surveys. Am J Clin Nutr;29:1238–41

51 Hampl, J.S., Taylor, C.A., & Johnston, C.S. (2004). Vitamin C deficiency and depletion in the United States: The third national health and nutrition examination survey 1988–1994. *Am J Public Health.* 94(5).

52 He, F.J., and MacGregor, G.A. (2008). Beneficial effects of potassium on human health. Physiol Plant;133(4):725-35. Retrieved from: http://www.ncbi.nlm.nih.gov/pubmed/18724413

53 Heimburger, D.C. et al. (2006). Clinical manifestations of nutrient deficiencies and toxicities: A resumé: In *Modern nutrition in health and disease* 10th edition, (Shils, M.E. et al. eds). Baltimore MD: Lippincott, Williams & Wilkins.

54 Hoffer, L.J., & Bistrian, B.R. (2012). Appropriate protein provision in critical illness: A systematic and narrative review. *Am J Clin Nutr.* 96(3).

55 Hoffer, L.J. (2006). Metabolic consequences of starvation. In *Modern nutrition in health and disease* 10th edition, (Shils, M. E. et al. eds). Baltimore MD: Lippincott, Williams & Wilkins.

56 Holick, M.F. (2006). Vitamin D. In *Modern nutrition in health and disease* 10th edition, (Shils, M.E. et al. eds). Baltimore MD: Lippincott, Williams & Wilkins.

57 Honein, M.A. et al., (2001). Impact of folic acid fortification on the US food supply on the occurrence of neural tube defects. *J. Am. Med. Assoc*; 285:2981–6.

58 HPS2-THRIVE Collaborative Group (2014). Effects of Extended-Release Niacin with Laropiprant in High-Risk Patients. N. Engl. J. Med. 371:203–212

59 Institute of Medicine (1997). Food and Drug Board. Dietary Reference Intakes for Calcium, Phosphorus, Magnesium, Vitamin D and Fluoride. Washington DC: National Academic Press.

60 Ishibashi, N., Plank, L.D., Sando, K., & Hill, G.L. (1998). Optimal protein requirements during the first 2 weeks after the onset of critical illness. *Crit. Care Med.* 26(9): 1529–35.

61 Jackevicius C.A., Tu J.V., Ko D.T., de Leon N., Krumholz H.M. (2013) Use of niacin in the United States and Canada. JAMA Intern Med;173:1379-1381

62 Johnson, C.S. et al. (2000). More Americans are eating 5-A-Day, but intakes of dark green cruciferous vegetables remain low. *J. Nutr.* 130(2): 3063–3067.

63 Kemi, V.E., Karkkainen, M.U.M., Rita, H.J, Laaksonen, M.M.L., Outila, T.A., & Lamberg-Allardt, C.J.E. (2010): Low calcium: phosphorus ratio in habitual diets affects serum parathyroid hormone concentration and calcium metabolism in healthy women with adequate calcium intake. *Br J Nutr*, 103:561–568.

64 Kennedy, D.O. (2016). B Vitamins and the braIn Mechanisms, dose and efficacy—a review. *Nutrients*; 8 (68): 2–29.

65 Kennel, K.A. et al., (2010). Vitamin D Deficiency in Adults: When to Test and How to Treat. Mayo Clin Proc. 2010 Aug; 85(8): 752–758. doi: 10.4065/mcp.2010.0138. Retrieved from: http://www.ncbi.nlm.nih.gov/pmc/articles/PMC2912737/

66 King, J.C. &Cousins, R.J. (2006). Zinc. In *Modern nutrition in health and disease* 10th edition, (Shils, M. E. et al. eds). Baltimore MD: Lippincott, Williams & Wilkins.

67 Kinney, J.M. (2006). Human Energy Metabolism. In *Modern nutrition in health and disease* 10th edition, (Shils, M. E. et al. eds). Baltimore MD: Lippincott, Williams & Wilkins.

68 Knochel, J.P. (2006) Phosphorus. In *Modern nutrition in health and disease* 10th edition, (Shils, M. E. et al. eds). Baltimore MD: Lippincott, Williams & Wilkins.

69 Kondrup, J., Allison, S. P., Elia, M., Vellas, B., & Plauth, M. (2003). ESPEN guidelines for nutrition screening 2002. *Clinical Nutrition* 22(4): 415–421.

70 Kudsk, K.A., Reddy, S.K., Sacks, G.S., Lai, H.C .(2003). Joint Commission for Accreditation of Health Care Organizations guidelines: Too late to intervene for nutritionally at-risk surgical patients. *JPEN J Parenter Enteral Nutr*;27(4):288–290.

71 Leshner R.T. (1981). Riboflavin deficiency—a reversible neurodegenerative disease. Ann Neurol;10:294–5.

72 Lee, R.D. & Nieman, D.C. (1996). *Nutritional Assessment* 2nd edition. New York: Mosby.

73 Levine, M., Katz, A., Padayatty, S.J. (2006). Vitamin C. In *Modern nutrition in health and disease* 10th edition, (Shils, M. E. et al. eds). Baltimore MD: Lippincott, Williams & Wilkins.

74 Lobo, V., et al. (2010). Free radicals, antioxidants and functional foods: Impact on human health. Pharmacogn Rev; 4(8): 118–126. doi: 10.4103/0973-7847.70902

75 Long, C.L. (1984). Nutritional assessment of the critically ill patient In *Nutritional assessment*, R. & Heymsfield, S. eds) Blackwell Scientific Publications, Boston.

76 Lowry, S.F. & Perez, J.M. (2006). The hypercatabolic state. In *Modern nutrition in health and disease* 10th edition, (Shils, M. E. et al. eds). Baltimore MD: Lippincott, Williams & Wilkins.

77 Maccubbin, D., et al. (2008). Lipid-modifying efficacy and tolerability of extended-release niacin/laropiprant in patients with primary hypercholesterolaemia or mixed dyslipidaemia. Int J Clin Pract;62(12):1959-70. doi: 10.1111/j.1742-1241.2008.01938.x.

78 Mackey, A.D., Davis, S.R., & Gregory, J.F., (2006).Vitamin B6. In *Modern nutrition in health and disease* 10th edition, (Shils, M. E. et al. eds). Baltimore MD: Lippincott, Williams & Wilkins.

79 Manson, A., & Shea, S. (1991). Malnutrition in elderly ambulatory medical patients. *Am. J. Public Healthr*; 81(9): 1195–1197.

[80] Matthews, D. (2006). Proteins and amino acids. In *Modern nutrition in health and disease* 10th edition, (Shils, M. E. et al. eds). Baltimore MD: Lippincott, Williams & Wilkins.

[81] McCormick, D.B. (2006). Riboflavin. In *Modern nutrition in health and disease* 10th edition, (Shils, M. E. et al. eds). Baltimore MD: Lippincott, Williams & Wilkins.

[82] Merck Manual for Health Professionals (2016). Hyperkalemia. Retrieved from: https://www.merckmanuals.com/professional/endocrine-and-metabolic-disorders/electrolyte-disorders/hyperkalemia

[83] Merck Manual for Health Professionals (2016). Hypokalemia. Retrieved from: http://www.merckmanuals.com/professional/endocrine-and-metabolic-disorders/electrolyte-disorders/hypokalemia

[84] Merck Manual for Health Professionals (2013). *Nutritional Disorders>Vitamin Deficiency, dependency and toxicity: Vitamin B6.* Retrieved from http://www.merckmanuals.com/professional/nutritional_disorders/vitamin_deficiency_dependency_and_toxicity/vitamin_b6.html

[85] Merck (2014). Karetomalacia. Retrieved from: https://www.merckmanuals.com/professional/eye-disorders/corneal-disorders/keratomalacia

[86] Merck manual for Health Professionals (2014b). Vitamin A. retrieved from: https://www.merckmanuals.com/professional/nutritional-disorders/vitamin-deficiency,-dependency,-and-toxicity/vitamin-a#v884888

[87] Merck Manual for Health Professionals (2012). *Overview of undernutrition.* Retrieved from http://www.merckmanuals.com/professional/nutritional_disorders/undernutrition/overview_of_undernutrition.html?qt=malnutrition&alt=sh#v882493

[88] Mock, D.M. (2006). Biotin. In *Modern nutrition in health and disease* 10th edition, (Shils, M. E. et al. eds). Baltimore MD: Lippincott, Williams & Wilkins.

[89] Moneti, F. and Yee, V. (1989). Mobilization for nutrition: results from Iringa. Mothers Child;8(2):1–3. Retrieved from: http://www.ncbi.nlm.nih.gov/pubmed/12342471

[90] Moore, J.C., DeVries, J.W., Lipp, M., Griffiths, J.C., & Abernethy, D.R. (2010). Total protein methods and their potential utility to reduce the risk of food protein adulteration. *Comprehensive Reviews in Food Science and Food Safety*; 9: 330–357.

[91] Moorthy, D. et al., (2012). Status of vitamin B-12 and B-6 but not of folate, homocysteine, and methylenetetahydrofolate reductase C677T polymorphism are associated with cognition and depression in adults. *J. Nutr*; 142 (8)1554–1556.

[92] Morley, J.E. (2014). Overview of undernutrition. *Merck Manual, Professional Version.* Retrieved from http://www.merckmanuals.com/professional/nutritional-disorders/undernutrition/overview-of-undernutrition

[93] Newsholme, E.A. & Leech, A.R. (1983). *Biochemistry for the medical sciences.* New York: John Wiley & Sons.

[94] NIH (2016). Vitamin A: Facts Sheet for Health Professionals. Retrieved from the National Institutes of Health website: https://ods.od.nih.gov/factsheets/VitaminA-HealthProfessional/

[95] Offitt, P. (2013). The vitamin myth. Why we think we need supplements. *The Atlantic*, July 19. Retrieved from http://www.theatlantic.com/health/archive/2013/07/the-vitamin-myth-why-we-think-we-need-supplements/277947/

[96] Paiva, S.A., and Russell, R.M. (1999). Beta-carotene and other carotenoids as antioxidants. J Am Coll Nutr; (5):426-33. retrieved from: http://www.ncbi.nlm.nih.gov/pubmed/10511324

[97] Patrick L. (2008) Iodine: deficiency and therapeutic considerations. *Altern Med Rev.* 13(2): 116–127.

[98] Pettifor, J.M. (2004). Nutritional rickets: Deficiency of vitamin D, calcium or both? *Am J Clin Nutr*, 80(suppl):1725S–9S.

99 Picciano, MF (1999). Iron and folate supplementation: an effective intervention in adolescent females (Editorial). *Am. J. Clin. Nutr.* 69:1069–1070.

100 Pinstrup-Andersen, P. & Cheng, F. (2007). Still hungry: One eighth of the world's people do not have enough to eat. *Scientific American* 297(3).

101 Popkin, B.M. (1994). The nutrition transition in low-income countries: an emerging crisis. *Nutr Rev* 52:285–298.

102 Pike, R.L., & Brown, ML. (1975). *Nutrition: An integrated approach*, 2nd ed. Toronto: Joh Wiley & Sons.

103 Quandt, S.A. (2006) Social and cultural influences on food consumption and nutritional status. In *Modern nutrition in health and disease* 10th edition, (Shils, M. E. et al. eds). Baltimore MD: Lippincott, Williams & Wilkins.

104 Raiten, D.J. & Fisher, K.D. (1995). Assessment of folate methodology used in the Third National Health and Nutrition Examination survey (NHANES-iii, 1988–1994). *J. Nutr*; 125: 137 S-98S.

105 Rand, W.M., Pellett, P.L., & Young, V. (2003). Meta-analysis of nitrogen balance studies for estimating protein requirements in healthy adults. *Am J Clin Nutr*; 77(1): 109–127.

106 Riaz, M.N. et al. (2009). Stability of vitamins during extrusion. *Crit Rev Food Sci Nutr.* 2009 Apr;49(4):361–8.

107 Riggs KM, Spiro A, III, Tucker K, Rush D. (1996). Relation of vitamin B-12, vitamin B-6, folate and homocysteine to cognitive performance in the normative aging study. *Am J Clin Nutr*;63:306–14.

108 Rose, W.C. (1957) The amino acid requirements of adult man. *Nutrition Abstracts and Reviews*, 27:631–647.

109 Ross, A.C. (2006). Vitamin A and Carotenoids. In: Modern Nutrition: In Health & Disease, 10th edition (Maurice E. Shils, Moshe Shike et al., eds). New York: Lippincott, Williams & Wilkins: 351–374

110 Rothman, D.L. et al. (1991). Quantitation of hepatic glycogenolysis and gluconeogenesis in fasting humans with 13C NMR. *Science* 254 (5031): 573–6.

111 Rude, R.K. & Shils, M.E. (2006). Magnesium. In *Modern nutrition in health and disease* 10th edition, (Shils, M. E. et al. eds). Baltimore MD: Lippincott, Williams & Wilkins.

112 Schlichtig, R. & Ayres, S.M. (1988). *Nutritional support of the critically ill.* Year Book Medical, Publishers, Chicago.

113 Semba, R.D. & Bloem, M.W. (2002). The anemia of vitamin A deficiency: epidemiology and pathogenesis. Eur J Clin Nutr;56(4):271-81. Retrieved from: http://www.ncbi.nlm.nih.gov/pubmed/11965502

114 Suttie, J.W. (2006) Vitamin K. In *Modern nutrition in health and disease* 10th edition, (Shils, M. E. et al. eds). Baltimore MD: Lippincott, Williams & Wilkins.

115 Torun, B. (2006). Protein energy malnutrition. In *Modern nutrition in health and disease* 10th edition, (Shils, M. E. et al. eds). Baltimore MD: Lippincott, Williams & Wilkins.

116 Traber, M.G. (2006). Vitamin E. In *Modern nutrition in health and disease* 10th edition, (Shils, M. E. et al. eds). Baltimore MD: Lippincott, Williams & Wilkins.

117 Turnlund, J.R. (2006). Copper. In *Modern nutrition in health and disease* 10th edition, (Shils, M. E. et al. eds). Baltimore MD: Lippincott, Williams & Wilkins.

118 Trumbo, P.R. (2006). Pantothenic Acid. In *Modern nutrition in health and disease* 10th edition, (Shils, M. E. et al. eds). Baltimore MD: Lippincott, Williams & Wilkins.

119 U.N.I.C.E.F. (2003) *Micronutrients iodine, iron and vitamin A.* Retrieved from http://www.unicef.org/nutrition/index_iodine.html.

120 USDA (2011). *National Nutrient Database for Standard Reference, Release 24. Nutrient Data Laboratory Home Page.* Retrieved from http://www.ars.usda.gov/Services/docs.htm?docid=23617

[121] Via, M. (2012). The malnutrition of obesity: Micronutrient deficiencies that promote diabetes. ISRN Endocrinol. 2012: 103472. Retrieved from http://www.ncbi.nlm.nih.gov/pmc/articles/PMC3313629/

[122] Wang, H.X., Wahlin, A., Basum, H., Fastbom, J., Winbind, B., & Fratiglioni L. (2001). Vitamin B (12) and folate in relation to the development of Alzheimer's disease. *Neurology*; 56: 1188–94.

[123] Weaver, C.M. & Heaney, R.P. (2006). Calcium. In *Modern nutrition in health and disease* 10th edition, (Shils, M. E. et al. eds). Baltimore MD: Lippincott, Williams & Wilkins.

[124] Weinsier, R. L., Hunker, E.M., Krumdieck, C.L., & Butterworth, C.. Jr. (1979). Hospital malnutrition. A prospective evaluation of general medical patients during the course of hospitalization. *Am J Clin Nutr*;32(2):418–426.

[125] Weissman, C. (1999). Nutrition in the Intensive Care Unit. Crit Care. 1999; 3(5): R67–R75. retrieved from: http://www.ncbi.nlm.nih.gov/pmc/articles/PMC137235/

[126] WHO (2008). Conclusions of a WHO Technical Consultation on folate and vitamin B12 deficiencies. Food and Nutrition Bulletin, vol. 29, no. 2 (supplement)

[127] WHO. (2007). Protein and amino acid requirements in human nutrition. *WHO/ FAO/UNU Joint Report*. WHO Technical Report Series 935 United Nations University. Produced by the Agriculture and Consumer Protection Department of the FAO.

[128] WHO. (2006). Guidelines on food fortification with micronutrients. Lindsay Allen, Bruno de Benoist, Omar Dary, & Richard Hurrell (eds).

[129] Whybro, A., Jagger, H., Barker, M., & Eastell, R. (1998). Phosphate supple-mentation in young men: Lack of effect on calcium homeostasis and turnover. *European Journal of Clinical Nutrition*; 52, 29–33.

[130] Williams, C.D. (1935). Kwashiorkor: A nutritional disease of children associated with a maize diet. *Lancet*. 226 (5855): 1151–2.

[131] Williams, C. D., (1933). A nutritional disease of childhood associated with a maize diet. *Arch Dis Child*. 8(48): 423–433.

[132] Williams, P. (1998) Food toxicity and safety. In Essentials of human nutrition. Mann, J. & Trustwell, S. (eds). New York: Oxford University Press.

[133] Wolf, G. (2004). The discovery of Vitamin D: The contribution of Adolf Windaus. *J. Nutr*. 134: 2015.

[134] Wolfe, R. R. (1996) Relation of metabolic studies to clinical nutrition—the example of burn injury. *Am. J. Clin. Nutr*. 64: 800–808.

[135] World Bank. (1993). *World Development Report*. Investing in Health New York: Oxford University Press.

CHAPTER 8 ANSWERS

1 Iodine

2 Vitamin B6 and maybe B12

3 Beriberi

4 Dr. Christian Eijkman

5 Polished rice

6 The Wernicke-Korsakoff Syndrome

7 Pellagra

8 NAD, NADH, NADP, NADPH

9 B6, B2, Iron, and copper

10 It inhibits lipolytic activity in adipose tissue and lipogenesis in the liver, thereby decreasing the synthesis of VLDLs

11 Vitamin B6

12 Biotin

13 Vitamin K

14 Vitamin K

15 Riboflavin

16 Retinol/Vitamin A

17 Vitamin A

18 Positive nitrogen balance = +1.18

19 (6.49g / 22.96) x 100 = 28.27%

20 Fe-deficiency anemia originating from Cu deficiency. Treatment should involve Cu supplementation

21 22.86 g of nitrogen or 143 g of protein

22 Osteoclasts

23 Activates osteoclastic cells in order to cause bone resorption

24 Increased calcium and phosphorus absorption

25 Causes increased calcium reabsorption from kidney tubules

The Problem of Anemias

© Image Point Fr/shutterstock.com

9.1. INTRODUCTION TO ANEMIA

Among hematological defects, anemia is possibly the most common disorder in medical practice. Anemias can be classified as either nutritional or non-nutritional, but, in general, they refer to a defective hemoglobin formation or low concentration in the peripheral blood, which may arise from iron deficiency, B-12 and/or folic acid deficiencies, thalassemic syndromes, sideroblastic anemia, and anemia of chronic disease. The risk of anemia also increases with vitamin A, riboflavin, and copper deficiencies, in addition to blood loss and parasitic infestation, like hookworm (de Benoist et al., 2008).

The most common forms of anemia are the nutritional anemias; specifically, iron deficiency anemia affects an estimated 1.62 to 2.0 billion people globally or between 25–30% of the planet's population, accounting for about 50% of all anemias (WHO, 2016; WHO, 2006; de Benoist, 2008). It is decidedly women, pregnant women, and preschool children who are mostly vulnerable, however, on average as many as 13–15% of men are anemic as well (de Benoit et al., 2008). Accurate international prevalence data is difficult to acquire because Chinese statistics are either inaccurate or unavailable most of the time (WHO, 2016; de Benoist et al., 2008). Nevertheless, 1992 WHO estimates, which included some Chinese statistics, suggests that 37% of all women around the world were anemic, whereas as many as 51% of pregnant women were afflicted with the condition (WHO, 1992). Moreover, in between 1990–1995, it had been surmised that industrialized countries, specifically, were also vulnerable with as many as 30–40% of children and pregnant women classified as iron deficient (WHO, 2001). Remarkably, despite improved education and greater accessibility to a more diverse and nutritious food supply, an estimated 23% of pregnant women in industrialized nations were diagnosed with anemia (WHO, 2001). A 2006 WHO report also found that 22.7% of women in industrialized nations suffered from iron deficiency anemia (WHO, 2006). When the data was stratified to Parisian female students attending university in the 1980s, a disturbing 75% were suspected of having depleted iron stores (WHO, 2001). More recently, 47.4% of pre-schoolers worldwide were classified as anaemic, whereas 30% of non-pregnant women and 42% of pregnant women were anemic (de Benoit, et al., 2008). Overall, given that there are 2.5% more people with depleted iron reserves than there are with outright anemia, it can be inferred that, at the turn of the Millennium, close to 75% of the world population was either Fe-depleted or suffered from Fe-deficiency anemia (WHO, 2001). Back in the 1970s, the incidence of iron deficiency anemia in England, Canada and the United States was 3% in men and 25% in women (Ali, 1976). Those values have since noticeably declined to 5% of women and 3% of men living in the United States, (Johnson-Wimbley, 2011). This drop in prevalence occurred more than likely from the widespread use of multivitamin supplements and the fortification of the food supply in the United States.

Clinically, the iron-deficient patient traditionally presents with low hemoglobin (<13 g/dl for men; <12g/dl for women) (WHO, 2001) accompanied by pallor, lethargy, fatigue, dyspnea, poor physical endurance, faintness, nausea, and anorexia. These symptomatic manifestations and causes of anemia may not always be limited to this classical picture, but could be compounded by other pathologies such as HIV, cancer, malaria and tuberculosis (de Benoist et al., 2008).

The objective of this chapter is not to become an expert in hematology, but rather to increase the recognition of hematological traits of iron, B-12 and folic acid deficiencies as well as to discern between acute and chronic iron deficiency anemias. This is likely the most helpful approach in getting students ready to tackle the assessment of nutrition-related anemias.

9.2 CLASSIFICATION OF ANEMIAS

In addition to being classified as nutritional and non-nutritional, anemias can be subdivided, by automated blood cell counters, into the three categories: 1) **hypochromic microcytic anemia**; 2) **normocytic normochromic anemia**; and 3) **normochromic macrocytic anemia**. This classification is based on determining the mean corpuscular volume (MCV), the mean corpuscular hemoglobin (MCH), and mean corpuscular hemoglobin concentration (MCHC) (Gibson, 1990).

Anemias that are hypochromic signify a problem in hemoglobin synthesis. And so it should not be surprising that the association between hypochromia and microcytic iron deficiency anemia is very strong (Johnson-Wimbley, 2011). In fact, approximately 25–50% of women and 15% of men, worldwide, are diagnosed with hypochromic anemia, and of these, 90% are iron deficient (Ali, 1976).

Normocytic and normochromic anemia tends to be linked to anemia of chronic disease, whereas macrocytic anemia is tagged to megaloblastic anemia, which originates from folic acid and/or vitamin B-12 deficiency. Macrocytic and megaloblastic anemias are diagnosed using the mean corpuscular volume (MCV). This red blood cell indices, refers to the size of the red blood cell. A small MCV would mean a microcytic cell, which occurs in more advanced forms of iron deficiency, whereas a larger than normal red blood cell would be referred to as macrocytic (Gibson, 1990).

MCV = Hematocrit (Hct) /red blood count/L

The MCH allows the determination of the hemoglobin cell count in the red cell. When the value is low—something that occurs only in the late phase of anemia (Gibson, 1990)—the red blood cell has a pale or diluted red color, and is therefore referred to as **hypochromic**. The MCHC also will tend to be low in advanced iron deficiency (Johnson-Wimbley, 2011); it refers to the concentration of hemoglobin rather than the cell count. It is the MCH that is most often used to confirm hypochromic anemia (Ali, 1976).

9.3 NON-NUTRITIONAL ANEMIAS

As previously shown, microcytic hypochromic anemia can be caused by iron deficiency, thalassemic syndrome, and congenital sideroblastic anemias, whereas in anemia of chronic disease, the tendency is to observe more of a normocytic erythrocyte. At this stage it may be advantageous to describe some of the non-nutritional anemias in terms of their hematological traits, as it can provide students with many of similarities seen in nutritional anemias. Students will likely find Figure 9.6 a helpful algorithm depicting the diagnosis and treatment of a broad assortment of nutritional and non-nutritional anemias.

9.3.1 Thalassemia

Thalassemia is a genetic disorder characterized by a failure in the synthesis of one or more of the globin chains (α, ß, γ, δ) of the hemoglobin protein, and commonly found in the Mediterranean, African, and Southeast Asian countries (Merck, 1987). The thalassemic syndrome can be expressed following a wide range of clinical variability, depending on whether globin chains are totally or partially affected. The heterozygote form (thalassemia minor) is referred to as the carrier with a mild to moderate microcytic manifestation, whereas the homozygous representation (thalassemia major) has the more severe microcytic and hypochromic anemia symptoms (HB ≤6 gm/dl) primarily resulting from hemolysis (Merck, 2013b). Both the major and minor forms are microcytic as evidenced by the smaller MCVs, however the thalassemia most likely to be confused with iron-deficiency is the heterozygous type (Ali, 1976) because it is the milder form that presents with less pronounced microcytic cells (Merck, 1987). The microcytic and hemolytic red blood cells, observed

in thalassemia, are related to an abnormality in hemoglobin production. The clinical features of the homozygous thalassemia, are jaundice, leg ulcers, cholelithiasis, hepato-splenomegaly, hemolysis, and absorptive iron overload, and are frequently represented with elevated bilirubin, serum iron, and ferritin (Merck, 2013b; 1987). Iron overload will tend to occur because of frequent blood transfusions (Merck, 2013b). Key to differentiating thalassemia from iron-deficiency anemia is that both serum iron and ferritin will increase in thalassemia, a very distinct presentation from the early decline of these markers in iron-deficiency (Merck, 1987).

9.3.2 Sideroblastic Anemias

Congenital sideroblastic anemia is characterized by inherited abnormalities in the production of the hemoglobin protein or in other words a dyserythropoiesis, the consequence of inadequately utilizing iron (Fe) from the bone marrow. This is the reason sideroblastic anemia is often referred to as an iron-utilization anemia (Merck, 2013). The repercussion is polychromatophilic red blood cells showing up as hypochromic and normocytic, which makes it easily confused with iron-deficiency anemia. However, this kind of anemia does not tend to be purely microcytic but rather dismorphic, that is to say, consisting of both large (macrocytic) and small red blood cells (microcytic) (Merck, 1987; Ali, 1976). So then, despite iron deposits in the mitochondria of the marrow (Wiseman et al., 2013), and an iron overload, this kind of anemia can nevertheless occur through genetic mutations and autosomal disorders.

Pyridoxine (vitamin B6) deficiency can increase the risk of developing sideroblastic anemia (Merck, 2013), and B6 has been shown to be somewhat therapeutic in partially reversing the anemia in some congenital cases (Merck, 1987; Bergmann et al., 2010). If the sideroblastic anemia is secondary to a hematological malignancy, one could expect abnormal leukocytes or thrombocytopenia. In addition, expect to find an elevated plasma ferritin and serum iron, in addition to high transferrin saturation (Merck, 1987). High ferritin occurs when there is excess iron; the unused iron is converted to ferritin and stored in the liver, spleen, and bone marrow. High levels of serum iron results from a disproportionally low concentration of hemoglobin for the available iron. This anemia can be distinguished from iron-deficiency anemia because the serum iron can be elevated, the transferrin concentration normal, and the percentage of iron saturation of transferrin elevated (Merck, 1987; 2013; Ali, 1976).

9.3.3 Anemia of Chronic Disease

On a worldwide basis, this is the second most common anemia, and within the hospital, medical and surgical settings, this form of anemia is certainly the most common. Anemia of chronic disease is mild and secondary to the acute/chronic response phase to infection, inflammation, and malignancy, and should therefore be considered normal for a clinical setting (Merck, 1987). There are several mechanisms occurring that may explain this mild anemia: reduced erythropoiesis and erythropoietin probably from disease-induced reactive oxygen species (ROS) derived from the synthesis of cytokines (Weiss & Goodnough, 2005). Additionally, there is a macrophage iron withholding, shortened red blood cell life span, a decline in iron absorption from the duodenum, and a small increase in plasma volume. The anemia in this setting acts as a compensatory mechanism to the trauma or infection by increasing the fluidity of the blood. In fact, the sequestration of iron into the reticuloendothelial system—earlier referred to as a macrophage iron withholding—may actually be beneficial as it keeps the iron from microorganisms, thus preventing the growth of pathogens (Weiss & Goodnough, 2005). It is therefore important to avoid an inappropriate diagnosis of iron deficiency anemia, but to closely study the multi-factorial dimensions of the problem. This mild anemia is often seen as a normocytic normochromic anemia (Weiss & Goonough, 2005; Ali, 1967) however, in the case of a chronic disease, persisting over many weeks and months, it is more likely to observe a microcytic hypochromic profile. At this advanced stage it becomes quite difficult to distinguish it from iron deficiency; doing a white cell differential and platelet count could help more clearly identify patients in an acute/ chronic phase reaction. The following laboratory markers represent the typical profile found in patients with an acute/chronic phase reaction:

1 MCV: normal or slightly reduced
2 Plasma ferritin: high or normal
3 Plasma iron: low
4 Transferrin: normal to low
5 Serum albumin: mildly reduced
6 Hyponatremia
7 Significant tissue damage: high lactate dehydrogenase
8 Total Iron Binding Capacity (TIBC): normal
9 Neutrophilia, lymphopenia and thrombocytosis (Gibson, 1990; Arthur & Isbister, 1987; Ali, 1967)

In anemia of chronic disease, there is a **mucosal block** at the level of the reticulo-endothelial (RE) cells, resulting in a reduced release of iron into the blood even though iron reserves overall may be satisfactory (Gibson, 1990). The reticuloendothelial (RE) system is a phagocytic network of fixed macrophages and monocytes located in the reticular connective tissue that surround the liver, kidney, and spleen (Encyclopedia Britannica, 2013; Strum et al., 2007). Because there is less iron released from the RE cells, the availability of iron to the red blood cells is reduced, therefore causing a build-up in erythrocyte protoporphyrin (EP), a precursor to heme. The reaction describing the role of iron (Fe) in hemoglobin synthesis is shown here (Ali, 1976):

$$EP + Fe \longrightarrow Hemoglobin$$

Hence, the rise in EP occurs in the absence of Fe and from the inability to completely form hemoglobin. The elevated EP mimics the response normally seen in iron-deficiency anemia. Contrary to the expected response, serum transferrin levels do not rise since iron reserves are not depleted. It is important to understand that transferrin concentrations generally increase in response to depleted iron reserves; in the anemia of chronic disease the iron reserves have not declined, therefore, transferrin synthesis is not stimulated. Also, in anemia of chronic disease, serum ferritin levels are not affected and nor is the MCV (Figure 9.6). Hence, in wanting to differentiate iron-deficiency anemia from anemia of chronic disease, a second level of testing is needed in order to get the desired confirmation before proceeding with treatment. The second step is done in concert with the patient's clinical history, thereby allowing the clinician to assess the impact of secondary underlying pathologies contributing to the patient's anemia. For instance, blood loss from GI inflammation or ulceration would confirm the likelihood of Fe-deficiency anemia. The "*four variable model*" has been successfully used to differentiate between anemia caused by inflammatory conditions and iron-deficiency anemia (Gibson, 1990). The four variables are outlined below:

a Serum ferritin

b Transferrin saturation and transferrin

c Erythrocyte protoporphyrin (EP)

d Mean corpuscular volume (MCV)

Iron-deficiency anemia can be diagnosed fairly accurately when the MCV or serum ferritin decline, concomitantly with one other abnormal parameter such as an elevated EP. A serum ferritin that declines to <25 ng/ml invariably implies a loss of iron reserves and therefore a high risk of iron deficiency anemia (Killip, 2007). A serum ferritin that varies between 30–100 ng/ml could indicate an anemia of chronic disease combined with true iron deficiency, and thus requires a third marker such as an elevated transferrin or low transferrin saturation to confirm iron deficiency anemia, or a normal to slightly reduced transferrin in the instance of an anemia of chronic disease (Weiss & Goodnought, 2005). On the other hand, a patient with a slightly elevated MCV or ferritin, and a high EP would not be diagnosed with Fe-deficiency anemia since the MCV and ferritin did not decrease. A patient presenting with a profile of low ferritin (<25mg/ml) and elevated erythrocyte protoporphyrin would likely be suffering from Fe-deficiency anemia. The decisive indication in the latter example is the low ferritin, since EP has also been found to increase in anemia of chronic disease (Killip, 2007; Gibson, 1990).

9.3.3.1 Uremia

This condition is seen in chronic renal failure and is associated with a decrease in renal excretory and regulatory function. Typically, anemia tends to develop when plasma creatinine increases to between 12–16 mg/dl or when the glomerular filtration rate (GFR) falls below 10% of normal (Merck, 2013d; Abuelo et al., 1992). There are a number of mechanisms contributing to the moderately severe normochromic and normocytic anemia typically seen in uremia: uremic toxins cause a suppression of bone marrow; the decrease in renal mass causes a deficiency in erythropoietin—a hormone produced by the kidney for the purpose of producing red blood cells in the bone marrow. Moreover, in renal dialysis (Figure 9.1), there is consistent blood loss. Hemolytic uremic syndrome and drug therapy can also be responsible for the occurrence of anemia (DHHS, 2014; Merck, 2013d).

9.3.3.2 Liver Disease

In 75% of the cases of chronic liver disease, anemia, resulting most often from blood loss, is frequently diagnosed. This is because of the deficiency of coagulation factors. Portal hypertension is also a common occurrence which generally leads to **splenomegaly** and to secondary hemolysis, increased blood volume, macrocytosis, and megaloblastic anemia. Alcohol can suppress bone marrow, and can cause malnutrition which can lead to folic acid deficiency. In addition, cirrhosis of the liver can cause a chronic haemorrhage into the GI tract, as well as a slow blood loss from gastric and esophageal varices. Over time the slow loss of blood produces iron deficiency anemia. In liver disease, anemia usually surfaces as a normochromic macrocytic anemia (MCV = 100–110 fL) (Gonzalez-Casas, et al., 2009).

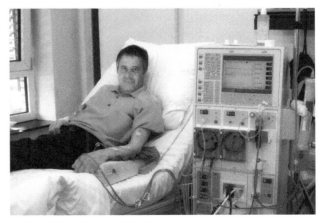

Credit © gopixa/shutterstock.com

Figure 9.1 *Patient undergoing dialysis*

9.3.3.3 Endocrine Disease

In hypothyroidism (myxedema) there is usually a mild anemia of unknown etiology that presents as normochromic and normocytic. A hypochromic anemia can occur that is caused by poor iron intake and absorption in addition to menorrhagia. The latter can go unnoticed or its severity can be masked because of a vasoconstriction, which occurs in order to reduce blood flow, and from a megaloblastic anemia derived from poor folate intake and/or absorption (Merck, 2012).

9.4 NUTRITIONAL ANEMIAS

9.4.1 Iron Deficiency Anemia

On the worldwide stage, iron deficiency anemia is the most common and most treatable of all anemias, affecting 24.8% of the world's population, and representing 50% of all types of anemias (de Benoist, 2008). It is also recognized as the single most important contributor to the burden of disease worldwide (WHO, 2002). The prevalence in developing countries among children is 46–51% and 42% among women (Pisciano, 1999). Although the preschool children and pregnant women, when expressed as a percentage, are most affected by iron-deficiency anemia, it is specially the non-pregnant women who encompass the greatest number of individuals—an estimated 468 million—suffering from iron-deficiency anemia (de Benoist, 2008). The causes appear to be associated with three main problems: 1) blood loss due to chronic bleeding typically seen in menorrhagia, slow GI and urinary tract bleeds, and blood loss from ulcers, colon polyps and cancers; 2) poor dietary intake of iron; and 3) an inability to absorb iron as seen in inflammatory bowel disease (DHHS, 2014). The most common presentation is fatigue, facial pallor, although the absence of pallor in ruling out anemia is not very reliable. Physicians will also check for pale gums and nail beds, irregular heartbeats, uneven breathing, and will conduct rectal and pelvic exams in search of internal bleeding (DHHS, 2014). Other symptoms such as koilonychia (spoon nails), glossitis, or dysphagia are uncommonly observed in the North American population (Killip et al., 2007).

9.4.1.1 Dietary Sources of Fe

Approximately 80% of the iron supplied by the North American diet is in the form of non-heme iron, which is abundantly found in legumes (lentils, soybeans, chick peas, navy beans), some fruits (prunes, apricots, raisins) and vegetables (spinach), grains, and cereals (DHHS, 2014), whereas the other 20% comes from animal protein-based heme iron. Breakfast cereals, enriched with iron, are sometimes a good source of iron, as they contain at least 10% of the RDA, but more often they are excellent sources of non-heme iron, with one serving containing 25%–50% of the RDA. The cereal brand "Total"® enriches many of their cereals with enough iron to meet 100% of the RDA; this is certainly a strategic way to meet daily iron requirements with very little effort (Figure 9.2). Animal sources of protein are elevated in heme-iron, which has a higher absorption rate. Red meats, liver, and eggs are examples of animal proteins rich in heme iron that are commonly found in the North American diet. Non-heme iron absorption is also facilitated by the ingestion of a protein compound found in meat, fish, or poultry, known as MFP factor. It functions by binding iron and forming a more easily absorbed complex (Stopler, 2004). Non-heme iron also has a

Credit © kiboka /shutterstock.com

Figure 9.2 *Breakfast rich in heme and non-heme iron.*

higher rate of absorption if consumed with a vitamin C-rich food sources such as citrus or orange juice (Gropper & Smith, 2013).

9.4.1.2 Those at Risk of Fe-Deficiency

Infants, children and women of child-bearing years are the three groups most vulnerable to iron deficiency. At birth, infants have between four to six months before the iron reserves of the body are depleted. It is for this reason that an infant cereal fortified with iron is usually introduced at that time. Infant formulas rich in iron are also available, but breast milk, though lower in iron content, has a much greater rate of absorption compared to infant formulas. It is however essential that breastfeeding mothers consume a diet rich in iron. Infants who consume junk food, or too much milk, can become iron deficient. The reason is that soft drinks, candies in addition to cow's milk are particularly poor sources of iron, and so, when consumed in excess, can displace good and excellent sources of iron out of the regular diet (DHHS, 2014). Women, who embrace weight-reducing diets, will tend to restrict meats, carbs and fats, in addition to avoiding breakfast in order to accelerate the weight loss process. This puts them particularly at risk of not ingesting sufficient iron. It is estimated that about 12% of women who live in industrialized countries suffer from iron deficiency anemia, and that the prevalence jumps to 43% among non-pregnant women residing in developing countries (Allen, 2000). In the United States 11% of women and 9% of adolescent girls and toddlers are believed to suffer from iron deficiency anemia (Looker et al., 1997). Surprisingly, as many as 54% of pregnant women, living in developing countries, and 18% residing in industrialized nations, have Fe-deficiency anemia, and thus are at greater risk of delivering low birth weight babies prematurely (DHHS, 2014; Allen, 2000). For this reason, most obstetricians working in the United States prescribe an iron supplement around the second trimester of pregnancy in compliance with the U.S. Preventive Services Task Force recommendations (USPSTF ,1996), which are consistent with current research findings (Killip et al., 2007). In developing countries, H. Pylori infestations are suspected of being associated with an increased risk of Fe-deficiency anemia, but the mechanism remains unknown (Wood & Ronnenberg, 2006).

With the increasing prevalence of bariatric surgical procedures to treat obesity, there is a documented rise in copper deficiencies—referred to as hypocupremia—which have been tied to a greater risk of iron deficiency anemias. It is specifically the involvement of copper in facilitating iron transport across the basolateral membrane of the intestine into the blood that is that is relevant to this discussion. The protein, haphaestin, found in the enterocytes of the GI tract is critical in oxidizing iron to is ferric form (Fe^{+3}) with the help of copper so that it can bind to the transferrin protein and be stored. In copper deficiency the body's ability to store iron is compromised (Chan & Mike, 2014)

The copper-transport protein, ceruloplasmin is also important in releasing stored iron from body reserves (Chan & Mike, 2014). Copper deficiency leads invariably to lower ceruloplasmin protein concentrations and less available iron.

9.4.1.3 Iron Metabolism

Dietary iron is absorbed mostly from the duodenum and combines with a glycoprotein, transferrin, which transports it to the bone marrow for the synthesis of hemoglobin, and for storage in tissue; residual iron is then attached to ferritin and stored in the liver, spleen, bone marrow, and reticulo-endothelial system (Gibson, 1990). There is no official excretory route for iron, therefore requiring that absorption be tightly controlled to ensure iron homeostasis and avoid toxicity. The amount of iron absorbed is pretty much dependent on the iron storage capacity and iron status of the body; the greater the deficiency in body stores, the more iron is absorbed from the duodenum. Indeed, up to 15% of non-heme iron and a maximum of 30–35% of heme iron intake can be absorbed when iron stores are low. In a non-deficient state only 5 to 10% of ingested iron (15 mg/d) is actually absorbed overall (Killip et al., 2007). Normally when there is a rich supply of iron stores, the body can slowly draw from this reserve to synthesize iron-rich erythrocytes (red blood cells). There are iron absorption enhancers that can be included in the diet, which enhance the non-heme iron absorption, most notably meat and vitamin C; there are also iron inhibitors, such as calcium and fiber, in addition to polyphenolic compounds such as the tannins found in wine, tea, and coffee that minimize the absorption of iron from the gut (Gropper and Smith, 2013; Killip et al., 2007). It is important to note the slowness at which iron can be mobilized for the synthesis of hemoglobin. In an acute hemorrhage, the rapid loss of iron from the body cannot be easily compensated, by reaching into body iron stores, even though there may be a rich reserve. The end result is the release, from the bone marrow, of a number of iron-deficient hypochromic erythrocytes in an acute blood loss; overall, however, the blood film may show either polychromatic or normochromic cells.

9.4.1.4 The Stages of Iron Depletion

Iron-deficiency anemia can have several causes: 1) poor dietary intake, especially in premature infants; 2) menstruation in women and hemo-dilution in pregnancy; 3) occult blood losses in men and postmenopausal women; 4) decreased iron absorption because of the gut infestation of hookworm, and the presence of phytates and phenolic compounds in the diet (de Benoist, 2008).

There are three main stages of iron depletion (Figure 9.3) and at each stage specific markers can be used to assess the degree of depletion of body iron reserves. The **first stage** is characterized by the gradual depletion of iron stores with which NO physical symptoms can be associated. Very promptly the serum ferritin decreases. This is considered the most sensitive marker of the depletion of iron reserves, and thus as an early screening for the risk of iron-deficiency anemia, but it is NOT the most specific. The **second stage** is referred to as "*iron deficiency without anemia.*" In this stage can be observed, the beginning of the transferrin saturation-declining phase, the gradual increase in erythrocyte protoporphyrin, and a mild decline in hemoglobin; levels may be slightly above or below the cut-off point. The second stage is short-lived, and the changes in blood markers may not be accentuated enough to raise any concern. The **third stage** is the most advanced and is referred to as "iron deficiency anemia." At this stage the hemoglobin has significantly decreased,

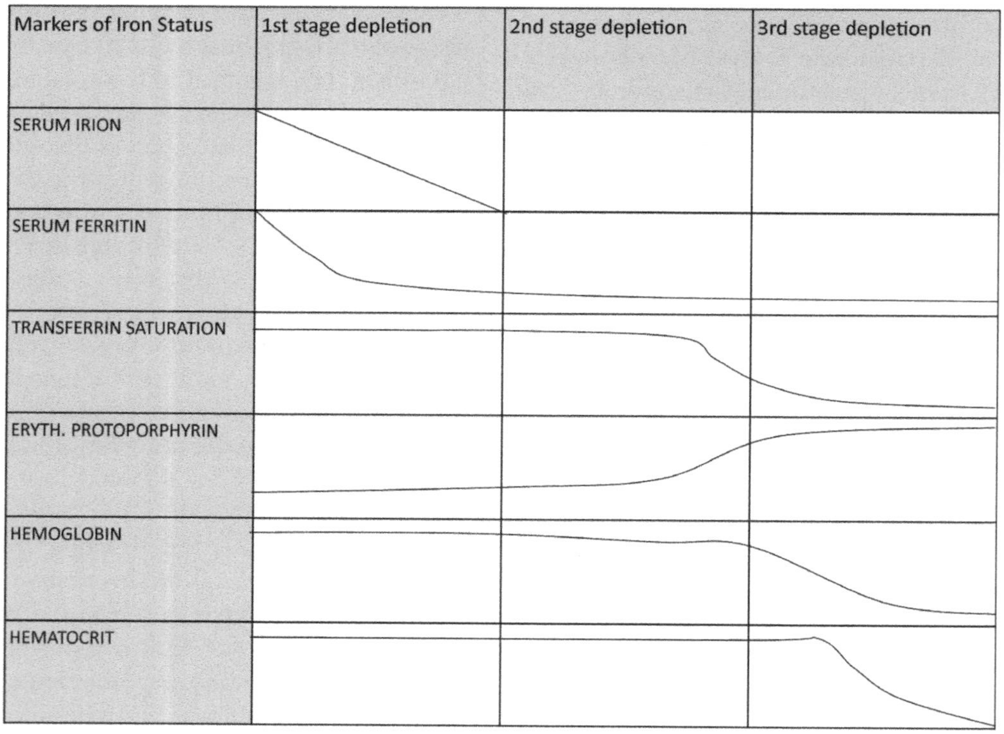

Markers of Iron Status	1st stage depletion	2nd stage depletion	3rd stage depletion
SERUM IRION			
SERUM FERRITIN			
TRANSFERRIN SATURATION			
ERYTH. PROTOPORPHYRIN			
HEMOGLOBIN			
HEMATOCRIT			

Source: Adapted from Gibson, 1990

[1] *Serum iron should be taken while fasting in the morning.*

Figure 9.3 *Effect of iron deficiency on specific markers of anemias.*

transferrin saturation is at its lowest, erythrocyte protoporphyrin (EP) is quite elevated, the MCV should be small, indicating a microcytic anemia, and the MCH should also be low, indicating hypochromia. The hematocrit is not all that sensitive and will only tend to decline once hemoglobin levels have plummeted (Gibson, 1990).

9.4.1.5 Markers of Iron-Deficiency Anemia

There are several markers used to assess iron deficiency anemia, however, none of them are specific enough to be used alone to identify iron deficiency with 100% certainty. In the assessment of anemias, the following markers are frequently used (see Figure 9.3 for marker vs. stage of iron depletion).

1 Hemoglobin
2 Hematocrit
3 Serum iron
4 Red cell indices
5 Erythrocyte protoporphyrin (EP)
6 TIBC + Transferrin saturation + Serum ferritin

Hemoglobin and **hematocrit** are considered very good markers of anemia, but abnormal values are not specific to iron-deficiency (Gibson, 1990) and it is not until the late stages of iron deficiency anemia that abnormal values become visible. In fact, hematocrit concentrations tend only to decrease once hemoglobin synthesis is impaired. The **serum-iron** Total Binding Capacity (TIBC) is done by most labs at the same time and from these values **serum-transferrin saturation** can be derived [(s-iron/ TIBC) x 100]. The transferrin saturation is by far the most sensitive to Fe-deficiency compared to serum iron and TIBC. The serum iron is a measure of the iron bound to transferrin; it is subject to both large day-to-day variability and within-day variability, so much so that serum iron in itself is not regarded as a reliable index as there can be up to 50% variability due to diurnal changes alone. The TIBC, on the other hand, is not subject to diurnal changes; it increases in states of iron depletion and decreases in cases of iron overload and in inflammatory conditions. The TIBC reflects the number of free iron-binding sites located on the transferrin protein. The **erythrocyte protoporphyrin (EP)** is a more stable marker of iron reserves than transferrin saturation. It begins to increase quite noticeably in the third

stage of iron depletion. This marker, however, is incapable of differentiating between a depletion of body reserves of iron and the impact of a mucosal block resulting from inflammation (Gibson, 1990).

The American Medical Association (AMA) guidelines recommend monitoring hemoglobin and hematocrit over four weeks following the prescription of an iron supplement. This is considered the most cost effective approach. The improvement of these markers (Hb >1–2 g/dl; Hct >3%) every two to three weeks with the iron challenge, confirms the iron deficiency anemia. Treatment involves a continuation of iron supplementation for another two months and referral to a dietitian who will teach nutritional guidelines for high iron intake. Should these markers be normal or not influenced by the challenge, consider the possibility of being in the early stage of anemia and monitor serum-ferritin (s-ferritin); a value <25 ng/mL confirms a depletion of iron stores (Figure 9.6). Serum ferritin >100 ng/ ml is recognized as indicative of normal iron stores. If hemoglobin concentrations remain low and unresponsive to supplements the likelihood of continued blood loss must also be envisioned or anemia of chronic disease (Figure 9.6). Many clinicians generally expect a normalization of hemoglobin after four months of daily supplement use (Killip et al., 2007). It is however noteworthy that a ferrous fumarate supplement is considered a redox-active form of iron that is capable of catalysing free radical production in the form of peroxides. In iron-deficient animals, studies have shown the intestine to be particularly susceptible to peroxidative damage with intake of iron supple-mentation. It appears that the manganese superoxide dismutase activity, the enzyme responsible for free radical detoxification in the mitochondria, tends to drop with iron supplementation (Picciano, 1999).

9.4.1.6 Avoiding the Misdiagnosis of Iron Deficiency Anemia

Some attention must be placed on minimizing the chances of misdiagnosing iron-deficiency anemia. Various pathologies or clinical situations can affect the typical markers that are relied on for the diagnosis of iron-deficiency anemia: **first**, iron-deficiency anemia and anemias resulting from genetic abnormalities (thalassemia, sideroplastic anemia) can influence similar blood markers. **Second**, anemias of chronic disease can often lead to a misdiagnosis of iron-deficiency anemia when, in fact, there can be more serious underlying infections, inflammations, or malignancies. Refer back to the earlier section that describes this anemia. The problem is that inflammatory conditions can mimic or mask some of the changes in iron deficiency anemia (Lichtin, 2013c). **Third**, copper (Cu) deficiency affects a variety of enzyme systems one of which causes a decrease in ceruloplasmin, a key transport protein, which carries iron to erythropoietic sites; the consequence is a hypochromic anemia. This should not be considered a major problem, as Cu deficiency is very rare. Incidences of Cu deficiency have, however, been reported in cases of chronic diarrhea, and chronic protein losses (nephritic syndrome, protein losing enteropathy (Gibson 1990). **Fourth**, anemia can result from blood loss. Initially the blood film will be polychromatic (some hypochromic) and the MCV will be slightly elevated because of compensatory reticulocyte activity (reticulocytosis), which is the production of large immature red blood cells. Afterwards, hemoglobin concentrations will begin to fall. As blood loss progresses, the iron stores are gradually depleted, leading to microcytic (small MCV) and afterwards, the MCH begins to fall (low MCH) and finally the MCHC decreases. The anemia profile typically seen in a hemorrhaging patient will also include the following changes:

a Serum iron: low
b TIBC: high
c Plasma ferritin: low

It is important that an underlying hemorrhage not go unnoticed. Generally, this is not a problem as the blood loss is usually associated with pain. However, there are exceptions to the rule, which may cause the blood loss to either be overlooked or delay its recognition: 1) in the case of psychiatrically disturbed patients or patients with head injuries, in whom pain and blood loss may not be noticed or reported; 2) an occult GI hemorrhage may not produce the typical episode of hypotension and the expected melena (black tar-like stool) may be delayed; 3) the initial stages of a retroperitoneal hemorrhage may be silent; 4) in trauma patients, undiagnosed occult hemorrhage can go unnoticed as the dark blood particulate leaks out gradually and imperceptibly. The gastroenterologist will order a fecal occult blood test to confirm the presence of blood; the key concept is that trauma can seize the peristaltic movements of the intestine and greatly lengthen the transit time of the stool creating constipation or fecal impaction; and finally 5) it may quite impossible to accurately localize pain in patients with multiple soft tissue injuries.

Fifth, anemia can also be the consequence of hemolysis: the separation of hemoglobin from the red blood cell and the rupture of the red blood cell membrane (Lichtin, 2013). This is a tricky domain to move into, yet it is also a very important diagnosis to establish since it may be present in such a wide range of diseases. For this level textbook, suffice to briefly review the different presentations of hemolysis. The first suspicion that hemolysis may be occurring is when the blood film reveals anemia with polychromasia (multiple colors). This often occurs when numerous reticulocytes—young red blood cells that are larger in size and different in color—are suddenly released from the bone marrow to compensate for the hemolysis of the erythrocytes; the consequence is **reticulocytosis** or overabundance of reticulocytes (Lichtin, 2013).

The presence of red or brown plasma, the consequence of abundantly circulating free hemoglobin, in concert with dark urine also suggests hemolysis; likewise yellow plasma, which occurs with unconjugated hyperbilirubinemia, and jaundice takes place when the rate at which hemoglobin is converted to bilirubin exceeds the liver's capacity (Lichtin, 2013). Acute hemolysis is commonly found in shock or septic patients who have an impaired bilirubin transport. In this scenario the bilirubin becomes conjugated and the blood profile shows a conjugated hyperbilirubinemia. In cases of acute or chronic intravascular hemolysis, one should expect to find hemosiderinuria or significant hemoglobin filtered through the kidneys into the urine (Rivera, 2013). A high circulating lactic acid dehydrogenase is also typically seen when there is red blood cell destruction as is expected in hemolysis or in an ineffective erythropoiesis (Lichtin, 2013b).

9.4.1.7 Strategic Steps in Diagnosing Fe-Deficiency Anemia

The final diagnosis of iron-deficiency anemia requires some competence in reading the various plasma markers. There are several steps to follow in attempting to diagnose iron deficiency anemia. The **initial screening** (previously described) involves deriving from the complete blood count (CBC) consisting of hemoglobin, hematocrit, white blood cell count (WBC), WBC differential, platelet count, and red blood cell morphology, information pertaining to the red cell indices. Based on the red cell indices, the anemia can be classified as either microcytic and hypochromic, normocytic and normochromic or as macrocytic and normochromic. The microcytic and hypochromic profile in the red cell indices is diagnosed when MCHC is < 320 g/L and the MCV is ≤ 80 fL (Johnson-Wimbley, 2011) (Table 9.1). This kind of anemia occurs usually when there is a severe depletion of the iron reserve, which takes place late in the second and into the third stages (Figure 9.3). These changes in the red cell indices can give the clinician the first hint that iron status is part of the etiology, but does not confirm it since thalassemia and congenital sideroblastic anemia also produce low MCV and MCH (Gibson, 1990). The second phase consists of monitoring serum hemoglobin and hematocrit. These a popularly measured, but they only reflect advanced (stage-3) depletion. Should these markers be suboptimal, then an improvement with iron supplement, will confirm Fe-deficiency anemia. The third phase should involved a few more markers that are more revealing. For instance, transferrin saturation <16% along with a TIBC >400 mcg/dl would infer a high likelihood of Fe-deficiency anemia, especially if the EP >70 mcg/dl (NIH, 2014; Gropper & Smith, 2013).

9.5 INTRODUCTION TO MEGALOBLASTIC AND MACROCYTIC ANEMIAS

The objective of this section is to further explore the nutritional-based anemias and thus, a logical progression is to move towards megaloblastic anemia. However, for the sake of clarity, it is important to point out that megaloblastosis comes under the much larger umbrella of macrocytosis. This is a more generalized state that refers simply to larger than normal erythrocytes. The causes of these large RBC are many, however it suffices for now, to mention that macrocytic anemia can be non-megaloblastic if it is secondary to the following conditions (Snow, 1999):

1 Alcohol, drugs, smoking
2 Liver disease
3 Reticulocytosis
4 Marrow disease
5 Myelodisplastic syndromes
6 Hypothyroidism
7 Dyserythropoiesis

Megaloblastic anemia is represented by large ovalocytic erythrocytes, and arises from defects in DNA synthesis, which affect nuclear maturity by preventing the mitotic division of the cell located in the marrow

Table 9.1
Standard Reference Ranges for Red Cell Indices

RED CELL INDICES	CALCULATION	HYPOCHROMIC MICROCYTIC	NORMOCHROMIC NORMOCYTIC	NORMOCHROMIC MACROCYTIC
MCV	HEMATOCRIT / RBC	≤80 fL	84–100 fL	> 100 fL
MCH	HEMOGLOBIN / RBC	low — 5–25 pg	normal — 26–32 pg	high — 33–53 pg
MCHC	HEMOGLOBIN / HEMATOCRIT	200-300 g/L	320–360 g/L	330-380 g/L

Klusek-Hamilton (Eds), H. (1984). Diagnostics: Nurses' Reference. *Springhouse PA: Springhouse Corporation, 1133 pp; Johnson-Wimbley. (2011).*

(Snow, 1999). In contrast, cytoplasmic mass and maturation continue to increase because of uninhibited RNA synthesis. Hence, there is advanced cytoplasmic hemoglobinization in comparison to the nucleus therefore resulting in a greater mean corpuscular volume (MCV). The megaloblastic state is almost always tied to folate and/or B-12 deficiencies. However, they can also result from the intake of some drugs and inborn errors of metabolism. If megaloblastosis can be established with elevated MCV (fl >130)—above this cut-off there is a greater certainty of low B-12 (cobalamin-Cbl), folate or both (Snow, 1999)—then it may not be necessary to do a bone marrow study in order to confirm the diagnosis. However, a bone marrow examination remains a helpful option in cases of multifactorial anemias. For instance, MCV is known to remain quite normal in a state of microcytic anemia combined with megaloblastosis (Snow, 1999).

9.6 ETIOLOGY AND PATHOPHYSIOLOGY OF B-12 DEFICIENCY

The main cause of B-12 deficiency is decreased absorption which, in 90% of patients with B-12 deficiency, is reflected by a serum B-12 <74 pmol/L (Snow, 1999). However, contrary to most other B vitamins, the body is able to store up to between 2–5 mg of cobalamin (Cbl), and will reutilize the Cbl via the enterohepatic circulation. Consequently, it takes between two to five years before neurological symptoms of deficiency begin to appear (Snow, 1999). There are many reasons why absorption could be compromised. From a medical/nutritional view point, the most likely causes of B-12 malabsorption are:

1 Failure of gastric parietal cells/mucosa to secrete IF
   – Gastrectomy
   – Chronic atrophic gastritis
   – Myxedema

2 Competition for available B-12 and cleavage of IF
   – Blind loop syndrome
   – Fish tapeworm infestation

3 Destroyed or absent ileal absorptive sites
   – Inflammatory enteritis
   – Surgical resection

4 Chronic pancreatitis

5 Malabsorption syndromes

6 Certain drug therapies (oral calcium chelating agents, aminosalicylic acid, biguanadines)

There are two relatively frequent causes of B-12 deficiency in North American society. The most prevalent occurrence is seen in gastric-bypass patients, who are now more numerous because of the obesity epidemic. There are about 113,000 bariatric surgeries performed every year in the United States at a cost of $1.3 billion per year (Livingston, 2010); the second most prevalent in Western society is related to an autoimmune disorder called Addisonian pernicious anemia. It is diagnosed mostly in those >50 years of age, who suffer from gastric mucosa atrophy of the fundus, which is associated with parietal cell antibodies seen in 90% of patients. It is noteworthy that very rarely are tests for gastric mucosa atrophy ever indicated. In addition, anti-thyroid antibodies, reported in 50% of patients and anti-intrinsic factor antibodies in 60% of cases characteristically describe this condition, and could help confirm the diagnosis of Addisonian pernicious anemia (Merck, 1987b).

9.6.1 Diagnostic Approaches to Identifying B12 Deficiency

In patients that present with unexplained macrocytosis, either folate or cobalamin deficiencies are generally suspected, but most often the cause is likely a B-12 deficiency causing **pernicious anemia**. Following a normal timeline, MCV size would tend to increase before any significant decline in hemoglobin became evident. MCV dimensions equal to or exceeding 100 fL tend to indicate macrocytosis, but clinical studies have shown that an MCV >130 fL, more accurately predicts low vitamin B-12 and/or folate concentrations (Snow, 1999). Caution is advised here, as it is possible to observe normal MCV values despite Cbl or folate deficiency, especially within the context of Fe deficiency anemia or thalassemia. In instances of neurological manifestations such as paresthesias and ataxia, Cbl deficiency is considered a very likely contributor to the etiology of pernicious anemia. It is generally accepted that hematological abnormalities show up before the onset of neurological symptoms, however, more than 25% of patients presenting with Cbl-based neurological symptoms have either a normal hematocrit or a normal MCV. In some cases, both the MCV and hematocrit are normal (Snow, 1999).

The advent of folic acid supplements, which are biologically active, has masked B-12 deficiency in many instances. Whereas it was possible for a physician, upon observing macrocytic erythrocytes to ponder whether the cause was folate or B-12 deficiencies or both, it is now more difficult to do so as megaloblastic cells are less prevalent now that folic acid supplements keep the problem of megaloblastosis in check. Nevertheless, folic acid supplements do not prevent the neurological anomalies associated with B-12 deficiency, and so the pernicious nature of B-12 deficiency goes unnoticed until later on, often years later (Snow, 1999).

Serum Cobalamin: The specificity of low serum Cbl as a predictor of B-12 deficiency is variable. Using a cut-off of <74 pmol/L, some have found a specificity of 90%. Translated into laymen terms, this means that 9 times out 10 a person without Cbl deficiency will not have a serum B-12 that is <74 pmol/L. **Specificity** refers to the proportion of individuals without the disorder who exhibit normal blood values or in other words negative results. This means that, should a patient's serum Cbl value fall <74 pmol/L, he would likely have a Cbl deficiency (Snow, 1999).

Schilling Test: This test is recommended once a B-12 deficiency has been confirmed, and the clinician wants to determine if the cause is B-12 malabsorption due to the absence of intrinsic factor (IF) (Gibson, 1990). Briefly the technique has two stages: **Stage 1** consists of administering an oral dose of crystalline Cbl, containing radioactive cobalt, and then, measuring the amount of radiolabeled Cbl in a 24hr urine collection. Patients with **pernicious anemia** excrete less than 3% of the dose, whereas non-deficient patients have greater than 8% of the administered dose in the urine (Gibson, 1990). If the value is abnormally low, then **stage 2** is implemented. In this second step, an oral administration of labelled Cbl and IF is given 3 to 7 days later. If urine values, subsequently collected are normal,

then it can be inferred that IF factor was truly missing (Snow, 1999).

Limitations of the Schilling Test: There could still be a problem even if the stage 2 results were normal. In instances of partial IF deficiency or gastric hypochlorhydria, crystalline Cbl—used in the Schilling's test—would likely be more easily absorbed than the protein bound Cbl normally encountered in food; the Schilling's test would, in this situation, be producing false negative results. Inadequate urine collection is another popular reason for false results. In cases of a dysfunctional ileum, caused by Cbl deficiency, the Cbl-IF complex is malabsorbed. This can however be reversed with prolonged Cbl administration. In renal insufficiency there is a delay in the urinary excretion of labelled Cbl, therefore producing false positive results (Snow, 1999).

Modified Food Schilling Test: Rather than using crystalline Cbl, radioactive B-12 is incorporated into food products like chicken, eggs or egg albumin and fed to patients. This method can correctly diagnose poor absorption of protein bound Cbl and would be relevantly applied to elderly with low gastric acidity (Fernández-Bañares et al., 2009; Gibson, 1990).

The **deoxiuridine (dU) Suppression Test** is capable of determining a B-12 and/or folate deficiency using bone marrow. The test is done by adding either cobalamin or methyl-tetra-hydrofolate to bone marrow culture. The vitamin that decreases the suppression of H-thymidine incorporation into DNA is the deficient vitamin (Gibson, 1990). The test can also be adapted to measure chronic B-12 and folate status using lymphocytes rather than bone marrow (Gibson, 1990).

Antiparietal Cell Antibodies: This is a fairly sensitive test as these antibodies are present in 85% of patients suffering from the autoimmune gastritis of pernicious anemia. They are very non-specific with detectable concentrations in patients with a variety of autoimmune endocrinopathies (Snow, 1999).

Anti-Intrinsic Factor Antibodies: This is an insensitive test as only 50% of patients with pernicious anemia have detectable levels of these antibodies. It is however very specific; thus it is possible to rule out pernicious anemia using this test. In other words, these antibodies are rarely seen in healthy individuals (Snow, 1999).

9.7 CHARACTERISTICS OF FOLATE

Folic acid is a term that refers to the chemical compound, pteroylglutamic acid, which is the synthetic and active form that is added to food by the food industry. Folic acid also refers to the more generalized class of compounds called folates, which exhibit similar nutritional activity. Folates are actively absorbed mostly from the jejunum, although the folate from milk tends to be absorbed in the ileum because of a specific folate-binding protein. Folate becomes active when its methyl group is removed; methyl-tetrahydrofolate (MTHF) becomes active de-methylated tretrahydrofolate (THF), and vitamin B-12 is critical in the removal of the methyl group from THF. Without B-12, folate remains trapped in an inactive form thus interfering with DNA synthesis, which is needed for mitotic red blood cell division. The absence of active folate is responsible for the generation of large immature red blood cells (megaloblastic), typically observed as large MCVs >100 fl, but is not linked to pernicious anemia; the latter is strictly the consequence of B-12 deficiency. Interestingly, a B-12 deficiency can however cause a deficiency in active folate, thus producing megaloblastic cells in addition to neurological impairment (Gibson, 1990). In that sense, megaloblastic and pernicious anemias can be morphologically identical, however, pernicious anemia can also be non-megaloblastic, exhibiting only neurological symptoms which are manifested as losses in sensation, loss of lower limb motor power from myelin degeneration in the spinal cord, therefore resulting in a disturbed gait. Although the preferred treatment for megaloblastic pernicious anemia is monthly intramuscular (i.m) 100 mg injections of vitamin B-12, megaloblastic anemia can also be overcome with large doses of folate; synthetic folic acid (pteroylglutamic acid) does not require cobalamin as a cofactor as it is already in its reduced active THF form. In contrast, large doses of dietary folate will do nothing to correct the neurological abnormalities if there is B-12 deficiency, since inactive folate requires B-12 to be activated to THF. Because the inactive methyl-tetrahydrofolate requires homocysteine in order to become demethylated and active, it is understandable that a folate deficiency will cause the buildup of homocysteine (Hcy) (Figure 9.4) in the blood, whereas the increase of both homocysteine and methylmalonic acid (MMA) (Figure 9.5) is usually indicative of a vitamin B-12 deficiency (Snow, 1999). This is illustrated in the case report described by Stabler (2013) in which a 57-year-old woman presented with serum MMA equal to 3600 nmol/L and a serum Hcy of 49.1 mcmol/L, both values significantly greater than normal—serum

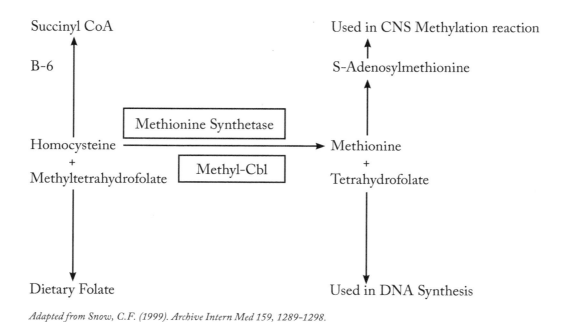

Adapted from Snow, C.F. (1999). Archive Intern Med 159, 1289-1298.

Figure 9.4 *Synthesis of methionine from homocysteine.*

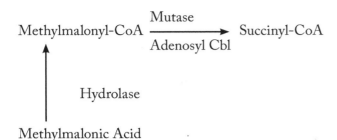

Figure 9.5 *Conversion of methylmalonyl-CoA to succinyl-CoA.*

MMA that is normal is <400 pmol/L, and normal Hcy is <14mcmol/L. Despite a serum Hcy indicative of a possible folate deficiency, the MCV was normal at 96fL. Even though the serum B-12 was not <74pmol/L, it was nevertheless suboptimal at 151 pmol/L. The absence of megaloblastosis in combination with a normal hematocrit of 42% precludes a normal MCV derived from microcytic anemia countering a megaloblastic anemia (Stabler, 2013).

The enzyme methionine synthetase (Figure 9.4) receives a methyl group from the donor, 5-methyl–THF, and transfers it to cobalamin for the generation of methyl cobalamin (Figure 9.4). The latter becomes the methyl donor to homocysteine for the production of methionine and THF. The activity of methionine synthetase requires adequate amounts of cobalamin.

A dietary folate deficiency therefore implies a poor availability of methyl-THF and thus a decreased availability of methyl groups; the consequence is a buildup of homocysteine. Notable, is the role played by pyridoxal phosphate (vitamin B-6) in favoring the chemical transformation of homocysteine to succinyl CoA (Gropper & Smith, 2013). Though it would be rare, this implies that a B-6 deficiency could ultimately cause a likely increase in serum homocysteine.

The graph (Figure 9.4) infers that a B-12 deficiency would prevent the methyl group transfer from occurring even though there may be abundant methyl THF in the diet; the consequence here is very little methyl-THF changing into the more active THF, again causing homocysteine concentrations in the blood to increase. It is essential to clearly point out that folate deficiency alone cannot result in neurological disorders; there must be B-12 deficiency, however a B-12 deficiency can cause both

neurological degeneration and megaloblastosis. Folic acid supplementation would bypass this problem. Since it is already biologically active, the synthetic folic acid would not require vitamin B-12 to gain the active form. Thus, neurological abnormalities would occur in the absence of an MCV >100 fl.

Cobalamin is also a needed co-factor in the conversion of methyl-malonyl-coenzyme A (CoA) to succinyl-CoA (Figure 9.5). Hence, in a Cbl deficiency state, methyl-malonyl-CoA and its hydrolysis product, methyl malonic acid (MMA) will increase; the latter is a useful diagnostic marker. Indeed, elevated MMA singularly occurs in only B-12 deficiency (Carmel, 2006; Snow, 1999).

9.8 ETIOLOGY AND PATHOPHYSIOLOGY OF FOLATE DEFICIENCY

The primary cause of folate deficiency is a suboptimal dietary intake, resulting from the inadequate intake of fruits and vegetable specifically, but also from the infrequent consumption of fortified breads, and breakfast cereals, and liver in particular. A deficiency can also occur by chronically overcooking vegetables, as folate is unstable at high temperatures (NIH, 2016; USNLM, 2015; Carmel, 2006).

There are multiple secondary causes for a folate deficiency, but only the most significant ones will be discussed here (Carmel, 2006; USNLM, 2015; NIH, 2016).

1 inadequate absorption: this is frequently seen in malabsorption disorders such as tropical sprue, celiac disease, and inflammatory bowel disease. Drugs such as sulfasalazine, contraceptives and aminosalicylic can interfere with absorption.

2 inadequate utilization: metabolic blocking of folate can occur with drugs like methotrexate and trimethoprim-sulfamethoxazole, pyrimethamine and triamterene, which are dehydrofolate reductase inhibitors.

3 increased requirements: pregnancy, lactation, premature infants, and patients undergoing hemodyalisis have heightened requirements for folate.

9.9 DIAGNOSTIC APPROACHES TO B-12 AND FOLATE DEFICIENCY

A strategic approach should always be about getting the right information in order to make a decision on the kind of treatment that is needed. To do so, the clinician must take into account the sensitivity of the test, the cost, and turnover time to run a particular test in addition to the value of the knowledge that can be derived from the test. In keeping with such a rationale, it is then advisable to begin by using a broad test, which can capture several problems and then proceed to a more specific test, which, in concert with physical symptoms, can help confirm the diagnosis. In the context of anemia, the first step would be to determine the existence of either macro or microcytosis and then attempt to determine if it is megaloblastic in nature.

The second step consists of a series of biochemical tests that can be used to confirm B-12 and folate deficiencies; these are listed below. In terms of practical and cost efficient approaches to diagnosing such deficiencies, serum values, although not indicative of the extent of body stores, can nevertheless be useful in predicting a likelihood of deficient stores, especially in cases when serum values fall below certain cutoff limits. The following markers can be used to monitor folate and cobalamin (Cbl) status (Snow, 1999; Gibson, 1990).

1 **Serum folate: reflects recent folate intake** (<3 ug/L is the lower cut-off limit, indicative of an acute low folate status).

   a Chronically low concentrations for longer than one month reflect a high likelihood of depleted folate stores.

   b Hemolysis may cause high serum folate.

   c Liver damage and renal failure equates to high folate levels.

   d Contraceptives + smoking equates to low folate.

   e Alcohol intake can cause short term decreases in serum folate.

   f Serum folate tends to increase in patients with Cbl deficiency. The impairment of the methionine synthetase pathway leads to an increase of the inactive MTHF, which is the principal form of serum in the blood

2 **Erythrocyte folate: reflect body stores** (<160 ng/mL is indicative of deficiency), however for an accurate interpretation it is important to consider the following (Snow, 1999; Gibson, 1990).

   a Not specific to folate deficiency, as values also decrease in B-12 deficiency. In fact, 60% of patients with pernicious anemia have low RBC folate

   b Important to assay for serum B-12 in addition to erythrocyte folate.

   c Erythrocyte concentrations of folate tend to increase in conditions involving hemorrhage or hemolysis, concomitantly with the rise in reticulocyte count and also in cases of Fe-deficiency anemia. The reticulocytes contain higher concentrations of folate compared to the older erythrocytes (Gibson, 1990).

   d There is a possibility of Fe-deficiency masking a folate deficiency.

   e Erythrocyte folate tends to be less sensitive to short term variances in dietary intake and therefore is more reflective of storage and status.

3 **Red cell indices**

   a MCV: Elevated in folate deficiency and sometimes in B-12 deficiency.

   b MCH: normal or slightly elevated: Cells are laden with hemoglobin but there are fewer cells.

4 **Serum Methylmalonic Acid.** Elevated values tend to mostly reflect Cbl deficiency however in 12% of cases folate deficiency is also reported. In cases of normal serum MMA, Cbl deficiency is rarely reported.

5 **Serum Homocysteine.** Elevated serum Hcy is invariably associated with Cbl and folate deficiencies. In the instance of normal Hcy, there is a small likelihood of either Cbl or folate deficiencies.

Iron-Define
ANEMIA ALGORITHM

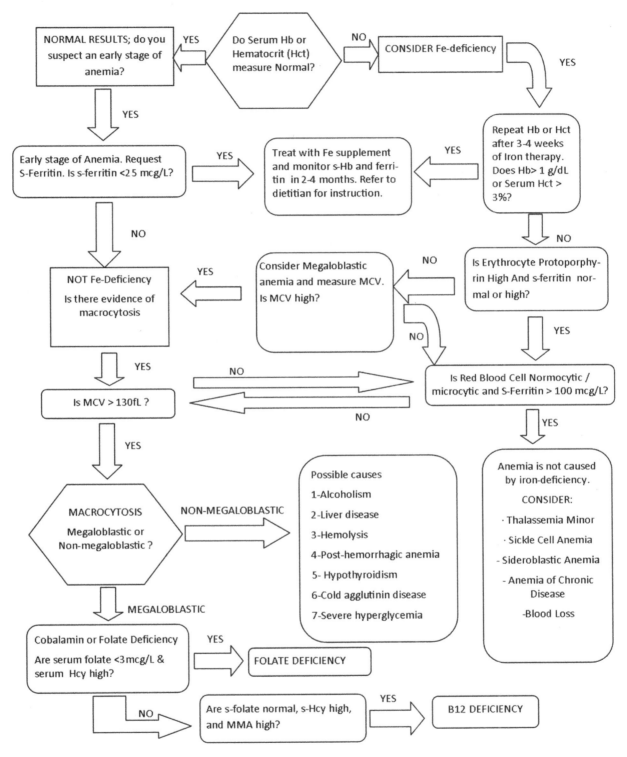

Adapted from Gibson, 1990; Killip, et al. 2007; Snow, 1999.

Figure 9.6 *Anemia algorithm.*

Table 9.2

Evaluation of Patients with Hematological Abnormalities and Normal Serum Cbl

SERUM FOLATE	SERUM MMA	SERUM HCY	INTERPRETATION
Normal	Normal	Normal	Neither Cbl or folate deficiency is likely
Normal	Normal	Elevated	Possible Cbl deficiency
Normal	Elevated	Normal	Possible Cbl deficiency
Normal	Elevated	Elevated	Probable Cbl deficiency
Low	Normal	Normal	Possible Cbl deficiency
Low	Normal	Elevated	High probability of folate deficiency
Low	Elevated	Normal	Possible Cbl deficiency or folate & Cbl deficiency
Low	Elevated	Elevated	High probability of B-12 & folate deficiency, but cannot distinguish type of deficiency. Need to consider a therapeutic trial *

1. Adapted from Snow, CF. Archiv of Internal Med. 1999; 159: 1289–1298.

* S–metabolite levels tend to normalize 7–14 d after nutritional replacement therapy

6 **S-Hcy, S-MMA and S-Folate:** Rather than rely on only one marker, there is greater diagnostic value in referring to a combination of three markers. Table 9.2 illustrates the diagnostic strengths in using these three markers.

7 **Polymorphonuclear leukocyte lobe count**. The hypersegmentation of the neutrophils generally precedes the development of macrocytosis and is a main early feature of folate and B-12 deficiencies. This test would become useful in attempting to confirm folate and B-12 deficiency in a situation involving a macrocytosis that is masked by iron-deficiency anemia—red blood cells appear normocytic. In such a case the MCV would be normal but other indices would be suggesting low iron reserves. The paradoxical normal MCV, in this context, should cause the clinician to question the findings.

9.10 PRACTICE PROBLEM SET IN ANEMIA

The two next problem sets will give students the opportunity to examine the blood profile of various types of anemias. The questions are the same for all three profiles. First, what can you conclude from the profile at hand, and second, what other markers would you need to confirm the diagnosis.

9.10.1 Problem Set-1. A woman age 20 presents with symptoms of tiredness and facial pallor.

The lab sends the physician the results of the blood test, who in turn reports them in the chart.

	Lab Values	Reference Values
Serum iron	0.62 mg/L	0.8–1.5 mg/L
TIBC	4.42 mg/L	3.0–4.5 mg/L
Erythrocyte protoporphyrin	1.10 mg/L	0.4–0.7 mg/L

What can you conclude from the blood values?

ANSWER: Serum Iron is low, which is consistent with iron deficiency anemia, however not reliable since serum iron is subject to diurnal variations. Serum iron is typically seen in chronic inflammation and pregnancy. Serum iron cut-off of <0.60 mg/L is almost stage-II iron deficient erythropoiesis (Gibson, 1990).

Erythrocyte protoporphyrin is elevated, which is consistently found in iron deficiency anemia and in a mucosal block defect observed in anemia of chronic disease; the latter prevents the release of iron from the reticulo-endothelial cells of the liver, spleen and bone marrow, and despite the abundance of iron reserves in the body. This mucosal block subsequently hinders the transport of iron to the erythrocyte, causing a rise in EP. The very high EP seen in this case should coincide with a transferrin saturation <16% if it is Fe-deficiency anemia. The transferrin saturation is calculated (s-iron/TIBC) x 100 and found to be = (0.62/4.42) x 100 = 14%. In addition, TIBC should increase in Fe-deficiency anemia.

TIBC: It is necessary to consider the TIBC as it remains within the normal range. This means the total number of free iron-binding sites on transferrin have not increased because more transferrin was not synthesized in response to depleted body iron reserves.

MOST LIKELY DIAGNOSIS: The evidence seems to point to a Fe-deficiency anemia. Facial pallor, elevated EP, and suboptimal transferrin saturation, having dipped below the cut-off limit of 16%, indicate possible stage-2 or 3 iron depletion (Gibson, 1990). The problem is that TIBC, normally higher in iron-deficiency anemia, is within the normal range. Moreover, % transferrin saturation is also known to decline in anemia of chronic disease.

It would be advisable to order an MCV to assess whether there were microcytic cells. However, the determining marker will be ferritin as it will tend to not decline in anemia of chronic disease, but rather increase.

9.10.2 Problem Set-2. A male age 55 complains of general weakness, tiredness and abdominal pain (Gibson, 1990)

	Lab Values	Reference Values
Transferrin	1.240 g/L	>2.00 g/L
Transferrin saturation	30 %	20–50 %
Plasma ferritin	12 mg/L	39.0–256.0 mg/L
Plasma iron	1.10 mg/L	0.8–1.5 mg/L

What can be concluded from the blood values?

ANSWER: The transferrin did not rise as is normally expected in iron deficiency. Rather the normal level suggests that the patient may be moderately protein deficient which causes a downward movement of transferrin concentrations (Gibson, 1990).

Transferrin saturation is within a normal range, but does not invariable rule out a problem since normal values are also seen in anemia of chronic disease.

S-ferritin is significantly low. Ferritin is secreted into the plasma from the reticulo-endothelial system and generally parallels the amount of stored iron. In chronic disease, the mucosal block defect results in an over-synthesis of ferritin from the reticulo-endothelial system. The low values, observed in this case, suggest the absence of chronic disease and suspiciously points towards early iron depletion.

The serum iron is normal, but does not by itself provide any conclusive results because iron tends to greatly shift with diurnal rhythms.

This patient does appear to suffer from depleted iron stores—possible early stage of depletion leading to anemia—that have not shown up in other markers yet. This suggests the first stage of iron depletion. There is some evidence as well of visceral protein deficiency.

What additional markers would you need in order to confirm a diagnosis?

To conclude whether there is protein deficiency, request retinol binding protein (RBP) as it is NOT affected by iron-deficiency anemia and has a short half-life of 12 hours. This protein is as sensitive to protein depletion as thyroxin-binding pre-albumin (TBPA) (Gibson, 1990). The latter is, however, too sensitive to minor stress. The dietitian should also complete a usual food assessment in order to determine the risk of the diet being suboptimal in iron. The physician could also order a CBC (NIH, 2012), which will include the hemoglobin (Hb), hematocrit, MCV and blood glucose among other markers, before inquiring about the patient's history of anemia. Not part of the CBC, but the erythrocyte protoporphyrin, would be relevant. Before proceeding to treatment, it is important that the physician proceed to rule out some relevant underlying causes for the anemia, should both the Hb and MCV be abnormal. Outlined below is an example of strategic steps that can be followed (Gerson, et al., 2015; NIH, 2014; Goddard et al., 2000; Merck,1987; Ali, 1976):

1 To rule out acquired sideroblastic anemia, a hematologist should be consulted. The MCV tends to be elevated in acquired sideroblastic anemia. This kind of anemia can present with low Hb and also as microcytic and hypochromic anemia, just like in Fe-deficiency anemia; the difference is that serum Fe, ferritin and transferrin saturation tend to be elevated (Merck,1987; Ali, 1976). Hence sideroblastic anemia can be ruled out based on the blood biochemistry.

2 A physical exam should be the next step after reviewing the patient's chart history. The goal is to look for abdominal pain, which, if present, should raise come concerns regarding the likelihood of a GI bleed. Hence the possibilities of overt or occult rectal bleeding should be considered. The presence of overt bright red blood or melena in the stool, should indicate the need for an upper and lower endoscopy in addition to a small bowel series. This kind of assessment should reveal inflammation and ulcerations in the stomach, in addition to polyps, cancer, ulcerations, lesions, fistulas, divertcula, and inflammation in small and large intestines which would be consistent with ulcers, ulcerative colitis, and Crohn's disease, diverticulitis, neoplasms, Meckel's diverticulum, or hemorrhoids. A negative endoscopic finding should lead to Meckel's small bowel series and to a radioactive chromium fecal blood loss study in search of occult blood loss (Gerson, et al., 2015; NIH, 2014).

3 Blood loss from non-GI sources such as the kidney—looking specifically for hematuria--and liver is considered only if there is evidence of systemic disease. Large menstrual blood loss needs to be documented as well.

4 Malabsorption is likely the last condition to rule out, by documenting the atrophy of the GI villi, gastritis, bacterial overgrowth, Celiac disease, and achlorhydria.

5 MOST LIKELY DIAGNOSIS: The low s-ferritin confirms early depletion of iron stores, while transferrin and transferrin saturation do not confirm anemia.

9.11 CASE STUDY 9.1— CHRONIC TIREDNESS

© Adam Gregor/shutterstock.com

Figure 9.7 *A 18-year-old woman, suffering from fatigue.*

Chronic Tiredness

CHIEF COMPLAINT		
Katherine is an 18-year-old emaciated and pale looking teenage girl who complains of low energy, difficulty concentrating, and being overly tired for the last six months. She claims to have lost 5 lbs in the last six to eight months and to have increasing difficulties concentrating. She is in her freshman year at university and presents with abdominal pain in the left lower quadrant and complains of chronic tiredness.		

PATIENT NAME	SEX	AGE
Katherine Canon	Female	18

OCCUPATION	MARITAL STATUS	NUMBER OF CHILDREN
Freshman college student	Single, lives alone	None

HISTORY OF PRESENT ILLNESS		
Katherine complains of poor appetite, tiredness, low energy, and decreased ability to concentrate for the last six to eight months. Prior to this time, she felt fine. She does not remember having similar symptoms previously.		

MEDICATIONS		
She reports taking no medication currently. She took antibiotics a few years ago for an ear infection.		

VACCINATIONS	SURGERIES
Up to date	No surgeries reported

PAST HISTORY	
Katherine had low body weight as a teenager and has never been very active physically. She did not participate in sports during her childhood.	

PERSONAL & SOCIAL HISTORY	
An 18-year-old girl, freshman in college. Lives alone for the past one year; the first time that she has lived away from home. Reports receiving high grades throughout her education. Has made a few friends but finds little time to socialize. Works weekends at a downtown bar.	

FAMILY HISTORY	
Katherine's father is an unemployed laborer with a long history of alcoholism. Her family has lived on social assistance for many years and receives frequent visits from social services. Her mother and father are alive.	

(Continued)

Chronic Tiredness

REVIEW OF OTHER SYMPTOMS
Poor appetite and frequent constipation, some mild abdominal pain in the left lower quadrant. Denies polyuria, polydypsia, and hyperphagia.
PHYSICAL EXAMINATION
GENERAL APPEARANCE
No apparent symptoms of distress.Pleasant, well-groomed, emaciated, and pale-looking girl. Appears somewhat depressed. Patient appears young for her age. There are signs of pallor in the face and conjunctiva and thinning hair, which are generally indicative of Fe-deficiency.

Examination of Regions of the Body

Chronic Tiredness	EXAMINATION FINDINGS	IS FINDING NORMAL? (Y/N)
Skin	Pallor, cold and extremely dry skin	N
Head, eyes, ENT	Pale conjunctiva, facial pallor, dry thinning hair	N
Neck	No palpable goiter	Y

Examination of Regions of the Body

Chronic Tiredness	EXAMINATION FINDINGS	IS FINDING NORMAL? (Y/N)
Lymph nodes	No lymphadenopathy	Y
Thorax and lungs	Lungs clear bilaterally, no wheezing	Y
Cardiovascular	Regular rate and rhythm	Y
Abdomen	Soft, non-tender, bowel sounds present, no hepatosplenomegaly	Y
Peripheral vascular	Warm extremities	Y
Musculoskeletal	No muscle wasting in upper and lower extremities, no edema, no temporal muscle wasting, triceps skinfold is in 10-25th percentile	Y
Neurological	Cranial nerves II-XII intact, sensorium intact throughout; reflexes slightly decreased in upper and lower extremities	Y

Vital Signs

Blood pressure,	130/70 mmHg, sitting
Pulse rate,	76 b.p.m. regular
Respiration rate	14/min
Temperature	97.5 °F (36.4 °C)
Height,	5'5" (164.5 cm)
Height for age percentile (for children),	N/A
Weight	111 lbs (50.60 kg)
Weight for age percentile	N/A
Weight for height percentile (for children),	N/A

Systems Review: Pain in the left lower quadrant suggests GI problems, possibly inflammatory bowel disease with some malabsorption. The patient presents as emaciated and depressed and has a high achiever profile typically seen among patients with anorexia nervosa; psychiatry should be consulted. The hematological profile shows abnormally low hemoglobin and hematocrit, thus intimating iron deficiency anemia.

Overall she appears to have grown normally as indicated by the rating of her height which is between the 50–75th percentile. Her weight for height is between the 10–25th percentiles which is still considered normal. There is no sense from these values that the patient is underweight (BMI = 18.7) especially since patient claims to have lost only 5 lbs in the last six months. This only represents a 4% weight loss, and therefore does not increase her risk of morbidity.

Review Blood Biochemistry: RBP, hematocrit and hemoglobin are all suboptimal indicating possible iron deficiency anemia and protein malnutrition. Hepatic and pancreatic functions are normal. Serum amylase and lipase are often ordered to assess pancreatic function.

Differential Diagnosis: Chronic infection, anorexia nervosa, inflammatory bowel disease, megaloblastic anemia, undernutrition, thyroid dysfunction, and diabetes mellitus.

Likely Diagnosis: Hypochromic and microcytic iron-deficiency anemia is likely because: s-Hb, Hct, MCV and MCH are suboptimal. The presence of facial pallor and pale conjunctiva are relatively strong physical symptoms. Women with heavy periods and those with poor dietary intakes are particularly susceptible. This is also a classic case of a young woman eating poorly as she learns to balance living on her own with school and social activities. Thalassemia is unlikely as there is no jaundice, splenomegaly, or hepatic siderosis, which are common symptoms. Moreover, it is more prevalent in African, Mediterranean, or Southeast-Asian women. Undernutrition should be considered here as there has been a loss of weight possibly tied to poor nutritional habits. The suboptimal retinol binding protein (RBP) level implies low protein status with the possibility of an underlying vitamin A (retinol) deficiency (Gibson, 1990). Moreover, the normal transferrin is suspicious given that it is normally elevated in Fe-deficiency anemia. This protein is also sensitive to nutritional status and will have a tendency to decline in malnutrition. It is likely that both malnutrition and anemia are keeping this serum protein normal. The abdominal pain is assumed to be from constipation since there are no hepatic or pancreatic disorders that are apparent, plus there is not indication of inflammation or infection as evidence by the absence of a fever, normal C-reactive protein and the normal WBC. The constipation can be confirmed with X-ray.

Laboratory Findings

LAB MARKERS	ACTUAL	NORMAL STD	INTERPRETATION
CBC (COMPLETE BLOOD COUNT)			
Hemoglobin (Hb)	9 g/dL	12–16 g/dL	Low
Hematocrit (Hct)	30%	38–46%	Low
Red Blood Cell (RBC)	3.2 million/mcL	4.2–5.4 million/mcL	Low
MCV (Mean Cell volume)	41 fl	84–99 fl	Low
MCH (Mean Cell Hemoglobin)	23 pg	26–32 pg	Low
WBC (White blood cell count)	8,300	4,500–10,000	Normal
C-Reative Protein	2 mg/dl	0–10 mg/dl	Normal
BLOOD PROTEINS			
Serum Albumin	3.4 g/dL	3.3–4.5 g/dL	Normal
Retinol Binding Protein (RBP)	2.1 g/dL	2.6–7.6 mg/dL	Low
Serum Transferrin	195 mg/dL	>188–341 mg/dL	Normal
LIVER FUNCTION TESTS			
Alkaline Phosphatase	100 U/L	90–239 U/L	Normal
Gamma-Glutamyl Transferase (GGT)	26 U/L	5–27 U/L	Normal
Alanine Amino Transaminase (ASAT) also (SGPT)	19 U/L	9–24 U/L	Normal
Amylase	95 SU/dL	60–180 SU/dL	Normal

Recommendations: The patient's diet needs to improve, both in terms of quality (micronutrients including Fe) and total energy because of her recent weight loss. The American Medical Association (AMA) recommends a repeat Hb or Hct after four weeks of iron supplementation to confirm iron-deficiency anemia. Traditionally, 60 mg of elemental iron is prescribed once/day or twice (b.i.d), in the form of ferrous-sulfate, gluconate or malate supplements (Lichtin, 2013d). If Hb increases by >1 g/dL and Hct increases by >3%, iron-deficiency anemia is confirmed, and iron supplementation such as iron fumarate, gluconate or sulfate (Lichtin, 2013d) should be continued for two months before further evaluation. If these markers are unresponsive to iron supplementation, then a differential with mean corpuscular or cell volume (MCV), RBC distribution width (RDW), and serum ferritin should be reordered. MCV will help diagnose if the size of the RBC have increased or normalized with the treatment of iron supplements. Ferritin should also normalize as iron stores are replenished. If neither of these markers improve with treatment, then a covert megaloblastosis should be suspected. Consequently, measuring serum homocysteine, serum folate and methyl malonic acid will be necessary to establish if it is a case of megaloblastic anemia due to vitamin B-12 or folate deficiency. The prescribed diet should include high quality protein in the amount of 40 g/day, needed to meet her physiological needs (0.8 g/kg BWT), and an adequate total energy to help her maintain her current body weight. The dietitian determines that the patient's TEE equals 1629 kcals/day using the Mifflin equation and an activity factor of 1.27. She initially prescribes a 1770 kcal/day diet which is close to the calculated TEE but also consistent with a second guideline of 35 kcal/kg recommended for undernourished patients. She will later increase her diet to 1880 kcal/day to ensure about a 1/2 lb of weight gain/week until she reaches a BMI of 20 and a corresponding body weight of 54.4 kg. Weight gain should be slow, allowing the patient to better adapt to dietary recommendations and ensure long-term compliance. The patient needs to increase the amount of iron-rich foods in her diet. The American Medical Association recommends consumption of iron-rich foods, and foods that enhance iron absorption, rather than iron supplementation, as the means of primary prevention and treatment. Patient should consume a high fiber diet in order to bring her daily fiber intake to at least 25 g/day, following an X-ray confirming that the pain in the lower left quadrant is from constipation.

It is advisable to begin the day with a high fiber breakfast cereal such as raisin bran, shredded wheat, bran flakes or bran buds in combination with raisins, and other dried fruits such as apricots, cranberries and prunes. Most of the high fiber raisin bran cereals will contain between 10 and 50% of the DRI for iron. Some breakfast cereals such as Total® will contain 100% of the DRI for iron in one serving. When combined with some kind of citrus juice or fruit such as orange or grapefruit, iron absorption is significantly enhanced. Often, a diet in combination with iron supplements helps replenish iron reserves more rapidly (Lichtin, 2013d; Merck, 1987; Gibson, 1990).

9.12 CASE STUDY 9.2— PATIENT COMPLAINS OF PARATHESIAS AND NYSTAGMUS

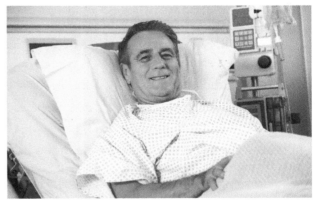

© *Monkey Business Images/shutterstock.com*

Figure 9.8 *Man Suffering from Parathesias and Nystagmus.*

Peripheral pins and needles paresthesias + spastic ataxia, intermittent diarrhea and fatigue

CHIEF COMPLAINT

Jim Rogers is a 43-year-old Caucasian businessman who lives alone. He has a five-year history of mild weight loss and anorexia. In the last year, he describes the anorexia as more pronounced and accompanied by nausea. In addition, he complains of feeling pins and needles and numbness in his legs, and a general lethargy that seems more pronounced over the last year. He describes feeling unsteady when standing as well as weakness in legs, arms, leg stiffness and some confusion. He has recently been experiencing spastic ataxia.

PATIENT NAME	SEX	AGE
Jim Rogers	Male	43
OCCUPATION	MARITAL STATUS	NUMBER OF CHILDREN
Businessman in pharmaceutical sales	Single and lives alone in an apartment	None

HISTORY OF PRESENT ILLNESS

J.R. complains of poor appetite, tiredness, lethargy, weight loss, and episodes of vomiting and intermittent diarrhea over the last year. He has experienced pins-and–needles in his lower limbs, and finds that he has recently, over the last year, become unsteady on his feet. He also reports stiffness in her legs, especially near the end of the day. His work performance in the area of pharmaceutical sales has declined over the last year as well. He finds it difficult to concentrate for long hours and becomes easily irritable. He reports a past history of inflammatory bowel disease (Crohn's) that has gone into remission since about 5 years.

MEDICATIONS

He reports not being on any medication or nutritional supplements at the moment.

VACCINATIONS	SURGERIES
He claims having received all childhood vaccinations.	Partial ileocolectomy 6 years ago involving 75% removal of the ileum.

PERSONAL & SOCIAL HISTORY

J.R is a 43 year-old male Caucasian living alone in Montreal for seven years and working 60 hrs/week as a sales representative in the area of pharmaceutical sales. J.R. has been living alone since the age of 20, and generally enjoys reading and cross-country skiing. He works out regularly at the gym since his surgery. He denies smoking and only occasionally drinks alcohol in social contexts.

FAMILY HISTORY

Mother is a high school teacher and father is a university professor in an MBA program. They live in Boston Massachusetts and are happily married. He has two younger brothers named Daniel and John, and one older sister, Joanne, who are all busy in their different careers.

(Continued)

Peripheral pins and needles paresthesias + spastic ataxia, intermittent diarrhea and fatigue

REVIEW OF OTHER SYMPTOMS

GI: Poor appetite. Some mild non-localized abdominal pain.

HEENT: thyroid not enlarged.

Rectal: Occasional episodes of soft watery stool 3-4 times /week, but generally stools are formed and regular. Stool test for occult blood is negative. No rectal bleeding observed.

Neurological: Alert, good memory. Evidence of ataxia, sensory loss of position and vibration sense in the lower extremities. In addition, there is a mild loss of reflex in legs and noticeable Babinski response.

PHYSICAL EXAMINATION

GENERAL APPEARANCE

No apparent distress symptoms. Tired-looking but well-groomed man complains of fatigue, lethargy and spastic ataxia. He reports losing 6% of usual weight over the last year, which he attributes to poor appetite.

Vital Signs

Blood pressure	130/90 mm Hg sitting
Pulse rate	76 p.m regular
Respiration rate	14 / min
Temperature	97.5 °F (36.4 °C)
Height	5' 9" (1.73 cm)
Triceps	7 mm
Height for age percentile	75th percentile
Present weight	154 lbs (70 kg)
Usual Weight	164lbs (74.4 kg)
Usual weight for height (percentile)	N/A
Present weight for age percentile	N/A
Present weight for height percentile	N/A
Present triceps skinfold percentile	N/A

Laboratory Findings

REGION OF BODY	EXAMINATION FINDINGS	IS FINDING NORMAL? (Y/N)	SUPPORTING MATERIALS
General	Pleasant well-groomed man who presents with no noteworthy physical findings. Complains of fatigue, lethargy, spastic ataxia, and unsteadiness. Not in acute distress	No	*The Merck Manual, Disorders of the Peripheral Nervous System, 1987*
Skin	Skin color normal, warm to touch	Yes	Stallings, V. and Hark, L. 1996
Head, eyes, ENT	Absence of bi-temporal wasting,	Yes	Stallings, V. and Hark, L. 1996
Neck	No palpable goiter	Yes	
Lymph nodes	No lymphadenopathy	Yes	*The Merck Manual, 1987 Pediatrics & genetics*
Thorax and lungs	Lungs clear bilaterally, no wheezing	Yes	
Cardiovascular	Regular rate and rhythm	Yes	
Abdomen	Soft, non-tender, bowl sounds present, no hepatosplenomegaly, occasional constipation and diarrhea, generalized abdominal pain	No	Lichtenstein, G.R. & Mueller, D.H., 1996 *The Merck Manual Anemias, 1987*
Genitalia and rectum	Soft pubic hair with full distribution, no perianal fistulas or rectal bleeding	Yes	*The Merck Manual, gynecology and obstetrics* 1987, 1690–1691
Peripheral vascular	Warm extremities, feet and hands	Yes	*The Merck Manual, Cardiovascular disorders*
Musculoskeletal	No muscle wasting in upper and lower extremities. No edema. No temporal muscle wasting; evidence of spastic ataxia and peripheral muscle fatigue.	No	Stallings, V. & Hark, L. 1996 *The Merck Manual,* 1987
Neurological	Cranial nerves II-XII intact, sensorium not intact throughout. Reflexes slightly decreased in lower extremities. Ataxia and moderate loss of propioceptive and vibratory sensations in the lower extremities. Babinski responses reported.	No	*The Merck Manual, Neurological disorders,* 1987, 1432–1433

Laboratory Values

NO.	TEST NAME	BASIC RESULTS	IS RESULT NORMAL?	EXPLANATIONS
1	Hemoglobin	110 g/L	No	Non-specific indicator that also falls in B12 deficiency
2	Hematocrit	42%	Yes	Close to lower limit of normal
3	S-Ferritin	175 g/L	Yes	Indicates that iron reserve is normal and along with normal MCV rule out Fe-deficiency anemia
4	S-albumin	43 g/L	Yes	
NO.	TEST NAME	BASIC RESULTS	IS RESULT NORMAL?	EXPLANATIONS
5	Spinal X-ray	No erosion, collapse or fracture	Yes	
6	S-glucose	4.0 umol/L	Yes	
7	WBC	9,000/uL	Yes	
8	Total lymphocytes	2.2×10^9/L	Yes	
9	GGT	30 U/L	Yes	
10	Serum B-12	60 pmol/L	No	Values <74 pmol/L indicate high likelihood of B-12 deficiency with high specificity (Snow, 1999)
11	T_4 RIA	110 nmol/L	Yes	
12	Abdominal Ultrasound	Normal	Yes	Pancreas not enlarged; no pseudocysts or cholelithiasis; and bile duct appears normal
13	Serum Amylase	130 U/dL	Yes	
14	MCV	98 fl	Yes	Normal
15	S-Folate	12 ng/ml (28 nmol/L) High	Yes	Values > 7nmol/L are considered normal

(Continued)

Laboratory Values

NO.	TEST NAME	BASIC RESULTS	IS RESULT NORMAL?	EXPLANATIONS
16	**Endoscopy**	Normal	Yes	No lesions or patchy ulcerations seen on mucosa. No fibrosis or edema observed. No sinus tracts or fistulas.

A Review of Case Findings

LIKELY DIAGNOSIS	EXPLANATIONS	REFERENCES
Inflammatory Bowel Disease	This is a patient at high risk of a resurgence of inflammatory bowel disease since there is a history in this patient, which resulted in the partial resection of ileum six years ago. Only infrequent episodes of watery stools and no debilitating abdominal pains reported, however, he does report a poorly localized abdominal pain. Patient has gained weight normally after ileum resection and maintained his usual expected weight up until one year ago. Referral to a gastroenterologist for an endoscopy followed by a barium contrast could be useful for the diagnosis of lesions, ulceration or inflammation of the GI tract.	*The Merck Manual*, gastrointestinal disorders, 1987, 711 *The Merck Manual*, gastrointestinal disorders, 1987; 743; 797- 817
Undernutrition	Poor eating habits and suboptimal energy intake due to anorexia and the 6% weight loss over the last year raises suspicions. Poor absorption intimates a very good likelihood of poor nutritional status	Mann & Trustwell. *The Essentials of Human Nutrition*, 1998, 271
Pernicious anemia	Resection of 75% of ileum could affect the reabsorption of bile and of intrinsic factor-B12 complex.	
Wernicke	Not likely thiamine deficiency arising from poor food intake and abundant alcohol consumption, which can lead to Wernicke-Korsakoff encephalopathy. It presents as mental confusion, aphonia and confabulation secondary to acute hemorrhagic polioencephalitis. There is no such manifestation documented in the medical history.	Truswell & Milne, The Vitamins In: *Essentials of Human Nutrition*, 1998, 197
Guillaine-Barré Syndrome	Presents as a rapid acute idiopathic polyneuropathy with segmental demyelination. There are symptoms similar to pernicious anemia such as paresthesias and ataxia. However, unlike pernicious anemia, Guillaine Barré characteristically causes the loss of deep tendon reflexes, in addition to heightened cardiac arrhythmias and respiratory paralysis, which can become life threatening.	*The Merck Manual*, 1987, neurological disorders, 1446

(Continued)

A Review of Case Findings

LIKELY DIAGNOSIS	EXPLANATIONS	REFERENCES
Multiple sclerosis	Likely: The symptoms most frequently reported are paresthesias in one or more extremities; weakness and clumsiness of a leg or hand. These are very similar to the neurological manifestations of pernicious anemia. Would need to test the cerebrospinal fluid (CSF). CSF is usually abnormal in 55% of case: elevated IgG, lymphocytes, and proteins (myelin active protein high during active demyelination)	*The Merck Manual*, 1987, neurological disorders, 1414

9.12 .1 Comments on Laboratory Findings

Hemoglobin value is low and neurological signs are quite visible. Normally an iron supplement is given as a challenge, and if hemoglobin concentration rises after four weeks, this would confirm Fe-deficiency anemia. This cost efficient procedure is approved and supported by the AMA. In the present case, the patient presents with overt neurological symptoms and a partial ileal resection. The focus here was to measure serum B12; value is< 74 pmol/L in the presence of normal or elevated serum folate concentrations, thus indicating there is a reasonable basis for inferring B12 deficiency and a likely **pernicious anemia**. There is, therefore, an impetus to promptly treat the neurological symptoms as if caused by pernicious anemia since the neurological disease may be irreversible should treatment be delayed. While treatment is being implemented, it's advisable to monitor the patient's CBC and red blood cell indices.

In this situation, the MCV is normal indicating no microcytosis or megaloblastosis. It is however important to indicate that although MCV may be normal, it could simply be the result of a combined microcytic anemia due to Fe-deficiency and megaloblastosis due to folate deficiency. However, the normal serum ferritin value confirms that iron stores are normal, which in facts rules out Fe-deficiency anemia.

The spinal X-ray can be done afterwards to rule out spinal injury. This is a likely differential diagnosis as some of the neurological symptoms reported here overlap those of spinal compression. The abdominal pain reported by the patient necessitates an abdominal ultrasound in order to rule out liver and spleen abnormalities. In addition, the endoscopy would be required to visualize and biopsy any abnormality of the GI tract such as ulcers, filling defects, and mass lesions. Poorly localized abdominal pain, intermittent diarrhea, and anorexia are symptoms frequently reported by patients suffering from pernicious anemia.

9.12.2 Final Diagnosis-Pernicious Anemia without Megaloblastosis

Pernicious anemia without megaloblastosis is the most reasonable diagnosis given the neurological symptoms secondary to the ileal resection (75%). The development of the disease over six years follows the likely time line for such a deficiency to occur. The neurological symptoms were distinct from Wernicke-Korsakoff syndrome, Guillaine-Barré syndrome and multiple sclerosis.

It is essential that B12 intramuscular injections be initiated as promptly as possible in order to avoid irreversible neurological damage.

9.12.3 Dietary Treatment and Rationale

Although he exercises and avoids smoking and excessive alcohol consumption, this patient still needs to decrease the number of hours he works in order to minimize stress. This is important, not only for general health, but also because he is at risk for a recurrence of IBD. It has been shown that psychosocial life stress is positively linked to the activity of IBS. The diarrhea can be caused by a variety of factors, however, the chronic diarrhea, in this case, suggests the possibility of at least a partial involvement of lactose intolerance, a frequent consequence of ileal resections. It would be a reasonable practice to impose a temporary restriction on lactose and document any alleviation of symptoms of diarrhea. The patient's diarrhea may also stem, in part, from "short bowel syndrome." Therefore, the goal is to increase frequency and decrease the size of meals in order to increase transit time and maximize absorption. Remember that following the resection, there is decreased absorptive surface that increases the likelihood of poor absorption.

Counseling the patient for the selection of foods high in B-12 is not helpful, given his condition. Food intake will never solve the problem, as the deficiency arises from poor absorption not intake. For this reason, intra-muscular injections of B-12 will have to be implemented.

Increasing the fat content of the diet would be contraindicated, given that patients with ileal resections are prone to fat malabsorption. The removal of most of the ileum, in this patient, has greatly decreased his ability to reabsorb bile salts through the enterohepatic circulation, thus compromising the absorption of fat and fat-soluble vitamins. Steatorrhea should have been reported as a symptom in this case, however, the patient's food intake may have been sufficiently reduced to mask the symptom.

Patient should be prescribed 50% carbohydrates, 25% protein and 25% fat, with a clear intent to limit the ingestion of simple sugars.

9.12.4 Pharmaceutical Treatments and Rationale

Intramuscular injections of vitamin B-12 are necessary to correct the neurological symptoms that Jim has been experiencing. It is imperative that such injections begin as soon as possible because the neurological damage could become irreversible if treatment is delayed. Afterwards, he should be changed to a lifelong regimen of cyanocobalamin vitamin B-12, 100–1000 micrograms intramuscular (i.m) injection once per month. In cases where the diagnosis is debatable, the risk-benefit ratio still favors treatment with vitamin B-12 injections until a neurological condition is identified. Moreover, cobalamin treatment is non-toxic. Folate treatment given concurrently with cobalamin is however, unlikely to be relevant, especially since megaloblastosis is not identified.

While hematological signs can be corrected within six weeks, especially in the case of folic acid insufficiency due to B-12 deficiency, it will take up to 18 months for neurological symptoms to subside. However, improvements in hematological and neurological symptoms have been reported after daily oral treatments (0.5 ug/d) of B-12 over three to five months.

A multivitamin is strongly recommended for middle-aged men because their eating habits tend not to meet nutritional guidelines. Jim also works long hours and lives alone, which may make him especially prone to poor eating habits. Moreover, high intake of antioxidants is recommended as it can decrease the risk of coronary heart disease, especially in men.

Iron-deficiency anemia is not an issue here. An anti-diarrheal agent could be recommended if diarrhea persisted after the restriction of lactose. The American Gastroenterological Association recommends Loperamide to reduce frequency of loose stools.

Antidepressants such as selective serotonin reuptake inhibitors (SSRIs) (e.g., fluoxetine, paroxetine, sertraline) are now commonly used in patients with IBS, as they have few side effects and can be useful in IBS patients with either severe or less severe refractory symptoms of pain.

REFERENCES

1 Abuelo, J.G. et al. (1992). Serum creatinine concentrations at the onset of uremia: higher levels in black males. *Clin Nephrol.* 37 (6): 303–7.

2 Ali, M.A.M. (1976) The hypochromic anemias. *Can. Fam. Physician* 22: 1530.

3 Allen, L.H. (2000). Anemia and iron deficiency: Effects on pregnancy outcomes. *Am. J. Clin. Nutr.* 71(5):1280–1284.

4 Arthur, C.K. & Isbister, J.P. (1987). Iron deficiency misunderstood, misdiagnosed, and misread. *Drugs*; 33 (2): 171–82.

5 Bergmann, A.K. et al. (2010). Systematic molecular genetic analysis of congenital sideroblastic anemia: Evidence of genetic heterogeneity and identification of novel mutations. *Pediatric Blood Cancer* 54(2): 273-278. Retrieved from http://www.ncbi.nlm.nih.gov/pubmed/19731322

6 Carmel, R. (2006). chapter 28: Folic Acid. In: Modern Nutrition in Health and disease. 10th Edition (Maurice E. Shils, Moshe Shike et al., eds). New York: Lippincott, Williams and Wilkins: 470-481

7 CDC (1998). Morbidity and Mortality Weekly Report (MMWR). Recommendations to Prevent and Control Iron Deficiency in the United States. Vol 47, No /RR-3.

8 Chan, L. N. & Mike, L. A. (2014). The science and practice of micronutrient supplementations in nutritional anemia: An evidence-based review. *Journal of Parenteral and Enteral Nutrition*, 38: 656–672.

9 de Benoist B et al., eds. (2008). *Worldwide prevalence of anaemia 1993-2005.* WHO Global Database on Anaemia Geneva, World Health Organization. Retrieved from http://www.who.int/vmnis/anaemia/prevalence/summary/anaemia_data_status_t2/en/

10 Encyclopedia Britannica. (2013). *Reticuloendothelial system.* Retrieved from http://www.britannica.com/EBchecked/topic/499989/reticuloendothelial-system

11 Fernández-Bañares, F. et al., (2009). A short review of malabsorption and anemia. World J Gastroenterol. 7; 15(37): 4644–4652. Retrieved from: http://www.ncbi.nlm.nih.gov/pmc/articles/PMC2754512/

12 Gallagher, P.G. (2011) Hemolytic anemias: Red cell membrane and metabolic defects In Goldman L, Schafer AI, eds. *Cecil Medicine.* 24th ed. Philadelphia, Pa: Saunders Elsevier.

13 Gerson, L.B. et al., (2015). ACG Clinical Guideline: Diagnosis and Management of Small Bowel Bleeding. Am J Gastroenterol; 110:1265–1287; doi: 10.1038/ajg.2015.246. Retrieved from: https://www.med.upenn.edu/gastro/documents/Whitson10.26.15.pdf

14 Goddarda, A.F., et al., (2000). Guidelines for the management of iron deficiency anaemia. Gut;46:iv1-iv5 doi:10.1136/gut.46.suppl_4.iv1

15 Gonzalas-Casas, R. et al. (2009). Spectrum of anemia associated with chronic liver disease. *World J Gastroenterol.* 15(37): 4653–4658. Retrieved from http://www.ncbi.nlm.nih.gov/pmc/articles/PMC2754513/

[16] Gropper, S.S. & Smith, J.L. (2013). *Advanced nutrition and human metabolism*, 6th edition. Belmont, CA: Wadsworth.

[17] Johnson-Wimbley, T.D. (2011). Diagnosis and management of iron-deficiency anemia in the 21st century. *Therap Adv Gastroenterol*; 4(3): 177–184.

[18] Killip, S. et al. (2007) Iron deficiency anemia. *Am Fam Physician*. 75(5):671–678.

[19] Klusek-Hamilton, H. (1984). *Diagnostics: nurses' reference*. Springhouse PA: Springhouse Corporation.

[20] Lichtin, A.E. (2013). *Overview of hemolytic anemia*. Retrieved from the Merck Manual Professional at http://www.merckmanuals.com/professional/hematology-and-oncology/anemias-caused-by-hemolysis/overview-of-hemolytic-anemia

[21] Lichtin, A.E. (2013b). Evaluation of anemia. Retrieved from the *Merck Manual Professional* at http://www.merckmanuals.com/professional/hematology-and-oncology/approach-to-the-patient-with-anemia/evaluation-of-anemia

[22] Lichtin, A.E. (2013c). Anemia of chronic disease. Retrieved from the *Merck Manual Professional* at http://www.merckmanuals.com/professional/hematology-and-oncology/anemias-caused-by-deficient-erythropoiesis/anemia-of-chronic-disease

[23] Litchtin, A.E. (2013d). Iron deficiency anemia: anemia of chronic blood loss, chlorosis. Retrieved from the *Merck Manual Professional* at http://www.merckmanuals.com/professional/hematology-and-oncology/anemias-caused-by-deficient-erythropoiesis/iron-deficiency-anemia

[24] Livingston, E.H. (2010). The incidence of bariatric surgery has plateaued in the *U.S. Am. J. Surg. 200* (3): 378–85.

[25] Looker, A.C, et al. (1997). Prevalence of iron deficiency in the United States. *JAMA*. 277:973–6.

[21] Merck. (2013). *The Merck Manual for healthcare professionals. hematology & oncology. Sideroblastic anemias.* Retrieved from http://www.merckmanuals.com/professional/hematology_and_oncology/anemias_caused_by_deficient_erythropoiesis/sideroblastic_anemias.html?qt=anemias&alt=sh

[26] Merck. (2013b). *The Merck Manual for healthcare professionals. hematology & oncology. Thalassemia.* Retrieved from http://www.merckmanuals.com/professional/hematology_and_oncology/anemias_caused_by_hemolysis/thalassemias.html?qt=thalassemia&alt=sh

[27] Merck. (2013c). *The Merck Manual for healthcare professionals. hematology & oncology. Anemia of chronic disease.* Retrieved from http://www.merckmanuals.com/professional/hematology_and_oncology/anemias_caused_by_deficient_erythropoiesis/anemia_of_chronic_disease.html?qt=anemia of chronic disease&alt=sh

[28] Merck. (2013d). *The Merck Manual of diagnosis and therapy. genitourinary disorders: Chronic kidney disease.* Retrieved from http://www.merckmanuals.com/professional/genitourinary_disorders/chronic_kidney_disease/chronic_kidney_disease.html?qt=uremia&alt=sh

[29] Merck. (2012). *The Merck Manual of diagnosis and therapy. endocrine and metabolic disorders: Hypothyroidism.* Retrieved from http://www.merckmanuals.com/professional/endocrine_and_metabolic_disorders/thyroid_disorders/hypothyroidism.html

[30] Merck. (1987). *The Merck Manual of diagnosis and therapy. hematology & oncology: Anemias.* Rahway, NJ: Merck & Co Inc.

[31] Merck. (1987B). *The Merck Manual of diagnosis and therapy. gastrointestinal disorders: Pernicious anemia.* Rahway, NJ: Merck & Co Inc.

[32] NIH (2016). Folate: Dietary Supplement Fact Sheet. retrieved from: https://ods.od.nih.gov/factsheets/Folate-HealthProfessional/

[33] NIH (2016b). B12: Dietary Supplement Facts Sheet. Retrieved from: https://ods.od.nih.gov/factsheets/VitaminB12-HealthProfessional/

[34] NIH (2014). How is iron deficiency anemia diagnosed? Retrieved from the National Heart, Lung & Blood Institute website: https://www.nhlbi.nih.gov/health/health-topics/topics/ida/diagnosis

[35] NIH (2012). Types of Blood Tests. Retrieved from the National Heart, Lung & Blood Institute website: https://www.nhlbi.nih.gov/health/health-topics/topics/bdt/types

[36] Picciano, M.F, (1999). Iron and folate supplementation: An effective intervention in adolescent females (Editorial). *Am. J. Clin. Nutr.* 69:1069–1070.

[37] Rivera, C. E. (2013). Hemosiderosis. Retrieved from the *Merck Manual Professional* http://www.merckmanuals.com/professional/hematology-and-oncology/iron-overload/hemosiderosis

[38] Snow, C. F. (1999). Laboratory diagnosis of Vitamin B-12 and Folate deficiency. *Archiv of Internal Med.* 159: 1289–1298.

[39] Stabler, S.P. (2013). Vitamin B-12 deficiency. *N Engl J Med* 368:149–160.

[40] Stopler, T. (2004). Medical nutrition therapy for anemia. In *Krause's food, nutrition, & diet therapy* (L. K. Mahan and S. Escott-Stump eds). Philadelphia: Elsevier.

[41] Strum, J. M., Gartner, L. P., & Hiatt, J. L. (2007). *Cell biology and histology.* Hagerstwon, MD: Lippincott Williams & Wilkins.

[42] U.S. Department of Health & Human Services. (DHHS, 2014)). National Heart, Lung and Blood Institute (NHLBI). *Iron deficiency anemia.* Retrieved from http://www.nhlbi.nih.gov/health/health-topics/topics/ida/

[43] U.S. National Library of Medicine (USNLM). (2015). Folate Deficiency. Retrieved from: https://medlineplus.gov/ency/article/000354.htm

[44] U.S. Preventive Services Task Force (USPSTF1996). Screening for iron deficiency anemia—including iron prophylaxis. *In Guide to clinical preventive services.* 2nd ed. Baltimore, Md.: Williams & Wilkins.

[45] Weiss, G. & Goodnough, L.T. (2005) Anemia of chronic disease. *N Engl J Med*; 352:1011-23.

[46] Wiseman, D.H. et al. (2013). A novel syndrome of congenital sideroblastic anemia, B-cell immunodeficiency [~].*Blood* 4;122(1): 112-23.

[47] WHO. (2016). *Micronutrient deficiencies: iron deficiency anemia.* Retrieved from the World Health Organization website http://www.who.int/nutrition/topics/ida/en/

[48] WHO. (2006). Guidelines on food fortification with micronutrients. Lindsay Allen, Bruno de Benoist, Omar Dary, Richard Hurrell (eds).

[49] Wood, R.J. and Ronnenberg, A.G. (2006). Chapter-12: Iron. In: Modern Nutrition in Health and disease. 10th Edition (Maurice E. Shils, Moshe Shike et al., eds). New York: Lippincott, Williams and Wilkins: 248–270,

[50] World Health Organization. (WHO, 2002). *The World Health Report 2002: Reducing risks, promoting healthy life.* Geneva, WHO.

[51] World Health Organization. (WHO, 2001) WHO/NHD /01.3). *Iron deficiency anemia: Assessment, prevention and control. A guide for program mangers*, Geneva.

[52] World Health Organization. (WHO, 1992). *The prevalence of anaemia in women: A Tabulation of available information.* (WHO/MCH/MSM/92.2).

INDEX

male, in U.S in 2010, **164f**
meat consumption, **25, 29**
medical expenses and, **2**
metabolic changes, **171–176**
    catabolic pathways during fasting, **172f**
    Cori cycle, **171f**
nausea, **178f**
nutrition therapy, **176**
    method of delivery, **176–178**
pathophysiology of, **167–168**
patient-generated Subjective Global
    Assessment (PG-SGA), **174f, 175f**
percutaneous endoscopic gastrostomy (PEGs)
    tubes, **178f**
polyp in colon, **168f**
prevalence of, **163–164**
prevention of, **1–2, 164–167**
protein requirements, **176t**
total energy expenditure, **182t–183t**
weight loss patient, **178, 178f**
    nutritional assessment of patient, **180–183**
    treatment of recommendations of
        patient, **183**
Carbohydrates, **6, 11, 20, 25, 40, 45–48, 55, 60,**
72, 77, 82, 154
    acceptable macronutrient distribution range
        (AMDR), **47**
    diet, Paleolithic era, **11**
    metabolism, **171**
    sucrose, chemical structure, **46f**
Carcinogenesis, **173**
Cardiovascular disease (CVD), **9, 40, 43, 86, 101**
    assessment of, **105**
    atherosclerosis, in arteries, **103f**
    blood cholesterol, ATP III classification
        of, **107t**
    case study, **109–154**
    causes of, **102**
        lifestyle habits, **103–105**
        lipid metabolism, abnormal, **104–105**
        poor diet, **102–103**
    dairy intake, **106**
    DASH diet, daily nutrient goals, **106t**
    dietary recommendations, **108**
    fats and oils, **108**
    fresh & frozen fruits, **115f**
    glycemic load (G.L.), **6**
    grains, **107**
    with heart attack, case study, **110–116, 110f**
        body composition assessment, **112**

        diet prescription, **114–116**
        food intake record, **112t–113t**
        lifestyle assessment, **112–114**
        medical assessment, **110–112**
        patient chart information, **111t**
        presentation, **111**
        weight maintenance, diet
            prescription, **114t**
    with hyperlipidemia, case study, **109t**
        body composition assessment, **109–154**
        diet assessment, **109**
        diet prescription, **110**
        medical assessment, **110**
        presentation, **109**
        recommendations, exercise
            prescription, **110**
    lean meats, **107**
    lipoprotein metabolism, **104f**
    medical tests, **110t**
    metabolic syndrome, **105**
    mortality rates, **10**
    polyunsaturated (n-6) fats, **10**
    saturated fats and, **9**
    strategies to control, **105–109**
    TLC diet, nutrient composition, **108t**
    triglycerides, ATP III classification of, **107t**
    United States, **24**
    with yogurt, **115f**
Carotene and retinol efficacy trial, **166**
Casimir Funk, **205**
CDC, *See* Centers for Disease Control and
    Prevention (CDC)
CDC 2010 report, **132**
Celiac sprue, **220**
Cellulose, **46**
Centers for Disease Control and Prevention
    (CDC), **21, 125**
Chadwick, Edwin, **5, 16, 17**
Chadwick report, **16**
Chemotherapy, **173**
Chlorine dioxide, **23**
Cholera epidemic, **16–17**
Cholesterol
    cardiovascular risk, **10**
    HDL, **27, 54, 102, 103, 110, 112**
    LDL, **27, 54, 103, 112**
    lowering drug, **145**
Cholic acid, **154**
ChooseMyPlate.gov, **29**
Chronic diseases, **1, 9, 10, 20–30, 43, 44, 56,**
    125, 126

high biological value, **49**
indispensable, **48**
polypeptide, **49**
Dietary recommended intakes (DRIs), **10, 28,
47, 49–54, 54f, 77, 78, 80, 89, 90, 134, 183,
203, 267**
    adequate intake (AI) value, **47, 52, 54–55**
    calories, **28, 29**
    estimate average requirement (EAR), **54**
    excessive, **77**
    for macronutrients, **50**
    recommended dietary allowance
        (RDA), **52, 54**
    suboptimal, **77**
    total sugar, **48**
    upper intake levels (ULs), **52, 54, 55**
Dietary reference intakes (DRIs), **28**
    determination of, **54–55**
Dietary selection, **22**
Dietary starches, **46f**
Dietitian, diet history, **77**
Diet prescription
    principles of, **59–60**
    weight maintenance, **114t**
Diet restrictions, **82**
Digestibility, **223**
25–Dihydroxy vitamin D (1, 25(OH)2 D), **217**
Disease prevalence
    chronic, prevalence and impact, **1–2**
    fatty acid composition, **9–10**
    glycemic load (G.L.), **6–9**
    macronutrient composition, **10–11**
    malnutrition, 21ᵗʰ-century
        nutritional guidance
    chronic disease prevalence in
        United States, **20–30**
    micronutrient density, **11–12**
    in Western societies, **5–13**
Diverticular disease, **147–148**
    of colon, **147f**
    fiber diet, recommendation, **148**
    GI diseases, **144–145**
    soluble and insoluble fibers, **148**
Diverticulitis, **147**
DNA mutation, **168**
Dopaminergic dysfunction, **73**
DRI, *See* Dietary reference intakes (DRIs)
Duel energy X-ray absorptiometry
    (DEXA), **75, 151**

E

Eat-5-A-Day Nutrition Campaign, **22f**
Eating patterns, **44**
Ebers papyrus, **4**
Economic development approach, **225**
EEG abnormalities, **210**
Empedoclean model, **2**
Empedocles of Agrigentum, **2**
Enterohepatic circulation, **154f**
Enterohepatic (EH) circulation, GI motility, **154**
Erythrocyte protoporphyrin (EP), **246, 247, 250**
Erythrocytes, **200, 214, 245**
Erythrocyte thiamin transketolase activity
    (ETKA), **206**
Esophageal cancer, from chronic esophagitis, **146f**
European Association for the Study of Diabetes
    (EASD), **90**

F

Fad diets, *See* Weight loss diets
Fasting plasma glucose (FPG), **90**
Fat burns, in flame of carbohydrate metabolism, **83**
Fat free mass (FFM), **91, 136, 197**
Fat intake, **25, 135**
Fatty acids
    composition, disease prevalence, **9–10**
    fat-soluble vitamins, **51**
    polyunsaturated, **51**
    saturated fatty acids, **51**
Fecal N, **224**
Fe-deficiency anemia, **244, 247**
Federal Meat Inspection Act (FMIA), **18**
Federal Physical Activity Guidelines for Americans
    2008, **86, 129**
Fermentation, **148**
Fiber, *See also* Dietary fiber
    insoluble, **47, 148**
    intake, **2, 114**
    soluble, **11, 47, 148, 149**
Fish consumption, omega-3 fatty acids
    (n-3 PUFAs), **10**
Fissures, from constipation, **149f**
Fistula, **148**
Flavin adenine dinucleotide (FAD), **208**
Flavin mononucleotide (FMN), **208**
Flaxseed, omega-3 fatty acids (n-3 PUFAs), **10**
Flaxseeds, **166**

Irritable bowel syndrome (IBS), **143, 150, 152–153**
    inflammatory bowel disease, **152**
    therapeutic strategies, **153**
    and ulcerative colitis, **150, 152**

K

Kakké, **204**
Keratomalacia, **227**
Ketone bodies, **83, 84f, 85, 126, 173, 193**
Ketone production, **46**
Korsakoff psychosis (KP), **206**

L

Laxative agents, **149**
Lean meats, **106**
Leptin, **84, 85**
    deficiency, **71**
Light-density lipoprotein (LDL), **27, 54, 104, 105, 111**
Linoleic acid, **52**
Lipid-mobilizing factor (LMF), **173**
Lipid peroxides (LPO), **166**
Lipids, **51–54**
    MUFAs, **54**
    polyunsaturated fats, **51**
Lipitor, **145**
Lipolysis, **172**
Liver
    enzymes, **178**
    glycogen concentrations, **193**
    irradiating, **199**
Low calorie diets (LCDs), **11, 76, 82**
Lymphatic system, **104**

M

McGovern, George, **24**
Macro/micro-mineral deficiencies, **216–221**
    calcium, **216**
    copper, **220**
    iodine, **220**
    magnesium, **218**
    phosphorus, **218**
    Selenium's role in human nutrition, **221**
    zinc, **219**
        superoxide dismutase, **221**
Macronutrient composition, disease
    prevalence, **10–11**
Macronutrient, proportions by age, **11t**

Magnesium, **216**
    in body, **218**
    deficiency, **218**
Malabsorption syndrome, **153**
Malnutrition, **13, 191**
    agricultural revolution in 18th-century, **14–15**
    central slaughterhouse in Chicago, **20f**
    in developing countries, **221–224**
    energy requirements of hospitalized
        patients, **197t**
    folate deficiency, **228**
        megaloblastic red blood cells, **214f**
    food impurity in 20th-century, **17–20**
    globalization of the food production, **231**
    in hospital
        assessment of, **194–195**
        prevalence of, **198**
        starvation, basic concepts, **192–194**
    impacts on society, **13**
    industrial revolution in 19th-century, **15–17**
    key micromineral deficiencies, **216**
    macro-minerals/micromineral
        deficiencies, **216–221**
        calcium, **216**
        copper, **220**
        iodine, **220**
        magnesium, **218**
        phosphorus, **218**
        selenium, **221**
        zinc, **219**
        zinc superoxide dismutase, **221**
    nitrogen balance, **224f**
    nutrient deficiencies, **213–216, 225–226, 229–230**
        ascorbic acid (vitamin C)
            deficiency, **201–203, 201f**
        cyanocobalamin (B12)
            deficiency, **215, 215f**
        niacin (vitamin B3)
            deficiency, **206–209, 206f**
        pyridoxine (vitamin B6)
            deficiency, **209–212, 210f**
        riboflavin (vitamin B2)
            deficiency, **208, 208f**
        thiamin (vitamin B1)
            deficiency, **203–206, 203f**
    nutritional guidance in 20th-century, **20**
    nutritional guidance in 21th-century, **20**
        chronic disease prevalence in
            United States, **20–30**
    nutrition transition, 231

Reactive oxygen species (ROS), **129, 246**
Recommended Dietary Allowances
(RDAs), **23, 54**
  adequate intake levels (AIs), **55**
  coefficient of variability (CV), **55**
  thiamin, **206**
Recommended nutrient intakes (RNIs), **54**
Rectal cancer, **28**
Red blood cells (RBC), **214**
Red meats, **248**
REE, *See* Resting energy expenditure (REE)
Refeeding syndrome, **177**
Regularly consuming milk, **217**
Relief soup, in Paris, **15f**
Renaissance, of European society, **14**
Resistant starches, **46**
Resting energy expenditure (REE), **57, 77, 177,**
  180, 192, 194
  calculations, **57, 77, 177, 180, 192, 194**
  for men, **58, 77**
  for women, **58, 77**
Reticuloendothelial (RE) system, **246**
Retinol binding protein (RBP), **262**
Riboflavin deficiency, **23, 206, 210**
Rickets
  children and, **22**
  vitamin D deficiency, **5**
ROME system, **144**

S

Saturated fats (SAFs), **9**
  and cardiovascular diseases, **9**
Scarsdale, **82**
Scarsdale diet, *See* Weight loss diets
Schilling test, **255**
School Meals Program, **5**
School Medical Service, **5**
Scurvy, **5, 16, 23, 201–203, 210, 230**
Selective serotonin reuptake inhibitor (SSRI), **145**
The Selenium and Vitamin E Cancer
  Prevention Trial, **167**
Selenium, role in human nutrition, **221**
Senate Select Committee on Nutrition and
  Human Needs, **24**
Sepsis, **196**
Serre, Michel, **14f**
Serum-iron, **251**
Serum-transferrin saturation, **251**

Short bowel syndrome (SBS), **153–155, 220,**
  See also Gastrointestinal (GI) diseases
Shortness of breath (SOB), **178**
Sibutramine, **85**
Skinfold measurements, **75, 89**
Sleep apnea, **133**
Smallpox, **16**
Sodium, **25**
Soluble fiber, **78**
Starches, **46**
  amylopectin, **46**
  amylose, **46**
  resistant, **46**
Stress factor (SF), **180**
Stroke, **85, 101**
Sugars, **25**
Symmetrical hyperostosis, **5**

T

"Taon" disease, **204**
TCA cycle, **83, 84f, 173**
TEE, *See* Total Energy Expenditure (TEE)
Thalassemia, homozygous, **245**
The Bienestar School-based Diabetes
  Prevention Program, **131**
Therapeutic lifestyle change (TLC), **108**
Thiamin (vitamin B1) deficiency, **4, 203–206, 203f**
Thiamin diphosphate (TDP), **206**
Thiamin pyrophosphate effect (TPPE), **206**
Thrifty gene phenotype hypothesis, **131**
Thyroid stimulating hormone (TSH), **220**
Thyroxin-binding prealbumin (TBPA), **262**
Timaeus (Plato), **3**
TLC diets, **114**
Total body weight (TBW), **91, 136**
Total energy expenditure (TEE), **57, 58, 58t, 76,**
  90, 112, 116, 134, 182t
  activity factors in, **57t, 58t**
  for men, **57**
  for women, **57**
Total iron binding capacity (TIBC), **251**
Total parenteral nutrition (TPN), **158, 211**
Trans-fatty acids (TFAs), **9**
Tricarboxilic acid (TCA) cycle, **104, 208**
Triceps skinfold (TSF), **173, 195**
Triglycerides (TG), **76, 104**
  ATP III classification of, **107t**
Trim and Fit program, **131**
Tuberculosis, **4, 16, 244**

Weight watchers, **82**

Wernicke encephalopathy (W.E.), **206**

Wernicke-Korsasyndrome-Koff syndrome, **272t**

Western societies, disease prevalence, **5–13**

    fatty acid composition, **9–10**

    glycemic load (G.L.), **6–9**

    macronutrient composition, **10–11**

    malnutrition, 21th-century

        nutritional guidance

        chronic disease prevalence in

            United States, **20–30**

    micronutrient density, **11–12**

White bread, **6, 22, 23**

Wiley, Harvey, **18**

Willett, Walter, **27**

Women's Health Initiative (WHI), **170**

World Bank, **225**

World Cancer Research Fund (WCRF), **28**

World Health Organization (WHO), **2, 10**

    omega-6 to omega-3 ratio, **10**

World systems theory, **225**

X

X-box, **133**

Xerophthalmia, **4, 227**

Xrophthalmia, **4**

Y

Yogurt, **217**

Yo-yo dieting, **76**

Z

Zinc

    deficiency of, **219, 220**

    in human health, **219**

    superoxide dismutase, **221**

ABOUT THE AUTHOR

DAVID BISSONNETTE is a registered dietitian and associate professor of nutrition at Minnesota State University, Mankato. He completed his doctoral work in the department of Nutritional Sciences at the University of Toronto's Faculty of Medicine, and has held academic positions at St. Francis Xavier University in Nova Scotia, Canada and McGill University in Montreal, Canada.